FOUNDATIONS IN ASIAN CHRISTIAN THOUGHT

Series Editor: Stephen T. Pardue

The Foundations in Asian Christian Thought series offers accessible and innovative introductions to key topics that are biblically rooted, contextually engaged and theologically rich. In each volume, a mixture of seasoned and rising scholars from all over Asia with a shared commitment to genuinely contextual reflection and the primary authority of Scripture introduce readers to major issues, identifying the key contributions of Asian Christians to the global theological conversation. In addition to introducing readers to the dynamic landscape of Asian Christian thought, each book also includes constructive proposals regarding how Christians can wisely advance the development of Asian biblical and theological reflection.

TITLES IN THE SERIES

Asian Christian Theology
2019 | 9781783686438

Asian Christian Ethics
2022 | 9781839730740

Exploring the Old Testament in Asia
2022 | 9781839732799

Exploring the New Testament in Asia
2023 | 9781839737114

Asian Christian Ethics: Evangelical Perspectives allows you to enter an energizing contemporary conversation in evangelical Christian ethics. The authors engage both personal and social ethics shaped by the particularities of their contexts. For them, "Asian" is not simply a colonial generalization but is produced through multiple specific histories and cultures. Embedded in the histories are ongoing dialogues between Christian and non-Christian religions, between those with power and those without, and between Christians who may deeply disagree. The resulting dialogue reshapes some of the dominant "Western" methods in Christian ethics and enriches ethical conversations in their home countries, their continent, and in the wider Christian world.

Elizabeth M. Bounds, PhD
Associate Professor of Christian Ethics,
Candler School of Theology, Emory University, Georgia, USA

Asia, the largest continent on earth, is marked by the similarity of its nations and yet its stark diversity. This collection of articles written by eminent scholars and thinkers makes an important contribution on the most crucial theme of ethics from the Christian perspective. Its comprehensive treatment of the topics from both personal morality and corporate ethical questions, makes it a must for the students of Asia and other continents. It provides a wide range of thinking at the cutting edge of challenges that face followers of Christ in these times. May I appeal to theological colleges and those interested in this vital theme to have this volume as a learning resource to be more impactful in the present turmoil of our nations.

Ashish Chrispal, PhD
Senior Advisor,
Overseas Council, United World Mission, South Asia

This collection of essays is a valuable work that demonstrates how Asian Christian ethicists are engaging their contexts seriously and discerning how to live faithful, integrated lives as disciples of Christ. It enriches our understanding of the gospel and inspires our imagination of what faithful discipleship can look like through diverse cultural lenses. The diverse expressions of faithful discipleship within global churches are a powerful witness to the catholicity of the gospel, for the gospel is for all nations and people in all cultures.

David Doong, PhD
General Secretary,
Chinese Coordination Centre of World Evangelism, Kowloon, Hong Kong

This book contains a treasure of Asian Christian ethical reflections from senior theologians and ethicists to younger thinkers and emerging leaders across Asia. The various essays show confidence in articulating Asian perspectives yet at the same time are critically self-aware of one's situatedness within a globally interconnected world. The essays do not shy away from engaging controversial social issues such as caste, homosexuality, poverty, political engagement, and religious violence, as well as the care of creation. In the midst of reading the analysis and proposals offered by the contributors, readers will be further challenged to avoid replacing an uncritical adoption of Western Christian ethical thinking with a romanticized version of Asian Christian ethics. This book is an important contribution that is not only relevant to the Asian context, but also to trans-contextual conversations concerning doing Christian ethics in a world full of unending conflicts and entangled complex causes that cannot be resolved with simplistic answers.

Rev. Sivin Kit, PhD
Program Executive for Public Theology and Interreligious relations,
The Lutheran World Federation, Switzerland

Given that Asia is the largest continent in the world and will have the fastest growth rate of Christians in the twenty-first century, we have good reason to do theology for ethical issues in this part of the world. Moreover, though there are many books on Christian ethics, Asian contextual theology, Asian evangelicalism, and evangelical ethics, there is a dearth of books on ethics from an Asian as well as evangelical standpoint. This book is thus unique among Christian publications. It deals with personal and social ethical issues arising in Asia's pluralistic context, which is a symbiosis of diverse cultural, religious, and racial identities. Its multidisciplinary and integrative approach recognizes the complexities of the ethical issues faced in Asia and deals with the subject matter head-on by grounding itself in biblical truth and a godly life in this fallen world.

Rev. Clement Mook-Soo Chia, PhD
Principal,
Singapore Bible College

Reading this book has challenged and corrected this Western evangelical ethicist in many ways! The rich collection of reflections by gifted Asian scholars in this volume is a gift to all of us who care about how obedience to the gospel can take shape in a diversity of Asian contexts.

Richard Mouw, PhD
President Emeritus,
Fuller Theological Seminary, California, USA

This book explores various ethical issues that Asians encounter in their daily lives. The voices we hear through this book come from different Asian contexts, rooted in the biblical tradition. Whether one comes from an evangelical background or otherwise, the book is a good read for students in Christian ethics, church leaders, and the people on the pew. The questions at the end of each chapter stimulate one to discern how to approach these moral issues in the private and public spheres.

Muriel Orevillo-Montenegro, PhD
Professor of Theology and Social Ethics,
Divinity School, Silliman University, Philippines

Asian Christian Ethics, edited by Aldrin M. Peñamora and Bernard K. Wong, is an outstanding reflection on Christian ethics in the Asian continent. Several works on ethics have come out in recent decades but the Christian evangelical perspectives this work has decisively given are a fresh contribution.

Three things attracted my attention. First is the definitive option to be holistic in its method. Eschewing unitary methodology and a Western secularist view of ethics, it incorporates not only the Bible – which is characteristic of all evangelical reflection – but also input from other Asian religions (e.g. Confucian, Buddhist, Gandhian, Dalit), and ethical wisdom from other indigenous religions. Some reflections are decisively personal but they are also social and cosmic. As the axiom goes: "the most personal is the most social."

Second, these ethical reflections start from everyday life relevant to Asia, and end with their relevance to the same: family, marriage, and sexuality; business and the market, corruption and politics; the sick, elderly, and people with disabilities; the question of suffering and the good life; and issues of peace and reconciliation in our violent and conflict-ridden world.

Third, these reflections have taken the option of the marginalized and the excluded by looking at their suffering, resistance, and wisdom through an ethics of care, embrace, and embodiedness prophetically proclaiming the suffering and risen Jesus as the ultimate *imago Dei*.

This book is a must-read for all Christian and non-Christian ethicists, theologians, religious thinkers, and practitioners in Asia and beyond.

Daniel Franklin E. Pilario, PhD
Dean,
St. Vincent School of Theology, Adamson University, Manila

Context, context, context. Context means everything for ethics. Goodness finds expression in how individuals and communities flesh out their vision of the moral life in particular contexts. Especially so for Christianity, for whom Christ's incarnation fleshes out God's goodness in the context of creation in all of its complexity and possibility. This wonderful collection of essays does all that for Asia, and takes the intimidatingly large category of "Asian Christian ethics" and beautifully brings it home in contexts that give new life to Christian moral reflection. I love this book, the very idea of it, the very possibility (and impossibility) of it, and certainly the actual expression of it.

Jonathan Tran, PhD
Associate Professor of Philosophical Theology,
George W. Baines Chair of Religion,
Baylor University, Texas, USA

True to the evangelical tradition, this work is Bible-centered while at the same time deeply conscious of, and sensitive to, the cultural and contextual situation of Asian societies. Here is a volume that broaches not only issues of personal transformation but also many momentous social, political, economic, and environmental questions of contemporary times. The authors and editors have attempted to chart a new Asian ethical course and navigate, in the light of God's word, many grey areas and complex moral issues. The contours of an Asian approach to ethics, different from the classical Western one, stand out in bold relief, especially by invoking Asian experiences of suffering, poverty, and marginalization. For all these reasons and its clarity and comprehensive presentation, this volume deserves to be an excellent textbook for Asian Christian ethics.

Felix Wilfred, PhD
Professor Emeritus,
School of Philosophy and Religious Thought,
State University of Madras, India

 FOUNDATIONS IN ASIAN CHRISTIAN THOUGHT

Asian Christian Ethics

GLOBAL LIBRARY

FOUNDATIONS IN ASIAN CHRISTIAN THOUGHT

Asian Christian Ethics

Evangelical Perspectives

Editors
Aldrin M. Peñamora and Bernard K. Wong

© 2022 Aldrin M. Peñamora and Bernard K. Wong

Published 2022 by Langham Global Library
An imprint of Langham Publishing
www.langhampublishing.org

Langham Publishing and its imprints are a ministry of Langham Partnership

Langham Partnership
PO Box 296, Carlisle, Cumbria, CA3 9WZ, UK
www.langham.org

Published in partnership with Asia Theological Association
ATA
QCC PO Box 1454 – 1154, Manila, Philippines
www.atasia.com

ISBNs:
978-1-83973-074-0 Print
978-1-83973-740-4 ePub
978-1-83973-741-1 Mobi
978-1-83973-742-8 PDF

Aldrin M. Peñamora and Bernard K. Wong hereby assert their moral right to be identified as the Author of the General Editor's part in the Work in accordance with sections 77 and 78 of the Copyright, Designs and Patents Act 1988.

All rights reserved. No part of this publication may be reproduced, stored in a retrieval system or transmitted, in any form or by any means, electronic, mechanical, photocopying, recording or otherwise, without the prior written permission of the publisher or the Copyright Licensing Agency.

Requests to reuse content from Langham Publishing are processed through PLSclear. Please visit www.plsclear.com to complete your request.

All Scripture quotations, unless otherwise indicated, are taken from the Holy Bible, New International Version®, Anglicised, NIV®. Copyright © 1979, 1984, 2011 by Biblica, Inc®. Used by permission. All rights reserved worldwide.

Scripture quotations in chapter 5 are taken from The Holy Bible, English Standard Version® (ESV®), copyright © 2001 by Crossway, a publishing ministry of Good News Publishers. Used by permission. All rights reserved.

British Library Cataloguing-in-Publication Data
A catalogue record for this book is available from the British Library

ISBN: 978-1-83973-074-0

Cover & Book Design: projectluz.com

Langham Partnership actively supports theological dialogue and an author's right to publish but does not necessarily endorse the views and opinions set forth here or in works referenced within this publication, nor can we guarantee technical and grammatical correctness. Langham Partnership does not accept any responsibility or liability to persons or property as a consequence of the reading, use or interpretation of its published content.

CONTENTS

Foreword xiii
Acknowledgments xvii
Introduction: The Quest for an Asian Evangelical Ethics 1
    Aldrin M. Peñamora and Bernard K. Wong

Part 1: Ethical Way of Life

Chapter 1: Identity, Local Wisdom, and Moral Formation 15
    Ethics of Embrace, Embodiedness, and Christoformation
    Florian M. P. Simatupang

Chapter 2: "Water is Thicker Than Blood" 39
    Family in the Changing Landscape
    Bernard K. Wong

Chapter 3: "Honor Your Father and Your Mother" 61
    Confucius and Jesus on Filial Obligations
    ShinHyung Seong

Chapter 4: Faithful Living 81
    Life in the Marketplace
    Jean Lee

Chapter 5: Corruption and Bribery 99
    Hwa Yung

Chapter 6: Human Dignity 121
    A Standard for Christian Life and Ministry
    Kiem-Kiok Kwa

Chapter 7: Ethics of Suffering for Asian Religiosity 143
    Dick O. Eugenio

Chapter 8: The Way of the Cross and the Good Life 165
    Evangelical Virtue Ethics in Asia
    Aldrin M. Peñamora

Part 2: Ethics in the World

Chapter 9: God's Story of Life 191
    Themes for an Asian Creation Care Ethics
    Athena E. Gorospe

Chapter 10: A Prophetic Voice in the Wilderness 217
   Church, Political Engagement, and Public Theology
   Agnes Chiu

Chapter 11: Homosexuality in Twenty-First Century Asia 235
   The Case of Taiwan
   Shang-Jen Chen

Chapter 12: The Eye of the Needle 255
   Wealth and Poverty
   Vinoth Ramachandra

Chapter 13: Renewed Action for Age-Old Concerns 275
   Caste and Indian Christian Ethics
   Nigel Ajay Kumar

Chapter 14: The Mission of the Church 301
   Just Peacemaking and Reconciliation
   Rula Khoury Mansour

Chapter 15: Religious Pluralism 327
   How Should Asian Christians Behave That Just Peace May Prevail?
   Paulus S. Widjaja

Contributors 351

FOREWORD

The title of this volume has five words: Asian. Christian. Ethics. Evangelical. Perspectives. To read these words assembled in plain linear fashion is momentarily like seeing five distinct oceans of reality, each in its own enormous, if roiling, bucket. To wrestle with the rich complexity of any one of them is more than a life's work. Of course, these five realities are not and cannot be approached so pristinely. The editors and authors of this book understand that deeply, and they daringly place them together in a simple five-word combination. This sets up the value and attraction of the book. The editors and writers know we come to these terms, as we do all terms, intersectionally. That is, we realize by daily experience, if not careful reflection, that all words are collections of meanings in contexts interacting with other words and contexts. The title sounds demanding – and necessary.

The book can be approached with at least two levels of interest: 1) the *explicit* topic of each essay on various ethical issues in diverse contexts. Generation by generation, the question remains – will the church live its identity and demonstrate its ethical convictions; and 2) the *implicit* implications of the volume as a whole.

The first is what is presented to the reader. The distinct voice of each author shows us their work and how they go about it, letting the differences or commonalities of interpretive approach be weighed in their own terms and compared to the approaches of others. The breadth of essay topics and writers here are gathered under two broad frames: a) *Ethical Way of Life*, which opens up questions for the personal and communal life of the church, aware of the fundamentally theological and human questions being considered; and b) *Ethics in the World*, which stands more in the public square where Christian points of view are among competing secular or religious assumptions and visions. This editorial organization allows the character of the essays to emerge for different contexts and gives the writers the freedom to use their different voices, with distinct purposes, and for the benefit of varied readers.

The second, implicit, and broader meaning of the book as a collection needs to be inferred without editorial definition or direction. No overarching hermeneutical assumptions are provided apart from the collection's title. The notes struck in each essay are valuable and the overtones produced by those notes are stimulating and interactive.

I am intrigued by questions that seem to underlie this book. What might Asian Evangelical perspectives bring to current ethical debates if such voices are centered and self-conscious? What if the church of Jesus Christ could understand and live out its faith amidst a flourishing diversity of ethnic, evangelical, and ethical perspectives?

The leading assumption of these essays then is that our understanding and practice of Christian ethics is thickly formed by and lived out in the context of ethnicity and culture. That is, ethnicity and culture are not veneers on otherwise "neutrally human" lives, but rather every human being is shaped by necessary, unavoidable, meaningful, and diverse realities of ethnicity and culture. While some aspects of ethnicity may have their superficialities, not least in a globalized world, the tectonic plates of self-perception, relationship, nature, and spiritual and moral values, arise from communities in locations.

By placing "Asian" as the first word in the title, the volume embraces these thick assumptions and puts them to work with all the appropriate self-consciousness, confidence, and humility that the task of Christian ethics requires. The word order does not necessarily mean its writers are first Asian and only secondarily Christian. Rather, the intent is to underscore that Christian ethics always and inescapably arise from and land in ethnically-shaped, culturally-shaped worlds and lives. By acknowledging the distinctive issues and perceptions of Asian Christian ethics, Asian and non-Asian readers can benefit from wider horizons than the dominant Western or White voices of history. Human life is always inescapably contextual and so are our ethical reflections. To recognize and admit this potentially produces more honest, sufficient, relevant, and challenging Christian ethical perspectives and practices.

If "Asian" acknowledges contextuality, "evangelical" has traditionally added theological claims of "supra-contextuality." That is, the theological knowledge of the evangelical tradition points to its understanding of God's revelation as essentialist and realist – Scripture testifies to the essence of God's being which is independent and universal in its reality, therefore not bound or defined by context. This means that the essays are holding on to the particularity of the *imago Dei* in human experience and the universality of God and God's revelation. Such is the inherent tension of the Christian faith and its trust in and knowledge of the God made flesh in Jesus Christ, strongly evident in evangelical theology and ethics. Here then is the crux of hope and challenge this book embraces; ethics that reflect the nature and reality of God, who is beyond and within context, overtly developed in relation to Asian evangelical

Foreword

Christian contextualities in the twenty-first century. The implications of such an approach are extensive.

As a White, Christian, evangelical man living in the United States, I am enriched and challenged by the varied Asian, Christian, evangelical voices here. As I read these essays, I feel like I am taking in air that is both familiar and unfamiliar. I am repeatedly stimulated to approach less or more familiar issues differently. These multi-ethnic, multi-contextual perspectives, grounded in the Scriptures and in the Evangel, raise vigorous questions and reshape the ethical matters under consideration.

It may be asked if this self-consciously ethnic and contextualized approach, despite evangelical affirmations, reduces its ethical approach to a relativistic smorgasbord of options? In other words, how does this ethnic paradigm affect the nature or possibility of Christian ethics making moral and reality claims beyond the particular ethnic or the contextual frame? How do the particularities of ethnic perspectives draw from or allow for the faithful character of God, the authority of the Bible, the incarnational revelation in Jesus Christ, and the life and witness of the church to make broader and deeper ethical appeals in evangelism or discipleship, in the personal or the public square?

These are among the questions I found stimulated by this collection, which I strongly commend. My gratitude for this set of essays is their thoughtful, self-conscious commitment to a necessary, timely, and complex task. I found myself repeatedly exhilarated by the labor being invested in such many-layered works. Thoughtful readers will be helped in the parts and in the whole of this volume, finding that the sheer commitment to this interpretive ethical work will be meaningful. *Asian Christian Ethics: Evangelical Perspectives*—five words that require simultaneous consideration and defy simplification. Work of this kind belongs to all of us seeking to think and act in ethical ways in the name of Jesus Christ.

Mark Labberton, PhD
President of Fuller Theological Seminary, California, USA
July 2022

ACKNOWLEDGMENTS

When the initial plans for this book were being laid out back in September 2019, little did we know that in just a few months we would all be entering a deadly stage in recent human history that would be brought about by the COVID-19 pandemic. This makes us even more appreciative of how the Lord has guided the completion of this volume in the midst of these trying times. We thank the key men and women, and the organizations that believed in the significance of this project in contributing to the growth of evangelical churches and the broader Christian communities in Asia and, hopefully, even beyond the Asian context.

We would like to first thank Dr. Steve Pardue, who shared with us the vision and his enthusiasm for this book, and who accompanied us in our writing and editing journey. We wish to thank Dr. Theresa Lua and Dr. Andrew Spurgeon for their support on behalf of ATA, and Dr. Sooi Ling Tan for highlighting the importance of ethics in Asia by making it the theme of ATA's General Assembly in 2021. We also appreciate the support of Langham Publishing, particularly Luke Lewis, Dr. Rico Villanueva, Vivian Doub, and Dr. Mark Arnold for encouraging Asian theologians to make their distinct contributions known to the global Body of Christ.

To the writers with whom we have journeyed with for the past three years: we express our gratitude for your close cooperation with us and the valuable contributions you have made to this volume. Each of you offer a unique voice from your own Asian context. When your voices come together, they become invaluable moral exhortations for Asian Christians, as well as an oratorio of praise to our Lord. To Professor Mark Labberton: you furnished us with a foreword even though you are well aware of being an "outsider." It is our wish that this book, though written by Asians and mainly for Asian Christians, may also make a humble contribution to the worldwide Christian community. We wish to thank our family members, Christine Ching-Peñamora, Clara Wong, Kristin Wong, and Josiah Wong, for being at our side and giving us much needed encouragement. Finally, we thank the institutions we serve, the Philippine Council of Evangelical Churches (PCEC) and China Graduate School of Theology (CGST), which help nourish our theological and ethical reflections and experiences, and have been greatly supportive of this endeavor.

INTRODUCTION

THE QUEST FOR AN ASIAN EVANGELICAL ETHICS

Aldrin M. Peñamora and Bernard K. Wong

PART 1

In the early nineteenth century when Protestant Christianity first entered China, the first Chinese pastor Liang Fa had high hopes. He believed that the mark of being a Christian is a wholehearted dedication to doing good. If everyone follows Jesus, he reasoned, evil will cease and peace would ensue. Therefore, Christians could count on improved morality to evangelize the Chinese people.[1]

Liang represents a prevalent Asian understanding of religion and ethics:[2] the two are inseparable and both should be beneficial for society. Liang's enthusiasm to evangelize the Chinese through superior morality, however, was met with surprises. Instead of embracing Christian faith, some who heard his message reported him to the magistrate. He was arrested and tried for preaching Christianity. The judge disregarded his arguments concerning improved morality and sentenced him to corporal punishment because of his faith in Jesus.[3]

Liang's story is an illustration of the complex relationship between religion and ethics. First, ethics is inseparable from religion. All religions expect their adherents to demonstrate certain virtues or even conform to specific behavioral norms. For example, Jesus teaches: "Let your light shine before others, that they may see your good deeds and glorify your Father in heaven" (Matt 5:16). Adherents have used this behavior-shaping character of religion to promote their own religion, as in Liang's advocacy of Christianity. On the other hand, those who fail to demonstrate upright morality may be shunned

---

1. Liang Fa, *Good Words to Admonish the Age*, from the Harvard University Collection (Taipei: Taiwan Student Publishing, 1965), 302, 312.
2. Although some authors clearly distinguish the two words "morality" and "ethics," their meanings are not strictly differentiated in this chapter.
3. Liang, *Good Words to Admonish the Age*, 304–6.

or excommunicated from their religious communities. In the early church, while Paul claimed that the church is an all-inclusive community (Gal 3:28), he admonished the Corinthian church to "put out of your fellowship" the person who commits sexual immorality (1 Cor 5:2).

Second, religion is not merely ethics. All religious traditions in the world are concerned with issues much wider than behavior, such as human well-being, suffering and death, the meaning of life, and worldviews. These wider issues frequently entangle with personal identity, social belonging, cultural expressions, and even ethnic or national loyalty. Therefore, the reception of a religion into any culture is a long and intricate process. When Liang narrowly understood religion as merely ethics, he failed to see why China – and other Asian countries – often resisted and banned Christianity for some periods in their history. Furthermore, different worldviews entail different notions of the "good"; behaviors deemed "good" for one religion may be considered repulsive for another. For instance, ancestor worship is a proper way to show respect for one's family in East Asia, but the same act has been condemned by Christian traditions as idolatrous. Therefore, behavioral change resulting from religious conversion can be considered detrimental to morality and the convert may even be persecuted.

Third, religious ethics often have political implications. When the Pharisees enforced behavioral codes among the Jews, they strengthened their political authority among the people. Jesus's clash with the religious leaders of his time was frequently over his "immoral" or "illegal" behaviors such as breaking the Sabbath law and mingling with sinners. These "sinful behaviors" of Jesus were not merely ethical but political: by defying the Pharisees' moral teachings, Jesus was considered politically subversive and had to be eliminated.

In modernity, religion, ethics, and politics continue to mingle together. Political leaders are concerned with the conduct of the people. Having the power to shape behavior, religions can become embroiled in politics. For instance, political rulers may use the predominant religion of their countries as political instruments to ensure social order. In the nineteenth century, the Rana regime that ruled Nepal used Hinduism – in particular the Vedic prescriptions of social order – to encourage national unity among diverse ethnicities.[4] Alternatively, political leaders may become suspicious over the power of religions shaping the behavior and even loyalty of their subjects.

---

4. Subho Basu, "Nepal: from Hindu Monarchy to Secular Democracy," in *Religion and Politics in South Asia*, ed. Ali Riaz (London: Taylor & Francis Group, 2010), 107.

The Quest for an Asian Evangelical Ethics

For instance, the sixteenth century Japanese feudal lord, Toyotomi Hideyoshi, was surprised that Christians in his territory were willing to defy his orders based on religious moral grounds.[5] Subsequent persecutions of the Catholic Church in Japan were partly due to Christians demonstrating loyalty to their faith more than to their political rulers.[6]

Clearly, religious ethics cannot be disengaged from the specific contexts as well as the actual lives of those who practice their religions. This is especially true if we focus on ethics that are Asian and Christian. Christianity has never been the predominant religion in most Asian countries. As such, any discussion of Asian Christian ethics involves contextualization of the Christian faith in particular Asian cultures, including the exchanges between Christianity and the predominant religion of the country.

However, we must be aware that "Christianity" in this discussion is also a product of contextualization. Christianity as commonly understood today – its practices, theology, ethics, etc. – originated from the Jesus movement that began in first century Palestine. Over the past two millennia, the Christian faith took root in Greco–Roman culture, then became the predominant religion in Europe and, subsequently, the Western world. Christianity in Asia today is largely the results of the missional efforts from this Western world. The history of Christianity in the West is not simply the gospel of Christ conquering the heathen, but Christianity being accepted by particular peoples, transforming their cultures, and itself being transformed at the same time. This lengthy process of contextualization results in Western Christianity embedded in the Greco–European philosophical traditions.

For our subject of Christian ethics, many textbooks today continue to follow this tradition and begin by laying out the historical development from the ancient Greek philosophers to postmodern theorists. Different theories – such as deontological, utilitarian, virtue – are then discussed, followed by the application of these theories to selected scenarios and cases. The layout of these ethics texts reveals the Western way to treat knowledge: first define the methodology, then use it with rationality to arrive at the desired result. For Christian ethics, Scripture, theology, tradition, and the church community

---

5. Xiaobai Li, *Faith, Profit, Power: The Christian Mission and the Choice of Japan* [*Xinyang, Liyi, Quanli*] (Zhangchun: Northeast Normal University, 1999), 54.
6. Samuel Hugh Moffett, *History of Christianity in Asia*, vol. 2, 1500–1900 (Maryknoll: Orbis, 2005), 79–81.

usually contribute to the methodology, and the desired result is the right choice or behavior expected of a Christian.

This Western approach to ethics has many advantages. The emphasis on methodology and rationality encourages reflection and dialogue in the face of ethical dilemmas. Laying out different theories helps decision makers to think from different angles. However, right behavior is not merely the result of ethical reflections. For example, communities may teach morality by explaining a tradition or cultivating certain habits rather than through the training of the mind.[7] Ancient Chinese, for instance, never developed a separate category of knowledge known as ethics, yet morality pervades all Chinese writing from this era, and everyone is instructed to behave in ways appropriate to "become human."[8] Instead of desiring to become rational decision makers, Asian traditions often look up to persons with cumulative experience and wisdom as virtuous models to emulate.[9] In the West, which tends to emphasize rational decision-making, the individual is often privileged over the collective. But in Asia, ethics is understood as "we-self" more than "I-self." The maintenance of social order, instead of the right decision of the individual, is the purpose of ethics.[10] The contextualization of Christianity in these cultures must consider the differences in approach between the West and Asia.

A textbook titled *Asian Christian Ethics* therefore, ought not to follow the layout of a typical Western ethics textbook that starts from methodology and ends with the practical. Even this introductory chapter does not aim to put forward a method, but to outline the contexts from which the chapters arise. However, as Christianity has long been contextualized in the West, having basic knowledge of the Western approach to Christian ethics will help readers understand this book.

It must also be mentioned that Asia, the largest continent in the world, is itself extremely varied. There is no such thing as "an" or "the" Asian Christian ethics that encompasses all Christian ethical approaches in Asia. To claim or develop such an all-inclusive notion would only result in a book that is too

---

7. Francis X. Clooney, "Practices," in *The Blackwell Companion to Religious Ethics*, ed. William Schweiker (Malden, MA: Blackwell, 2008), 78.
8. Eske Møllgaard, "Chinese Ethics?" in *The Blackwell Companion to Religious Ethics*, ed. William Schweiker (Malden, MA: Blackwell, 2008), 369.
9. John Ross Carter, "Buddhist Ethics?" in *The Blackwell Companion to Religious Ethics*, ed. William Schweiker (Malden, MA: Blackwell, 2008), 279.
10. Wilson Muoha Maina, "Public Ethical Discourses and the Diversity of Cultures, Religions, and Subjectivity in History: Can We Agree on Anything?" *Journal of the Study of Religions and Ideologies* 11, issue 32 (Summer 2012): 22.

general to be truly useful for anyone living in a particular Asian culture. This is not to say that there are no common features in Asian ethical reflections that are uniquely Asian; but such commonalities, in our view, do not amount to an Asian ethical metanarrative. Thus, in this volume you will read writings of authors from different regions and from diverse evangelical backgrounds. When viewed together the resulting mosaic hopefully exhibits truthful aspects of how Christian ethics is being done in Asia. Therefore, the title of this book, *Asian Christian Ethics*, does not mean that the book refers to a single, unified ethical approach or perspective, but more accurately means "a selection of Christian ethical approaches in Asia." Due to the vastness of Asia and a plethora of ethical issues worth addressing, the fifteen chapters are therefore only representative topics. They are only a small sample of how leading Asian Christian ethicists grapple with moral issues that arise in their particular Asian settings. Despite such limitations, it is our hope that anyone reading this book, whatever their cultural background and situation, would find valuable insights to address the ethical issue that they face.

The subtitle of this book is *Evangelical Perspectives*. The meaning of "evangelical" must be explained, for it bears different meanings in different parts of the world. This book is a kind of sequel to *Asian Christian Theology: Evangelical Perspectives*,[11] and we follow that volume in understanding "evangelical" to refer to a commitment of the gospel as the work of the triune God. John Stott avers that evangelical Christians are committed to speak and live before God, insisting on "the primacy of Scripture, the centrality of the atoning work of Christ, and the power of the Holy Spirit to transform us as God's people."[12] Life transformation and sanctification are core pursuits of evangelical Christians; thus ethics has always been important in evangelical churches worldwide. Oliver O'Donovan rightly argues that Christian ethics must arise from the gospel; faith and morality must not be separated. Disregarding ethics renders the gospel incomplete. Yet commitment to ethics does not weaken our proclamation of the gospel as glad tidings for all.[13] The chapters of this book discuss what the contextualization of the gospel in Asia entails in terms of ethics, and how Christian ethics can be good news for the peoples of Asia's cultures.

---

11. Timoteo D. Gener and Stephen T. Pardue, *Asian Christian Theology: Evangelical Perspectives*, ed. Gener and Pardue. Carlisle: Langham, 2019.
12. Gener and Pardue, "Introduction," in *Asian Christian Theology*, 5.
13. Oliver O'Donovan, *Resurrection and Moral Order: An Outline for Evangelical Ethics*, 2nd ed. (Grand Rapids: Eerdmans, 1994), 11–12.

PART 2

As coeditors, we had to decide how to arrange this selection of Christian ethical approaches in Asia in a coherent manner. Immediately we recognized that grouping the chapters by subject matter is unsatisfactory, for many chapters defy simple and clear categorization. Ethics is, after all, highly interdisciplinary and integrative. Instead of imposing an external order onto the chapters, we proceeded to listen to the authors themselves. It became noticeable that our authors either explore their subjects from a more personal angle or from a predominantly social perspective. So we decided to arrange the chapters following these contrasting but complementary approaches.

The first eight chapters mainly deal with themes related to the sphere of the moral life as it connects to *individual or personal ethics*, while the second part – chapters nine to fifteen – focuses on broader societal issues that characterize *social ethics*. The two dimensions are, of course, interrelated. For instance, the ethical issues that an individual grapples with in the personal sphere are embedded in particular social contexts. Even the variables that shape a person's decisions and character have a social dimension. The same can be said regarding social ethics, for issues concerning the social, structural, and the wider public often require the decision-making of individual moral agents.[14] In other words, while distinctions can be made between the two dimensions, personal and social ethics are basically intertwined. In fact, for us Christians and for adherents of other Asian religions such as in Hinduism, Buddhism, and (in some ways) Confucianism, ethics is even entwined with the cosmic dimension, over which, for us Christians, God is sovereign. It will be helpful to keep in mind the interrelated nature of these dimensions in reading the chapters in this book. For whether a chapter has a marked emphasis on the personal, social or cosmic sphere, it ultimately concerns how we Christians in Asia are called to live moral lives by embodying our Christian faith concretely as we seek, in various ways and situations, to give glory to our triune God.

Asian Christian Ethics: Evangelical Perspectives begins with a chapter, written by Florian M. P. Simatupang, which emphasizes the importance of local wisdom in shaping a person's Christian moral life. Simatupang focuses particularly on how Christian faith can bring restoration and healing to conflicts arising from Asia's pluralistic context. As exemplifications, Simatupang gives an overview of four Christian theologians, two each from Indonesia and the Philippines, whose ethical approaches toward cultural and religious "others"

---

14. Robin Gill, *A Textbook of Christian Ethics*, 3rd ed. (New York: T&T Clark, 2006), 341.

have deep influences from their culture. He then constructs a contextual evangelical ethics that is not defined by opposition or isolation in relation to such "others"; instead, informed by local wisdom, Simatupang describes a Christocentric ethics that is embracing, hospitable, and accepting in ways that demonstrate how Christ, through the Spirit, is being formed in the believer.

Chapters Two and Three examine key issues about the family, which is certainly one of the most important influences – in some Asian cultures it is *the* most important influence – that help cultivate a person's moral life. Bernard Wong first tackles the issue of divorce and remarriage, which Asian Christians now increasingly face due to significant challenges and reconfigurations to the traditional notion of family. It is the theology of marriage, Wong avers, not ethical rules regarding divorce, which should especially inform Christians in such matters. This theology, while resisting the breakdown of marriages and families, also challenges certain Asian concepts of "familism" which are undergirded by oppressive cultural structures and practices, such as patriarchy. Wong therefore calls for a deep engagement with Scripture and culture, and counters oppressive Asian familial structures by presenting a moral vision of the family based on biblical images of the church. In ShinHyung Seong's essay, filial obedience and obligation are examined in light of Confucian and biblical teachings. As the Confucian concept of family is a central moral influence in the private and political spheres of many Asian cultures, Seong therefore sees the importance of transforming Confucian notions to reflect biblical ideals. To achieve this, he recovers Confucius's original teachings on the family that aimed to promote harmonious human relationships, and which stand in contrast to the repressive social hierarchy that came to be associated with later iterations of Confucianism. This perspective from early Confucianism shares some key features of the biblical concept of family and filial obligation and opens the way toward a contextualized Christian ethical understanding of filial piety and obedience that demonstrates love for God and Christian discipleship.

Chapters Four and Five of the book deal with how Asian Christians can be faithful and transformative disciples in the fields of business and the marketplace. Jean Lee articulates the challenges deriving from the general orientation of the marketplace toward self-interested profitability and efficiency. She warns how the strong forces at play in the marketplace can lead Christians to develop a double morality, justifying immoral business practices while leading moral lives privately. Lee rejects such an approach, maintaining instead that Christians are called to faithful and integrated lives. As the challenges in the marketplace are unpredictable, she emphasizes the building of genuine character that is rooted in Christ, a character that is also suffused with imagination, hope, and the ability to see the good amid the fallenness of the marketplace.

Hwa Yung's essay particularly focuses on the issue of corruption at the micro level of personal interaction. He notes it is crucial for Asian Christians to carefully pursue a biblically contextualized ethical response to corruption. In particular, he highlights the dangers of dualistic thinking, uncritical acceptance of Western approaches, superficial understanding of the biblical material, and an inadequate approach to social engagement. Crucial for Hwa is an incarnational approach to corruption that requires biblical and cultural sensitivity; this is quite challenging given the gray areas and tensions that exist not only in applying biblical truths and principles, but within the biblical material itself. Hwa navigates through these difficulties as he proposes helpful and realistic guidelines for transformative social engagement.

The next three chapters (Chapters Six, Seven, and Eight) that end this section of the book analyze themes which in one way or another run throughout all the essays of this volume – the theme of human dignity which Kwa Kiem-Kiok addresses in her essay and the theme of *suffering* which Dick O. Eugenio and Aldrin M. Peñamora examine in their respective chapters. Kiem-Kiok contemplates the plight of marginalized people such as the sick, the aging, and those with disabilities, having in view Asian cultural norms and values that bestow dignity to some people, but which sometimes foster mistreatment and neglect of the vulnerable. Kiem-Kiok looks to the Scriptures for ethical guidance and sees how its teachings on human dignity reject social exclusions; instead, the Scriptures promote treating every person with equal dignity, for all human beings bear the image of God. From this biblical conviction, Kiem-Kiok urges Asian Christians to be discerning of the ways their culture promotes marginalization, and to cultivate a counterculture of hospitality and openness to the needy.

In his essay, Eugenio gives a broad view of suffering and outlines some of the main religious perspectives on suffering in the region. Christians in Asia face not only pervasive suffering, but remarkable diversity regarding how suffering is viewed across various religious traditions and cultures. To respond to suffering of others with genuine compassion, Christians must come to their aid in a way that demonstrates the love of Jesus with sensitivity to their worldview.

Peñamora's chapter deals with suffering through the lens of virtue ethics. He gives an overview of the Confucian and Gandhian approach to virtue ethics, and contrasts some of its key features with a Christocentric conception of virtue ethics that is cruciform. Based on biblical conceptions of Jesus as the God who suffered, Peñamora points out that in light of the immense suffering in Asia, a Christian ethical view of *eudaimonia* or the good life, can be none other than cruciform: that is, characterized by a willingness to suffering for the sake of others.

The second part of the book, which focuses on the wider sphere of social ethics, begins fittingly with Athena Gorospe's essay on the care of creation, within which all personal and social ethical interactions are conducted. Recognizing the need for a deeply contextual engagement of this issue for the Asian evangelical context, Gorospe sets out and grounds her vision of ecological engagement in the biblical narrative of creation centered on the theme of life – a theme that is central to the biblical story and which also occupies a prominent place in many Asian faith traditions. For Gorospe, this conceptual interconnectedness is necessary so that Asian evangelicals can have a deeper sense of the importance and urgency of caring for the environment. By focusing on life, Gorospe hopes to empower the agency and participation of Asian evangelicals for the flourishing of all life.

In the following essay by Agnes Chiu, the question of the church's role in the public sphere is examined from the perspective of public theology. Drawing from the teachings of Abraham Kuyper (and like Gorospe), Chiu sees the Genesis creation narrative as foundational in the church's engagement with the wider society. From this biblical foundation she describes the church's responsibility for advancing the common good in the public sphere. Important in this regard is the church's prophetic role of providing moral guidance and vision to society and government. While this may prove difficult when the government is unjust, Chiu nonetheless calls the church to fulfill its prophetic function, noting how the South Korean church has exemplified this calling effectively, if imperfectly.

The essays in Chapters Eleven, Twelve and Thirteen grapple with ethical issues involving particular groups in society. Considering Taiwan's recent decision to legalize same-sex marriage, Shang-Jen Chen examines key biblical passages that address the issue of homosexuality from an evangelical point of view. Chen reviews the primary contentions of Christians who promote an "affirming" perspective on same-sex relationships. Chen observes that while liberal ideologies were a factor in the legalization of same-sex marriage, other social factors were also crucial, such as the evangelical church in Taiwan's general unpreparedness for the legal, political, and religious challenges that the legalization campaign introduced. Chen proposes key ways in which the

Taiwanese church – and others in the region – can respond to the rapid changes in norms surrounding gender and sexuality.

Vinoth Ramachandra's essay deals with ethical concerns related to Asia's poor and downtrodden social classes, who continue to live miserably and work under exploitative conditions even in Asian countries with powerful economies. Ramachandra analyzes some of the key features of conventional economic arrangements that produce such inequalities among Asia's people. Pointing to the teachings of the Bible as well as the writings of the early church Fathers, he emphasizes the centrality of pursuing justice in a way that concretely addresses social inequality and oppression. Asian Christians must put their faith into action by rejecting the culture of exploitative consumerism that has become increasingly pervasive in the region.

Nigel Ajay Kumar reflects on India's social hierarchical system of caste in his essay to aid in shaping an Asian evangelical response to this age-old concern that has also entered Indian churches. Toward this end, Kumar underscores the importance of learning about recent paradigm shifts and counter-narratives in studying caste, which reveals how colonialism and Christian missionary endeavors reinforced caste discrimination. Along with this, he calls for a deeper study of biblical themes and concepts such as the *imago Dei*, as well as the reconfiguration of Christian practices that tend to perpetuate discrimination. Central for Kumar's ethical response is the Pauline notion of "unity in Christ" that can undergird ecclesial practices aimed at bringing people together regardless of social distinctions.

In the closing chapters of this volume (Fourteen & Fifteen), the need for just peace is discussed in relation to conflict situations that are socially exemplified in two distant Asian locales, Palestine and Indonesia. Rula Khoury Mansour emphasizes the interconnectedness of mission and peacemaking. By mission, Mansour points to the church's prophetic role in confronting social injustice and, by peacemaking, she emphasizes the importance of a contextualized reconciliation theology and practices that characterize the just peacemaking paradigm. Mansour offers an analysis of this interconnection in three case studies, looking at the responses of oppressed Christians during the American civil rights movement, the struggle against South Africa's apartheid system, and especially in the ongoing conflict between Palestine and Israel. While these different contexts each call for different ethical responses from the oppressed church, for Mansour they express most importantly the church's attempt to embody God's shalom and love for all human beings as incarnated through Jesus Christ.

The Quest for an Asian Evangelical Ethics

In the final essay, Paulus S. Widjaja deliberates on how Asian Christians ought to act toward religious others in ways that cultivate just peace. He observes that in Asia's context, which is marked by religious pluralism, excessive concern for one's religious identity and truth claims could lead to the pursuit of political power for the purpose of marginalizing, persecuting, and even eliminating adherents of other faith traditions. In such a hazardous context, Widjaja calls the Asian church to cultivate an ethic of peacekeeping, peacemaking, and peacebuilding that is rooted and intertwined in the peaceable, loving, and just nature of Jesus Christ's calling. Indeed, for Widjaja it is through deeply identifying with Christ's calling that the Asian church can avoid becoming entangled in a cycle of religious violence and can instead become an alternative community that is embracing, non-condemning, and transformative.

Having thus outlined the chapters of this book, we would like to express how we are truly privileged and thankful to be bringing you this collection written by incisive evangelical thinkers who are committed servants of Christ. We are deeply honored to have collaborated with them, as well as to have learned from them during this writing process. It is our hope that you will find these essays helpful as you reflect upon and address ethical concerns in your specific context, whether you are from Asia or any other part of our global community.

BIBLIOGRAPHY

Basu, Subho. "Nepal: from Hindu Monarchy to Secular Democracy." In *Religion and Politics in South Asia*, edited by Ali Riaz, 98–118. London: Routledge, 2010.

Carter, John Ross. "Buddhist Ethics?" In *Blackwell Companion to Religious Ethics*, edited by William Schweiker, 278–85. Malden: Blackwell, 2008.

Clooney, Francis X. "Practices." In *Blackwell Companion to Religious Ethics*, edited by William Schweiker, 78–85. Malden: Blackwell, 2008.

Gener, Timoteo D. and Stephen T. Pardue. "Introduction." In *Asian Christian Theology: Evangelical Perspectives*, edited by Timoteo Gener and Stephen Pardue, 1–9. Carlisle: Langham, 2019.

Gill, Robin. *A Textbook of Christian Ethics*. 3rd ed. New York: T&T Clark, 2006.

Li Xiaobai. *Faith, Profit, Power: The Christian Mission and the Choice of Japan*. Zhangchun: Northeast Normal University, 1999.

Liang Fa. *Good Words to Admonish the Age, from the Harvard University Collection*. Taipei: Taiwan Student Publishing, 1965.

Maina, Wilson Muoha. "Public Ethical Discourses and the Diversity of Cultures, Religions, and Subjectivity in History: Can We Agree on Anything?" *Journal of the Study of Religions and Ideologies* 11, no. 32 Summer (2012): 18–36.

Moffett, Samuel Hugh. *History of Christianity in Asia*, vol. 2, 1500–1900. Maryknoll: Orbis, 2005.

Møllgaard, Eske. "Chinese Ethics?" In *Blackwell Companion to Religious Ethics*, ed. William Schweiker, 368–73. Malden: Blackwell, 2008.

O'Donovan, Oliver. *Resurrection and Moral Order: An Outline for Evangelical Ethics*, 2nd ed. Grand Rapids: Eerdmans, 1994.

PART 1

ETHICAL WAY OF LIFE

CHAPTER 1

IDENTITY, LOCAL WISDOM, AND MORAL FORMATION

Ethics of Embrace, Embodiedness, and Christoformation

Florian M. P. Simatupang

INTRODUCTION

If there was ever a time when the word "evangelical" needed ethical redemption, it is now. In certain parts of the world, the meaning is almost automatically associated with voters of a particular political leaning, an alignment to "hot-button" issues, and even a gravitational attraction to conspiracy theories.[1] As an Indonesian theologian and ordained Pentecostal minister who does consider himself to be evangelical in the broadest sense of the word, it is one that I have avoided and resisted being associated with as of late. For one thing, in Indonesia, there is a continuous tension between evangelicals of a particular persuasion with other Christians, including Pentecostals. Although there are exceptions, as a Pentecostal theologian, it is often much easier to have a charitable theological conversation with peers coming from a "mainline" background. For another, the worldview of evangelicalism of particular expressions, such as fundamentalism, dispensationalism, and Zionism, is incompatible with the enchanted sacramental worldview of the Asian people – a worldview that is inherent in Pentecostalism. That is why I not only believe Asian voices have something to offer to the development of Pentecostal theology that embraces its

---

1. See Mark A. Noll, *The Scandal of the Evangelical Mind* (Grand Rapids: Eerdmans, 1995); and D. L. Mayfield, "In Push to Reopen, American Evangelicals Fall Prey to Political Strategy," *Sojourners*, May 11, 2020, https://sojo.net/articles/push-reopen-american-evangelicals-fall-prey-political-strategy.

strong sacramental instinct, but I also believe those same voices have something to contribute to the ethical redemption of the word "evangelical."[2]

This chapter seeks to present an approach to Christian ethics in Asia from the angle of the rediscovery of local wisdom that brings a sense of restoration and healing. I maintain that evangelical ethics in Asia requires an appreciation of such wisdom to inform a genuine Christian moral formation. Rather than basing it from what is commonly known as the Bebbington Quadrilateral,[3] my definition of an evangelical perspective is any reflection within the Chalcedonian Christological boundaries. The local wisdom and the ethics deduced sit within the broad area defined by the four walls of Chalcedon.[4] After all, what makes an ethic *Christian* is that it leads to the concrete formation of the character of Christ in individuals and the community. After this introduction, this chapter contains two major sections: first, a survey of the current landscape of how identity and social ethics display and inform a process of restoration and healing; second, a constructive proposal built around three themes – embrace, embodiedness, and Christoformation.

A SURVEY OF THE CURRENT LANDSCAPE

Vietnamese–American theologian Peter Phan maintains that the most urgent task for Asian churches is to become the church that is "*in* Asia [and] also *of* Asia" that manifests as "a transparent sign of and effective instrument for the

---

2. I see the worldview of Asians as inherently closer to the worldview of the biblical authors and quite different than the Western worldview, making it in a sense, inherently evangelical. See Simon Chan, *Grassroots Asian Theology: Thinking the Faith from the Ground Up* (Downers Grove: IVP Academic, 2014), who argues that Asians still have a "primal religious view" that is "holistic and communal" in contrast to the Western separation of secular and supernatural, 34.
3. For an explanation of the content of the Bebbington Quadrilateral see "What Is an Evangelical?," National Association of Evangelicals, accessed January 17, 2022, https://www.nae.org/what-is-an-evangelical/.
4. The Chalcedonian Definition is a declaration adopted at the Council of Chalcedon in AD 451 of Christ's two natures, truly human and truly divine. The declaration addressed several beliefs considered heretical known as Nestorianism (a denial of the unity of the divine person in Christ), Apollinarianism (a denial of the fullness of Christ's human nature), and Eutychianism (a denial of the duality and distinction of the divine and human natures of Christ). The creed affirms both the human and divine nature of Christ existing "without confusion, without change, without division, without separation," while leaving a room, as Alister McGrath states, for "a plurality of interpretations regarding their relation." The four "withouts" make what is sometimes known as the four walls of Chalcedon. I see the four walls as bordering a large area that I can use for redefining the idea of evangelical focusing on Christ as the evangel (good news) himself. For a brief explanation on the Council of Chalcedon and the debates surrounding it see Alister E. McGrath, *Christian Theology: An Introduction*, 6th edition (Chichester, West Sussex; Malden: Wiley-Blackwell, 2016), 22, 224–27.

saving presence of the reign of God, the reign of justice, peace, and love."[5] How have theologians in Asia affirmed what Phan said? The vastness of Asia requires me to limit myself, and as an Indonesian, naturally, I chose to survey Indonesia. I also decided to survey the Philippines because, although due to foreign influence we are quite different (for example, Indonesia is predominantly a Muslim country and the Philippines Roman Catholic), Indonesians and Filipinos share many cultural similarities. In this survey, I chose a woman and a man representing each country. The *leitmotif* traceable in their reflections is *restoration* and *healing*, whether personal, communal, or relational – all involving a process of drawing on local wisdom.

Joas Adiprasetya

I begin with the Indonesian theologian, Joas Adiprasetya, who experienced living with "a burden of rejection (as the impact of in-betweenness) as well as quasi-acceptance (as the impact of in-bothness)."[6] This theme of in-betweenness (neither one nor the other) and in-bothness (sort of, but not really of one or the other) is found throughout Adiprasetya's work, a theme he would develop into a "liturgy in-between" maintaining that the task of theology is to explore and construct one from the place of in-between.[7] Such a liturgy, he argues, compels the church to experience the freedom to be "little Christ," the victim and the healer, reconciling places of fragmentation.[8] For this chapter, we will look closer at how he used the concept to reconcile his identity theologically.[9]

As an Indonesian of Chinese descent raised in Javanese culture, it was difficult for him to be comfortable with his ethnic identity.[10] Events in Indonesia that occurred not long before he was born caused this struggle. After what was commonly known as the Indonesian Communist Party (PKI) revolution in 1965, the New Order regime led by then-President Soeharto implemented a massive assimilation program throughout the country. All things suspected of having any relationship with communism and the PKI were banned. One of them was the eradication of all things related to China and Chinese

---

5. Peter C. Phan, *In Our Own Tongues: Perspectives from Asia on Mission and Inculturation* (Maryknoll: Orbis Books, 2003), 15.
6. Joas Adiprasetya, "Following Jesus the Clown," *Theology Today* 69, no. 4 (January 2013): 420.
7. Joas Adiprasetya, "The Liturgy of the In-Between," *Scottish Journal of Theology* 72, no. 1 (2019): 83.
8. Adiprasetya, 94.
9. Adiprasetya, "Following Jesus the Clown," 419.
10. Adiprasetya, 420.

culture. Indonesia's diplomatic relationship with The People's Republic of China was frozen in 1967 because the Indonesian regime was convinced the Chinese played a role in the rebellion. Chinese-Indonesians were forced to adopt Indonesian names, prohibited from Chinese religious activities, speaking Chinese, and writing using Chinese characters.

The entire process brought with it a host of negative by-products that Adiprasetya experienced firsthand. Even after adopting an Indonesian name, like many Chinese-Indonesians, he was subjected to racial mistreatments. Among these was being made the object of racial slurs that made him feel like a clown, an experience that greatly traumatized him.[11] A challenging response from fellow participants at a conference in Korea became a wakeup call, forcing Adiprasetya to rethink his personal theological construct in light of his long-suppressed Chinese-Indonesian identity. To reconcile his "in-betweenness" and "in-bothness," he reflects on the character of Semar, the Javanese clown, whom he finds fascinating and helpful in illustrating these concepts.[12]

Semar is the main comic relief character in Javanese mythology which is greatly influenced by two Sanskrit epics, the *Ramayana* and the *Mahabharata*, and is often portrayed through the *wayang* plays. A widely accepted meaning of his name is *samar*, which translates to "vague" as there is vagueness about his character. Adiprasetya maintains that ambiguity is the commonality between clowns across diverse cultures. For example, in their "total otherness," clowns seem to always be in their own world, quite often misunderstood in terms of their gender, and typically perceived as rude or vulgar in their persona. Another commonality among clowns is their double sidedness, meaning that they can criticize and express solidarity all at once. The final common feature in clowns is their ability to be victim and healer at the same time, meaning the role of the clown often involves becoming a victim of a particular circumstance not of their own making yet, at the same time, not only be vindicated but also offering "healing" in terms of solution and resolution to the situation. Adiprasetya contends these characteristics are found in the character of Semar, the clown.[13]

Furthermore, Adiprasetya also argues that the characteristics of a clown are also found in the person of Jesus of Nazareth. First, the kenosis act Jesus performed is not unlike that seen in Semar; it is an action that is "a reversal

---

11. Adiprasetya, 419.
12. Adiprasetya, 420.
13. Adiprasetya, 421–24.

of human and worldly paradigms."[14] The self-emptying of Jesus that ends in his crucifixion is folly in the eyes of the world, but it redefines what power is from the perspective of his Father's kingdom (1 Cor 1:8). Second, like Semar, Jesus also displays a double-edgedness. Jesus criticizes structures of power, embraces those on the margins, the poor, the outcasts, women, children, and by doing so, brings liberation through the "intertwining [of] criticism and solidarity."[15] Finally, we can see in Jesus a victim and a healer – found climactically in his suffering on the cross. He became the victim through the collusion of the religious and the political centers of powers, making "the marginal clown . . . more marginalized."[16] Yet as the victim, he also became the healer. As Adiprasetya explains,

> It is exactly in the suffering of Jesus that God's humor reaches its climax. God hides himself. He is *deus absconditus*, God who hides, but, at the same time, in the suffering of Jesus, He shows solidarity with the suffering people who have been marginalized. In Jesus's suffering, therefore, God is absent as well as present and revealed (*deus revelatus*). On the cross, the tragedy and comedy coexist. And only by this humorous clowning can we be healed: as Peter also reminds us, "By his wounds you have been healed" (1 Pet 2:24; cf. Isa 52:5).

By way of the story of a Javanese clown, Adiprasetya was able to make peace with his previously ignored identity as an ethnic minority in Indonesia. He accepted the clown-ness of his identity as a mark of following Jesus, the clown. Adiprasetya contends that only by such acceptance can one "relieve [oneself] from the *bondage* of marginalization of any kind, [so that one] . . . will be able to follow Jesus the clown freely."[17]

Septemmy E. Lakawa

Septemmy Lakawa is an Indonesian theologian involved in conversations with people who experienced religious violence and its aftermath in Indonesia, and whose work tries to reconstruct and reconfigure a way to do theology having

---

14. Adiprasetya, 425.
15. Adiprasetya, 426.
16. Adiprasetya, 426.
17. Adiprasetya, 427.

those conversations in mind.[18] At the turn of the millennium, after the fall of Soeharto, many areas in Indonesia were marred by religious violence. Among those was the island of Halmahera, where the violence took place from late 1999 to early 2002.[19] In 2004, Lakawa was invited to lead a workshop to help pastors of the Evangelical Christian Church denomination in Halmahera, many of whom had experienced the brutal violence firsthand, to read the Bible afresh in light of seeking peace and reconciliation.[20] This was challenging according to Lakawa; for these pastors turning the other cheek was equal to surrendering to the violent injustice committed to them. Lakawa explains,

> It was hard for them to understand that Jesus calls them to "give the other cheek" while in reality they "do not have the other cheek any more since the violence done against them had taken both their cheeks." Reading the Bible through the eyes of the survivors of religious violence raises the question of the ambivalence of the Bible. It is a question of how to relate to the biblical message of "loving your enemies" to their unresolved and unhealed anger, hatred, and anxiety.[21]

In visiting a church where over one hundred members were slaughtered, she recalled looking at graves in the church courtyard. All the graves were marked white and bore the name of the person and the words, *Martir Jemaat*, meaning a martyr of the congregation.[22] Lakawa focused her studies about how Christians can respond in the aftermath of religious violence by suggesting that Christians should look back and "find within our histories the narratives that speak about the possibility of living a peaceful, just, and reconciling life."[23]

Lakawa argues that the proper Christian response in the aftermath of religious violence remains one of hospitality, precisely the kind that takes risk. Her further research proposes this as a model, calling it "risky hospitality," which provides an opportunity for healing of the community through traditional

---

18. Septemmy Eucharistia Lakawa, "A Woman Becoming: On Pain, Dancing and Doing Theology with Those Who Face Religious Violence," *Reformed World* 56, no. 3 (September 2006): 284.
19. Lakawa, 290.
20. Lakawa, 290.
21. Lakawa, 291.
22. Lakawa, 291.
23. Lakawa, 287.

Identity, Local Wisdom, and Moral Formation

public mourning and public testimony.[24] She maintains that practicing the local traditions of hospitality is particularly relevant in contributing to missional practices in a post-violence experience. In constructing risky hospitality, she employed five images used to analyze and present the complex and fragile process of healing and rebuilding an interreligious relationship in the aftermath of violence.[25] They are "journeying, creating space, remaining, breathing, and extending hands," illustrating "a dance movement that is embodied in the religious communities' various ways of reconnecting with each other."[26] These images are connected to two concepts, namely, improvisation and imagination. Through improvisation, the "dance movement" will take on new forms beyond the traditional understanding; imagination provides a lens that comes from the cultural and faith stories that shaped the Christian community and which will influence how they recreate interreligious relationships.[27] Space limitation prohibits us from looking deeper into her construction of risky hospitality, which includes the use of public mourning, public testimony as healing practices, and the creation of public space for risky hospitality through the house of prayer. It is crucial for our discussion, however, that the inspiration of the dance movement that includes journeying, creating space, remaining, breathing, and extending hands, comes from her own experience of healing.

Lakawa recalls that, although she did not have a terrible experience performing the traditional dances of Indonesia with their particular gender construction, and she admired seeing her two sisters perform traditional dances, since childhood she has told herself (and her body) that dancing is not her thing. Through this experience, she asked herself, "[I]s there any way to do different movements that could still be considered beautiful?"[28] The question remains buried all through her adult life, partly because physically she was struggling with painful scoliosis. The question of the possibility of creating different dance movements that are still considered beautiful came back to her during her doctoral coursework when grappling with the subject of theological aesthetics. She recalled she had a strong desire to give dancing another try even though that desire came with a very frightening realization of the severe back

---

24. Septemmy Eucharistia Lakawa, "Risky Hospitality: Mission in the Aftermath of Religious Communal Violence in Indonesia," ThD diss, Boston University School of Theology, 2011, xxi.
25. Lakawa, 357.
26. Lakawa, 357.
27. Lakawa, 358.
28. Lakawa, "A Woman Becoming," 293.

problem that she has and the pain that can come as a result.²⁹ Through encouragement from her professor and advice from her physical therapist, she composed a dance called "The Dance of the Broken Beauty." This dance consists of three parts, namely "obedience, suffering, and the desire for abundant life"; the movements were a combination of her therapeutic exercises and elements of traditional dances once performed by her sisters.³⁰ This dance experience became for her a place to begin "to imagine the possibility of re-creating and reconfiguring theology by connecting [her] personal struggle with that of the struggle of the people and the churches in Indonesia," solidifying her vocation as "a witness to the possibility of the life, peace, justice, and reconciliation" testified and exemplified by Christ.³¹

Melba Padilla Maggay

Melba Maggay is a Filipina social anthropologist and social activist who has done extensive work around the interface of religion, culture, and development in the Philippines.³² Much of Asia has been influenced by colonialism in one way or another. Because of that, engagement with local wisdom often brings us a risky encounter of otherness "where we contend with strangeness, and are in danger of being hit, not only by the enemy but also by friendly fire."³³ Like all cultures, Filipino culture is resilient, so that even with outside influences, its core values and buried structures often continue to exist unscathed.³⁴ She maintains that to engage our own culture within its own context of categories is an essential prerequisite to make sense of our history.³⁵ Maggay proposes an evangelism effort that is more congruous with the indigenous mindset of the Philippines. In the past, Western missionary practices have neglected local cultural assumptions; thus, the process of evangelism comes in "packaged formulations" that assume immediate cross cultural relevancy.³⁶ The result is an incongruity of the gospel message that is being transmitted to the indigenous consciousness of the Filipinos. There should be another way, more sensitive to

---

29. Lakawa, 294.
30. Lakawa, 294.
31. Lakawa, 295.
32. Melba Padilla Maggay, "Engaging Culture: Lessons from the Underside of History," *Missiology* 33, no. 1 (January 1, 2005): 62.
33. Maggay, 63.
34. Maggay, 67.
35. Maggay, 65.
36. Melba Padilla Maggay, "Towards Sensitive Engagement with Filipino Indigenous Consciousness," *International Review of Mission* 87, no. 346 (July 1998): 361.

the Filipino mind, so that proclamation of the good news can be "genuinely incarnated in the cultural reality" of the people of the Philippines.[37]

Maggay maintains that, historically, conversion to Christ could be described as superficial. Superficial conversion has created what is called "culture Christianity" (for example, the replacement of old Filipino wooden statues with statues of saints with Caucasian features).[38] This was partly because the Catholicism that first came to the Philippines, the Iberian variety, was one that was hardly affected by the aftermath of the Reformation and the scrutiny of the age of reason that came not long after that. It was a medieval Catholicism that was tied with the idea of totalitarian faith, where the church is synonymous with the state.[39] The result was a form of Catholicism that was deficient in its Catholic paradigm. The Filipinos then simply assimilated this new element into their religious paradigm. An example would be the absence of God the Father in Catholic churches because the Father is seen as *Bathala*, who is distant and is mediated by ministering spirits, not unlike the *anitos* (spiritual beings that populated the worldview of pre-colonial indigenous Filipinos).[40]

This superficiality did not change after the arrival of American evangelical missionaries. Unlike the Spanish missionaries who taught in the vernacular, they prioritized transmission using the English language. This not only ignored the indigenous imagination but also set in motion assimilation of the American ethos among the converts so that "their mission efforts were . . . far removed from the reality of the Filipino people."[41] A Filipino trained in the American Bible Belt school of thought ends up lacking the ability to grapple with the theological questions that arise from Filipino culture.[42] One of the most regrettable aspects of this outcome is the preoccupation with theological controversies instead of fighting unjust social-economic order, not to mention the promotion of a demythologized version of Christianity. The arrival of the Pentecostal/charismatic movement has, according to Maggay, softened the naturalism that plagued this Christian witness. However, it too brought a new set of problems such as the tendency to "demobilize new believers and to generate mere spiritual 'highs.'"[43]

---

37. Maggay, 362.
38. Maggay, 362; Maggay, "Engaging Culture," 67.
39. Maggay, "Towards Sensitive Engagement with Filipino Indigenous Consciousness," 363.
40. Maggay, 363; Maggay, "Engaging Culture," 67.
41. Maggay, "Towards Sensitive Engagement with Filipino Indigenous Consciousness," 363.
42. Maggay, "Engaging Culture," 68.
43. Maggay, "Towards Sensitive Engagement with Filipino Indigenous Consciousness," 364.

Maggay posits that evangelism which acknowledges the religious consciousness indigenous to Filipinos and includes recognizing and engaging the Spirit's power will make the proclamation of the gospel come alive. This evangelism paradigm should contain three things. First, it requires a renewed awareness of the power of "signs and wonders" to accompany verbal proclamation as the culture is used to correlating anyone speaking for God, whether priest or *babaylan* (shamans), as someone with power.[44] This is demonstrated in the rapid spread of the Pentecostal/charismatic movement in the Philippines. The demonstration of power must be in the sense of divine presence that connects with the local reverence for mystery or *lihim ng karunungan* that will allow an experience of spiritual insight and healing.[45]

Second, it necessitates a correction from the overemphasis of an individualized Western view of sin – which, according to Maggay, leans more toward viewing sin as individual offenses such as infidelity, lying, or violating the rights of others – to a more holistic view of sin.[46] In the Filipino consciousness, the concept of *sala* is understood as having one's relationship with the community or with the cosmos disrupted.[47] When this happens, there is a rupture in the harmony of relationships, which the community views as a fundamental failure. Theologically, this will help redefine sin as cosmic disharmony and repentance as an act of regaining harmony, connecting with the Christian concept of *koinonia*.[48]

Third, the dominant image of Christ as forever suffering has not helped empower people, especially the poor, because the image perpetuates a sense of powerlessness on their part. Therefore, Maggay maintains that the alternative images, such as Christus Victor, need to be emphasized to counter this feeling of helplessness. To speak more powerfully to the Filipino indigenous mind, the gospel will also need a recentering to understand Jesus Christ as the "Lord of the spirits" who is bringing his redemptive work throughout creation.[49]

Finally, authentic evangelism requires taking into account critical cognitive differences between the Filipino and the Western mind. First is the idea of holism, which is the unity of the natural and supernatural, sacred and secular, public and private. The Filipino mind does not split the person into body and

---

44. Maggay, 365.
45. Maggay, 366.
46. Maggay, 366.
47. Maggay, 366.
48. Maggay, 367.
49. Maggay, 367.

soul; instead, Filipinos see the body (*katawan*) as persona (*katauhan*) bound to their soul (*kaluluwa*).⁵⁰ The other crucial cognitive difference is in the concept of time, *pa* and *na*; these refer to the idea of "roundness, of completion, as well as to sensitivity to what is still in process," which is closer to the Hebrew idea of "appointed" or "opportunity" [*sic*] time.⁵¹ This indigenous concept of time can help understand the work of the Holy Spirit in a better sense in contrast to the time-bound constraints of the Western mind. Keeping indigenous consciousness will make evangelism efforts more integrated and authentic to the Filipino people.

Aldrin Peñamora

We proceed to look at the work of Aldrin Peñamora, one of the editors of this volume. He is a theologian from the Philippines who has done quite an extensive peacebuilding work with the Bangsa Moro (the Muslim minority indigenous to the southern Philippines), calling the church to be their true neighbor.⁵² In seeking justice for the Moros, Peñamora employs at least two different approaches. The first is to construct "a Christian ethic of responsibility" which looks at the Filipino concept of *kapwa* (neighbor), and the second is to look into the Christian ritual of the Eucharist as a resource for "Christian justice and peacemaking ethics."⁵³

The Muslim–Christian relationship in the Philippines, commonly referred to as the "Moro Problem," has been marked by pain. Christians in the Philippines have committed injustice toward the Moros. Peñamora maintains that if Christians were to be honest with the whole issue, the Moro Problem "is really about the Christians being the problem of the Moros."⁵⁴ Throughout their history, the Moros have been the recipient of injustice committed first through the colonialization of Spain and the United States, followed by the Western–Christian oriented government of the Philippines. This systemic marginalization comes in the form of "economic destitution, political marginalization, religious intolerance, and threats to Moro identity."⁵⁵

---

50. Maggay, 368.
51. Maggay, 371.
52. Aldrin M. Peñamora, "Ethics of Responsibility: Christ-Centered Personal and Social Ethics for Church and Society," *Journal of Asian Evangelical Theology* 19, no. 1 (March 2015): 107.
53. Aldrin M. Peñamora, "Eucharistic Justice: A Christ-Centered Response to the Bangsamoro Question in the Philippines," *Asian Journal of Pentecostal Studies* 19, no. 1 (February 2016): 32.
54. Peñamora, 33.
55. Peñamora, "Ethics of Responsibility," 101.

In constructing his Christian ethic of responsibility, Peñamora looked to the Filipino concept of kapwa that emphasizes shared identity between *ako* (self) and *iba* (other) as offering a possibility to look at another person as a brother or a sister of whom we are called to be their keeper.[56] The option can be manifested when Filipinos deepen their understanding of Christ as someone who is ontologically for others, as explained by Bonhoeffer.[57] This ontological "for others" being formed individually and collectively is the focus of Peñamora's Christian ethics. He explains:

> These two *person*-al categories, the personal and the communal, cannot be separated, for the individual "I" only emerges in sociality; Christian personal life is possible only within the communal life of the church. Thus, in a sense, the individual owes his or her to the Other. This "I-You" relationship is central to the notion of a Christian ethic of *responsibility*, for the You, bearing in itself the image of the divine You, places a necessary demand on the personal I, this giving rise to responsibility. In this, the I experiences reality through the claim of the Other. It is in responding to the Other's claim that the personal I exists in reality and acts ethically.[58]

According to Peñamora, this has been translated into a Filipino Christology that portrays Jesus as the "God of Struggle" from the word *pakikibaka*, meaning struggle. This theology of struggle can prove to be helpful to deal with the Moro situation because it is more than about the struggle of the oppressed. Instead, it is "primarily a theology *in* and *of* struggle that is generated through solidarity with the struggling Filipino people."[59]

The resource to practice this theology of struggle, which seeks to alleviate the plight of the Moros who have suffered due to the "swords and the Christian cross," can be found in the Eucharist, which Peñamora maintains is "a crucial resource for a Christian justice and peacemaking ethic."[60] Peñamora looked into the paradigm for justice, specifically economic justice, presented by Anabaptist John H. Yoder and Roman Catholic Monika Hellwig. Drawing

---

56. Peñamora, 107.
57. Peñamora, 93.
58. Peñamora, 94–95.
59. Peñamora, 99.
60. Peñamora, "Eucharistic Justice: A Christ-Centered Response to the Bangsamoro Question in the Philippines," 31–32.

from Yoder, Peñamora points out that the Eucharist is paradigmatic for "equitable economic distribution" and "revolutionary" in propelling the church to follow Jesus in his Luke 4:18–20 ministry of jubilee, which includes canceling debts and redistribution of property.[61] From Hellwig, Peñamora stresses that the Eucharist alleviates poverty not just in the physical sense, but also in affective and spiritual terms, and maintains the Eucharist addresses a greater hunger than physical hunger – which is the hunger for "creative love."[62]

This Eucharistic justice proposal is not about inviting the Moro neighbors to celebrate the breaking of bread in an ecclesiastical context; instead, what he is proposing is that when Christians celebrate the Eucharist, they ought, first, to lament because of the injustice suffered by their neighbors. Second, when celebrating the Eucharist, we need to respond to the "call for [Christians] to act justly toward our Muslim neighbors."[63] The Eucharist should remind Christians that scripturally the celebration is "paradigmatic for the preferential for the poor."[64] The Eucharist can then enrich the indigenous concept, kapwa, that emphasizes shared identity between ako (Self) and iba (Other) so that Filipino Christians can carry out their ministry of reconciliation as new creations. The Eucharist, along with the concept of kapwa, will enable Christians to regard Christ not from a worldly power point of view any longer (2 Cor 5:16). Instead, they can take on the mind of Christ that understands greatness and power are expressed fully by being the servant and slave to all (Phil 2:1–11; Matt 20:26–27).

CONSTRUCTIVE PROPOSAL

I construct my proposal for an Asian evangelical ethics around three themes. First, *an ethics of embrace* modeled after the Trinitarian embrace into which we have been invited to enter. Second, *an ethics of embodiedness* that takes its cues from Confucianist philosophy. Such ethics, made possible by perichoretic embrace, allow us to see embodied practices that offer formation in light of that embrace.[65] Embodied practices are necessary, even required, as it is in them that Christians in Asia can have an opportunity to experience and extend

---

61. Peñamora, 36–37.
62. Peñamora, 38.
63. Peñamora, 40.
64. Peñamora, 37.
65. Perichoresis is a word used to describe the mutual indwelling and interpenetration of the persons of the Trinity. It conveys relational ideas such as interchange, reciprocity, being drawn to one another, giving to and receiving from one another, and contained in one another that exists in the Triune God. The perichoretic embrace, found in the salvific story narrated in

the embrace of the triune God. Third, *an ethics of Christoformation* for the Trinitarian embrace that enables local embodied practices to be included in that embrace has a *telos* (end-goal), the formation of Christ in a person. Before proceeding, I would like to discuss the need for such an ethics.

WHY ASIAN CHRISTIAN ETHICS?

The idea that Christianity is a Western religion still needs to be dismantled. It is partly through Christian ethics that are genuinely Asian that Asian Christians will be able to feel at home as Christians who have made peace with their cultural identity. It is disheartening to see Asian Christians who identify themselves as evangelicals often possessing an "us against them" attitude. In describing different models of Christian encounter in India, theologian M. Thomas Thangaraj presented this reality. He shows that the Syrian Orthodox in Kerala were the only Christians able to live alongside their Hindu neighbors in the predominantly Hindu community. On the other hand, Protestants have, for the most part, seen the "Other" as either enemies, potential converts, or people with primitive superstitions.[66] This is unfortunate! This attitude denies the fact that at Pentecost the disciples experienced in time and space the promise given through Joel that the Spirit is poured out on all flesh (*epi pas sarx*), a reality that Paul affirms when declaring that God has not left himself without a witness (Acts 2:17; 14:17). The attitude also creates a situation where Asian Christians find themselves, unnecessarily, in a disadvantaged place similar to what Phan calls "betwixt-and-between" but in their own native land.[67]

From the mid-twentieth century, many theologians in Asia began to let go of that assumption, opting instead for another way of engagement that is no longer an encounter *between* cultures but rather *among* cultures.[68] This is encouraging! Thus, Thangaraj shows that diverse ways to engage the Other have emerged in India. The Other is now seen as a storehouse of culture.

Scripture, invites us to enter into this relationship. Later in this volume Paulus S. Widjaja offers a different nuance of perichoresis. His definition and mine are different but do not contradict each other, 340.
66. M. Thomas Thangaraj, "Religious Pluralism, Dialogue and Asian Christian Responses," in *Christian Theology in Asia*, ed. Sebastian C. H. Kim, First Edition (Cambridge; New York: Cambridge University Press, 2008), 159–60.
67. Peter C. Phan, "Betwixt and Between: Doing Theology with Memory and Imagination," in *Journeys at the Margin: Toward an Autobiographical Theology in American-Asian Perspective*, ed. Peter C. Phan and Jung Young Lee (Collegeville: Liturgical Press, 1999), 113.
68. Peter C. Phan, *Christianity with an Asian Face: Asian American Theology in the Making* (Maryknoll: Orbis Books, 2003), 10.

Practices of other religions have been adapted to enrich the Christian spiritual life and worship, providing language and concepts.[69] Yet another mode of engagement is to see the Other as a companion in struggle, especially in the struggle for independence and the development of a new nation.[70] Later on, this engagement branches into a different form: Christians working hand-in-hand with the Other in bringing liberation and freedom to those who are marginalized. The final type of engagement is to see the Other as a partner in inter-religious dialogue. This effort is at least noticeable in academia throughout Asia.[71] I maintain that these different modes of engagement are indicative of the "personal and societal enrichment and transformation" that "betwixt-and-between" provides as an opportunity. That is, not being disadvantaged by their in-betweenness, Christians have a chance to think from both sides, using "memory and imagination . . . contemplating the past and creating the future at the same time."[72]

An Ethics of Embrace

Christian theology understands God as triune, expressing hospitality by embracing the whole created order through the Son and the Spirit. Space does not permit me to discuss in-depth the idea of Trinitarian embrace and hospitality.[73] For our discussion, I want to emphasize that as people who have experienced this divine embrace, we are invited to participate in embracing the world, offering and extending God's hospitality to others. In constructing an ethics of embrace, I benefited from the understanding of embrace of Miroslav Volf, who used the term as a "metaphor for reconciliation."[74] Volf maintains that an embrace consists of four essential and integrated movements, namely, "opening the arms, waiting, closing the arms, and opening them again."[75] We will look at these four movements and how they can contribute to an ethics of embrace. First is the act of *opening the arms*. Volf maintains that this gesture of reaching

---

69. Thangaraj, "Religious Pluralism, Dialogue and Asian Christian Responses," 162.
70. Thangaraj, 162.
71. Thangaraj, 163.
72. Phan, "Betwixt and Between: Doing Theology with Memory and Imagination," 114.
73. For a good discussion of Trinitarian hospitality see Amos Yong, *Hospitality and the Other: Pentecost, Christian Practices, and the Neighbor* (Maryknoll: Orbis Books, 2008), 99–128; Daniela C. Augustine, *Pentecost, Hospitality, and Transfiguration: Toward a Spirit-Inspired Vision of Social Transformation* (Cleveland: CPT Press, 2012), 43–72.
74. Miroslav Volf, *Exclusion & Embrace: A Theological Exploration of Identity, Otherness, and Reconciliation*, First Edition (Nashville: Abingdon Press, 1996), 140.
75. Volf, 141.

for the Other signals a "discontent with [our] own *self-enclosed* identity" (emphasis mine) coupled with a "desire for the other" by creating a space for the Other to come in because the opening of arms is also an invitation.

The second movement is *waiting*, a significant movement as it tells the Other that in our previous movement we are not trying to invade them, but rather that the intent of the interaction is one of mutual reciprocity. In waiting, we "wait for the desire in the other to arise" and to make a move into the created space.[76] The third movement is *closing* the arms, a movement that is impossible without reciprocity because it requires "two pairs of arms for one embrace."[77] Closing of the arms would also require a "soft touch" to prevent a too tight of an embrace that would be crushing, invading, and overpowering. Through this, "the identity of the self is both preserved and transformed, and the alterity of the other is both affirmed as alterity and partly received into the ever-changing identity of the self."[78] The final movement is again *opening the arms*. Volf explains that the embrace does not weld the two bodies together into one; instead, it comes about as the arms are put around the other person.[79] Therefore, for the embrace to remain an embrace, the arms are required to open up again to let go of the Other so that the conversation of differences can continue when the next opportunity for an embrace arises.

I maintain that it is in this idea of embrace, and the four movements within an embrace, that an Asian Christian can have an advantage by being "betwixt-and-between" as opposed to being disadvantaged. This advantage is similar to what Korean theologian Sang Hyun Lee argues is a move from marginality, which is a place of exclusion, to liminality, which is a place of creativity.[80] This will enable Asian Christians to be ministers of reconciliation precisely from their in-between location. By opening our arms to the Other who are our neighbors, we begin to show our discontentment with our self-enclosed identity as a church, perhaps due to the myopic vision of Christianity we have inherited, and we begin to see the Other as those to whom Christ opens his arms. In waiting, we open our ears and prepare to listen attentively to what the Other is going to say as they enter the shared space, recognizing that God has always been present in their space. As they come into the shared space, they

---

76. Volf, 142.
77. Volf, 143.
78. Volf, 143.
79. Volf, 144.
80. Sang Hyun Lee, *From a Liminal Place: An Asian American Theology* (Minneapolis: Fortress Press, 2010), ix–x, 5, 31–33.

are also bringing the presence of God. By closing the arms, we acknowledge God's presence that both they and we bring into the shared space. The "soft touch" ensures that as we understand that we bring the presence of God, we do not invade the Other with our presence. Finally, the opening of the arms again acknowledges our differences while committing to continue the conversation that will be mutually enriching for both sides in another embrace.[81]

I maintain that the process of embrace that turns the disadvantage of "betwixt-and-between" into an advantage is traceable, at least implicitly, in the thoughts of all four theologians surveyed above. In Adiprasetya, we see his process of reconciliation and healing of self-identity was found by embracing his clown-ness, a reflection of the clown-ness of Jesus, seen initially through a Javanese clown character. For Lakawa, an imaginative embrace of a "dance movement," performed through painful physical debilitation, enabled her to construct an idea of a "risky hospitality" as one way to rebuild interreligious relationships strained by victims' painful memories of religious violence. Maggay embraced the indigenous mindset of the Filipinos to construct authentic evangelism in the Philippines. Peñamora investigated the indigenous Filipino concept of neighbor (kapwa) and the Eucharist as resources that enable Filipino Christians to embrace their Moro neighbors who have been the victims of injustice.

An Ethics of Embodiedness

Asian Christian ethics must not be limited to abstract moral principles; instead, it is a construct that must envision the holistic transformation of the people of God, which requires embodiedness. This is only natural because of our allegiance to the incarnate God. In proposing the possibility of the liturgy of the Eucharist countering the liturgy of torture practiced by the state, William T. Cavanaugh points out that when "meaning" is given to the Eucharist, it often becomes "Gnostic internalization" that completely misses the formative aspect of the celebration itself.[82] Christian ethics that are strictly about moral principles are in danger of becoming Gnostic, which will result in alienating

---

81. Without using the concept of embrace I have discussed the possibility of hospitality not from the position of power, but also from the position of weakness (where Christians are the minority) in Florian Simatupang, "Christian Hospitality in the Celebration of 'Id al-Fitr: Participating in Halal Bi-Halal as a Way for Indonesian Christians to Learn Reconciliation from Their Muslim Neighbors," *Pneuma* 41, no. 2 (2019): 233–34.
82. William T. Cavanaugh, *Torture and Eucharist: Theology, Politics, and the Body of Christ*, First Edition, Challenges in Contemporary Theology (Oxford; Malden: Blackwell Publishing, 1998), 12.

people, rendering them powerless, and unable to answer the questions of the everyday human condition of the people of Asia, including questions that relate to suffering and injustice. Hence what is needed is an ethics that is embodied.

According to Korean theologian Jung-Sun Oh, as the most Christianized society in East Asia, the Korean social fabric and the way society functions is still characteristically very Confucian even if the ideology of Confucianism itself is somewhat fading. The permeation of Confucianist philosophy is so profoundly thorough in South Korea to the point that classic Confucian texts are often quoted by Christian preachers, including those who would be considered conservatives.[83] Oh maintains that one of the reasons for this is the fact that Confucianism is more about lived realities than abstract principles.[84] The understanding of religiosity in Confucianism is about the transformation of the individual within a community that comes as a result of a faithful encounter with the divine.[85] Oh further maintains that there is no conflict between the Christian message and the nature of the Korean mind as influenced by Confucianism because both are about "restoring human dignity or self-realization" toward the salvation of the whole person.[86] Much of Oh's work then is to construct, by process of retrieval, what it means to be a Christian in a Korean context where one does not just simply adopt a Western expression of Christianity and superimpose it onto the Korean cultural and societal precepts, but instead seeks "to sow the seed of Christian message in the field of Korean soil" so that it will bring forth indigenous fruit.[87]

I maintain that the survey above has shown to us the indigenous fruits that come from retrieving and adapting embodied local wisdom and traditions. These fruits, I will add, are harvested within the embodied context of each of the theologians. Mediated by the character of the local Javanese clown, Adiprasetya experienced an encounter with the divine – Jesus the clown – that resulted in the transformation of the self. In the story of Lakawa's embodied practice, a dance movement of journeying, creating space, remaining, breathing, and extending hands became part of her physical healing process and the healing process of a community in the aftermath of religious violence. Maggay, seeking to find a way for Christian conversion to move beyond the

---

83. Jung-Sun Oh, "A Hermeneutics of Korean Theology of Filial Piety: A Global Theology," *The Asia Journal of Theology* 24, no. 2 (October 2010): 331.
84. Oh, 331.
85. Oh, 332.
86. Oh, 334.
87. Oh, 334.

superficial that only produces either "culture Christianity" or a "demythologized Christianity" (which are both unable to answer the concerns of Filipinos), retrieved, among other things, the indigenous way of seeing the body (*katawan*) as persona (*katauhan*) bound to the soul (*kaluluwa*). Last, Peñamora, in retrieving the embodied Filipino concept of *kapwa* (neighbor) which emphasizes shared identity between ako (Self) and iba (Other) and connecting it with the Christian ritual of the Eucharist as a resource for Christian justice and peacemaking ethics, sees the possibility of regarding the Moros as brothers and sisters, for whom we are called to be their keepers.

An Ethics of Christoformation

The telos of Asian Christian ethics is always about seeking the Christoformation of persons and communities.[88] The process of Christoformation is always the work of the Holy Spirit, the Spirit of Christ, who has been poured out on all flesh, allowing *all flesh* to participate in the life of the Word made flesh (cf. John 1:14). An ethics of Christoformation is a lens through which we can see how, by the work of the Spirit, Christ is formed in all. This Christoformation first takes place in the church, not so much as an order of priority, but more importantly, as enabling the community to be Christlike, which includes the ability to discern the work of Christ forming his character in all people who are participants of his flesh-ness. Daniella Augustine maintains that on the day of Pentecost, the Spirit of God Christoformed the church, enabling it to become "an extension of the koinonia of the Trinity in-fleshed in the redeemed human community."[89] It is precisely as an extension of that Trinitarian fellowship that the church discerns and affirms the Christoformative works of the Spirit outside of the church.

Scripture testifies the characteristics of Christ to us, such as the fruit of the Spirit, hospitality, self-emptying (*kenosis*), and image bearer (cf. Col 1:15), to name a few. If any of these characteristics is taking shape in a person or community, we must acknowledge that as Christoformation taking place because these characteristics can only be the work of the Spirit. I maintain that these characteristics are easily visible in the survey above. Lakawa's and Peñamora's peacebuilding efforts require, at the very least, a posture of kenosis to be an

---

88. Frank D. Macchia in, *Baptized in the Spirit: A Global Pentecostal Theology* (Grand Rapids : Zondervan Academic, 2006), 106, maintains that "[t]he transformative power of the kingdom . . . has a *Christoformic* goal and direction," (italics original).
89. Augustine, *Pentecost, Hospitality, and Transfiguration*, 16.

extension of the triune God's hospitality. Enabled by the Spirit to self-empty oneself, one can value the Other above oneself (Phil 2:3) and see the Other as one whom the triune God embraces with hospitality. In Adiprasetya and Maggay, the restoration of the image bearer-ness is being realized by the Spirit. For Adiprasetya, the Spirit is realizing a restoration of the self as image bearer by embracing, through a Javanese clown, his once rejected clown-ness. In Maggay's work, the Spirit is seeking Christoformation in the Filipino people using local wisdom to move them to a more genuine, yet indigenous conversion to Christ.

CONCLUSION

Are we dealing with syncretism or contamination of the Christian faith? That is probably a question that comes up in the reader's mind. I would argue that the answer to both possibilities is "no." First, Edward Said argues that it would be a mistake to see a proposal like this as contamination; instead, we need to understand "all culture as hybrid . . . and encumbered, or entangled and overlapping with what used to be regarded as extraneous elements," which prohibits us from seeing the progression of something (in our case, Christian ethics) as merely linear.[90] As Oh has argued, our self-awareness, including our awareness of Christian understanding, is always the fruitful result of the ever-expanding and dynamic network of human relationships.[91] With regards to syncretism, Simon Chan citing Lamin Sanneh, sees Christianity as a "translated religion" that is highly adaptable in the receiving culture and argued that what is required is a theological nuance[92] hence the three themes I constructed; these offer us ethical nuances to understand the process of translation that is taking place. These three themes should help us; first to understand the hybridity of cultures, and then to accept the process of contextualization.

QUESTIONS FOR DISCUSSION

1. Do you think the word "evangelical" needs rescuing from how it has been perceived? If so, do you think Asian Christians can

---

90. Edward W. Said, *Culture and Imperialism* (New York: Vintage, 1994), 317.
91. Oh, "A Hermeneutics of Korean Theology of Filial Piety," 340.
92. Simon Chan, "Folk Christianity and Primal Spirituality: Prospects for Theological Development," in *Christian Movements in Southeast Asia: A Theological Exploration*, ed. Michael Nai-Chiu Poon (Singapore: Armour Publishing Pte Ltd, in collaboration with the Centre for the Study of Christianity in Asia, Trinity Theological College, 2010), 4, 9.

contribute to the process of restoring the word "evangelical", and how?
2. What would be some of the ways we can understand the word "evangelical" that are closer to the enchanted worldview of Asians? Out of the four theologians discussed in this chapter, which do you find most helpful from their engagements with their respective traditions, cultures, and rituals in shaping an enchanted evangelicalism? Which do you find least helpful? Why?
3. Should evangelical Christians in Asia have an "us vs. them" attitude, or should we continue to seek ways of engaging traditions, cultures, and rituals? Other than the directions the four theologians have taken, what would be some different possible ways you might consider?
4. Aside from embrace, embodiedness, and Christoformation, what would you suggest should also be included in creating a framework to look at Asian identity, rituals, relationality, and vocabulary?
5. Do you think the themes of embrace, embodiedness, and Christoformation are enough to safeguard from the fear of syncretism or contamination? Why or why not?

BIBLIOGRAPHY

Adiprasetya, Joas. "Following Jesus the Clown." *Theology Today* 69, no. 4 (January 2013): 418–27.

———. "The Liturgy of the In-Between." *Scottish Journal of Theology* 72, no. 1 (2019): 82–97.

Augustine, Daniela C. Pentecost, Hospitality, and Transfiguration: Toward a Spirit-Inspired Vision of Social Transformation. Cleveland: CPT Press, 2012.

Cavanaugh, William T. *Torture and Eucharist: Theology, Politics, and the Body of Christ*. First Edition. Challenges in Contemporary Theology. Oxford; Malden: Blackwell Publishing, 1998.

Chan, Simon. "Folk Christianity and Primal Spirituality: Prospects for Theological Development." In *Christian Movements in Southeast Asia: A Theological Exploration*, edited by Michael Nai-Chiu Poon. Singapore: Armour Publishing Pte Ltd, in collaboration with the Centre for the Study of Christianity in Asia, Trinity Theological College, 2010.

———. *Grassroots Asian Theology: Thinking the Faith from the Ground Up*. Downers Grove: IVP Academic, 2014.

Lakawa, Septemmy Eucharistia. "A Woman Becoming: On Pain, Dancing and Doing Theology with Those Who Face Religious Violence." *Reformed World* 56, no. 3 (September 2006): 284–95.

———. "Risky Hospitality: Mission in the Aftermath of Religious Communal Violence in Indonesia." ThD, Boston University School of Theology, 2011.

Lee, Sang Hyun. *From a Liminal Place: An Asian American Theology*. Minneapolis: Fortress Press, 2010.

Macchia, Frank D. *Baptized in the Spirit: A Global Pentecostal Theology*. Grand Rapids: Zondervan Academic, 2006.

Maggay, Melba Padilla. "Engaging Culture: Lessons from the Underside of History." *Missiology* 33, no. 1 (January 1, 2005): 62–70.

———. "Towards Sensitive Engagement with Filipino Indigenous Consciousness." *International Review of Mission* 87, no. 346 (July 1998): 361–73.

Mayfield, D. L. "In Push to Reopen, American Evangelicals Fall Prey to Political Strategy." *Sojourners* (May 11, 2020). https://sojo.net/articles/push-reopen-american-evangelicals-fall-prey-political-strategy.

McGrath, Alister E. *Christian Theology: An Introduction*. 6th edition. Chichester; Malden: Wiley-Blackwell, 2016.

National Association of Evangelicals. "What Is an Evangelical?" Accessed January 17, 2022. https://www.nae.org/what-is-an-evangelical/.

Noll, Mark A. *The Scandal of the Evangelical Mind*. Grand Rapids: Eerdmans, 1995.

Oh, Jung-Sun. "A Hermeneutics of Korean Theology of Filial Piety: A Global Theology." *The Asia Journal of Theology* 24, no. 2 (October 2010): 325–46.

Peñamora, Aldrin M. "Ethics of Responsibility: Christ-Centered Personal and Social Ethics for Church and Society." *Journal of Asian Evangelical Theology* 19, no. 1 (March 2015): 91–107.

———. "Eucharistic Justice: A Christ-Centered Response to the Bangsamoro Question in the Philippines." *Asian Journal of Pentecostal Studies* 19, no. 1 (February 2016): 31–44.

Phan, Peter C. "Betwixt and Between: Doing Theology with Memory and Imagination." In *Journeys at the Margin: Toward an Autobiographical Theology in American-Asian Perspective*, edited by Peter C. Phan and Jung Young Lee, 113–33. Collegeville, MN: Liturgical Press, 1999.

———. *Christianity With an Asian Face: Asian American Theology in the Making*. Maryknoll, NY: Orbis Books, 2003.

———. *In Our Own Tongues: Perspectives from Asia on Mission and Inculturation*. Maryknoll, NY: Orbis Books, 2003.

Said, Edward W. *Culture and Imperialism*. New York: Vintage, 1994.

Simatupang, Florian. "Christian Hospitality in the Celebration of 'Id al-Fitr: Participating in Halal Bi-Halal as a Way for Indonesian Christians to

Learn Reconciliation from Their Muslim Neighbors." *Pneuma* 41, no. 2 (2019): 218–35.

Thangaraj, M. Thomas. "Religious Pluralism, Dialogue and Asian Christian Responses." In *Christian Theology in Asia*, edited by Sebastian C. H. Kim, First Edition, 157–78. Cambridge, UK; New York, NY: Cambridge University Press, 2008.

Volf, Miroslav. *Exclusion & Embrace: A Theological Exploration of Identity, Otherness, and Reconciliation*. First Edition. Nashville: Abingdon Press, 1996.

Yong, Amos. *Hospitality and the Other: Pentecost, Christian Practices, and the Neighbor*. Maryknoll: Orbis Books, 2008.

CHAPTER 2

"WATER IS THICKER THAN BLOOD"

Family in the Changing Landscape

Bernard K. Wong

THE CURRENT LANDSCAPE

Families in Asia have been undergoing significant changes in the past few decades. The nature and degree of these changes vary with the socioeconomic, political, and cultural contexts of each region, but recent studies reveal several major trends common to all Asian countries. First, the age of marriage is increasingly postponed, and wealthier countries see the highest percentage of unmarried young adults. For example, over ninety percent of young adults aged 20–24 in Hong Kong, Japan, South Korea, Taiwan, and Singapore are still single. Second, the percentage of divorced persons has increased, though the figure is still lower compared to the West. Third, the number of never-married mature adults has risen significantly. For example, over twenty-eight percent of Japanese men aged 40–44 in the year 2010 had never been married; this percentage had jumped sharply from just under three percent in 1970. People who remain single at this age are unlikely to start their families or to have children at all.[1] These common trends indicate that Asians increasingly deviate from the traditional norm – marrying young, giving birth, and raising children to continue the family lineage, and staying in the same marriage for life. Remaining unmarried for life, co-habitation, divorce, remarriage, single-parenthood, blended families, and marriages with no children are becoming more common. While the more economically developed countries are leading these trends, other Asian countries are tracing along the same path.

Evangelical Christians generally uphold the traditional marriage and family norm. Marriage is defined as the "one flesh union" between a man and a woman. Lifelong and stable marriage is considered the foundation of a good

---

1. Stella R. Quah, "Families in Asia: A Kaleidoscope of Continuity and Change," in *Routledge Handbook of Families in Asia*, ed. Stella R. Quah (Oxon: Routledge, 2015), 3–22.

family for the benefit of the couple and their children. As the traditional family is on the decline, the church responds by protecting the sanctity of marriage. Homosexuality and divorce are fervently addressed and opposed.[2] While homosexuality attempts to redefine the heterosexual nature of the marriage union, the issue of divorce and remarriage addresses the stability of this union. Other less prominent ethical issues are also related to marriage stability. For example, mixed marriage between a Christian and non-Christian is frowned upon as it may lead to more divorces.[3] In addition, marriage, when defined as a "one flesh union," requires that sexual relationship should only happen within marriage. Therefore, pre-marital sex, co-habitation, and extra-marital affairs are morally wrong. The church places heavy emphasis on these ethical issues. For example, the discipline guidelines of a major evangelical denomination in Hong Kong list seven specific moral failures. Four among them are related to marriage and family: homosexuality, pre-marital sex and extra-marital sex, divorce and remarriage, and marriage between a Christian and a non-Christian.[4]

In the rapidly changing world, these ethical teachings of the church will increasingly be challenged. As young adults in Asia further postpone their marriages, the church's insistence on the sinfulness of pre-marital sex and co-habitation may appear legalistic and stifling. As more people remain single into their mature adulthood and finding a spouse becomes more difficult, the church's disapproval of mixed marriage may be perceived as a harsh imposition on those who desire to marry. Therefore, Christians in Asia should continually refresh the ethical framework for marriage and family while remaining faithful to our cultural and biblical traditions.

Moreover, the church must remain conscious that the nature and purpose of the family revealed in the Bible differs from traditional Asian understandings of family. Although the Bible affirms some family values associated with Asian cultural norms, it challenges others. If the church embraces the traditional family too readily, she tends to overlook these challenges. For example, the Christian vision of singleness as a worthy vocation challenges the church's sweeping advocacy of marriage and family. Recovering this vocation is

---

2. See, for example, the inclusion of "divorce and remarriage" and "homosexuality" in John Jefferson Davis, *Evangelical Ethics: Issues Facing the Church Today* (Phillipsburg: P&R Pub., 2004).
3. Mook Kuk Arnold Yeung, *Feng zhi wo: Fengyu tong lu hua jiating* [*Shelter in the Wind: Weathering the Storm in the Family*] (Hong Kong: Gengxin ziyuan chuban she, 2013), 43–44.
4. The remaining three ethical issues are abortion, fraud, and false teaching. Christian and Missionary Alliance Church Union Hong Kong, *Xuandao hui jilu shouce* [*C&MA Discipline Guidelines*], (Hong Kong: C&MA, 2015).

especially relevant as more Asians remain single for life. Likewise, the church's advocacy for stable families should not entail a return to the traditional form of stable family, lest the church unwittingly collude with the Asian patriarchal cultures and bring harm to weaker family members. As Christ is the head of all Christian households, the traditional patriarchal family should be challenged. Christian ethical reflections on the family in contemporary Asian contexts must consider these challenges.

Due to the limited length of this essay, only a few of these ethical issues will be discussed in detail. The most prominent issue – divorce and remarriage – will first be investigated to show how Asian Christians use biblical, theological, and cultural resources to discourage them. One factor that contributes to the rising rates of divorce is the weakening of traditional forms of patriarchy, a trend that should be celebrated. Our discussions will then turn to the relationship between Christianity and patriarchal Asian cultures. Christianity in the West frequently invokes love as the moral principle to enhance familial relationships and resist harmful patriarchy. But I contend that in Asian cultures, a properly understood ecclesiology offers a moral vision that appeals to Christians better.

DIVORCE AND REMARRIAGE

Asian evangelical Christians share with other evangelicals around the world a deep conviction that the Bible must be the primary norm for the ethical management of family life. As a result, one factor in responding to divorce and remarriage is the application of biblical texts related to the issue. Jesus's sayings in the Gospels (Matt 5:31–32; 19:3–9; Mark 10:2–12; Luke 16:18) and Paul's teaching in 1 Cor 7:12–16 are the major texts of concern. Old Testament texts are also sometimes referenced (Exod 21:10–11; Deut 22:13–29; Deut 24:1–4; Ezra 9–10; Mal 2:10–16) but are usually given less weight. However, the different scriptural texts by no means offer a unified view on the issue. For instance, Jesus's teaching against divorce in Mark 10:11–12 mentions no exceptions, but the same teaching in Matthew includes an exception clause, "except for sexual immorality" (Matt 5:32; 19:9), which, in itself, is difficult to interpret. The Old Testament speaks against divorce in one place (Mal 2:10–16) yet seems to commend it in another (Ezra 9–10). Faced with this variety of voices within the canon, a person may be able to find biblical support for the particular view of divorce and remarriage being advocated. In such cases, although the Bible is cited, biblical authority is undermined when its teachings are applied only selectively and without appreciation for the spirit of the whole of the Christian scriptures.

A closer look at the relevant biblical texts reveal that they arise from their specific contexts to address differing concerns. For example, it has been suggested that the Gospel of Mark emphasizes the high cost of discipleship, so that divorce is disallowed, while the exception clause in the Gospel of Matthew serves to address the debate over the grounds of divorce within Judaism.[5] In other words, Mark focuses on marriage as an aspect of Christian discipleship while Matthew demonstrates how Jesus understands the spirit of the Mosaic Law through divorce and remarriage. Discipleship and law, not divorce and remarriage, are the more fundamental concerns of the respective biblical texts. Another example can be found in the Old Testament. Malachi spoke against divorce to admonish covenantal faithfulness while Ezra commanded Israelites to separate from their gentile wives to demonstrate their faithfulness toward God.[6] While both passages are concerned with Israel's fidelity toward God, two opposite ethics of divorce emerge depending on the situation. These examples explain why the Bible contains apparently different teachings at various places. A corollary is that we should not directly apply a specific teaching in the Bible into our own contexts without appropriate interpretive care.

Therefore, Christian ethicists frequently approach the subject of divorce and remarriage by first constructing a theology of marriage from Scripture, then deduce ethical principles from this theology. The "one flesh union" that Jesus retrieves from the Genesis narratives is the basis of such a theology. The creation of man and woman sets the stage for marriage. As "It is not good for the man to be alone" (Gen 2:18), marriage overcomes this deficiency by uniting the man and the woman. "A man will leave his father and mother" (Matt 19:4) suggests a shift in allegiance from parents to spouse at marriage, and the marriage union is the strongest bond among humans. The statement, "They are no longer two, but one flesh" has sexual, social, and spiritual meanings, which suggest that husband and wife should be united in body, heart, mind, and will. "Therefore what God has joined together, let no one separate" suggests that marriage should be permanent, not just for the good of humans,

---

5. Richard Hays, *The Moral Vision of the New Testament: Community, Cross, New Creation: A Contemporary Introduction to New Testament Ethics* (New York: HarperOne, 1996), 349–53.
6. Wallace Louie, "Shengjing zhong lihun yu zaihun si guan [Four views on 'Divorce and Marriage' in the Bible]," in *Lihun yu zaihun: jidutu de guandian* [*Divorce and Remarriage: Christian Perspectives*], 4th ed., edited by Lawrence Chan (Hong Kong: China Alliance Press, 2014), 73–78.

but also according to God's will.⁷ Christians in general agree that it is not good for marriages to break up. Their difference is in whether divorce should be allowed, and if so, under what circumstances and for what reasons. The options fall broadly into four views, and each ethicist's choice often reflects a primary concern. These views are described below from the most stringent to the most permissive.⁸

1. Divorce is not allowed at all.

Man-Kei Ho holds this view and avers that in the face of secularization and crumbling morality, the church should make no compromise with the world by naming any divorce justified.⁹ Couples in troubled marriages can only separate and should not seek legal divorce. Christians who divorce their spouses sin against God. Remarriage is also not allowed. While this view upholds the sanctity of marriage, it can be particularly challenging to put into practice. In addition, biblical interpretation that supports this view is often rather strained. For instance, Ho argues that the clause "except for sexual immorality" in Matt 19:9 is not a condition to allow husbands to divorce their wives, but is simply an insertion that bears no particular weight to the command.¹⁰ But the exception clause is obviously a quotation from Deut 24:1 and it is likely that Jesus would not preclude the possibility of divorce in the fallen world.¹¹ While it is commendable to maintain that divorce is not good, insisting that the Bible allows for no divorce is difficult to substantiate.

2. Annulment is allowed, not divorce.

To annul a marriage means to declare it as invalid and therefore that it should not have been contracted in the first place. For the Roman Catholic Church, annulment is the only way to separate a married couple as they consider

---

7. Lawrence Chan, "Shengjing zhong de hunyin guan [Biblical View of Marriage]," in *Lihun yu zaihun: jidutu de guandian* [*Divorce and Remarriage: Christian Perspectives*], 4th ed., ed. Lawrence Chan (Hong Kong: China Alliance Press, 2014), 3–11.
8. Louie, "Four views on 'Divorce and Marriage' in the Bible," 68–69.
9. Man-Kei Ho, *Practical Christian Ethics* (Taipei: Taosheng Publishing House, 2010), 159–160.
10. Ho, *Practical Christian Ethics*, 156–8. Ho's interpretation is rather unique. Some scholars interpret the preposition "except" in the Matt 19:9 clause to mean "including," thus arriving at the same conclusion as Ho, but Ho does not opt for this interpretation. See Louie, "Four views on 'Divorce and Marriage' in the Bible," 68.
11. Peter Chang, "Cong Ma tai fuyin shijiu zhang san zhi jiu jie kan lihun [Divorce: An Interpretation of Matt 19:3–9]," in *Lihun yu zaihun: jidutu de guandian* [*Divorce and Remarriage: Christian Perspectives*], 4th ed., ed. Lawrence Chan (Hong Kong: China Alliance Press, 2014), 43–53.

marriage a sacrament that should never be broken.[12] In modern times, valid grounds for annulment may include the couple being too closely related by blood, someone coerced or deceived into marriage, or a party unable or unwilling to complete sexual intercourse.[13] As annulled marriages are not lawful marriages to begin with, the separated spouses can remarry afterward. It should be noted that some marriage separation can be interpreted as either divorce or annulment. For example, some consider that in Ezra 9–10, the marriages between Israelites and gentiles to have been invalid to begin with, so that Ezra simply announced the annulment of unlawful marriages instead of asking the Israelites to divorce their lawful wives.[14] Others assert that the Israelites were divorcing their gentile wives.[15] Nevertheless, the grounds of annulment should be restricted, lest people use it as an excuse to find an easy way out of an unpleasant marriage.

3. Divorce is allowed for certain limited conditions.

Many evangelicals embrace this view and the most common grounds for doing so are the "Matthean exception" and "Pauline privilege." The former is based on the clause "except for sexual immorality" (Matt 5:32; 19:9) and is frequently interpreted to mean adultery. Therefore, if a spouse commits adultery, the innocent party may seek divorce. The latter is derived from Paul's discussions of the unbelieving spouse (1 Cor 7:12–16). The ethical principle that ensues stipulates that if an unbelieving spouse seeks divorce, the believer may passively agree. Moreover, desertion for a considerable duration can be considered an instance of the unbelieving spouse actively seeking divorce. Many evangelicals consider adultery and desertion the only two grounds of divorce since only these two have biblical support.[16]

Advocates of this view are, in fact, using a particular method to read the Bible for ethics. On the one hand, the "one flesh" theology of marriage stipulates that marriage should be permanent. But on the other hand, the Bible contains certain exceptions to this ideal. To uphold biblical authority, marriage should be deemed permanent while the Matthean exception and Pauline privilege are the only two valid grounds for divorce.

---

12. John Witte, Jr., *From Sacrament to Contract: Marriage, Religion, and Law in the Western Tradition*, 2nd ed. (Louisville, KY: Westminster John Knox, 2012), 111–12.
13. Witte, 328.
14. Louie, "Four views on 'Divorce and Marriage' in the Bible," 73–74.
15. Alexander Mak, "Divorce and Remarriage in the Bible," *Hill Road* 27 (July 2011): 51.
16. Cheng Ji, "Reflections on the Legitimate Grounds for Divorce and Remarriage among Chinese Christians," *China Graduate School of Theology Journal* 48 (January 2010): 88–100.

Two assumptions underlie this thinking. First, the Old Testament, which contains examples of divorce and may be read as recommending it in certain circumstances, must be read in light of the New Testament's teaching on the subject, given the need to interpret the whole Scripture in light of Jesus. Second, the two grounds of divorce found in the New Testament are considered the limit beyond which Christians should not transgress. In other words, the two grounds are not examples arising from specific contexts within the early church that invite other deviations from the marriage ideal; they are themselves universal ethical principles and so Christians today should continue to abide with them.

It is beyond the scope of this essay to evaluate the validity of these two assumptions – they are explicated here for the readers to decide. However, advocates of this view must decide how to manage other cases arising from their own contexts. One such case is spousal abuse and domestic violence, which is widely accepted as a valid reason for divorce today. Some exclude it as a valid ground for divorce by being faithful to the New Testament tradition.[17] Others argue that as abuse breaks up marriage, it is effectively desertion under "Pauline privilege."[18] Yet the case of the unbelieving spouse seeking divorce in the Corinthian church is rather different from a person contemplating divorce while suffering abuse from his or her spouse. If biblical support is to be found for spousal abuse as a valid ground of divorce, Exod 21:10–11 is more relevant than 1 Cor 7:12–16.[19] But advocates of this view usually limit the valid grounds of divorce to the New Testament texts.

4. Divorce is allowed for a variety of reasons.

The above discussions lead to the view that includes cases other than adultery and desertion as valid grounds for divorce while maintaining the ideal of marriage permanence. Some ethicists advocate this view through biblical interpretation. While considering resources from both Old and New Testaments, Alexander Mak argues that marriage is a covenant in which both parties have rights and duties. Although both ought to abide by the covenant, failure of one party to keep the covenant may free the other party of their obligations. This concept of covenant is consistent throughout the canon, and so does not

---

17. Ji, "Reflections on the Legitimate Grounds," 94–5.
18. Peter and Esther Chow, *Xin wang ai: Shengjing lunli xue daolun* [*Faith, Hope, Love: Introduction to Biblical Ethics*] (Taipei: CCLM Publishing, 2014), 207–8. Chun-Ming Fong, *Christian Ethics* (Hong Kong: Chinese Baptist Press, 2001), 135.
19. Mak, "Divorce and Remarriage in the Bible," 70.

require privileging the New Testament over the Old. The "Matthean exception" and "Pauline privilege" are only two examples where the marriage covenant may be broken; other grounds for divorce can also be accepted as valid. These include failure to provide for material and psychological needs, as well as spousal abuse. On this view, God's justice and mercy – rather than rules and principles – should be the main consideration in deciding whether a married person may divorce his or her spouse.[20]

Pastoral concern is another reason to support the more permissive view. For instance, Johnson Lim argues that as Jesus would have welcomed divorcées and people who have been remarried, the church should do the same. The more restricted view of divorce and remarriage, he claims, are only held by "'ivory tower' teachers, theologians, pastors, and church leaders rather than grass-root pastors who minister to broken and hurting people in a fallen world."[21] Although divorce is never good, the church should bear witness to God's grace instead of passing harsh judgments. Agnes Liu, on the other hand, employs a consequentialist approach to the issue and arrives at the same permissive view. She first affirms that God wills marriages to be permanent and argues that divorce is harmful for the couple, their family, and society. Yet sometimes divorce may be the right decision and leads to lesser evil, for both the couple and even their children. She opines that ethical decisions are not simply right versus wrong. They may be tragic but understandable, forgivable, or even acceptable. The decision to divorce or to remarry, though not always ideal, may be the right one.[22]

MARRIAGE IN ASIAN CULTURES

Asian Christians quite often borrow resources from their Western counterparts in constructing a theology of marriage and discussing divorce and remarriage. But some intentionally use their own cultural resources in the exercise. For example, Peter and Esther Chow frame their interpersonal ethics – including familial and social ethics – in the language of traditional Chinese virtues. They discuss divorce under the concept of *zhen*, which means chastity or fidelity. In the familial context, this word describes a married woman who remains

---

20. Mak, 69–71.
21. Johnson Lim, "Divorce and Remarriage in Theological Perspectives," *Asia Journal of Theology*, 20, no. 2 (October 2006): 278.
22. Agnes Tat-Fong Liu, "Lihun yu zaihun de lunli caijue [Ethical Decision for Divorce and Remarriage]," in *Lihun yu zaihun: jidutu de guandian* [*Divorce and Remarriage: Christian Perspectives*], 4th ed., ed. Lawrence Chan (Hong Kong: China Alliance Press, 2014), 103–21.

faithful to her husband even after his death. For the relationship between husband and wife, the word *cong* is used, which literally means "to follow" or "to obey" and is used in the Chinese culture to encourage women to follow their husbands' headship.[23] Zhen and cong conjure up the image of stable and harmonious familial relationships and are considered virtues to pursue. Using these concepts has the benefit of correlating Christian morality with traditional Chinese morality and can help Chinese to accept Christian ethical teachings. Moreover, as divorce has become increasingly common in recent decades, retrieving traditional Chinese virtues can help promote stable marriages.

However, the Christian theology of marriage is rather different from traditional Chinese concepts of marriage. This is evident in how the Chows qualify zhen and cong in their discussions. Instead of exhorting women to be faithful to their husbands, zhen is linked to Jesus's teaching on adultery – "I tell you that anyone who looks at a woman lustfully has already committed adultery with her in his heart" (Matt 5:28). The virtue is transferred from women to men, and from behavioral conformance to the transformation of desire.[24] Similarly, cong in traditional Chinese culture demands wives obey their husband at all costs. But the Chows change the object of obedience from husbands to Christ and exhort Christian wives to place God above their husbands and parents.[25] Therefore, although the traditional Chinese ethical resources are used to emphasize the importance of familial virtues, the contents of these ethical teachings are derived from the Bible.

In fact, the traditional Chinese marriage and familial culture is far from ideal. Although the patriarchal family structure, the honor-shame system, and the glorification of female chastity ensured ultra-stable marriages for centuries, most modern Chinese consider these elements of traditional culture to be malicious, especially to women. Chinese Christian ethicists also use the Bible to criticize their own culture. They notice that traditional Chinese society was rather like the Old Testament Jewish society in the matter of marriage and family. While a Jewish man could divorce his wife if she displeased him (Deut 24:1), a Chinese husband could do the same for any of seven reasons, such as infertility, unwillingness to serve his relatives, gossiping, jealousy, or sickness. Therefore, Jesus's critique of the Jews – that this was an allowance given only because their "hearts were hard" – is equally applicable to the Chinese. In

---

23. Chow, *Faith, Hope, Love*, 148, 207.
24. Chow, 207–8.
25. Chow, 148–9.

addition, polygamy and concubinage were widely practiced in ancient cultures that have not been transformed by Christianity, Jewish, and Chinese cultures included. Gender inequality was also severe, as only husbands could put off their wives, but wives had no such privilege. While the livelihood of women depended totally on their husbands, divorced women found it difficult to survive. These traditional marriage and familial norms caused much harm and injustice to women and should be criticized and transformed by Christianity.[26]

In fact, Chinese society began to change in the late nineteenth century, and Christianity played a part in these developments. Historian Sau-Wah Leung attributes this change to two main factors: the exposure of Chinese to Western ideas through trade and the evangelical, educational, charitable, and publishing work performed by Western missionaries. The early missionaries into China first sowed the seeds of women's liberation, not only by speaking highly of women but also by opening schools and orphanages for girls. Chinese reformists of the early twentieth century, many of them non-Christians, followed in their footsteps to continue the women's liberation movement. The evil behind the traditional patriarchal family was continually exposed and criticized, and Chinese society became more and more open to women's rights and gender equality. Women's liberation continues today, and the economic and political status of women has greatly improved.[27]

As the status of women rose, so did the rate of divorce. This is the unfortunate reality all societies must face, not just Chinese. Leung opines that it was because the liberation movement only knows "destruction without reconstruction." The old system of marriage and family was dismantled and liberation from bondage was exalted as the only ideal. In the twentieth century, humanism and companionship marriage stepped in to fill the moral void but could hardly curb the rising rate of divorce.[28] This is the context in which Asian Christians must navigate the issue of divorce and remarriage today. On the one hand, challenging patriarchy and empowering women alleviates injustice. But on the other hand, the same social change generally results in more divorce. Christians must also know that missionaries did play a part in challenging patriarchy, though no Christian would celebrate the unfortunate rise in divorce rates that followed. Nevertheless, to address the issue of divorce

---

26. Ming-Tao Wang, *Christians and Marriage* (Hong Kong: The Alliance Press, 1967), 51–55.
27. Sau-Wah Leung, "Zhongguo shehui bianqian zhong de lihun wenti [Divorce in the Changing Chinese Society]," in *Lihun yu zaihun: jidutu de guandian [Divorce and Remarriage: Christian Perspectives]*, 4th ed., ed. Lawrence Chan (Hong Kong: China Alliance Press, 2014), 125–50.
28. Leung, 157–59.

and remarriage today, the church must avoid advocating a return to traditional patriarchy. Moreover, given the changing culture, appealing to ethical rules alone may not be adequate. A moral vision of the family is needed. We will revisit this subject later.

CHRISTIANITY AND PATRIARCHY

Societies do not follow a simple progression from patriarchy to liberation. Leung observes that while the divorce rates of Chinese societies are quickly catching up with those of the West, traditional patriarchy is still deeply-felt in modern China. Divorcées are still stigmatized, especially women.[29]

Patriarchy remains prominent in many parts of Asia. Gender inequalities – in educational opportunities, career advancements, wage differences, and property inheritance – are often considered normal. More harmful expressions of patriarchy may include sex-selective abortion, female infanticide, selling female children, and violence against wives. Christians generally resolutely oppose such offenses, but at times they may also reinforce versions of patriarchy that bring harm to families. In his study of domestic violence in India, Mhonyamo Lotha names "misinterpretation of the Scriptures" as one factor that contributes to the offense. For instance, the exhortation for wives to submit to their husbands (Eph 5:21–33) is misinterpreted to mean husbands have the right to beat their wives. Being beaten is perceived as the cross that wives should bear, so that seeking help from outside of the family is discouraged.[30] Jesus's teaching to "turn to them the other cheek also" (Matt 5:39) is used to admonish wives to tolerate their husbands' abuse. The perception of an inferior status of women aggravates the situation, but many Christians interpret the Genesis 2–3 narratives to support this view. Eve's creation as Adam's "helper" is often thought to mean that women should assume a lower status, though the Bible actually says that Eve was created to alleviate Adam's loneliness (Gen 2:18), and the language of helper is not indicative of a lower status. God's judgment on Eve after the fall – "he will rule over you" (Gen 3:16) – is interpreted to support a natural gender hierarchy instead of as the result of sin.[31]

---

29. Leung, 158.
30. Mhonyamo Lotha, "An Appraisal of Domestic Violence," in *Voices Against Domestic Violence: Biblical, Theological and Sociocultural Appraisal of the Experiences of the Oppressed Tribal, Children, Men, and Women*, ed. A. Tali Ao (Bali Nagar, New Delhi: Clark Theological College/Christian World Imprints, 2016), 43.
31. Wai-Yin Wong and Man-Yee Chan, *Lantian xingdong: Jiaohui fangzhi jia bao shi gong yan jiu bàogào* [*Operation Blue Sky: Research Report on Church's Prevention of Family Violence*] (Hong Kong: Hong Kong Women Christian Council, 2006), 33–35.

Asian evangelical Christians are generally against divorce. But their opposition may have originated from ideologies foreign to the Bible. In her study of Christianity in Korea, Nam-Soon Kang observes that some Korean theologians blend the Confucian notion of the family, or "Confucian familism," with that of Christianity. They understand the relationship among family members to be hierarchical according to gender and age. The Father–Son relationship in the Godhead, they assert, is primary, and so the father–son relationship in the human family should take precedence over the husband–wife relationship. Similarly, individuals should be subservient to their families, as one acquires status only in familial relationships.[32] Confucian familism elevates harmonious and stable families and may appear similar to Christianity in certain aspects, but there is more to it. Its heavy emphasis on male family lineage and stable relationships causes all people – Christians included – to desire a "normal" life of getting married, having at least one biological son, and staying in a stable family for life. Anything outside of this norm, such as remaining single for life, separating from one's spouse, or adopting a non-biological child, are considered aberrant and even shameful. Women are also subdued to inferior positions in family, church, and society. While Korean Christians are deeply influenced by Confucian familism, their denunciation of divorce may have been mingled with notions of the traditional patriarchal family structure. In this case, the church risks falling into the danger of perpetuating harmful patriarchy.[33] For instance, if pastors value stable families at the expense of the well-being of individuals, they may counsel against divorce at all costs. They may be ready to offer spiritual, emotional, economic, and counseling support to victims of domestic violence, but would be reluctant to consent to divorce. Victims generally face greater dangers in such situations.[34]

Kang points out that Christianity does not advocate a single familial norm. Jesus relativizes the traditional family by emphasizing the spiritual dimension of its members, so that family is not limited to biological relationship. Jesus also deconstructs the patriarchal family and challenges the subordination of women.[35] This discussion reminds Asian Christians to be careful when employing cultural resources to champion certain forms of marriage or familial ethics.

---

32. Nam-Soon Kang, "Confucian Familism and Its Social/Religious Embodiment in Christianity: Reconsidering the Family Discourse from a Feminist Perspective," *Asia Journal of Theology* 18, no. 1 (April 2004): 177–78.
33. Kang, 172–74.
34. Wong and Chan, *Operation Blue Sky*, 24–26.
35. Kang, "Confucian Familism and Its Social/Religious Embodiment in Christianity," 175–76.

It does not mean that cultural resources must be avoided. But as all cultures are tainted by sin, Asian Christians must first use the Bible to challenge our traditional notions of marriage and family before advocating them.

CHRISTOLOGY AND THE FAMILY

Our discussions of the family began with divorce and remarriage. The Bible admonishes against divorce and the theology of marriage stipulates the permanent "one flesh" union as the ethical ideal. Yet actual situations in a fallen world may require making allowances for deviations from this ideal. In the case of domestic violence, the right decision may even be for the victim to divorce the abusing spouse. Behind these ethical decisions is the desire for human persons to flourish. Poling Sun argues that the gist of Jesus's teaching is not merely outward behavior, but an inner life and value system aligned with God's kingdom.[36] The ethics of marriage and family is not merely about conformity to a set of rules or behavioral norms, but the establishing and maintaining of relationships.

For Christians, these relationships must be understood through Christ, who stands at the center of all. For instance, all family members – including wives, children, and slaves – are related to Christ as human persons and are of equal worth. The oldest male is no longer the head of the household, but Christ. Traditional patriarchal families are challenged; Christ comes in to fill the moral void. Christian husbands and wives are to "submit to one another out of reverence for Christ" (Eph 5:21). Children should still obey their parents but "in the Lord" (Eph 6:1). For Christians married to non-Christian spouses, Christ's suffering and forbearance encourages them to live a life of purity so that their spouses may be won over with their behavior (1 Pet 3:1–2). But if the unbelieving spouse wishes to leave, the believer should let him or her go for God calls us into peace (1 Cor 7:15). A Christian may choose to remain single to focus on serving Christ (1 Cor 7:32–35). The church should acknowledge Christ's sovereignty in the community in its ethical teachings concerning sex, marriage, and family. How Christians live out familial relationships is an integral part of their Christian discipleship.[37]

If Christ is at the center of all familial relationships, then his love becomes the guiding principle among family members. "Husbands," Paul exhorts, "love

---

36. Poling Sun, *New Testament Ethics* (Hong Kong: Hong Kong Baptist Theological Seminary, 2009), 117.
37. Sun, 120–37.

your wives, just as Christ loved the church and gave himself up for her" (Eph 5:25). The love of Christ for the church also unites the husband with his wife in their "one flesh union." As Ephesians 5:31–32 states, "'For this reason a man will leave his father and mother and be united to his wife, and the two will become one flesh.' This is a profound mystery – but I am talking about Christ and the church." Union between Christ and the church, founded upon Christ's love for the world, is the basis of Christian marriage.[38] The biblical exhortations against divorce and the "one flesh" theology of marriage stem from this understanding of marital union. The marital ethics that ensue are not foremost a debate over the legitimate grounds of divorce and remarriage, but about how Christ's love for the church, received by members of the church, can enable Christian marriages to bear witness to this uniting love.

Drawing an analogy between the Christ–church union and the marital union does not mean that all human marriages must remain undissolved at all costs. Jesus says, "At the resurrection people will neither marry nor be given in marriage" (Matt 22:30), demonstrating that marriage is a penultimate reality. This eschatological perspective of marriage gives rise to several implications. First, all human marriages will end one way or another. Death of a spouse definitely ends it. In the fallen world, adultery, abandonment, or abuse may also be reasonable grounds of divorce. Second, given that time is short, married couples should treasure their time together and try their best to work out their marital union. Third, the ultimate termination of all marriages in fact brings hope to those mired in extremely difficult marital relationships, for they will certainly be released from their burden sometime in the future. Fourth, those who remain single for life are no less dignified than married persons and should make use of their time and freedom to serve the Lord.[39]

Besides empowering Christian couples to bind together, Christ's love is also suggested as an antidote against domestic violence. Eyingbeni Hümtsoe-Nienu identifies the power imbalance embedded in social structures and cultural conditions to be the root cause of intimate partner violence. Without addressing this imbalance, domestic violence would not cease even if the community and the church condemn it as wrong. The theological response to domestic violence, avers Hümtsoe-Nienu, begins with naming God's omnipotence not as absolute power but as absolute love. God's love revealed through Christ

---

38. Bernard Wong, *Beginning from Man and Woman: Witnessing Christ's Love in the Family* (Carlisle: Langham Monographs, 2017), 239–40.
39. Chan, "Biblical View of Marriage," 16–17.

invites all to live peacefully with him. This peace was made possible by Christ, who accomplished reconciliation between God and humans. Those who share Christ's love are reconciled vertically with God and horizontally with others. This notion of love challenges the power imbalance in society by shifting the basis of relationship from power to love. Hümtsoe-Nienu writes, ". . . de-centralizing power with the reconciling love of God is significant for cementing human relationship. In the context of [domestic violence] it is expressed in the ability to resist negative influence of power that results in brokenness of relationship between household members."[40]

ECCLESIOLOGY AND THE FAMILY

Love is frequently invoked as the ethical principle that governs interpersonal relationships; family included. This is especially prominent in the Western theological traditions. Yet love is generally not accentuated as much in Asian cultures. For instance, Confucian ethics emphasizes the cultivation of a person's character in concrete communal settings. One crucial moral teaching states that a person should pursue an eight-step process of "investigating things, extending knowledge, being sincere in thoughts, rectifying their hearts, cultivating their persons, regulating their families, ordering their states, and making the world peaceful."[41] The concept of love is notably absent in this teaching. Moreover, the collective and communal is emphasized over the individual for the maintenance of a hierarchical relational structure.[42] Confucianism underscores a person's position in the collective – families and states – more than her individual practice of love for others. Therefore, collective concepts may appeal more to Asians who have come under Confucian influence. The church, as a collective concept, can serve as an effective image to address the moral issues related to the family among Asian Christians.

The New Testament names the church the "household of God." Familial language – such as "brothers and sisters" and "God's children" – is used to describe relationships within the church. The family is a favorite metaphor that Chinese Christians use to imagine the church. A study reveals that

---

40. Eyingbeni Hümtsoe-Nienu, "Theological Response to Domestic Violence," in *Voices Against Domestic Violence: Biblical, Theological and Sociocultural Appraisal of the Experiences of the Oppressed Tribal, Children, Men, and Women*, ed. A. Tali Ao (Bali Nagar, New Delhi: Clark Theological College/Christian World Imprints, 2016), 115.
41. Tang Kailin and Zhang Huaicheng, *Cheng ren yu cheng sheng: Rujia lunli daode jingcui* [*Becoming Human and Becoming Sage: The Essence of Confucian Ethics*] (Changsha: Hunan University Publishing, 1999), 87.
42. Kailin and Huaicheng, 74.

"church-as-family" and "family-as-church" are important concepts that Chinese churches embrace in their ministries.[43] It is true that Confucian concepts of the family may adversely influence the church, leading to closed-off and homogeneous communities, hierarchical relationships, and paternalistic leadership.[44] But I contend that ecclesiology, when correctly constructed, can offer Asian Christians a moral vision to address the issues that the contemporary family faces. Here I offer a cursory description of such moral vision based on three images of the church found in the Bible: the bride of Christ, the body of Christ, and the household of God.

The Church as the Bride of Christ

The church as the bride of Christ means that it is the eschatological community (Rev 21:2). The nuptial image suggests that the church is a covenantal community characterized by faithfulness and love. Christians should bear witness to the total peace and reconciliation of the new heaven and new earth. Therefore, the church should resist the culture of easy divorce and help married couples to remain faithful and family members to love one another. But on the other hand, the reality that perfect peace is eschatological means that humanity is always marred by sin before Christ returns. Yahya Wijaya contends that on this side of the eschaton, "Just as the church was unable to avoid fragmentation, so many families have been unable to resist divorce."[45] When divorce becomes inevitable, the church should not simply condemn or avoid the divorcées. As a community of reconciliation, the church should continue to accept them and help them build respectful relationships, though not as husbands and wives. This is even more important because divorcées, single-parent families, and blended families often need support – and the church should not neglect this duty.

The Church as the Body of Christ

The church as the body of Christ means that different members are of equal dignity but are called into distinct roles, receiving different gifts to serve one another for the benefit of the whole community (1 Cor 12). Families modeled

---

43. Shuling Peng and Ruth C. Chang, "Church-as-Family, Family-as-Church: Chinese Churches' Perception and Practice of Family Ministry," *Jian Dao* 53 (2020): 126.
44. Tobias Brandner, "The Church as Family: Strengths and Dangers of the Family Paradigm of Christianity in Chinese Contexts," *Theology Today* 76, no. 3 (2019): 218–21.
45. Yahya Wijaya, "Broken Church for Broken Couples: How the Divided Church Should Take Care of Divorced Persons," *Asia Journal of Theology* 33, no. 1 (April 2019): 25.

after this concept subvert the Asian patriarchal family. As Christ is the head of the household, any power imbalance between husband and wife is challenged. The role of each member should be decided according to the gifts each receives, so Christian couples need not conform to the fixed gender roles stipulated in their cultures. What is important is that each member uses their gifts for the benefit of the whole family. The headship of Christ and equal dignity among members, however, does not entail equal authority between parents and children. Parenthood is a calling from God and parents are given authority over their children to guide them toward maturity in Christ. In turn, children should obey their parents in Christ (Eph 6:1–4). But when a child is mature enough to "leave his father and mother and be united to his wife" (Matt 19:5) parents should let go of their authority. Parental authority is highly regarded in Asian cultures, and this notion can help Christian families navigate the relationship between parents and children.

The Church as the Household of God

The church as the household of God means that all are included: "There is neither Jew nor gentile, neither slave nor free, nor is there male and female, for you are all one in Christ Jesus" (Gal 3:28). The flesh-and-blood family is relativized. Unlike the adage "blood is thicker than water," the church is a community where "water is thicker than blood" – the water of baptism is more important than blood relationships.[46] A person's familial role is contingent and does not define identity. Instead, familial roles are God's callings (1 Cor 7:17), and each should accept their own calling in joy and gratitude. Singleness is an equally dignified calling, as demonstrated by Jesus and Paul. Childlessness is not shameful, and every adult in the church is a spiritual parent to the children of others. This understanding of the family challenges the "familisms" of Asia – the ideal that each person must marry and produce a male heir to continue the bloodline.

Moreover, when members of God's household are not necessarily related by blood, the church can become surrogate families for those who lack economic or emotional support from their biological families.[47] The early Christians realized that they belonged to the same family, so "all the believers were together

---

46. Jana Marguerite Bennett, *Water Is Thicker Than Blood: An Augustinian Theology of Marriage and Singleness* (Oxford: Oxford University Press, 2008).
47. Nanlai Cao, "The Church as a Surrogate Family for Working Class Immigrant Chinese Youth: An Ethnography of Segmented Assimilation," *Sociology of Religion* 66, no. 2 (2005): 183–200.

and had everything in common. They sold property and possessions to give to anyone who had need" (Acts 2:44–45). This notion of the church is especially relevant for families having members who work or study overseas, a phenomenon that is becoming more common in Asia. The church then becomes these people's surrogate family while their family members are not around.

The Apostle John had a glimpse of the new heaven and new earth:

> I saw the Holy City, the new Jerusalem, coming down out of heaven from God, prepared as a bride beautifully dressed for her husband. And I heard a loud voice from the throne saying, "Look! God's dwelling place is now among the people, and he will dwell with them. They will be his people, and God himself will be with them and be their God." (Rev 21:2–3)

All humanity will become one with Christ at the final wedding. The biological family will give way to the all-inclusive family in the new heaven and new earth. While we wait for Christ's return, the church, as the eschatological community, is the spiritual family in which Christians learn to accept all and love one another. The biological family, as a penultimate reality, should bear witness to Christ's love in today's world.

QUESTIONS FOR DISCUSSION

1. On the issue of divorce and remarriage, what is the ethical position that your church adopts? What are the arguments that support this position? How would you revisit the issue?
2. Is patriarchy evident in your society? In your church? How can Christians challenge patriarchy without falling into individualism?
3. How are people not following the norm of familism (e.g. single, childless, divorced) perceived in your society and in your church? What are the biblical and theological resources to address familism?
4. Who are the people in need of a "surrogate family" in your society? Is your church serving as a "surrogate family" for those in need? How can it do this better?

BIBLIOGRAPHY

Bennett, Jana Marguerite. *Water Is Thicker Than Blood: An Augustinian Theology of Marriage and Singleness*. Oxford: Oxford University Press, 2008.

Brandner, Tobias. "The Church as Family: Strengths and Dangers of the Family Paradigm of Christianity in Chinese Contexts." *Theology Today* 76, no. 3 (2019): 217–223.

Cao, Nanlai. "The Church as a Surrogate Family for Working Class Immigrant Chinese Youth: An Ethnography of Segmented Assimilation." *Sociology of Religion* 66, no. 2 (2005): 183–200.

Chan, Lawrence. "Shengjing zhong de hunyin guan [Biblical View of Marriage]." In *Lihun yu zaihun: jidutu de guandian* [Divorce and Remarriage: Christian Perspectives], 4th ed., edited by Lawrence Chan, 3–21. Hong Kong: China Alliance Press, 2014.

Chang, Peter. "Cong Ma tai fuyin shijiu zhang san zhi jiu jie kan lihun [Divorce: An Interpretation of Matt 19:3–9]." In *Lihun yu zaihun: jidutu de guandian* [Divorce and Remarriage: Christian Perspectives], 4th ed., edited by Lawrence Chan, 43–54. Hong Kong: China Alliance Press, 2014.

Chow, Peter, and Esther Chow. *Xin wang ai: Shengjing lunli xue daolun* [Faith, Hope, Love: Introduction to Biblical Ethics]. Taipei: CCLM Publishing, 2014.

Christian and Missionary Alliance Church Union Hong Kong. *Xuandao hui jilu shouce* [C&MA Discipline Guidelines]. Hong Kong: C&MA, 2015.

Davis, John Jefferson. *Evangelical Ethics: Issues Facing the Church Today*. Phillipsburg: P&R Pub., 2004.

Fong, Chun-Ming. *Christian Ethics*. Hong Kong: Chinese Baptist Press, 2001.

Hays, Richard. *The Moral Vision of the New Testament: Community, Cross, New Creation: A Contemporary Introduction to New Testament Ethics*. New York: HarperOne, 1996.

Hümtsoe-Nienu, Eyingbeni. "Theological Response to Domestic Violence." In *Voices Against Domestic Violence: Biblical, Theological and Sociocultural Appraisal of the Experiences of the Oppressed Tribal, Children, Men, and Women*, edited by A. Tali Ao, 107–21. Bali Nagar, New Delhi: Clark Theological College/ Christian World Imprints, 2016.

Ji, Cheng. "Reflections on the Legitimate Grounds for Divorce and Remarriage among Chinese Christians." *China Graduate School of Theology Journal* 48, January (2010): 87–102.

Kang, Nam-Soon. "Confucian Familism and Its Social/Religious Embodiment in Christianity: Reconsidering the Family Discourse from a Feminist Perspective." *Asia Journal of Theology* 18, no. 1 (2004): 168–89.

Leung, Sau-Wah. "Zhongguo shehui bianqian zhong de lihun wenti [Divorce in the Changing Chinese Society]." In *Lihun yu zaihun: jidutu de guandian* [Divorce and Remarriage: Christian Perspectives], 4th ed., edited by Lawrence Chan, 125–65. Hong Kong: China Alliance Press, 2014.

Lim, Johnson. "Divorce and Remarriage in Theological Perspectives." *Asia Journal of Theology* 20, no. 2 (2006): 271–84.

Liu, Agnes Tat-Fong. "Lihun yu zaihun de lunli caijue [Ethical Decision for Divorce and Remarriage]." In *Lihun yu zaihun: jidutu de guandian* [Divorce and Remarriage: Christian Perspectives], 4th ed., edited by Lawrence Chan, 103–122. Hong Kong: China Alliance Press, 2014.

Lotha, Mhonyamo. "An Appraisal of Domestic Violence." In *Voices Against Domestic Violence: Biblical, Theological and Sociocultural Appraisal of the Experiences of the Oppressed Tribal, Children, Men, and Women*, edited by A. Tali Ao, 39–48. Bali Nagar, New Delhi: Clark Theological College/Christian World Imprints, 2016.

Louie, Wallace. "Shengjing zhong lihun yu zaihun si guan [Four views on 'Divorce and Marriage' in the Bible]." In *Lihun yu zaihun: jidutu de guandian* [Divorce and Remarriage: Christian Perspectives], 4th ed., edited by Lawrence Chan, 66–102. Hong Kong: China Alliance Press, 2014.

Mak, Alexander. "Divorce and Remarriage in the Bible." *Hill Road* 27, July (2011): 47–71.

Man-Kei Ho, *Practical Christian Ethics* (Taipei: Taosheng Publishing House, 2010), 159–60.

Peng, Shuling, and Ruth C. Chang. "Church-as-Family, Family-as-Church: Chinese Churches' Perception and Practice of Family Ministry." *Jian Dao* 53 (2020): 109–30.

Quah, Stella R. "Families in Asia: A Kaleidoscope of Continuity and Change." In *Routledge Handbook of Families in Asia*, edited by Stella R. Quah, 3–22. Oxon: Routledge, 2015.

Sun, Poling. *New Testament Ethics*. Hong Kong: Hong Kong Baptist Theological Seminary, 2009.

Tang, Kailin, and Huaicheng Zhang, *Cheng ren yu cheng sheng: Rujia lunli daode jingcui* [Becoming Human and Becoming Sage: The Essence of Confucian Ethics]. Changsha: Hunan University Publishing, 1999.

Wang, Ming-Tao. *Christians and Marriage*. Hong Kong: The Alliance Press, 1967.

Wijaya, Yahya. "Broken Church for Broken Couples: How the Divided Church Should Take Care of Divorced Persons." *Asia Journal of Theology* 33, no. 1 (2019): 20–33.

Witte Jr., John. *From Sacrament to Contract: Marriage, Religion, and Law in the Western Tradition*, 2nd ed. Louisville, KY: Westminster John Knox, 2012.

Wong, Bernard K. *Beginning from Man and Woman: Witnessing Christ's Love in the Family*. Carlisle: Langham Monographs, 2017.

Wong, Wai-Yin, and Man-Yee Chan. *Lantian xingdong: Jiaohui fangzhi jia bao shi gong yan jiu bàogào* [Operation Blue Sky: Research Report on Church's

Prevention of Family Violence]. Hong Kong: Hong Kong Women Christian Council, 2006.

Yeung, Mook Kuk Arnold. *Feng zhi wo: Fengyu tong lu hua jiating* [Shelter in the Wind: Weathering the Storm in the Family]. Hong Kong: Gengxin ziyuan chuban she, 2013.

CHAPTER 3

"HONOR YOUR FATHER AND YOUR MOTHER"

Confucius and Jesus on Filial Obligations

ShinHyung Seong

INTRODUCTION

"Why are ethics necessary for Christians?" Bonhoeffer's explanation about the differences between what he called "cheap grace" and "costly grace" is helpful in answering this question. He highlighted the ethical degradation of many Christians and stressed that Christians need to live ethically because of the costliness of grace. Bonhoeffer elaborated, "Such grace is *costly* because it calls us to follow, and it is *grace* because it calls us to follow *Jesus Christ*."[1] That is, humans cannot be justified by their merit in terms of ethics, but by the grace and forgiveness of God; this is the immovable foundation of Christian faith. This truth leads us to discuss the meaning of obedience and filial obligation for Christian ethics.

Obedience and filial obligation are important in East Asian ethics, not only for individuals but also within public life. The ethic of obedience and filial obligation was developed in Asia alongside the tradition of Confucianism; it involved concepts and practices that govern the relationships between kings and subjects, parents and children, among brothers, and between spouses. These ideas have deeply shaped how Asians perceive human relationships in the familial, social, and political spheres. As such, contemporary Christians cannot disregard filial piety as an outdated virtue but should recover and transform it with the help of Christian theology. Christianity and theology are fundamentally contextual since the nature of theology involves cultural

---

1. Dietrich Bonhoeffer, *Nachfolge* (Chr. Kaiser Verlag München, 1937), trans., by R. H. Fuller, *The Cost of Discipleship* (New York: Macmillan, 1959), 45. Italics original.

encounters.² Understanding the moral value of obedience in terms of filial piety is important for contextualizing Christian ethics in Asia.

In this chapter, we will first discuss the original Confucian notion of filial piety, which did not intend to support social hierarchies but aimed to emphasize human relatedness and the ethical virtue of obedience. Then we will delve into the biblical material concerning filial obligation. A close look at the Bible reveals similar traditions in the Old and New Testaments regarding this morality, though with crucial differences as well. This section will discuss that the Bible's commands are similar to, but also in essential ways different from, the Confucian model. Last, we will develop a notion of obedience by comparing the interpretations of filial obligation in Confucianism and the Bible. The purpose is to transform the ethical value of filial piety in Asia with Christian theology.

FILIAL OBLIGATION IN CONFUCIANISM

Filial obligation (*xiao*) is one of Confucianism's fundamental virtues. Confucius (551–479 BC), the originator of Confucian thought, lived during China's Spring and Autumn periods (722–476 BC). Due to the ongoing wars and power struggles during this time, Chinese society was in turmoil and people were suffering greatly. Survival was the most important concern.³ The continual warring of ancient China inspired Confucius to become involved in politics to improve the people's well-being. After holding a minor position in his hometown – the state of Lu – for two years, Confucius was still not promoted to a higher position and could not even retain a political position in his hometown due to numerous political opponents. He traveled across many states in an attempt to hold a political position, but ultimately returned home in his old age to die without having gained a superior political position. He developed his political philosophy based on the idea of *ren* (humanness), which became known as ren-politics, and he also concentrated on "the Way" (*tao*) to appreciate humanity for its sense of community and society. Although he did not intend to formulate any kind of political ideology nor religious tradition, his followers, such as Menzi, Xunzi, Donn Shongshu, and Zhu-zi, developed the tradition of Confucianism.

---

2. Stephen Bevans, *Models of Contextual Theology* (New York: Orbis Books, 2002), Introduction.
3. See, Xinzhong Yao, *An Introduction to Confucianism* (Cambridge: Cambridge University Press, 2012); Yu-LanFung, ed., Derk Bodde, *A Short History of Chinese Philosophy* (New York: The Free Press, 1997).

"Honor Your Father and Your Mother"

There are three main periods in the development of Confucianism: the establishment, the renaissance, and the contemporary. Confucius (551–479 BC), Menzi (371–289 BC), Xunzi (310?–211? BC), and Dong Zhongshu (170?–120? BC) were the founders of Confucianism from the Spring and Autumn period to the Later Han dynasty.[4] Dong Zhongshu established the political foundation for the Earlier Han dynasty as he established belief in an ontological natural order of hierarchy. Thereafter, Chinese rulers adopted Confucianism as their primary ideology due to its emphasis on social hierarchy. Neo-Confucian scholars initiated the renaissance period during the Song Dynasty (960–1279). Zhu Xi (1139–1193) is considered the great scholar of neo-Confucianism due to his establishment of the philosophical foundation of Confucianism.[5] After him, neo-Confucianism became the dominant ideology in East Asia, especially in the Joseun Dynasty of Korea.

Confucianism and Its Encounter with the Western Tradition

Matteo Ricci (AD 1552–1610), an Italian Jesuit missionary, arrived in China in 1582, and tried to find a Chinese religious tradition that could relate to Christianity. After his first consideration of Chinese culture, he thought that Buddhism could do the job. But he found that correlating Buddhism and

---

4. Yao, *An Introduction to Confucianism*, Introduction. Menzi and Xunzi were known as the great disciples of Confucius. They argued different theories about human nature. Menzi argued that human nature is innately good so individuals can develop their goodness (*ren*) autonomously; however, Xunzi argued that society must be founded on a sound law and education system since human nature is innately evil. Xunzi's idea was developed as the school of law, with the founder Hanfeizi. *Qin*, the first unified empire in China, accepted Hanfeizi, and the emperor of *Qin* persecuted other Confucius scholars. Unfortunately, the *Qin* dynasty ended quickly, then, the *Han* dynasty reunified China. The surviving Confucius scholars supported the *Han* dynasty. One of these was Dong Shongshu. He gave up the ideas of Xunzi, but he manipulated Menzi's idea of basic relationship order of humanity (king-servant, father-son, male-female, and the old-the young), which is functional, as being ontological. Thus, Menzi's idea of human relationships was distorted by Dong Zhongshu and became the foundation of social and political hierarchy in China.

5. Yao, *An Introduction to Confucianism*, 1–15. According to Yao, the first period represents the origin of Confucianism and the tradition's acceptance in mainstream ideology, which lasted from the Spring and Autumn periods (770–476 BC) to the end of the Later Han dynasty (AD 25–220). During the second period, Confucianism spread to other parts of East Asia from the renaissance period to the eighteenth century, but this period ended with the abolition of Confucianism's dominance in both China and East Asia during the nineteenth century. Then, the third period began with a critical reflection of the tradition, which was initiated in the May Fourth Movement (AD 1919) and remains ongoing. A significant feature of the third period is that modern Confucian scholars propagate and reinterpret Confucian doctrines in light of Western traditions. As Confucianism is being spread worldwide, the world, in turn, impacts Confucianism.

Christianity was challenging. Instead, he focused on Confucianism and discovered its significant alignment with Christianity. He met with Chinese scholars and officials to translate Confucian texts, which he introduced to European countries. After Ricci, many missionaries (William Carey in India, Adoniram Judson in Myanmar, and William Baird and Horace Underwood in Korea, etc.) visited Asian countries in an attempt to contextualize Christianity within Asian traditions like Confucianism and Buddhism. At the same time, Sinology ("Sino" means China and "logy" means study. So, it is the study of Chinese culture, history, and philosophy) developed among Western scholars such as Voltaire, Leibniz, Tindal, and Jaspers, with various fields of scholarship analyzing the similarities and differences between Western and Eastern societies.[6]

In the nineteenth century, Confucianism began to lose its political influence in many Asian countries due to colonialization by Western powers. Asian cultures also became receptive to the idea of democracy. However, a new renaissance of Confucianism occurred in the 1970s in the United States of America, leading to an increased interest in Sinology in both Eastern and Western cultures.[7]

Confucian Ethics

Confucian morality can be categorized as a form of virtue ethics. Four significant works describe Confucius's virtues: *The Analects of Confucius*, *The Words of Mencius (Mengzi)*, *The Great Learning*, and *The Book of Mean (Zhongyong)*. These present an approach to ethics with concepts similar to Aristotelian theories of virtue, emphasizing, for example, self-cultivation, habituation, and the praxis of humanity.[8] In the contemporary scholarship of Sinology, Confucian philosophy focuses more on moral character than moral acts, as Confucian tradition values moral agency and moral characteristics such as goodness, benevolence, and propriety.[9] In particular, issues of identity and human relatedness are the foundation of the Confucian ethical framework.

A common criticism of this framework is that it does not support individuality and self-identity. Instead, it is said to exclusively emphasize a sense

---

6. Yao, 2.
7. Yao, 3.
8. Edward Slingerland, "Virtue Ethics, the *Analects*, and the Problem of Commensurability," *Journal of Religious Ethics* 29, no. 1 (2001), doi:10.1111/0384-9694.00070. Also see, Aristotle, *Nicomachean Ethics*; McIntyre, *After Virtue*.
9. D. C. Lau, trans. *Confucius: The Analects* (Hong Kong: Chinese University Press, 1983), introduction.

of community while demanding the individual's sacrifice for the sake of society. Moreover, critics argue that its application in a modern democratic social system is impossible since it places such significant value on familial relationships, creating an authoritarian social hierarchy incompatible with democratic values.[10]

For instance, Kang argues that Confucianism has oppressed women by valuing the patriarchal system and formulating a social hierarchy.[11] In Asian countries like China, Vietnam, Myanmar, Thailand, Korea, and Japan, Confucianism has been utilized as the main political ideology. Confucianism occupied mainland China for over two thousand years, from the Han dynasty (206 BC) to the Qing Dynasty (AD 1911). In Korea, the ruling ideology during the Joseon Dynasty (AD 1392–1910) was neo-Confucianism.[12] Again, Confucianism has been criticized as a political ideology that does not fit into modern-day democratic society. In a sense, this criticism is legitimate because a hierarchical ruling ideology indeed developed under Confucianism.

At the same time, it is notable that primitive Confucianism in terms of Confucius's original ideas was not based on social hierarchy but on human relatedness.[13] This contrast is clear when we look more closely at the idea of humanity and the interpretation of hierarchy in primitive Confucianism. There are two ways to understand hierarchy: ontological and functional. The ontological understanding of hierarchy argues that everyone assumes a fixed role in a human association and a person's role determines one's identity. Although stable communities can be formed in such systems, the ontological understanding of hierarchy frequently leads to oppressive social structures and is objectionable.

In contrast, a functional understanding of hierarchy focuses on the way in which the specific social roles each person plays are necessary for meaningful relationships to occur (teacher and student, parents and children, king and

---

10. Nam-Soon Kang, "Confucian Familism and its Social/Religious Embodiment in Christianity: Reconsidering the Family Discourse from a Feminist Perspective," *Asia Journal of Theology* 18, no. 1 (2004). Also read Canglong Wang, "Individuality, Hierarchy, and Dilemma: The Making of Confucian Cultural Citizenship in a Contemporary Chinese Classical School," *Journal of Chinese Political Science*, no. 21 (2016) and Romeyn Taylor, "Chinese Hierarchy in Comparative Perspective," *The Journal of Asian Studies* 48, no. 3 (1989).
11. Kang, "Confucian Familism and its Social/Religious Embodiment in Christianity: Reconsidering the Family Discourse from a Feminist Perspective," 169–72.
12. For the historical background of Confucian tradition, see Xinzhong Yao, *An Introduction to Confucianism* (Cambridge: Cambridge University Press, 2000); Yu-Lan Fung, *A Short History of Chinese Philosophy*, ed. Derk Bodde (New York: The Free Press, 1976).
13. ShinHyung Seong, *Otherness and Ethics* (Eugene: Wipf & Stock, 2018), chap. 5.

civilians, etc.). Thus, roles and hierarchy are flexible and are set up to serve the broader purpose of human relationship. Primitive Confucianism supports this notion as it prescribes an approach to human relatedness designed to help every person maintain goodness (*ren*) for the sake of others. For instance, Menzi insists that a king must care for his people by adhering to ren and proposed a radical remedy by which people may change their king's position if he fails to do so.[14]

Yet over time Confucianism in China declined into an ontological understanding of hierarchy, and the socio-political system gradually lost the ideals of primitive Confucianism. Confucianism prevailed as the ruling ideology as it emphasized ontological social hierarchy from the Han dynasty onwards. This long history of ontological hierarchy eventually became permanent. Contemporary scholars have tried to distinguish the ideas of social hierarchy and human relationships in the Confucian tradition.[15]

The Ethical Implication of Filial Obligation (Piety)

The criticisms of Confucianism, especially in its contemporary form, are legitimate; however, the recovery of its ethical value is important for Asian Christians to contextualize our faith and approach to ethics. The first step is to recover the basis of Confucian ethics: ren. Ren emphasizes human goodness and relatedness as it encourages people to achieve humanity through self-cultivation and "the Way" (*tao*) to build an ideal society. Confucius emphasized tao when he said, "all that I teach can be strung together on a single thread."[16] The original Chinese text refers to the phrase, "All that I teach," as "my Way (tao)." Thus, Confucius conceived of tao in his teachings as being the core of humanness. This single thread involves understanding (*shu*)[17] others, which is the foundation of Confucius's golden rule. When Zigong asked, "Is there one word that can serve as a guide for one's entire life?" Confucius answered, "Is

---

14. Bryan Van Norden, trans. *Mengzi* (Indianapolis/Cambridge: Hackett Publishing Company, 2008), 26; Book 1 B8.1.
15. Donald J. Munro, *The Concept of Man in Early China* (Ann Arbor: University of Michigan, 2001), chapters 1–3; William Theodore De Bary and Tu Wei-Ming eds., *Confucianism and Human Rights* (New York: Columbia University Press, 1998), chapters 3–7.
16. *Analects*, 34, Book 4:15. See also the repetition of this metaphor in 174, Book 15:3.
17. In the English translation of *Confucius Analects*, *Shu* has been translated into various meanings i.e. altruism (by Chan), reciprocity (by Tu and de Bary), understanding (Slingerland), empathy (Brooks), and deference (Hall and Ames).

it not 'understanding' (shu)? Do not impose upon others what you yourself do not desire."[18]

Confucius emphasized that the basis of goodness is filial obligation or piety (xiao) and respect for elderly brothers (ti).[19] He valued filial obligation and brotherly love not to promote social hierarchy but to demonstrate the importance of human relatedness, which, he believed, begins with familial relationships. It is from the smallest unit of the family that larger human associations, including nations, are formed.[20] Furthermore, ritual propriety (li) is the source of filial piety. Li is not the simple practice of rituals but the process of respecting others by participating in the rituals, which is a practical service for people. In this sense, Confucius argued that filial piety refers to the lifelong obedience of and respect toward parents in terms of ritual propriety rather than a simple sacrifice for them. For instance, when Meng asked about filial piety, Confucius answered, "Do not disobey . . . when your parents are alive, serve them in accordance with the rites; when they pass away, bury them in accordance with the rites and sacrifice to them in accordance with the rites."[21] Confucius said, "Nowadays 'filial' means simply being able to provide one's parents with nourishment. But even dogs and horses are provided with nourishment. If you are not respectful, wherein lies the difference?"[22] Based on this understanding of the relationship between li and xiao, several important ethical virtues are embedded in the notion of xiao.

Harmony is the first source of xiao, and Confucius argued that harmony does not simply mean that one agrees with others about everything. However, it involves maintaining ritual propriety with one another, just as one maintains their social roles through harmony.[23] Filial obligation is also based on the notion of harmony within the family in terms of human relationships. Confucius summarized this concept: "Let the lord be a true lord, the ministers true ministers, the fathers true fathers, and the sons true sons."[24] With this sense of harmony, Confucius emphasized the golden rule ("Do not impose upon others what you yourself do not desire") and taught his disciples: "When in public, comport yourself as if you were receiving an important guest, and

---

18. *Analects*, Book 15:24, 183.
19. *Analects*, Book 1:2, 1.
20. *Analects*, Book 1:2, 1.
21. *Analects*, Book 2:5, 9.
22. *Analects*, Book 2:7, 10.
23. *Analects*, Book 13:23, 149.
24. *Analects*, Book 12:11, 130.

in your management of the common people, behave as if you were overseeing a great sacrifice."[25]

Politeness is the second foundational aspect of xiao – politeness refers to respecting others by adhering to humility rather than being extravagant or boastful. For instance, Confucius served in royal rituals at the Great Ancestral Temple while he held a political position in Lu State. While he asked about everything he needed to do to master the ritual, other politicians criticized him for not knowing the ritual well. Confucius replied, "This asking is, in fact, part of ritual."[26] This example demonstrates his politeness, carefulness, and humility. Confucius appreciated the overall ritual more than its specific elements. One day, Zigong attempted to practice a sacrifice without using a lamb, but Confucius rebuked him: "Zigong! You regret the loss of lamb, whereas I regret the loss of the rite."[27] Thus, Confucius highlighted the kernel of the ritual rather than the formality of xiao.

Sincerity is the third foundation of xiao and refers to endurance and consistency in practicing the virtue. Sincerity is important because some people may find it difficult to practice xiao as a lifelong process. For instance, Zai Wo once objected to the lengthy three-year mourning period required after the death of one's parent: "Surely one year is long enough. If the gentleman refrains from practicing ritual for three years, the rites will surely fall into ruin; if he refrains from music for three years, this will be surely disastrous for music." This seemed to be a practical suggestion, so Confucius answered, "Do it as you wish if you feel comfortable." Yet, he continued to explain the meaning of a three-year mourning period to his disciples: "A child is completely dependent upon the care of his parents for the first three years of his life – this is why the three-year mourning period is the common practice throughout the world. Did Zai Wo not receive three years of care from his parents?" Finally, Confucius reprimanded Zai Wo for lacking goodness.[28] Thus, we must learn how to maintain li and xiao in our everyday ren practice by sincerely understanding our parents.

To summarize, filial piety in Confucianism is not a simple obligation that is meant to support social hierarchy but is a key virtue based on human relatedness. It is necessary to practice it habitually in one's daily life to cultivate

---

25. *Analects*, Book 12:2, 126.
26. *Analects*, Book 3:15, 23.
27. *Analects*, Book 3:17, 24.
28. *Analects*, Book 17:21, 209–19.

goodness (ren) and to follow "the Way" (tao). Practicing filial piety also helps a person appreciate harmony, politeness, and sincerity. While harmony is the foundation of human relationships, politeness encourages people to follow the virtue of xiao and sincerity disciplines people into endurance and consistency.

THE BIBLE AND FILIAL OBLIGATION

Both the Old and New Testaments emphasize a vision of filial obligation that is similar to the concept of filial piety in Confucianism. While the Confucian understanding of filial obligation is based on a humanistic approach, the biblical tradition is based on divine commandments.[29] Thus, a kind of filial piety is required of Christians – not because parents have divine authority, but because it is a part of Christian discipleship.

Filial Obligation in the Old Testament

The Old Testament, especially the Torah, emphasizes filial piety as an ethical practice for Israel's community.[30] Moses's familial experience was unique since he was adopted by the princess of Egypt on the one hand and had his biological mother serve as his nanny on the other hand. He had a dual identity as the son of Egypt's princess and a person of Hebrew ethnicity. Because of his identity as a Hebrew, God called him to liberate his people from slavery. This was a special experience for Moses because he realized that he was a descendant of Abraham, Isaac, and Jacob, which gave him a unique sense of family within God's chosen community. When he received the Decalogue at Mount Sinai, filial piety was stipulated in the fifth commandment. The first to the fourth commandments concern the relationship between God and humans and the sixth to the tenth commandments focus on relationships among humans. The commandment about filial piety lies in the middle, as if God is saying to His people: "Unless you obey your parents, you cannot examine yourself as a good follower of the law of God. Your relationship with your parents reveals how you follow God with all your heart."[31]

---

29. Daniel Qin, "Confucian Filial Piety and the Fifth Commandment: A Fulfillment Approach," *Asian Journal of Pentecostal Studies* 16, no. 2 (2013): 139–64.
30. Moon Sang Kwon, "Honoring Parents and Jewish Community Consciousness: A Comparative Study of Biblical Parent Care and Confucian HYO (filial piety)," *A Study of Systematic Theology*, 33 (2019), 140–75.
31. As discussed above, Jesus also pointed out this truth in his debate about the tradition of corban on Mark 7:11 and Matt 15:5.

Obedience to parents is a divine commandment because of the preciousness of the familial relationship. For instance, when God called upon Abraham, central to God's many promises was that his offspring would be as numerous as the "stars in the sky." Furthermore, when God called upon Moses in the desert, Moses asked who he was and God replied, "I am the God of your ancestors, the God of Abraham, Isaac, and Jacob." It is significant that at these major moments of calling in salvation history, familial relationship was emphasized.[32]

The fifth commandment states: "Honor your father and your mother, so that you may live long in the land the Lord your God is giving you."[33] God did not create the Decalogue to be a conditional contract with the Israelites but as a holy covenant that his chosen nation must follow. As noted in Ephesus 6:1–3, God does not offer any compensation for the other commandments, he promises a blessing in the fifth commandment on filial piety. The path toward being blessed in the Promised Land is to honor one's parents. Whether the fifth commandment is a conditional promise may not be the main concern. The commandment clearly teaches that God desires his people to build a sound relationship – not only with God but also with others.

Moreover, the fifth commandment may be understood as a bridge that demonstrates how people form positive relationships with God as well as others. If one can build this kind of relationship with their parents while honoring them, it is representative of a blessed life bestowed by God. God emphasized the holiness of his chosen people and told them, "Each of you must respect your mother and father, and you must observe my Sabbaths. I am the Lord your God."[34] As God mentioned honoring parents alongside other holy rules, such as performing the Sabbath, not worshipping idols, and having sacrifices, we can infer that it is not only a principle for ethical living, but one with religious implications with substantial prescribed punishments for disobedience, similar to other religious violations (see also Deut 21:18–21; 27:16).[35]

---

32. Seong-kwon Park, "Biblical *hyo* (filial piety) as Respect for Parents," *Study of Hyo (Filial Piety)*, no. 7 (2008), 24–35.
33. Exod 20:12. According to Deut 5:16, "Honor your father and your mother, as the Lord your God has commanded you, so that you may live long and that it may go well with you in the land the Lord your God is giving you."
34. Lev 19:3.
35. Seung-jin Hahn, *The Ethics of Filial Piety and the Reality of Aging Society* (Paju: Korean Study and Information, 2011), 151–163. Hahn emphasized the meaning of filial piety with two bases like Christian ethics and God's commandment. To begin with, it has individual and social ethical implications since it promotes individual virtue as well as social responsibility. Also, the law was made by God to guide his people (Christians) toward holiness and sincerity.

Filial Obligation in the New Testament

Filial obligation is not only a moral virtue, but it also demonstrated the way of discipleship in the New Testament.[36] While Jesus debated the meaning of law in the Torah with Israel's religious leaders, he rebuked them as hypocrites because they did not serve their parents in accordance with the corban tradition.[37] Meanwhile, the Apostle Paul also accentuated filial piety in his letters: Romans 1:30; Ephesians 6:1–3; Colossians 3:20; 1 Timothy 5:4; and 2 Timothy 3:2. These verses illustrate that Paul considered filial obligation an important aspect of Christian life in terms of practicality and spirituality.

Jesus emphasized filial obligation not only in words but also in action. According to biblical archaeologists,[38] as the oldest son in his household, Jesus had to serve his family and work as a carpenter after his father died until he started his ministry at about thirty years old. A superior example that demonstrates his filial obligation is that during his crucifixion Jesus asked John, one of his disciples, to be his mother's son. Afterward, John served Mary as his mother.[39] Paul also taught the importance of honoring parents and elders in his letters. He retrieved the Old Testament tradition and explained that the virtue is beneficial for Christians to follow because God would bestow blessings upon those that obey their parents.[40] On the other hand, disobeying parents is considered a sin against God in Romans 1:30 and 2 Timothy 3:2. Paul followed the Old Testament when he described the blessings that would result from filial obligation. However, he developed a different interpretation of this concept from the Old Testament, as he argued about sin in the world. Paul categorized many sins and one of these involved disobeying one's parents.

Jesus and Paul emphasized filial piety not simply to promote moral virtue, but to teach Christian discipleship. In Luke 14:26–27, Jesus taught "If anyone comes to me and does not hate father and mother, wife and children, brothers and sisters – yes, even their own life – such a person cannot be my disciple. And whoever does not carry their cross and follow me cannot be my disciple."

---

36. Dong-soo Kim, "New Testament and Filial Piety," *Theological Forum* 43, no. 2 (2006), 389–409.
37. Mark 7:11 and Matt 15:5. Corban is material (money) that was designated as an offering for God in the Jewish tradition. Jewish people misused this tradition to avoid serving their parents since they did not need to spend this money on them if they called it "corban." They also did not use this money as an offering. Jesus severely criticized this situation.
38. Jack Finegan, *The Archeology of the New Testament: The Life of Jesus and the Beginning of the Early Church* (Princeton: Princeton University Press, 2014).
39. John 19:25–27.
40. Eph 6:1–3, Col 3:20, and 1 Tim 5:4.

This passage has been misunderstood by some Christians who assume that families must be given up for the Church.[41] But this interpretation contradicts Jesus's other teachings on filial obligation.

Instead, it is better to understand Luke 14:26–27 as serving to emphasize the priority of Christian life and discipleship. As discussed above, when the Israelites ignored the law of filial piety, replacing it with their tradition, Jesus rebuked them sternly. After Jesus emphasized the meaning of filial piety, Jesus taught his discipleship from these passages. More seriously, Jesus told them that they would find themselves against their family members while they tried to be a disciple.[42]

Jesus also told a follower who wanted to join in the funeral service for his parents before coming with Jesus, "Follow me, and let the dead bury their own dead."[43] In order to grasp this teaching, we have to understand the urgency and priority of discipleship.[44] It does not mean that we must ignore family to follow Jesus, but it means that the way of being a disciple, loving God and your neighbor, is a very difficult task.[45] Likewise, Paul also emphasized filial piety similarly, instructing to obey your parents "in the Lord." He says further that a father must instruct his children under the Lord.[46] This is mutual love for Christians, with caring and respect for others in the Christian community.[47] Thus, in the New Testament tradition, filial obligation is not only an important virtue for Christian life, but it is also broadened to include the realm of discipleship.

The Ethical Meaning of Filial Obligation in the Bible

The Christian biblical tradition teaches the ethical meaning of filial obligation. Most importantly, it is one of the divine commandments that Christians must follow. However, unlike in the Old Testament law, God did not make this a condition for acquiring his blessing. Instead, it is based on an ethical foundation for Christians that helps shape a sound relationship with God as well as others. We learn from the Decalogue that parents are a bridge between God and each child, so showing obedience toward parents is an example of one's

---

41. Yong-soo Hyun, "Why Jesus told disciples to leave their parents and brothers?" *The Character & shema* 2 (2010), 14–15.
42. Matt 10:21.
43. Matt 8:22; Luke 9:60.
44. Kim, "New Testament and Filial Piety," 394.
45. Dong-soo Kim, "New Testament and Filial Piety," 393–94.
46. Eph 6:1–4.
47. Dong-soo Kim, "New Testament and Filial Piety," 401–2.

attitude toward God. To reiterate, the Torah is not predicated upon contractual relationships, but illustrates the way God's people should live in the world, whether or not they receive God's blessing.

This is ultimately based on the call to holiness, as God said, "Be holy as I am holy."[48] Because honoring our parents is categorized alongside performing the Sabbath, not worshipping idols, we can conclude that filial piety is a way to practice the religious piety.[49] The better we can honor our parents, the deeper our relationship with God becomes. This is a part of what the Apostle Paul means when he urges Christians to offer our bodies as living sacrifices, which represents a way that we can please God in our daily lives.[50]

Once we understand filial piety as an element of daily faithfulness, we can also recognize that, like any moral decision, we must be conscious of the temptation to disobedience and insincerity. Jesus's debate with the Jewish leaders cautions us not to become hypocritical, creating numerous excuses to evade filial obligation. For example, we may say that we have other needs to fulfill, we are busy, or we already have many others to care for. The Bible exhorts us to practice the virtue of filial piety in our daily life. Although some of Jesus's teachings appear to contradict the notion of filial piety, he expected his followers to practice the virtue as part of discipleship. This is the basis of the Christian understanding of filial piety.

CONFUCIANISM VERSUS CHRISTIANITY: CHRISTIAN PRACTICES IN FILIAL OBLIGATION

What are the similarities and differences between Confucianism and Christianity in the understanding and practice of filial piety? Three similarities are noted.

First, in both systems, filial piety offers a clear moral standard for social relationships, especially in the family. Both traditions value the relatedness of humans and understand the family as the essential unit of society. For Confucianism, the relatedness of the family is broadened into society and even the whole nation. On the other hand, Christianity does not only highlight this social aspect of filial piety. Obeying one's parents is also related to

---

48. Lev 19:2.
49. Hahn, *The Ethics of Filial Piety and the Reality of Aging Society*, 210–211; Moon Sang Kwon, "Honoring Parents and Jewish Community Consciousness: A Comparative Study of Biblical Parent Care and Confucian HYO (filial piety)," 148–52.
50. Rom 12:1.

the divine sphere, underscoring the meaning of holiness as well as resistance against sin and evil.

Second, both traditions consider filial piety a moral virtue, and a community narrative is the foundation of this virtue. Confucianism and Christianity have similar goals in their communities, including sincere efforts to build relationships. Confucius and Jesus equally stress the significance of sincerity over hypocrisy. Confucius argued that sincerity is derived from consistency, as he maintained ritual propriety as best as he could. Similarly, Jesus argued that sincerity is even more crucial than the Torah's tradition. When addressing Israel's religious traditions, Jesus argued that it was useless for a person to practice filial piety without a sense of sincerity.

Third, filial piety in both traditions has religious connotations. For Confucianism, the religious connotation is reified most clearly in ancestor worship. In Christianity, the meaning of respecting one's parents is broadened into the realm of honoring God as well as an act of discipleship.[51] Yet having religious connotations also results in the most significant difference between the two traditions: Confucianism is humanistic, Christianity is theistic. Simply put, filial piety is a humanistic virtue in Confucianism but a divine command in Christianity.[52]

This difference between humanistic versus theistic understanding of filial piety created controversy over ancestor worship when Christianity was brought into Asia. When Ricci first came to China, he had the chance to meet Confucian scholars. The Chinese Emperor did not worship the Christian God but venerated Christianity and appreciated its moral teachings. Gradually, however, the Roman Catholic Church started to consider filial rite as superstition and banned it in 1742. In response, the Chinese Emperor K'ang-Xi expelled their missionaries. It was not until 1939 that the Catholic Church reversed the decision about filial rites. Robert Morrison, the first Protestant missionary to China in 1807, followed the Catholic Church's attitude toward ancestral rites. Then, Protestant Christians in China tried to moderate their position, debating it at three conferences on 1877, 1890, and 1907. But the fundamental problems between the two belief systems could not be solved

---

51. Daniel Qin, "Confucian Filial Piety and the Fifth Commandment: A Fulfillment Approach," 151–53.
52. Qin, 153–56.

because of the different notions regarding religion and deity between the Chinese traditions and Christianity.[53]

The same issue arose in Korea. When Catholicism entered Korea in 1784, the ban on filial rites adopted in China was followed. As in China, the ban was eventually lifted in 1939. As of today, the issue of filial rites causes no conflicts between the Korean Catholic Church and Korean society. For the Korean Protestant Church, memorial worship (*choo-do-yee-bae* – a worship service in which ancestors are remembered and gratitude expressed to God for them) instead of ancestral rites were encouraged beginning from the early twentieth century. However, the issue of ancestral rites is still causing much conflict among Koreans.[54] The debate is about whether the ancestral rites violate the first commandment in the Old Testament.

While all Asian cultures highly regard filial obligation and the honoring of ancestors, many Asians consider Christianity unethical in this respect. At the same time, some Christians may still consider the Asian expression of filial obligation and the practice of ancestral rites to be idolatry. A cultural approach is required on this issue, and Asian Christians should approach this issue with humility and understanding.[55]

The theistic understanding of Christianity indeed creates conflict with the humanistic understanding of Confucianism regarding ancestor rites. But on the other hand, the same theistic understanding can help Confucianism maintain the humanistic notion of functional hierarchy. As discussed, primitive Confucianism emphasized human relatedness. Equal dignity among all persons is assumed and roles within hierarchical structures are flexible and are set up for human relatedness and the benefit of everyone in the community. But when Confucianism was adopted in the Han dynasty by the political establishment, its functional hierarchy gradually morphed into an ontological hierarchy. The

---

53. Lung-kwong Lo, "The Nature of the Issue of Ancestral Worship among Chinese Christians," *Studies in World Christianity* 9, no. 1 (2003), 30–42.
54. Keun-won Park, "Korean Christian churches and Ancestral Rite," *Korean Journal of Christian Studies* 8, no. 1 (1991), 346–53.
55. David M. Park and Julian C. Müller, "The challenge that Confucian filial piety poses for Korean churches," *HTS Theological Studies* 70, no. 2 (2014), 6–8; Keun-won Park, "Korean Christian churches and Ancestral Rite," 356–58. As Stephen Bevans emphasized "contextualization," it is important for Christians to understand the relation between the gospel and culture. To begin with, Keun-won Park argued that the Christian needs to give up triumphalism and exclusivism toward other cultures, and to have humble conversation with other traditions. On the other hand, Park and Müller suggest a creative method to practice the Christian way of filial piety, such as a "Christian Memorial Service" that makes Christians honor ancestors in a Christian way.

underlying assumption was changed from equal dignity for all, to the one on top having a higher ontology than others. The role and position of persons then became fixed, and abuse and oppression ensued.

As Christians believe God is superior to all, and that all human beings are created equal, the notion of ontological hierarchy among humans is resisted. In fact, the biblical understanding of Christians as "parts of the same body having the same head – Jesus Christ" (1 Cor 11:12–31) agrees well with the notion of functional hierarchy in primitive Confucian. The biblical exhortation: "Children, obey your parents in the Lord, for this is right" and "Honor your father and mother" (Eph 6:1–2) recognizes equal dignity between children and parents but unequal function and authority between them in the family. This is the Christian notion of filial piety. At the same time, in the contemporary world where all types of hierarchy are frowned upon and the virtue of filial piety is disparaged, Asian cultures can help Christians recover the importance of the virtue.

PRACTICAL CHALLENGES

Finally, as Christians in contemporary Asia seek to put these ideas into practice, we should be mindful of the practical challenges created by the contemporary ethical landscape. We can expect challenges in three areas: changes in contemporary family structures, the issue of abusive parents, and the spiritual resources to practice filial piety.

First, as other chapters in this volume note, the meaning and structure of the family has been changing. In the past, the family was understood as a much bigger community than the nuclear family consisting of just the married couple with their children. In Asian cultures, the traditional family was more like a clan made up of relatives descending from the same ancestor. Yet, because of Westernization and globalization, the family in many Asian countries nowadays is understood as the nuclear family. In addition, many more people remain single for life, and living in single-parent and blended families has become more common. The notion of filial piety may also shift with these changing family patterns. For Christians, the church as the spiritual family should also inform our understanding of filial piety. Filial piety may be perceived as not a simple obligation for parents, but a moral action that stems from the understanding that humans are relational beings. In this case, our obligation is not only toward our parents, but other family members as well, such that a sound community can be built (1 Tim 5:1–2).

A second challenge relates to the very real problem of abusive parents. For children of abusive and even violent parents, what does filial piety mean? As love is the greatest commandment, filial piety should be understood through love. Love aims at well-being, justice, and reconciliation. Therefore, children of abusive parents may have to maintain distance from them until they are no longer violent. Yet a relationship with their parents should be maintained, even if it does not involve meeting in person. For older children, continued support for their parents is an important way to continue honoring them, even in less-than-ideal relational circumstances. Reconciliation and restoration toward fellowship between parents and children is always the goal, and this involves forgiveness. But it can be difficult for children to forgive their parents, especially in Asian cultures where parents are frequently reluctant either to admit the guilt of hurting their children or to apologize. However, Jesus has forgiven our sins through sacrificing himself, and God also forgives everyone, including our parents.[56] It is in experiencing God's forgiveness that we may forgive others, though protection of victims of abuse must also always be given the highest priority.

This leads to the spiritual resources to practice filial piety. As a virtue, practicing filial piety is itself a dimension of sanctification and Christian discipleship. God's grace and the transformative power of the Spirit is indispensable. But along this spiritual journey, we realize that the more we love our parents, the more deeply we love God. Obeying our parents is thus a way to glorify God. Our spiritual journey is also a pilgrimage toward freedom, as Martin Luther wrote: "A Christian man is the most free lord of all, and subject to none; a Christian man is the most dutiful servant of all, and subject to everyone."[57] In this sense, and with the biblical framework in mind, obeying one's parents is in fact the way to freedom, and Christian ethics is thus liberating.

QUESTIONS FOR DISCUSSION

1. The meaning of "family" has gradually changed from that of an extended family to a nuclear family system. Even a one-person family is incredibly popular in modern times. So, how

---

56. ShinHyung Seong and Seon-wook Kim, "A Study of the Biblical Meaning and the Christian Social Ethical Interpretation of Forgiveness," *The Korean Journal of Christian Social Ethics* 46 (2020), 136–41.
57. Martin Luther, "Dedicatory Letter of Martin Luther to Pope Leo," in *On the Freedom of a Christian*, http://www.fordham.edu/halsall/mod/luther-freedomchristian.html, last modified January 21, 2020.

can we develop a sound sense of family through the idea of filial obligation?
2. It may be burdensome to serve your parents, and you may wonder: "Why not 'me' first and 'parents' second? Also, if I receive more money, can I serve my parents better than if I am living in poverty?"
3. You may think, "I fully understand that I must obey my parents wholeheartedly, but I cannot because they are often violent. Since I do not want to personally meet them anymore, what should I do?"
4. You may be facing this dilemma: "My parents do not believe in Jesus Christ and have persecuted me in various way so that I will not be Christian. Frankly, I do not know how to maintain my filial obligation. Is there any beneficial method that I could implement?"

BIBLIOGRAPHY

Bevans, Stephen B. *Models of Contextual Theology: Faith and Cultures*. New York: Orbis Books, 2002.

Bonhoeffer, Dietrich. *Nachfolge*, Chr. Kaiser Verlag Müchen, 1937, trans., by R. H. Fuller, *The Cost of Discipleship*. New York: Macmillan, 1959.

De Bary, Wm. Theodore and Tu Wei-Ming eds., *Confucianism and Human Rights*. New York: Columbia University Press, 1998.

Finegan, Jack. *The Archeology of the New Testament: The Life of Jesus and the Beginning of the Early Church*. Princeton: Princeton University Press, 2014.

Fung, Yu-Lan. *A Short History of Chinese Philosophy: A Systematic Account of Chinese Thought from its Origins to the Present Day*. Edited by Derk Bodde. New York: The Free Press, 1976.

Hahn, Seung-jin. *The Ethics of Filial Piety and the Reality of Aging Society*. Paju: Korean Study and Information, 2011.

Hyun, Yong-soo. "Why Jesus told disciples to leave their parents and brothers?" *The Character & Shema* 2 (2010): 13–55.

Kang, Nam-Soon. "Confucian Familism and its Social/Religious Embodiment in Christianity: Reconsidering the Family Discourse from a Feminist Perspective." *Asia Journal of Theology* 18, no. 1 (April 2004): 168–89.

Kim, Dong-soo. "New Testament and Filial Piety." *Theological Forum* 43 (2006.2), 389–409.

Luther, Martin. "Dedicatory Letter of Martin Luther to Pope Leo." In *On the Freedom of a Christian*. Accessed July 13, 2020. http://www.fordham.edu/halsall/mod/luther-freedomchristian.html.

Moon, Sang Kwon, "Honoring Parents and Jewish Community Consciousness: A Comparative Study of Biblical Parent Care and Confucian HYO (filial piety)," *A Study of Systematic Theology* 33 (2019): 140–75.

Lau, D. C., trans. *Confucius: The Analects*. Hong Kong: Chinese University Press, 1983.

Lo, Lung-kwong. "The Nature of the Issue of Ancestral Worship among Chinese Christians," *Studies in World Christianity* 9, no. 1 (2003), 30–42.

Munro, Donald J. *The Concept of Man in Early China*. Ann Arbor: University of Michigan, 2001.

Park, David M. and Julian C. Müller. "The challenge that Confucian filial piety poses for Korean churches," *HTS Theological Studies* 70, no. 2 (2014): 1–8.

Park, Keun-won. "Korean Christian churches and Ancestral Rite." *Korean Journal of Christian Studies*, 8/1 (1991): 340–59.

Park, Seong-kwon. "Biblical hyo (filial piety) as Respect for Parents." *Study of Hyo (Filial Piety)*, no. 7 (2008): 21–42.

Qin, Daniel. "Confucian Filial Piety and the Fifth Commandment: A Fulfillment Approach." *Asian Journal of Pentecostal Studies* 16, no. 2 (2013): 139–64.

Seong, ShinHyung. *Otherness and Ethics: An Ethical Discourse of Levinas and Confucius (Kongzi)*. Eugene: Wipf & Stock, 2018.

Seong, ShinHyung and Seon-wook Kim. "A Study of the Biblical Meaning and the Christian Social Ethical Interpretation of Forgiveness." *The Korean Journal of Christian Social Ethics*, 46 (2020): 115–45.

Slingerland, Edward, trans. *Confucius Analects*. Indianapolis/Cambridge: Hackett Publishing Company, 2003.

———. "Virtue Ethics, the Analects, and the Problem of Commensurability." *Journal of Religious Ethics* 29, no. 1 (Spring 2001): 97–125. doi: 10.1111/0384–9694.00070.

Taylor, Romeyn. "Chinese Hierarchy in Comparative Perspective." *The Journal of Asian Studies* 48, no. 3 (August, 1989): 490–511.

Van Norden, Bryan W., trans. *Mengzi*. Indianapolis/Cambridge: Hackett Publishing Company, 2008.

Wang, Canglong. "Individuality, Hierarchy, and Dilemma: The Making of Confucian Cultural Citizenship in a Contemporary Chinese Classical School." *Journal of Chinese Political Science* 21 (2016): 435–52.

Yao, Xinzhong. *An Introduction to Confucianism*. Cambridge: Cambridge University Press, 2000.

CHAPTER 4

FAITHFUL LIVING

Life in the Marketplace

Jean Lee

THE MARKETPLACE CHRISTIAN

Christian faith asserts that all aspects of life, including participation in the marketplace, are within the Creator God's reign, and serve as platforms for community and interaction of human persons. However, due to the fallen nature of humankind, societal and commercial activities have deteriorated into independent contractual exchanges based on calculative personal interests. The marketplace hence has become a place where sinful human nature takes priority. Accordingly, an integral part of Christians' mission is to function as an agent for marketplace and commercial transformation according to God's will.

In the commercial world, business ethics are often understood in abstraction to mean doing right or wrong, or making moral choices. This view is particularly inadequate for Christians seeking to walk in faith in the marketplace, as they may need to stand firm and tackle demands that do not align with Christian values on a daily and continuing basis. This means their choices are not isolated incidences. Christians in the marketplace are not isolated decision-making agents but are challenged to live a perpetual life articulating their Christian identity and values. Accordingly, Christians do not merely seek to respond ethically to the challenges of the marketplace issues; they are called by God to their vocation and sent by Christ to live as children of God in the secular world. They walk in faith under the reign and values of the kingdom of God, rather than powers of the secular world. They act morally along this path not just to satisfy ethical demands, but to become persons who please God.

While the world is no doubt twisted and broken, it is highly complex and retains its created goodness. As God the creator continues to uphold the world via his word and grace, glimpses of light shine through darkness. Goodness resides in the human heart and is present in many forms and places. There are no specific rules or perfect solution to issues in the marketplace because it is a highly dynamic environment. This means no single theory or framework can fit all contexts and decisions. The variety of professions and contexts provide a platform for articulation of faith, taking Christians on the path of continuous spiritual growth. In this regard, Christ sends his disciples to live Christian lives in every profession within society. They are granted different forms of competence, as well as the presence of the Holy Spirit, to walk in faith daily in the marketplace.

Asia consists of various countries where cultures and business practices differ greatly. On the one hand, many local communities are developing, struggling to find means for shelter and to feed their people. On the other hand, people in commercially developed cities enjoy higher living standards, while struggling on issues such as law enforcement, bribery, and corruption. Many Asian cultures prioritize familial and friendship ties in ways that raise perplexing questions about fairness and justice. In many Asian nations that have experienced rapid economic development, the pressure to do well financially is heightened, creating key challenges for Christians, who seek to serve one master above all (Matt 6:24). To this end, life in the marketplace takes on many shapes and forms. This article attempts to lay a foundation for faithful Christian life in the marketplace in the Asian context, arguing that Christians must intentionally articulate their faith, which is not merely an ethical decision-making process, but based on an improvisation of their character and identity in Christ.

MARKETS AND MORALITY

In pursuit of economic development, the logic behind the market exchange mechanism leads to the economic person (*Homo economicus*) model. The market assumes human persons make rational choices, always aiming at maximizing their benefits. It also assumes enterprises maximize profits in a rational manner. A combination of such assumptions contributes to the development of economic markets, creating the marketplaces in which we reside.

The modern market based on trade and commercial exchange has been developed over the years with the development of capital, contract, and business laws. Modern markets, driven by economic growth, become more and more complex with the introduction of financial instruments and banking systems. A pervasive focus on autonomy, profits, and wages potentially erodes the value of human quality and connections.¹ Business organizations run on a standard principal-agent model that assumes employees need to be monitored and controlled. Organic communities of cooperative living that used to be based on mutual care and support are replaced by autonomic or mechanical interaction in the modern exchange markets. However, no matter what form or stage of development markets are at, commercial activities need to be moral to sustain their basic functions.² For example, trades must be based on mutual trust, while cheating leads to unnecessary transaction costs. Individuals who enter the marketplace through employment or other forms of participation often find themselves within hierarchical structures that impose certain cultural norms, demands, and values, depending on the social group they encounter.

In describing the social structure of managerial work, Jackall asserts that

> the hierarchical authority structure that is the linchpin of bureaucracy dominates the way managers think about their world and about themselves. Managers do not see or experience authority in any abstract way; instead, authority is embodied in their personal relationships with their immediate bosses and in their perceptions of similar links between other managers up and down the hierarchy.³

This hierarchical culture is even more apparent in Asian companies, where people tend to look upon authorities to provide direct instructions or answers. Although the market is merely a mechanism that facilitates cooperative living, the systems, structures, and priorities aggregate to a complex human mechanism that in turn affect the participants within. Life in the marketplace can mean either active participation with efforts to build character, or passive responses by participants who choose to go with the crowd. Most often, participants linger somewhere along the spectrum of effort, and struggle onwards. Besides battling the constant demand for productivity, they need to

---

1. The impact of the market environment on morality has undergone significant discussions over the years. In 2008, the views of thirteen scholars were presented at a John Templeton Foundation debate, on the question: "Does the Free Market Corrode Moral Character?" (The views can be seen here: https://bethimpson.files.wordpress.com/2018/02/does-the-free-market-corrode-moral-character.pdf.) Scholars are split on the issue, some arguing that either way is possible.
2. A detailed discussion of markets and morality is beyond the scope of this article. For more details, refer to Paul J. Zak, ed., *Moral Markets: The Critical Role of Values in the Economy*. Princeton: Princeton University Press, 2008.
3. Robert Jackall, *Moral Mazes: The World of Corporate Managers* (Oxford: Oxford University Press, 2010), 18.

find their place within relationships that go alongside the struggle for power and authority.

PERSONAL AND COMMUNAL

Life in the marketplace takes on both a micro (personal) and a macro (communal) aspect. At the communal level, we face systemic limitations and adversities that overshadow our activities within society. Many of these are structural – hierarchical power struggles, systemic poverty, labor abuse, etc. The magnification of sinful human nature, taken in aggregate over the years, contributes to systems that focus on profits and efficiencies, driving people into a survival mode that thrives on egocentric self-interest. In time, the self-interested economic system and culture becomes entrenched and taken for granted as the only way to survive. People who intend to do good face a kind of helplessness that in turn pushes them back into taking self-protective measures. In Asia, where many family-run businesses have grown into large conglomerates, relationships often take priority over capabilities. This tends to create injustices in terms of power, opportunity, and the like.

At a personal level, individuals enter the workforce or enact marketplace transactions daily. Christians who strive to live faithfully in this arena filled with twisted human nature and sinfulness are constantly challenged by secular values. Some of these values, such as "only results matter" or "just follow the norm," may run directly opposite to Christian values and are easily identified, although not easily tackled. Worse still, many secular values have already been taken for granted or have become part of culture. The infiltration of secular values calls for the diligent Christian to be attentive to biblical teachings and to be able to respond to marketplace issues with sound biblical knowledge and theological instincts. Often, practices taken as the norm in their profession may contradict Christian teachings. One example is the practices of businesses bluffing during a negotiation process in the sale of property. Property agents have a strong motive to bluff about pricing when trying their best to narrow the price gap between a seller and buyer. Will Christian property agents do the same, telling white lies that help to close the deal? If they remain honest and refuse to do so, can they survive in a competitive industry that rewards results rather than integrity?

Another challenge at the personal level relates to the individual's development over time as a marketplace participant and disciple of Christ. A typical person may enter the marketplace as worker, employee, businessperson, etc., before becoming a Christian. Even for those who have grown up as Christians, little practical knowledge has been taught at church to prepare them to enter the marketplace. Instead, they spend years acquiring professional knowledge that is by and large "secular" in nature. This does not mean secular knowledge is entirely evil. In fact, quite the opposite. Secular knowledge is generated by people striving to understand the world and the truth. The sciences help explore nature and the logic of things. Art stimulates creativity and is uplifting. Yet knowledge from human sources alone always remain incomplete, missing the last step that takes one to the Creator God. As such, a return to God is necessary to uphold spirituality and the human heart – that is, to reconcile with the self and to attain true life. This means one is a Christian before being a participant in the marketplace, not vice versa. This fundamental positioning reminds the Christian to uphold one's identity in the marketplace, as well as other arenas in life. Life in the marketplace takes on an entirely different perspective once the participant's identity as Christian is maintained.

COMPARTMENTALIZATION AND DUAL MORALITY

One common way of dealing with ethical challenges in the marketplace is to operate with different persona or mindsets in the marketplace verses the private life. This is quite common, especially when one is not alert about the need to actively integrate faith and work. Wong and Rae describe this as the compartmentalization strategy, where we follow different sets of values within different spheres of our life. Compartmentalization allows us to act differently in the competitive marketplace while maintaining higher virtues privately. Research suggests that compartmentalization is a critical component in the acceptance of perpetuation of corruption. In particular, organizations that emphasize adherence to social norms tend to create conditions for compartmentalization.[4]

Yet for Christians, compartmentalization is not an option. Not only does this practice create a dichotomy, it also clearly works against the principle that the lordship of Christ extends over every aspect of our lives. Integrity in the marketplace is not only necessary, but a test of our true faith and obedience. For Christians, faith is not tied to financial advantage but to life and all its goodness. Wong and Rae remind us that ethics is about the values that drive a person or organization, not merely laws and compliance.[5]

---

4. Kenman L. Wong and Scott B. Rae, *Business for the Common Good: A Christian Vision for the Marketplace* (Downers Grove: IVP Academic, 2011), 167–68.
5. Kenman, 170–88.

Similar to compartmentalization is the concept of dual morality – a separation of personal and professional ethics.[6] The idea comes from cultural relativism, asserting that the marketplace, like any given culture, has self-defining moral standards. Renowned economist Milton Friedman advises that it is the duty of businesses to focus entirely on maximizing profits for shareholders.[7] Managers are to do everything possible within the law to do so, setting personal values aside. This form of dual morality can be taken further to the agency concept, in which employees are simply expected to obey commands from their superior without exception. Considering oneself only as an instrument conducting the work of the organization, the employee frees oneself of any moral obligations. This is seen most vividly in work that requires taking orders without questioning, such as the armed forces. What do Christians do when ordered to do things contradictory to the Christian faith? Different Christians may differ in their position and response to such questions. Ultimately, a focus to the personhood, calling, and vocation of the individual Christian is needed to resolve the particularities of each decision appropriately.

One common Christian approach to living ethically in the marketplace is a three-step application of biblical values: recognize, analyze, and resolve.[8] It anticipates a continuous exposition of the Bible, critical analysis of the issue at hand, and an attempt to do the best possible thing under the given circumstances. The ultimate goal is to live a blessed life, do good for our neighbors, and to please God.[9] This approach is simple and easily understandable, but may only work well for some professions or work environments without too many conflicting values and demands. For others who constantly face external and internal struggles in the marketplace, this three-step application may be too simplistic.

Hill presents Christian ethics in the marketplace in terms of the "changeless character of God." Thus, Hill proposes that "when we behave in a manner

---

6. Alexander Hill, *Just Business: Christian Ethics for the Marketplace* (Downers Grove: IVP Academics, 2008), 69–70.
7. Milton Friedman, "The Social Responsibility of Business is to Increase Its Profits," in *Ethical Theory and Business*, ed. Denis Arnold, Tom Beauchamp and Norman Bowie (Cambridge: Cambridge University Press, 2020), 207–10.
8. Gill illustrates this approach through a study of the Ten Commandments in his book: David Gill, *Doing Right: Practicing Ethical Principles* (Downers Grove, IL: InterVarsity Press, 2004), 79–321.
9. Gill, *Doing Right*, 25–43.

consistent with God's character, we act ethically."[10] This approach does not draw on egoism, utilitarianism, or casuistry, but rests in an ultimate goal of living a life that emulates God's character. Accordingly, Hill points to three divine characteristics – holiness, justice, and love – as ethical decision-making bearings repeatedly emphasized in the Bible. All three characteristics are to be considered since they complement each other.[11] This approach recognizes that actions must be substantiated not only by rational thought, but by the whole person. The Christian striving to live a faithful life must do so in an integrated way, with a focus not on earthly riches but on the kingdom of God.

AN INTEGRATED LIFE

Eldred points out that in God's economy personal success has nothing to do with earning but is connected instead to hearts and relationships. Success in God's kingdom is how we serve others to his glory in the sphere of influence to which God calls and sends us.[12] In this sphere, we strive to become our true selves, reflecting all the goodness of the *imago Dei* (the image of God), and seeking to enact and participate in the *missio Dei* (the mission of God) by becoming a servant to others. Earthly success is not guaranteed, but such a faithful and integrated life points to an eternal hope greater than any other.

Life in the marketplace at the communal level means that the church, overall, is called by God and sent to every sphere of life in the marketplace. The missio Dei is thus implemented via his people, penetrating all businesses and professions at all ranks and files. In aggregate, God works through the church to redeem businesses and transform the marketplace. Marketplace Christians often find themselves in positions far from being able to make a difference. This is indeed true if one remains at a self-sufficient level in the attempt to live faithfully. Transformation of the world is something that belongs to God, willed by God, and enacted in his time. Nevertheless, where God calls and sends his people, Christians are to exert their influence by living faithfully in their respective spheres, no matter how insignificant the impact may be.

The modern marketplace is indeed overshadowed by systemic sinfulness and unethical practices. This is even more apparent in underdeveloped

---

10. Alexander Hill, *Just Business: Christian Ethics for the Marketplace* (Downers Grove: IVP Academics, 2008), 14.
11. Hill describes the three characteristics as legs on a three-legged stool, each balances the other two. For more details, refer to Hill, 14–17.
12. Ken Eldred, *The Integrated Life: Experience the Powerful Advantage of Integrating Your Faith and Work* (Colorado: Manna Ventures, 2010), 50.

countries where corruption may be part of business norm. To tackle unethical practices at a systemic level is a greater task that may often be seen as next to impossible at the personal level. Here we need to return to a wider picture of God's call and commissioning of the whole people, before returning to a reflection of how each does one's own part. Eldred presents a practical picture of a threefold ministry in our work life: a ministry *at* work, a ministry *of* work, and a ministry *to* work.[13] A ministry *at* work points those around us to God, a ministry *of* work serves and creates, while a ministry *to* work redeems the practices, policies, and structures of institutions. This threefold vision for ministry integrates Christian practice in the workplace and allows the marketplace Christian to make an impact at both the personal and systemic levels.

In the Reformed tradition, the threefold ministry reminds us of the messianic offices of Christ as prophet, priest, and king.[14] Karl Barth points out that Christ in Galilee revealed his prophetic office, Christ's passion presented his priestly office, and his exaltation showed his kingship. These three offices of Christ "all find their secondary continuation in those who are sent by him."[15] In the marketplace context, the prophetic office calls upon the Christian to enact righteousness, to speak the truth, and to exert the values of God's kingdom. This is a ministry *at* work that points people to God. Priesthood parallels the Christian's ministry *of* work – serving, creating and caring in similar ways as Christ the mediator. The responsibility of the kingship office is *to* work positively towards a society and system that governs in a manner pleasing to the will of God. A ministry to work attempts to do so by rebuilding or transforming society's practices, policies, and structures.

FAITHFUL DAILY LIVING

We have already seen that faithful Christian living is complex and dynamic thus, not to be confined to simple rules or formulas. Nevertheless, humans are attracted to simplicity and predictability, especially when it comes to the marketplace which demands effective and efficient results. Here, the law and order take on vital impact. "The law contributes to the marketplace by ensuring predictability and by providing a level playing field for all competitors.

---

13. Ken Eldred, *The Integrated Life: Experience the Powerful Advantage of Integrating Your Faith and Work* (Colorado: Manna Ventures, 2010), 107.
14. For a detailed discussion of the threefold office of Christ and its implications for marketplace Christian, refer to R. Paul Stevens, *The Other Six Days: Vocation, Work and Ministry in Biblical Perspective* (Grand Rapids: Eerdmans, 1999), 163–89.
15. Karl Barth, *Church Dogmatics* (Edinburgh: T&T Clark, 1957), II.2.431.

Predictability is vital because it enables companies to effectively plan for the future."[16] The legal system focuses on what people must not do and the processes to prevent such laws from being broken. To the Christian who lives under an alternative set of values within the kingdom of God, relying on the secular law as a moral pointer may not be sufficient. In fact, mere compliance with the law does not make people morally good. Rather, law-abiding behavior is the minimum acceptable standard in society.

Thus, ethics in the marketplace differs from simply observing the law in a particular way that is critical to the Christian pursuing discipleship. This is especially true for Asian countries where the legal and judicial system is immature. While law and general ethics can be analyzed and dealt with in an overall manner through deriving one's stance and advocating the arguments, life in the marketplace takes on a different form. There is no time to pause and analyze when the boss makes demands. Business opportunities may slip away quickly if not acted upon. Pressure to deliver results is real and continuous. All these daily occurrences in the marketplace may be normal practices that nobody questions. To stand firm on the Christian faith in such circumstances, Christians must have the courage to form character and habits that respond to continuous demands in a biblical manner.

Besides a good framework and theological ground to build morality, Christians need to develop an ethical or theological instinct that becomes part of their thought system and habitual behavior. In addition to studying God's Word and knowing what is to be done, they must assimilate such knowledge into their lives, becoming a person pleasing to God. Everyday marketplace challenges form a platform whereby Christians learn and grow spiritually by practicing, improvising, and articulating their faith. The marketplace thus becomes a sphere where they can learn to persevere and stand firm where things seem impossible, thus experiencing God's help and presence when upholding God's Word.

Hill recognizes the disparities between knowing and doing. He distinguishes between the concepts of "sin" and "sins," stating that "while the former term describes our defective moral character, the latter includes actions that naturally follow – lying, promise breaking, stealing, and so on." Accordingly, fallen human nature leads to sinful actions that magnify in the marketplace, where pressure and competition provide strong incentives to rationalize

---

16. Hill, *Just Business*, 85.

unethical behavior.[17] To combat this, Christians must learn to articulate or improvise their faith.

RELEVANCE OF THE IMPROVISATION MODEL

Wells proposes the practice of improvisation in the theater as a model for the church to live faithfully without fear when encountering the unknown of the future.[18] Theatrical improvisers often experience uninhibited freedom during the improvisation process. The story and practice of the church shape and empower Christians in similar ways.[19] I assert that the improvisation model is particularly valuable for marketplace Christians, who need both the theological framework and the improvisational space for articulating the Christian faith under unpredictable situations. Not only is the marketplace environment rapidly changing, but so also are the demands that the participant react immediately to the given changes or requests. Seeing oneself as an improviser within the Christian discipleship framework encourages the development of Christian character and theological instincts on a continuous basis when confronted with marketplace issues.

The improvisation model pursues an ecclesial ethics that resides with the traditions and practices of the church, as well as the character and acts of God.[20] As opposed to the universal or subversive strands, it contains a liberating power that allows Christians to embrace the unconventional. As Wells asserts,

> they – almost invariably – accord authority to Scripture, and generally to some other forms of discernment, perhaps tradition, or reason, or experience, or something similar. These provide the boundaries of their performance, their stage, as it were. And on this stage they strive to enact a faithful drama.[21]

The moral life is more about tiny episodes of implementation. This idea of a continuous stream of "moments of decision" or "situations" resembles the marketplace environment closely.[22] Contemporary ethics offer cases or

---

17. Hill, *Just Business*, 17.
18. The improvisation model includes features such as habit, status, questioning givens, over-accepting and incorporating the lost, that are beyond the scope of this article. For details, refer to Samuel Wells, *Improvisation: The Drama of Christian Ethics* (Grand Rapids: Brazos Press, 2004), 73–153.
19. Wells, *Improvisation*, 11.
20. Wells, *Improvisation*, 34.
21. Wells, *Improvisation*, 65–66.
22. Wells, *Improvisation*, 73.

dilemmas that require careful analysis and discernment, presenting boundaries or extremities that may not reflect reality. Life in the marketplace involves not only dilemmas, but inner struggles for the participants, as well as possible negotiations or possibilities that reach beyond a fixed case scenario. Only when Christians see possibilities or hope when their faith is being challenged can they retain strength and endurance to strive on in the narrow path.

Traditionally, the image of Christian soldiers matching for war has been rather vivid for the church when describing the Christian mission. In this regard, the marketplace can be seen as the frontline of the battlefield. Nevertheless, marketplace Christians are not constantly at war, fighting tiring battles daily. Instead, they are soldiers continuously in training, getting ready for the spiritual battles that confront them on particular occasions. Challenges are like obstacles that strengthen the soldiers as they form habits to face and tackle them with a Christian worldview and constantly make faithful decisions.

Wells describes the formation of theological instincts as requiring imagination. In addition to the ordinary imagination that enables one to develop an instinct, there is also a creative dimension to see simultaneously what might yet be. During this process, the Christian experiences the slow development of moral formation.[23] The marketplace is solid ground for learning and practicing faith, taking the Christian on the path to continuous moral formation and spiritual growth. During this process, the concept of improvisation triggers an awareness of the active process of forming habits, and at the same time provides a buffer or space for struggle, discernment, and alternate choices.

TAKING GIVENS AS GIFTS

As we have described, the macro aspect of marketplace life presents systemic problems to its participants. Wells suggests that Christians should see these limitations and problems as "given" – "gifts" or opportunities that God grants each person. This viewpoint will change attitudes and thoughts, encouraging Christians to seek new ways of improvising despite boundaries and limits confronting them. Wells further asserts that to the people of God, the only "given" is God's story of creation, election, redemption, and consummation. All else can become "gifts."[24]

In reality, what the Christian encounters may be lies or unrighteousness, pressures that demand compromise. In the face of such adversities, faith may

---

23. Wells, *Improvisation*, 76.
24. Wells, *Improvisation*, 115–26.

appear to have no place in the marketplace. However, Christian ethics do not ask for arguing or giving up, but present a subversive paradigm that transforms given limitations through faithful discernment and action. This is because, for every situation, there is a fundamental human aspect that is not covered by functional or task-oriented means alone. Human ignorance and sinfulness are givens. These lead to concrete difficulties and sufferings as humans attempt to cooperate in the marketplace. Christians must learn to embrace these as the life that God grants, confronting difficulties and suffering to experience life in its fullness within God's grace.

EMBRACING LIFE

As Christians seek to develop their theological and ethical instincts in the marketplace, they must find ways to keep in mind the deeper commitments of the Christian worldview, especially the goodness of the created order. God created the cosmos and all beings within it, seeing that all is good. Although humankind has fallen and now lives in brokenness and sin, God remains faithful and loving to his people. One can only become fully satisfied when returning to his embrace. This view asks that Christians respect and embrace life in its fullness – and strive to regain the goodness and abundance of creation.

One simple yet practical model for the marketplace Christian is the "Habit-Unlearn-Gift" (HUG) framework that reminds us to embrace life granted by the loving and faithful God. God embraces his people and reveals himself even in the darkest moments, so long as Christians continue to reside and abide in Him. HUG proposes that marketplace Christians form habits that allow them to articulate the Christian faith naturally. Forming habits that are biblical is particularly important in the marketplace environment where competition and efficiency drive participants to quick and timely responses, often without much opportunity for detailed analysis. Christians' natural instincts and responses need to be theologically sound. This can only be learned through continuous spiritual reflection and putting faith into practice, the formation of habits, and the building of godly character as time goes by. Humans can be rational and make intentional choices. At the same time, humans are often emotional. Many choices are not entirely rational. When facing pressures or challenges that threaten our well-being, job security or personal image, it is difficult to make faithful choices. Forming habits not only allows Christians to make faithful choices, but also helps to reduce the struggles involved.[25]

Second, Christians need to unlearn the "givens" of this world. In particular, the commercial practices and norms of various professions present all sorts of "givens" that attempt to govern life in the marketplace. Not all these norms and practices are against the Christian faith. Some may be partial truth. Others can be directly against Christian values. These form an environment that demands participants adhere to its views and processes. Christians must have the faith and courage to identify improper practices, unlearn the ways taken for granted, and derive creative solutions to the problems at hand. This necessitates belief that God shall grant wisdom to find the righteous alternatives that are always present. It also means that the Christian must have faith to accept undesirable outcomes that may result from a strong stance on biblical grounds.

I do not advocate extreme measures or that Christians subvert all traditions. Rather, the call to "unlearning" in this context is a reminder that Christians need to be alert, step out of their comfort zone, and be ready to practice the truth. God grants wisdom and creativity for working toward common goals via many different means. Faithful marketplace Christians work hard with all the wisdom and gifts God has granted, at the same time trusting that God's Word and his presence shall guide them on the righteous path.

Third, "gifts" remind Christians to transform "givens" to "gifts." When facing tough demands and conflicts, it is easy for marketplace Christians to accumulate negative emotions from their continuous daily struggles. These negative emotions can lead to helplessness or depression on one end or create anger or bitterness at the other end. The concept of "gifts" reminds us that all strength and goodness come from God. There will always be a way out in times of troubles, turning givens into gifts.[26]

The HUG framework is based on an articulation or improvisation of the Christian life which focuses on the character or the "being" of the person and leads to the performance or the "doing" of the person. It refuses to give in to the givens of marketplace life, while reminding us to turn to the goodness and gifts from God.

---

25. The concept of "forming habits" is discussed in Wells, *Improvisation*, 73–85. The application to the marketplace context is my own addition.
26. The concepts of "questioning givens" and "incorporating gifts" are discussed in Wells, *Improvisation*, 115–42. Again, the application to the marketplace context is my own addition.

ASIAN CULTURAL CHALLENGES

The culture in Asia affects life in the marketplace in myriad ways. These may include general concerns such as leadership styles and cultural ethos, as well as common problems such as deception and lies. A few examples are highlighted below.

Paternal management style and obedience are rather common in Asian organizations. On the one hand, traditional small family businesses can build strong ties and a warm organizational environment that enhances internal stability, allows quick responses to changes, and strengthens employee job security. On the other hand, paternal leadership styles can prevent implementation of proper policies, hinder organization growth, or lead to abuse of leadership power. Although it is difficult to change such leadership styles, the marketplace Christian is ideally positioned to assert influence on a given organizational culture by being part of it and through building healthy working relationships with all those involved. As the Christian climbs the corporate ladder, the sphere of influence widens.

Asia is the birthplace of many religions and numerous types of local religious practices. These practices tend to tie closely to our daily lives and implant a transactional logic of exchanging spiritual rituals for money and prosperity. When it comes to Christianity, this fundamental misunderstanding leads to easy acceptance of the prosperity gospel, especially in the marketplace, where money and prosperity are prominent goals. Accordingly, it is important to teach a solid foundation of Christian values and enactment. We need to strengthen virtues such as endurance, courage, and perseverance among Christians. Speaking up is not a form of disobedience but a way to witness and dialogue for the common good. As in the HUG framework, Christians can unlearn the prosperity gospel logic and practice total surrender to God's guidance in faith that God's way is the way of truth and life.

Deception, corruption, and lies are more prominent in Asian workplaces than the West. A Christian once shared her struggles when entering the marketplace. She started working at a construction company where many practices appeared to be at odds with her Christian values. She then decided to change jobs and work for the government, thinking that compliance work would allow her to uphold good standards. To her astonishment, she found that bricks submitted for compliance checks were not the ones used for actual construction. Since substandard building materials may cause buildings to collapse, she had many sleepless nights pondering the issue. There is no single solution to thorny situations such as this. In this Christian's situation, the challenge was (and is) to pray for a way out, observe opportunities for change, and to speak up according to the Spirit's prompting. In the worst case, she may need to change jobs again, if she is forced to act outside of her convictions. This is a typical example of someone who needs support and encouragement from Christians around her to not give up prematurely, and to form a habit of continuously discerning the next step. This "given" can turn into a "gift" if those around her become aware of the danger of using substandard building materials, or if her faith in Christ is strengthened during the process.

POWERS AND PRINCIPALITIES

A discussion of life in the marketplace is not complete without tackling the issue of powers and principalities that confront Christians head on in the marketplace. These may include fallen social structures, sinful spiritual beings, and systemic evil.[27] In particular, many Asian cultures operate on a fear of spiritual beings, as demonstrated by the importance of feng shui and spirit worship in Chinese businesses. Here we acknowledge in the first instance that Christ has claimed victory over all powers and principalities through his resurrection. Nevertheless, the reality that sinful powers and darkness are so apparent in marketplace life means Christians can easily lose hope and knowing or unknowingly sway away from the truth.[28] Stott asserts that the Bible's description of evil power is a personified reality. Such a cosmic view of evil needs to be preserved. Only when we properly acknowledge the presence of evil powers in the human society can we explain why these systems get easily twisted or become evil forces.[29] The Bible never shies away from descriptions involving evil power, spirits, and adversities. We see obvious penetration of unrighteousness into all aspects of society. To face this challenge, a proper view of the experience and presence of the Holy Spirit is vital to life in the marketplace.

The Holy Spirit is not an external force or power Christians draw from to fight adversities. Rather, the Holy Spirit is a person of the triune God, living and present within Christians to guide and direct them in their daily walk. The Spirit gives strength and heals along the way, as God wills and in God's time. Therefore, when confronted with sinful power, marketplace Christians stand firm upon the truth, striving to act according to God's Word. They may

---

27. Stevens, *The Other Six Days*, 220–25.
28. For a discussion on powers and principalities, refer to Marva J. Dawn, *Powers, Weakness, and the Tabernacling of God* (Grand Rapids: Eerdmans, 2001), 1–34.
29. Dawn, *Powers, Weakness, and the Tabernacling of God*, 10.

succeed or fail at different times but should always continue to steer toward the truth through repentance and perseverance.

Knowledge of powers and principalities does not necessarily lead Christians to battle and strength; it places them in a humbling posture before the triune God, realizing that all glory, power, and honor belongs to him. The marketplace Christian proclaims God's reign and the presence of God's kingdom – first in one's life, then in businesses and professions, and ultimately in the world and the whole cosmos. God chooses to work in an amazing way beyond human comprehension. He calls upon human weakness to reveal his might, working through the church community to penetrate the darkness, letting his true light shine through the life of the faithful in every dark corner in the marketplace. In this already-but-not-yet era Christians ask not when Christ shall return, but how the people of God can live faithfully to enact kingdom values.

GOING FORWARD

We have seen that living faithfully in the marketplace is a process of character-building and continuous spiritual growth. It is important for faithful Christians to be able to articulate their faith when confronted with marketplace values and demands. Traditionally, church life tends to focus more on the inner or spiritual aspects of its congregation and the gathering for worship within the church. We teach the Bible and think about applications. We care for the sick and support families. However, seldom do we go deep into how we confront challenges in the marketplace. The faith and work integration that had largely been neglected in the past has gradually developed into a marketplace movement during the past decade. It is a highly missional arena that the global churches must carry forward into the future.

Miller traces the history of this "Faith at Work" movement from its sociological and ethical aspects, documenting both the surprising abdication of this field by the church and how it has developed despite all the challenges.[30] Evolution of the movement prompts us to look further and deeper into an essential integrative approach to life in the marketplace, moving beyond ethical struggles to an articulation of faith that is missional. In Asia, the Faith and Work movement has also started with an emphasis on the Asian context of

---

30. Besides a detailed study of the history of the Faith at Work movement, Miller also provides a comprehensive list of reference materials on the subject. For details, refer to David W. Miller, *God at Work: The History and Promise of the Faith at Work Movement* (Oxford: Oxford University Press, 2007), 197–218.

business dealings. Launch of the Chinese, Korean, and Vietnamese versions of the Theology of Work Project website (theologyofwork.org) mark major steps in consolidating materials that focus on the Asian context.[31]

In Asia, where different countries present many varieties of commercial structures and business practices, the marketplace is not only a place for Christians to enact their faith, but also to contribute to the development and well-being of cities and localities. Christian vocation is closely tied with Christian mission, and with the integral mission of the church. Where Christians live integrated and faithful lives in their localities, and assert influence within their sphere of influence together, the marketplace can be transformed into an environment that promotes the common good.

Further studies of life in the marketplace can take the forms of survey and analysis of Christians in different professions and contexts. The faith integration of Christians within each professional context will also provide meaningful insights for other Christians entering such professions. In the past decade, the global church has been moving from an awareness of the need for integration of life in the marketplace to questions about the enactment and practices of faithful Christian life in these arenas. Asian churches have much to contribute from their experiences of living their faith in rapidly changing, dynamic marketplace environments.

QUESTIONS FOR DISCUSSION

1. What are the challenges and difficulties unique to life in the marketplace as opposed to other daily contexts?
2. What are the different approaches Christians take to tackle marketplace problems? Which of these do you find most appropriate and why?
3. What is the improvisation approach? Why is it particularly applicable to life in the marketplace?
4. Describe the HUG framework and give an example of how it may apply to a marketplace situation.

BIBLIOGRAPHY

"About." The Theology of Work Project. https://www.theologyofwork.org/about.

---

[31]. For a description of the Lausanne Movement Theology of Work Project, refer to https://www.theologyofwork.org/about.

Arnold, Denis, Tom Beauchamp, and Norman Bowie. *Ethical Theory and Business* 10th edition. Cambridge: Cambridge University Press, 2020.

Barth, Karl. *Church Dogmatics*. II.2. *The Doctrine of God*. Edinburgh: T&T Clark, 1957.

Dawn, Marva J. *Powers, Weakness, and the Tabernacling of God*. Grand Rapids: Eerdmans, 2001.

Eldred, Ken. *The Integrated Life: Experience the Powerful Advantage of Integrating Your Faith and Work*. Colorado: Manna Ventures, 2010.

Gill, David. *Doing Right: Practicing Ethical Principles*. Downers Grove: InterVarsity Press, 2004.

Hill, Alexander. *Just Business: Christian Ethics for the Marketplace*. Downers Grove: IVP Academics, 2008.

Jackall, Robert. *Moral Mazes: The World of Corporate Managers*. Oxford: Oxford University Press, 2010.

Miller, David W. *God at Work: The History and Promise of the Faith at Work Movement*. Oxford: Oxford University Press, 2007.

Stevens, R. Paul. *The Other Six Days: Vocation, Work and Ministry in Biblical Perspective*. Grand Rapids: Eerdmans, 1999.

Wells, Samuel. *Improvisation: The Drama of Christian Ethics*. Grand Rapids: Brazos Press, 2004.

Wong, Kenman L. and Scott B. Rae. *Business for the Common Good: A Christian Vision for the Marketplace*. Downers Grove: IVP Academics, 2011.

CHAPTER 5

CORRUPTION AND BRIBERY

Hwa Yung

Corruption is a universal problem although some countries have been able to deal with it more effectively than others. This chapter will begin with an introduction to the nature and scale of the problem and briefly look at how Christians in Asia have tended to respond to it. We will then look at how to develop a proper theological framework to address the issue. The final section of the essay will provide some proposals on how to deal with the issue from a Christian perspective. It should be made clear that this chapter is not primarily about addressing corruption at the macro level of national politics and economics. This is a huge subject and there are other resources readily available.[1] Instead, the focus of this chapter is humbler and aims at laying some pastoral guidelines at the micro level for Christians who have to face this issue in their daily work and life.

INTRODUCTION

Defining Corruption

What is corruption, what is the scale of the problem, and how have Christians tended to respond to it in Asia? The description of corruption by Transparency International (TI) is probably as good as any. It states:

> We define corruption as the abuse of entrusted power for private gain. Corruption erodes trust, weakens democracy, hampers economic development and further exacerbates inequality, poverty, social division and the environmental crisis . . . Corruption can take many forms, and can include behaviours like: public servants demanding or taking money or favours in exchange for services, politicians misusing public money or granting public jobs or

---

[1]. Transparency International has an easily accessible online library at "Library," (n.d.), https://www.transparency.org/en/library (accessed 21 Jul 2022). Further, for a useful introduction to some of the issues involved see Ronald Wraith and Edgar Simpkins, *Corruption in Developing Countries* (London: George Allen & Unwin, 1963; reissued, London & New York, Routledge, 2010).

contracts to their sponsors, friends and families, corporations bribing officials to get lucrative deals. . . . Corruption can happen anywhere: in business, government, the courts, the media, and in civil society, as well as across all sectors from health and education to infrastructure and sports. Corruption can involve anyone: politicians, government officials, public servants, business people or members of the public.[2]

Moreover, TI further points out that corruption usually "happens in the shadows" and constantly evolves and "adapts to different contexts and changing circumstances."[3] Furthermore, it involves a huge cost to everyone in any society. Specifically, it includes:

Political costs: Your freedom and rule of law.

Social costs: Your participation and even your trust in government.

Environmental costs: Your chance for a healthy environment and a sustainable future.

Economic costs: Your opportunity to build and grow wealth.[4]

The Scale of the Problem

An International Monetary Fund paper in 2016 estimated that corruption in the public sector alone (i.e. private sector excluded) costs the global economy USD1.5 trillion to USD2 trillion annually in bribes, which is about two percent of the global gross domestic product. These figures do not include the resulting indirect costs to a country in lower economic growth, lost tax revenue, and reduced public funds for infrastructure, health care, and education.[5] Overall, there is general agreement that corruption correlates negatively with economic growth and development.[6]

---

2. Transparency International, "What is Corruption?" (n.d.), https://www.transparency.org/en/what-is-corruption (accessed 21 Jul 2022).
3. Transparency International, "What is Corruption?"
4. Transparency International, "What is Corruption?"
5. International Monetary Fund, "Corruption: Costs and Mitigating Strategies," *International Monetary Fund, Staff Discussion Notes No 16/05* (May 11, 2016), https://www.imf.org/en/Publications/Staff-Discussion-Notes/Issues/2016/12/31/Corruption-Costs-and-Mitigating-Strategies-43888 (accessed 29 Apr 2021). See further, Tom Burgis, *Kleptopia: How Dirty Money is Conquering the World* (London: William Collins, 2020) for a recent global overview.
6. Marie Chêne, "The Impact of Corruption on Growth and Inequality," *Transparency International Anti-Corruption Helpdesk* (15 Mar 2014), https://www.transparency.org/files/content/corruptionqas/Impact_of_corruption_on_growth_and_inequality_2014.pdf (accessed

In the latest TI Corruption Perception Index 2021 which ranks the least corrupt nation highest, countries in Asia (excluding those in the Middle East) have not done very well. Out of a total of 180 nations surveyed, only 14 from Asia are ranked within the top 100: Singapore – 4, Hong Kong – 12, Japan – 18, Bhutan and Taiwan – 28, Korea, South – 32, Malaysia – 62, China – 66, India and Maldives – 85, Timor Leste – 86, Vietnam – 87, Sri Lanka – 94 and Indonesia – 96. All others ranked below 100.[7]

How Have Christians Responded in General?

The above shows clearly that corruption is a major challenge for Christians in Asia. Generally speaking, not much has been written about how Christians ought to deal with the problem in a manner that carefully wrestles with biblical teaching and sound ethical reasoning.[8] This leaves many Christians floundering between two alternatives, neither of which is Christian or pastorally helpful.

First, many take the attitude that Christianity deals primarily with spiritual matters but life outside the church must be managed in more worldly-wise ways. Probably a vast majority of Christians, from the poorest church members to Christian billionaires, adopt this approach in some form or other. Like everybody else, if you have to pay, you just pay! The result is a dualistic Christianity wherein life is split into two parts – the spiritual and the practical or, alternatively, the sacred and secular.

The other response may appear prima facie to be more Christian but, in fact, may even be worse. The church and its leaders will openly teach that, according to the Bible, all forms of corruption and bribery are wrong and therefore Christians must not be tainted by it in any way. The church member hears what is taught and says to himself, "The pastor is right, but I just have to ignore them. Otherwise, how can I feed my family and survive?" The result is

---

21 Jul 2022); Elvin Mirzayev, "How Corruption Affects Emerging Economies," *Investopedia* (17 Dec 2021), https://www.investopedia.com/articles/investing/012215/how-corruption-affects-emerging-economies.asp (accessed 21 Jul 2022).

7. Transparency International, "Corruption Perceptions Index 2021" (2022), https://www.transparency.org/en/cpi/2021 (accessed 21 Jul 2022). See further, Syed Hussein Alatas, *Corruption and the Destiny of Asia* (Singapore: Simon & Schuster, 1999).

8. I have written in greater detail on the subject in Hwa Yung, *Bribery and Corruption: Biblical Reflections and Case Studies for the Marketplace in Asia*, 2nd edn., ed. Soo-Inn Tan (Singapore: Graceworks, 2018), which also contains some very helpful responses from business practitioners. See also Bernard T. Adeney, *Strange Virtues: Ethics in a Multicultural World* (Downers Grove: InterVarsity Press, 1995), 142–62; David W. Gill, *It's About Excellence: Building Ethically Healthy Organizations* (Eugene, OR: Wipf & Stock, 2011).

twofold. First, the Christian is left with a bad conscience; second, and worse, he will eventually conclude the Bible is a good book, but irrelevant to life!

DEVELOPING AN ADEQUATE APPROACH: FOUR PRINCIPLES

To address the issue of corruption adequately we need to deal with at least four basic issues.

Rejecting Dualism in Our Theology

First, we need to reject dualism or a dualistic worldview in our thinking. Most of us have basically adopted a Western theology. But underlying this theology is a fundamental dualism.

At the simplest level, we see this in the Platonic separation of the human being into the body which belongs to the imperfect phenomenal world (the real world we live in) and the soul which belongs to the perfect world (Plato's world of "forms"). Whereas the Bible conceives of the human person as holistic, Christian theology under the influence of Greek philosophy increasingly saw the human in dualistic terms, with the soul being treated with greater importance than the body.

The Chinese scholar, Carver Yu,[9] argues that this in fact goes back to the way in which reality is conceived of in Greek philosophy, as something which is "complete-in-itself, self-subsistent, and self-motivating."[10] A thing or being therefore becomes, by definition, self-subsistent by and of itself, without any need for relation to other things or beings. This laid the foundation for the development of individualism in Western thought. This individualistic understanding of being became incorporated into modern Western philosophy through Descartes. In his famous statement "I think, therefore I am," the "I" is a being or substance (using Aristotelian language) who finds meaning and existence in and of itself, without the need of any reference to the external world. With this, individualism became fully established in Western thought.[11]

This individualism in turn further helped accentuate the individualization and spiritualization of salvation, a tendency which has been endemic in Western theology since Augustine.[12] Salvation for him is both other-worldly

---

9. Carver T. Yu, *Being and Relation: A Theological Critique of Western Dualism and Individualism* (Edinburgh: Scottish Academic Press, 1987).
10. Yu, 67; see 64–98.
11. Yu, 98–106.
12. David J. Bosch, *Transforming Mission: Paradigm Shifts in Theology of Missions* (Maryknoll, NY: Orbis, 1991), 215–17.

and individualistic, with primary emphasis given to the redemption of the soul rather than the reconciliation of the world. This, as David Bosch puts it, "could not but spawn a dualistic view of reality, which became second nature in Western Christianity – the tendency to regard salvation as a private matter and to ignore the world."[13] Thus, eventually Platonic body-soul dichotomy combined with Cartesian individualism to firmly establish the dualistic view of reality in Western thought, as well as the individualization and spiritualization of Christian salvation in Western theology.

Many Christians, especially twentieth-century evangelicals, have bought into this Greek dualism and accepted the tendency to spiritualize and individualize the doctrine of salvation, and turn salvation into a purely other-worldly affair with little serious relationship to real life in this world. Therefore, the tendency for them is to advocate a withdrawal from the "public square" and its concomitant of a "life-boat ethics." The world, being sinful, is perceived as a sinking ship, hence there is no point in trying to save it. Instead, we are to jump into the "life-boat," which is the church, and leave the world to sink![14]

Consequently, because of our dualistic evangelical mindset, many Christians lack a serious theology of social engagement that informs and guides us in constructive ethical action in a sinful world. To put it in another way, for many our ethics tend to be pietistic and personal, emphasizing the "don'ts" more than the "dos." To the extent that ethics is taken seriously – which is not always the case – we tend to emphasize personal holiness in private life rather than social holiness in public.

Formulating a Culturally and Contextually Sensitive Ethics

Second, we need to guard against assuming that answers worked out in Western textbooks can be applied in total in the Asian contexts without further qualification. On some issues this may be in order, but not in others. This is because, although moral principles in the Scriptures are God-given and therefore valid across time and cultures, the way in which these principles apply may differ in different socio-political and cultural settings.

For example, Christian moral thinking formulated in the West tends to prioritize principles over relationships, on the assumption that moral decisions

---

13. Bosch, 216.
14. This is basically the position of D. L. Moody and of twentieth century fundamentalism. See, e.g., Richard F. Lovelace, *Dynamics of Spiritual Life: An Evangelical Theology of Renewal* (Downers Grove, IL: InterVarsity Press, 1979), 355–400, esp. 377.

must be made without regard to relationships. But in Asian cultures, relationships are fundamental. Indeed, Duane Elmer suggests that "the majority of the people in the world value relationships above most other values."[15] How then do moral principles work out in such situations? Further, in many cultures, relationships are built through gift-giving. But how do we draw the dividing line between a bribe and a gift given in appreciation for help given?[16] A further complication in this problem is that family ties in many Asian societies require us to help family members. But doing so in public life often results in charges of nepotism. Yet, if a Christian fails to "take care" of family members when in a position to do so, he or she is also condemned in the eyes of his or her culture. This presents a real moral dilemma.

I am not hereby suggesting that we do away with ethical principles for the sake of relationships or justifying nepotism in Asian societies. Clearly these are non-starters. But the point being made is that answers developed in the West often need to be reworked in a culturally sensitive manner before they can be applied in other contexts.[17] In particular, much work needs to be done on how we can move Christian ethics from being primarily shaped by a pervasive individualism and cold moral principles to one that also takes relationships and community seriously.[18]

Reading of the Bible Carefully

If the second issue concerns the need to be culturally and contextually sensitive in applying biblical principles in ethics, the third concerns the need to read the Bible more carefully and not just through alien eyes. The Bible and Christian moral teachings down the centuries provide a wealth of ethical resources for us to draw on. But to use them constructively involves careful in-depth study of the Bible because these biblical principles are set in cultures and socio-political contexts alien to ours. In other words, before we can even apply the Bible's teaching to the issues before us in a contextually and culturally sensitive

---

15. Duane Elmer, *Cross Cultural Conflicts: Building Relationships for Effective Ministry* (Downers Grove: InterVarsity Press, 1995), 178–79.
16. For a helpful introductory discussion on Christian ethics and relationship, see Tan Che-Bin. "Ethical Particularism as a Chinese Contextual Issue," *The Word among Us: Contextualizing Theology for Mission Today*, ed. Dean Gilliland (Dallas, TX: Word, 1989), 262–81.
17. See Bernard T. Adeney, *Strange Virtues*, for a good example of doing ethics in non-Western cultures.
18. The crucial importance of relationship is now increasingly being reemphasized in life and work even in the Western world. See, for example, Michael Schluter and David Lee, *The R Factor* (London: Hodder, 1993).

manner, we need first to delineate these principles through a culturally and contextually sensitive reading of the Bible itself.

For example, the Old Testament is absolutely clear on the prohibition of the use of a bribe to pervert justice (Exod 18:21; 23:8; Deut 16:19; Amos 5:12; Mic 7:3; etc.).[19] At the same time, it also recognizes that in traditional cultures, gifts are often used to secure favors which may not involve acts of perversion of justice (e.g. Gen 43:11; Mal 1:8). This latter point is often missed out in Western discussions. Furthermore, as we have already noted earlier, the line between a bribe and a gift is not always easy to draw in many cultures. Serious theological reflection, which also involves a thorough study of cultures and customs, is therefore required. This is one task that must be done by the Asian church if we are to develop an adequate theology that properly informs Christian engagement in the world.

Thus, the task before us involves a double challenge: we need to be culturally and contextually sensitive, both in reading the Bible and in applying its principles in our ethics. For example, consider the issue of bribery before us. A bribe has been defined as "an inducement improperly influencing the performance of a public function meant to be gratuitously exercised." However, "What counts as 'an inducement,' what counts as 'improperly influencing,' what counts as 'a public function,' what functions are 'meant to be gratuitously exercised' have changed as culture has changed."[20] And when we add to this the place of gifts both in the Old Testament and in various cultures noted earlier, the double challenge becomes clear. The issues are often not straightforward.

A Theology of Social Engagement – The Incarnational Principle

This brings us to the fourth and final issue, the incarnational principle. In his book, *The Secular Saint*,[21] Robert Webber sums up neatly the approaches that have been developed in Christian thought historically and by which Christians engaged with the world. These are the *separational* model, the *identificational* model, and the *transformational* model, each of which draws on some specific aspects of biblical teaching.

---

19. All biblical references in this chapter are based on the ESV.
20. John T. Noonan, Jr., "Bribery," *A New Dictionary of Christian Ethics*, eds. John Macquarrie and James Childress (Philadelphia, PA: Westminster Press, 1986), 65–66.
21. Robert E. Webber, *The Secular Saint: The Role of the Christian in the Secular World* (Grand Rapids: Zondervan, 1979).

The separational model draws on biblical teaching that Christians are "aliens and exiles" in the world (1 Pet 2:11) and called not to "love the world" (1 John 2:15). Exemplified by the pre-Constantinian church and the Anabaptists, it emphasizes the Christian's separation from the world and withdrawal from engaging it publicly.[22] The identificational model draws on Old Testament examples of God's people like Joseph and Daniel in public life. Represented by the Constantinian church and civil religion, this model sees the Christian living simultaneously under God's law in two realms, the church and the state (the world). However, caught between the two, the danger here is for the Christian to slide into compromise with the world.[23] The transformational model draws on images like Christians being "salt" and "light" (Matt 5:13–16), and on the overall thrust of biblical teaching. Supremely identified with Augustine and Calvin's teachings, it also recognizes that the Christian lives in two separate realms, the church and the world. Nevertheless, it believes that the church is in position to change the world for good.[24]

Webber notes that the basic thrust of each of the three models is rooted in some aspects of biblical teaching, and to emphasize one at the expense of others is inadequate. They should therefore be integrated under the *incarnational* model, which is the way that Jesus related to the world. He "identified with the world; was separate from the ideologies that rule it; and by His death, resurrection, and second coming assured its transformation."[25]

Webber's proposal for an incarnational approach makes a lot of sense. With respect to corruption, none of us wish to identify fully with the world. But none of us can avoid some entanglement with it in an imperfect world, however indirect, unless one chooses a hermit's existence or a rigid separation model. Just consider how much of the money you paid for your house was for the purpose of greasing palms? Or what percentage of the price you paid for a piece of merchandise went into various corrupt practices before it reached the market? But all of us also recognize that separation is a Christian principle. Yet, although we are not of the world, we remain in the world, living with all its contradictions (John 17:14–19; 1 Cor 5:10). As for transformation, the fact remains that until Christ returns corruption will continue in one form or other. Nevertheless, we all should do whatever we can to check it.

---

22. Webber, 75–104.
23. Webber, 105–34.
24. Webber, 135–65.
25. Webber, 188.

AN INCARNATIONAL APPROACH TO THE CHALLENGE OF CORRUPTION

How does the incarnational model work in practice in dealing with corruption at the micro level? Before laying out the basic guidelines, two points need clarifying.

First, we need to be clear about the difference between the incarnational model and the separational model. In real life we can only avoid corruption altogether if we follow the separational model rigidly. In practice, very few have succeeded in living this way, like a hermit completely cut off from the world. The vast majority of Christians will find themselves "in the world," though not wanting to be "of the world" as well. But once we are "in the world," we cannot pretend that we can remain untouched by it. This needs to be clearly stated.

Once we have chosen the second option of being "in the world" and therefore opting for the incarnational model, we have two alternatives. One, which we will call "Alternative One," is to opt for jobs wherein it is possible to avoid corruption as much as possible. This would usually mean certain jobs in the government sectors where we can choose not to be touched by corruption if we so desire. But even there, things are not always smooth sailing. Temptations abound, and even when we wish to keep above them, we will face intense pressure from colleagues or superiors who do not share our convictions. It could also include certain types of jobs in the marketplace wherein one is relatively shielded from corrupt practices. This would be true of some professions such as medicine or law. But even here there are all sorts of problems involved when it comes to getting permits to operate, or getting files moving through the bureaucracies, etc.

The other option, "Alternative Two," is the one which a majority of people in the marketplace find themselves. Here corruption ranges from the relatively mild to the serious, depending on our fields of work. Examples of these include accountancy, banking, manufacturing, building industry, construction, import-export business, etc. Those working in these sectors will find it impossible to avoid some entanglement with corrupt practices, whether directly or indirectly.

The second point that needs clarifying is this. Some people in both alternatives have attempted to resolve the issue by taking one of the following three ways out. One is, "If I am the boss, and paying is the only way to get things moving, I will ask one of my subordinates, a 'friend' or an 'agency' to do it. I don't want to be directly involved." Or "If the boss asks me to do it, I will do it. But I am not responsible." Or again, "If the boss asks me to, I still will not do it. But I will ask him to get someone else to do it. I just don't wish to dirty my hands." Careful analysis of each of the above apparent solutions will show that, whether you like it or not, you have to bear part of the responsibility, directly or indirectly. I do not think that we can so easily salve our consciences by putting things in such black-and-white terms.

In other words, we must be clear about our alternatives. Most of us do not have the luxury of the separational model. We are then left with the incarnational model. But once we adopt this model, there is no way we can avoid some forms of entanglement with corruption, however indirect. Further, within the incarnational model, we can choose either alternative. With Alternative One we will find it relatively easier to keep away from some direct entanglement with corruption at most times, but not necessarily all the time. With Alternative Two we will invariably find ourselves being caught up in situations where bribes will be asked for in some form or other. The following is a set of proposed guidelines for those who have adopted the incarnational model, especially those in Alternative Two.

Guideline 1: All Forms of Active Corruption Be Absolutely Prohibited

The first guideline is that under the separation principle all forms of active corruption should be prohibited. It is helpful to make a distinction between *active corruption*, which involves paying a bribe to get something done either illegally or immorally, and *passive acceptance* within a corrupt system, which involves paying to get something legitimate moving faster or paying under duress. All Christians would affirm that the former must be strictly prohibited. This would include, for example, the following:

- Receiving bribes in any form for oneself to do something unjust or illegal for someone else
- Giving bribes in any form to secure something unjustly or illegally for oneself
- Outright lies and dishonesty, including the failure to honor contracts and debts
- Sexual immorality
- Failure to provide adequately for staff's welfare and outright exploitation of workers
- Knowingly producing and distributing defective products.

Guideline 2: As Much as Possible, We Should Avoid Any Form of Passive Acceptance of Corruption

If the separation principle requires the strict prohibition of all kinds of active corruption, it also insists that any form of passive corruption should also be avoided as much as possible, even though total avoidance is impossible. I am aware that I am advocating a position here that does not view everything in black-and-white terms. For lack of a better term, I have used the term *passive acceptance* to describe this position. Many will balk at any suggestion of such a thought because it looks like moral compromise. Perhaps the following comments will help.

First, I have already argued that once we adopt the incarnation model, we cannot avoid some forms of passive acceptance of corruption in life. To think otherwise is to be untruthful to the facts of life.

Second, a careful reading of the Bible shows that while God's moral demands are absolute, nevertheless a certain degree of accommodation to human weaknesses is found in the way they are applied in real life situations. For example, the Bible is consistent throughout that monogamy is God's ethical ideal for humanity. Yet, there is not a single direct condemnation of polygamy in the Old Testament. But in time, the Jews came to clearly see the full implications of Old Testament teachings, and monogamy was the norm by Jesus's time. God appears to have been prepared to wait more than a thousand years for his Word to have its leavening effect on Israelite culture.

Or consider the problem of slavery. Nowhere do we find any direct criticisms on the institution of slavery even in the New Testament. But there are clearly indirect critiques in Galatians 3:28 and Philemon. Yet, after some two thousand years, there is now unanimous agreement among Christians that slavery is immoral. Perhaps the most relevant example to our subject is Jesus's attitude to the Roman taxation system. The latter was a widely known form of corruption by which the collection of taxes was farmed out by the Romans to tax collectors, who often made loads of money on the side (cf. Zacchaeus in Luke 19:1–10). Yet, having challenged the corruption of the system through the conversion of Zacchaeus, Jesus nevertheless stated that taxes (with all the extras going toward corruption) must still be paid in his saying that we are "to give to Caesar what belongs to Caesar" (Luke 20:25).

In each of the above examples, we find a form of passive acceptance of corruption in the world. Radical as the Christian message is, there is also a recognition in the Bible that not everything can be changed overnight. There appears to be situations in which God seems prepared to give a society time to work at changes gradually. Recognition of the above means that, in dealing with the second form of corruption in the marketplace, that of passive acceptance, Christians will need a similar wisdom and honesty.

Third, as already noted, the line between a gift and a bribe is often not clear in non-Western cultures. The law may say that the latter is illegal, but social customs require giving as an expression of appreciation. Many Christians do not realize that the tension surrounding this complex tension is also seen in the Old Testament. For example, in six references to gifts or bribery in Proverbs, three (15:27; 17:23; 22:16) condemn it, but three others (17:8; 18:16; 21:14) extol it in positive terms. More importantly, every condemnation of bribery in the Bible is directed either at those who practice it to pervert justice, or those who use their positions of power to oppress others, especially the poor. We *do not* find a single condemnation of those who must pay because they are in a position of weakness and are forced to do so. As Bernard Adeney explains:

> Such equivocation in the Old Testament seems to reflect a recognition of the power differential between a poor person who gives a gift in order to stave off injustice and the rich who uses his power to exploit the poor. The powerful and the powerless are not judged by the same abstract absolute, but by the relationships and intentions of their situation.[26]

Considering the above three comments, the way forward appears to be that, as far as possible, we should avoid even the passive acceptance of corruption. This would mean, that if we are in the position of the boss, we should always view passive acceptance as the very last resort. It should never be used as a shortcut to avoid the hard work of seeking every legitimate means of solving the problem. Or, if we are under orders, we may need to say to the boss, at the risk of incurring his wrath, "Please get someone else to do it."

However, in doing so we must always remember two things. First, when taking this position, we must avoid any sense of personal moral superiority on our part, which allows us to be judgmental toward those who are directly involved. For whether we are directly or indirectly involved, we share in the sinfulness of that action – in so far as it is less than God's ideal. Second, by saying that we would rather not do it, we are making a point that we do not believe that this is ultimately good for our society and that there is something

---

26. Adeney, *Strange Virtues*, 152.

improper about such actions. Ultimately, it is still our hope that such practices be wiped out for the good of all. This leads to the third guideline.

Guideline 3: We Practice Identification Only to the Extent That It Allows Us to Work for Transformation

The incarnational model would require that we practice identification only to the extent that it allows us to work for transformation. Some systems are so inherently corrupt that it would seem impossible to effect any transformation from within. The Gestapo of Nazi Germany or the ex-Soviet KGB would be good examples from recent history. In the early church, by the end of the second century, the church generally took the line that Christians should not be in the civil service, the military, or in the Roman entertainment industry (charioteers, gladiators, etc.). This was because these occupations involved idolatry, emperor worship, extreme cruelties, and often killing which equals murder. Today Christians should take the same stand against businesses and corporations which are founded on an inherently corrupt basis. The only Christian course of action in such situations is to get out.

In other situations which are greyer, one would have to weigh the various options carefully. Would staying allow me to effect some socioeconomic or even moral transformation for the common good? For example, would accepting a low level of passive corruption mean my ability or my company's ability to provide employment for some needy persons who would otherwise be unemployed or better quality of service for the general public?

To many Christians this raises an ugly question. Are we compromising our ethical principles? The answer is "Certainly not!" Apart from all the other arguments I have already put forward earlier, allow me to draw attention to another principle in Scripture. Consider the episode in the life of the prophet Jeremiah (Jer 38:14–28) when he lies (vv. 24 & 27) to a group of evil men to protect the king and safeguard his own life. This appears to be morally justified. It is comparable to telling an enraged man with a gun looking for a particular person to kill that the person is somewhere else, even when you know that is not true. Your responsibility to save life in that situation takes precedence over your responsibility to tell the truth.

Norman L. Geisler speaks of the need of a "graded absolutism" in our ethical thinking.[27] God's various moral commands are absolute, but they are not all at the same level of importance. To tell a lie to save a life in certain

---

27. Norman L. Geisler, *Christian Ethics: Options and Issues* (Grand Rapids: Baker, 1989), 113–32.

circumstances (and not just any) is to recognize that life-saving is more important than truth-telling in God's hierarchy of values. This does not mean that lying is right in and of itself. Neither does it mean that we are compromising God's law, "You shall not bear false witness." But in exceptional circumstances, not telling the truth is the lesser of two evils! A "tragic choice" is involved. The right answer in such a situation comes only through careful consideration of the issue, coupled with much prayer and wisdom.[28]

In seeking a solution to the problem of corruption, we need to recognize that the same principle of a "graded absolutism" is applicable here. Does our Christian responsibility to the wider public take precedence over the acceptance of a relatively low level of passive acceptance of corruption in the system? Does it allow me to work in the longer term to effect some genuine transformation in society, based on Christian values? Or have I to opt out of the marketplace altogether because it has become so inherently corrupt that the only legitimate form of Christian witness is the separational model? These are tough questions. But Christians should diligently consider them, not just as individuals, but together as members of a prayerful and pastorally supportive community.

This last point is often forgotten when we struggle with this issue. Trying to resolve such issues by oneself opens one up to all sorts of folly and pitfalls. As members of the community of God's kingdom, Christians must help each other to work through such issues together. Apart from the theological point that this is how Christians should live, there are at least three distinct advantages with this: collective wisdom in approaching the problems, honest discussions that protect us from slipping into easy compromises and foolish rationalizations, and communal and pastoral support for every individual who must take tough decisions.

As a good illustration of how the second and third guidelines apply in practice, one marketplace practitioner, Sherman Lam,[29] tells of the dilemma faced by a friend. In the context of the economic downturn in Southeast Asia caused by the burst of the dot-com bubble in the late 1990s, this person was leading a team that was bidding for a contract in Vietnam. But getting the contract involved paying a twenty percent "consultation fee" to another company overseas which had nothing to do with the project. When he informed his boss

---

28. See Adeney, *Strange Virtues*, 153–56, for another perspective.
29. Sherman Lam, "Case Study by Sherman Lam," in Hwa Yung, *Bribery and Corruption: Biblical Reflections and Case Studies for the Marketplace in Asia*, 2nd ed., ed. Soo-Inn Tan (Singapore: Graceworks, 2018), 74–77.

about this matter, his boss had no interest in his moral scruples and warned him instead that, without the contract, his whole team would be retrenched. Of course, his team members pleaded with him to give in to the bribery demand out of concern for their personal livelihoods. Moreover, in Asian cultures, the leader is the "big brother" who must take responsibility for the rest.

After careful consideration as a Christian and out of concern for his team members and their need to provide for their families, he signed the contract. He arranged for the "consultancy fee" to be paid into the overseas account and then further made sure that the account was closed after the transaction. His company got the contract, and the livelihoods of his whole team was saved. With everything settled, he then put in his resignation to his employer.

Did this person do the right thing as a Christian? This brings us to the fourth guideline.

Guideline 4: We Must Avoid Being Judgmental to Fellow Christians Who Take Different Approaches to Corruption

It may be that different Christians, after genuinely seeking God's mind, find themselves emphasizing different aspects of the incarnational model and end up taking different approaches to corruption. In such a situation, we must avoid being judgmental toward others. God often calls us to different callings. God's gifts to us are different and so is his calling. Some may find that the marketplace is altogether too distasteful and opt for a model of total separation. For example, the Anabaptists and their spiritual descendants today, the Mennonites, have always tended toward this position. It may be that God is calling forth some in the Asian church to do the same, setting up Christian counter-communities as a means of showing to the world something more of what the values of the Kingdom of God are like. Catholic monastic orders have always tended in this direction. And when we think of Mother Theresa's ministry, for example, we may well need to ask: Why are we so slow in developing Christian counter-cultural communities within Protestant churches today? And is our slowness an indication of our reluctance to follow our Master in radical obedience?

On the other hand, Christ calls others to be fully immersed in our fallen world, caught up constantly in all its contradictions. But even so, we may be called to different paths of Christian obedience. For example, I am aware that some Christians have been able to tell marvelous stories of how they have been able to avoid corruption in situations where bribery is unavoidable. This is certainly highly laudable and must be encouraged at every point. However, certain things must be borne in mind before we make this into an absolute standard by which we judge everyone else.

First, those in this category are usually Christians who are more matured in their faith and have grown deep in their prayer life. Many other church members are still struggling to arrive at that level of spiritual maturity and will need time to grow in faith and trust. We must be careful not to lay an impossible load upon their fragile consciences before they are ready. That would be pastorally irresponsible.

Second, such people are often in the upper echelons of the business world. They have friends in high places with whom they fraternize regularly at business or government functions, or in golf clubs. Through prayer and such avenues of influence, they find that they can get many things done without paying (anything?). But, again, we need to remember that most of the population does not have such privileges. This is particularly true of blue-collar workers, like taxi-drivers and those running small businesses. These people have a different power relationship to those in positions of authority. When they are victimized by having to pay to get their licenses renewed, for example, they cannot call on their friends in high places to settle the matter for them. And if they do not pay, their license renewals are held up for long stretches. How then do they feed their families?

Each Christian, with the support of his or her church, must decide what approach to the problem God is calling him or her to take. Whichever approach God calls us to, when it is conscientiously followed, that approach could be just as difficult and costly to enact as other approaches, but it may well end up being equally as powerful in its witness.

Guideline 5: We Must Never Lose Sight of Our Calling to Be Salt and Light

It is essential that we never lose sight of the transformation principle which is built on the Christian's calling to be "salt" and "light" in the world. I need to emphasize that the position advocated here is not one of unprincipled compromise. Rather, it is one firmly rooted in principled arguments. Further, it is also a position that takes seriously the facts on the ground and does not try to pretend that in some ways we can live in a sterilized world, untouched totally by its moral contradictions. It does not provide easy straightforward answers in many cases, but neither is it meant to be taken as a license for unbridled corruption in the world. In all these, the goal of moral and socio-political transformation must always be kept in sight.

CORRUPTION AND BRIBERY

But several questions must be asked: Is transformation possible? Can a situation of endemic corruption be turned round? What hope is there long term? A lesson from history is helpful. In their book, *Corruption in Developing Countries*, Ronald Wraith and Edgar Simpkins note that Britain at the beginning of the nineteenth century was as corrupt as many developing countries today. Yet, by around 1880, it came to attain "a standard of public integrity which is perhaps without precedent."[30] This came as a result of the emergence of what has been called "Victorian morality," which persisted till after the Second World War. The British historian, Harold Perkins, described the moral change in England around this period rather humorously (and cynically too): "Between 1780 and 1850 the English ceased to be one of the most aggressive, brutal, rowdy, outspoken, riotous, cruel, and bloodthirsty nations in the world and became one of the most inhibited, polite, orderly, tender-minded, prudish, and hypocritical."[31] What brought about these changes?

Wraith and Simpkins recognized that a range of factors contributed to the widespread eradication of corruption, including political, socioeconomic, educational, and other changes and advances. Nevertheless, they also drew attention to the underlying religious influences that led to the moral changes and deep-seated integrity in the personal and public life of many individuals. They argued that "It seems that whatever may have been the political and economic reasons for the decline of corruption, the puritanical thread in the fabric of Victorian England was important."[32] This puritanical thread of course goes back to the seventeenth century Puritans who had sought to revive English Christianity. But the more important and immediate influence in this thread was the eighteenth-century evangelical revival under John Wesley and his fellow Methodists. As Wraith and Simpkins sum up, "The Methodist movement and its aftermath coincided with the Industrial Revolution and was more largely responsible than any other influence for the integrity and thrift of a large section of the working class."[33]

They further argue that the influence of the Methodists and their fellow nonconformists[34] was augmented in the nineteenth century by groups within

---

30. Wraith and Simpkins, *Corruption in Developing Countries*, 9.
31. Harold Perkin, *The Origins of Modern English Society*, 2nd ed. (London & New York: Routledge, 2002), 280.
32. Wraith and Simpkins, *Corruption in Developing Countries*, 62.
33. Wraith and Simpkins, 181.
34. The term "nonconformist" in English history applies to non-Anglican Protestants including the Congregationists, Baptists, Quakers, and Methodists.

the Anglican Church which impacted much more the upper classes.[35] These were the evangelicals led by William Wilberforce, the High Churchmen, and the Christian Socialists under F. D. Maurice. About this time, the radical philosophers or Utilitarians, under Jeremy Bentham and J. S. Mill, also came onto the scene.[36]

Wraith and Simpkins sum up their discussion of the above influences by arguing that all these flowed as different tributaries into one powerful stream and, working together, eventually helped eradicate corruption from public life. Without these forces working in Britain in the nineteenth century, "it is questionable whether corruption would have been virtually destroyed by the century's end." They further suggest that corruption in many developing countries can be eradicated only if "influences as profound as these have worked themselves into the national consciousness."[37]

It is not possible in this short treatment to discuss in detail Wraith and Simpkins' thesis here. But for those of us who identify ourselves as evangelicals, it is important to recognize that both Wesley and Wilberforce played crucial roles in this story. Wesley and early Methodists with their strong "holiness" teachings helped shape the morality of the working class and the emerging middle class. Wilberforce and the Clapham Sect labored for a whole generation to abolish slavery and promote moral reform among the upper classes.[38] Both groups thereby contributed significantly toward the eradication of corruption in Britain. Christians in general – and evangelicals in particular – must ask ourselves what lessons we can learn from their stories.

Corruption will continue to be rife unless there is a fundamental change in the private morality of individuals and the public conscience of the nation. What can Christians do about this? First, we must labor for the spread of the gospel and revival in the church so that many will come to know true repentance and holiness in life, thus contributing to moral transformation in our societies. Second, we must do away completely with a dualistic theology which prevents us from applying the values of the kingdom of God to the burning ethical and socio-political issues of our day. Third, recognizing that there are many non-Christians who are similarly concerned with corruption

---

35. Wraith and Simpkins, *Corruption in Developing Countries*, 180–82.
36. Wraith and Simpkins, 182.
37. Wraith and Simpkins, 182.
38. For the work of Wilberforce and the Clapham Sect, see Ian Bradley, *The Call to Seriousness: The Evangelical Impact on the Victorians* (London: Jonathan Cape, 1976); and Stephen Tomkins, *The Clapham Sect: How Wilberforce's Circle Transformed Britain* (Oxford: Lion Hudson, 2010).

in our respective nations, we must find ways to collaborate with them to fight corruption in public life.

With respect to the last point one of the most effective things that Christians can do, especially those in politics, civil society movements, or any other sphere of public influence, is to lobby and campaign for the setting up of independent anti-corruption bodies in our respective countries. To achieve this goal, Christians will need to work in cooperation with peoples of other faiths, who are similarly concerned, to exert maximum public pressure. In Hong Kong, the Independent Commission Against Corruption (ICAC) was established in February 1974 because of agitation by the people because of rife corruption then.[39] Over the years it has helped Hong Kong fight public corruption significantly, making it one of the least corrupted societies in world rankings.

However, it should be noted that such anti-corruption bodies can only be effective if they are fully independent and free from government influence, as is the case of Hong Kong's ICAC. That, unfortunately, is not the case in most Asian countries. Moreover, given the current political changes in Hong Kong, it remains to be seen whether the ICAC's independence will be compromised in future.

One last thought. Does it mean that a whole nation must become Christian before corruption can be eliminated? Not at all! The former Berkeley sociologist, Robert Bellah, has suggested that we often underestimate the influence of a small committed minority in society. He suggests that "the quality of a culture may be changed when two percent of its people have a new vision."[40] Surely this is a challenge worth taking up!

QUESTIONS FOR DISCUSSION

1. Do you agree with the five guidelines given in this chapter? What are your reasons for agreeing or disagreeing?
2. In your national context, where do you see Christians in general, and businesspeople in particular, getting involved directly or indirectly in corrupt practices for their own personal gain? Give

---

39. Independent Commission Against Corruption, Hong Kong SAR, "About ICAC: Brief History" (27 Aug 2019), https://www.icac.org.hk/en/about/history/index.html (accessed Feb 4, 2021).
40. Robert Bellah, "The Sacred and the Political in American Life," *Psychology Today* 9 (8) (1976): 58–65.

specific examples. How should you and your church address that in a pastoral manner?
3. Within your cultural context, how would you as a Christian distinguish between a gift and a bribe? In what kinds of situations would giving a gift in appreciation be appropriate and morally right?
4. How would you go about planning a workshop for your church or a group of Christians in working life to help them deal with corruption in your national context?
5. In your particular situation, do you think it is possible to reform the system to reduce corruption? What can be done to bring moral transformation?

BIBLIOGRAPHY

Adeney, Bernard T. *Strange Virtues: Ethics in a Multicultural World.* Leicester: Apollos, 1995.

Alatas, Syed Hussein. *Corruption and the Destiny of Asia.* Singapore: Simon & Schuster, 1999.

Bellah, Robert. "The Sacred and the Political in American Life," *Psychology Today*, Vol. 9 (8) (1976): 58–65.

Bosch, David J. *Transforming Mission: Paradigm Shifts in Theology of Missions.* Maryknoll, NY: Orbis, 1991.

Bradley, Ian. *The Call to Seriousness: The Evangelical Impact on the Victorians.* London: Jonathan Cape, 1976.

Burgis, Tom. *Kleptopia: How Dirty Money is Conquering the World.* London: Harper Collins, 2020.

Chêne, Marie, "The Impact of Corruption on Growth and Inequality." Transparency International Anti-Corruption Helpdesk (15 Mar 2014), https://www.transparency.org/files/content/corruptionqas/Impact_of_corruption_on_growth_and_inequality_2014.pdf (accessed 21 Jul 2022).

Elmer, Duane. *Cross-Cultural Conflicts: Building Relationships for Effective Ministry.* Downers Grove: InterVarsity Press, 1995.

Geisler, Norman L. *Christian Ethics: Options and Issues.* Grand Rapids: Baker, 1989.

Gill, David W. *It's About Excellence: Building Ethically Healthy Organizations.* Eugene, OR: Wipf & Stock Publishers, 2011. See also Gill's website www.ethixbiz.com on the same subject.

Independent Commission Against Corruption, Hong Kong, SAR, "About ICAC: Brief History" (27 Aug 2019), https://www.icac.org.hk/en/about/history/index.html (accessed 4 Feb 2021).

International Monetary Fund, "Corruption: Costs and Mitigating Strategies," *International Monetary Fund, Staff Discussion Notes No 16/05* (May 11, 2016), https://www.imf.org/en/Publications/Staff-Discussion-Notes/Issues/2016/12/31/Corruption-Costs-and-Mitigating-Strategies-43888 (accessed 29 April 2021).

Lam, Sherman. "Case Study by Sherman Lam," in Hwa Yung. *Bribery and Corruption: Biblical Reflections and Case Studies for the Marketplace in* Asia, 2nd ed., ed. Soo-Inn Tan. Singapore: Graceworks, 2018, 73–80.

Lovelace, Richard F. *Dynamics of Spiritual Life: An Evangelical Theology of Renewal*. Downers Grove: InterVarsity Press, 1979.

Mirzayev, Elvin. "How Corruption Affects Emerging Economies," *Investopedia* (17 Dec 2021), https://www.investopedia.com/articles/investing/012215/how-corruption-affects-emerging-economies.asp (accessed 21 Jul 2022).

Noonan, John T. Jr., "Bribery." In *A New Dictionary of Christian Ethics*, ed. John Macquarrie and James Childress. Philadelphia, PA: Westminster Press, 1986, 65f.

Perkin, Harold. *The Origins of Modern English Society*, 2nd ed. London & New York: Routledge, 2002.

Schluter, Michael and David Lee, *The R Factor*. London: Hodder, 1993.

Stott, John. *Issues Facing Christians Today*. Basingstoke: Marshall, Morgan, and Scott, 1984.

Tan, Che-Bin. "Ethical Particularism as a Chinese Contextual Issue." In *The Word among Us: Contextualizing Theology for Mission Today*, ed. by Dean Gilliland. Dallas: Word, 1989, 262–81.

Tomkins, Stephen. *The Clapham Sect: How Wilberforce's Circle Transformed Britain*. Oxford: Lion Hudson, 2010.

Transparency International, "Library" (n.d.), https://www.transparency.org/en/library (accessed 21 Jul 2022).

Transparency International, "What is Corruption?" (n.d.), https://www.transparency.org/en/what-is-corruption (accessed 21 Jul 2022).

Transparency International, "Corruption Perceptions Index 2021" (2022), https://www.transparency.org/en/cpi/2021 (accessed 21 Jul 2022).

Webber, Robert E. *The Secular Saint: The Role of the Christian in the Secular World*. Grand Rapids: Zondervan, 1979.

Wraith, Ronald, and Edgar Simpkins. *Corruption in Developing Countries*. London: George Allen & Unwin, 1963; reissued, London & New York: Routledge, 2010.

Yu, Carver T. *Being and Relation: A Theological Critique of Western Dualism and Individualism*. Edinburgh: Scottish Academic Press, 1987.
Yung, Hwa. *Bribery and Corruption: Biblical Reflections and Case Studies for the Marketplace in Asia*, 2nd ed., ed. Soo-Inn Tan. Singapore: Graceworks, 2018.

CHAPTER 6
HUMAN DIGNITY

A Standard for Christian Life and Ministry

Kiem-Kiok Kwa

Ali is a migrant worker in your city. He does heavy manual labor, working ten to twelve hours each day. He gets paid about US$10 each day and is given two meals a day by his employer. He shares a small room in a large dormitory with seven other men where there are cooking and cleaning facilities. Every month, he tries to send about US$250 back to his family in Bangladesh.

Lanny is fifteen years old and the only child of your good friend from church. She has Down syndrome. Though Lanny can function quite independently, your friend is especially concerned about her now that she begins to experience hormonal and physical changes. Furthermore, while there is currently a school for Lanny to attend, that will end when she reaches sixteen years old, and your friend is worried about what Lanny can do after that.

Uncle Lim, a widower, is seventy-four years old, and lives with his son and his family. He recently tells you that the family is not treating him well – he claims that they are not feeding him – and he has to go out to find his own meals. The son maintains that in recent months his father has become forgetful and, as Uncle Lim has diabetes, it is not healthy for him to eat out.

These situations are common across many cities and families in Asia today and raise many questions. For example, who are the people on the margins in our societies, like Ali? Are they even noticed? There are many migrant workers in Asian cities, legal and illegal; many come from the rural areas into the cities for work. Others could be refugees, or overstayers in the country who try to eke out a living doing odd jobs. Who are the people at the geographic, economic, and social margins of Asian cities, and what structures are there for their care and welfare?

People with disabilities are often hidden or unseen. Some families may find it shameful to have a member who has a disability, and so will withdraw from the wider community. A family member with a disability also needs much emotional and physical resources for their care, and it takes all a family has to take care of them. Tragically, there are also disabled people who are abandoned by their families and left to fend for themselves.

Many Asian societies are aging; Japan, Korea, and Singapore are some of the fastest aging countries in the world. There are many faces of the elderly – they can be well or sick, they could be physically or financially independent or dependent, with or without chronic diseases, mentally capable or incapacitated. They can be part of loving families or estranged from them or without close families. In the Asian context, the cultural norms and expectations are for families to care for the elderly in their midst, hence public social networks for such services may not be mature. However, not all families can care for an elderly parent, or more than one depending on their situation, and they will need community resources to help them.

FRAMING THE ISSUES

While people at the margins or with disabilities such as those described above may arouse our Christian compassion, what warrants their care is that they are people, human beings. In Christian anthropology, each person is made in the image of God, and so is to be treated as with dignity. While at first glance such care may seem self-explanatory, there are aspects of Asian culture, such as shame, which may negate dignified care for them. Furthermore, while Christian compassion may inspire care, caring so as to give others dignity, and not merely by patronizing them, should be a distinguishing mark of Christians. Conversely, when the church sees every person as made in God's image, this unique perspective could be the motivation for service and ministry to all people, producing a holistic ethic toward those on the margins and those with disabilities. That is, beyond caring for their immediate needs, does a Christian anthropology demand more?

These are issues surrounding the understanding of human dignity. For Christians, it is easy to give a glib answer that every person, including the poor, the disabled, and the elderly with dementia, is made in the image of God and so should be treated with respect. In this chapter, we will explore the concept of image of God and its connection to human dignity from Scripture and tradition.

In this chapter, we will first consider what "human dignity" means. Since human dignity is derived from people being made in the image of God, we explore the concept of "image of God" in Scripture and Christian tradition. We shall then consider what this means in the light of prevailing cultural values in the Asian context, and thus seek to provide practical guidance for relationships with people like Ali, Lanny, and Uncle Lim.

DEFINITIONS

The term "human dignity" is dense, and notoriously difficult to define, even if we have a sense of what it means. While word dictionaries do not have definitions for the term, "human dignity," some, like the Merriam-Webster dictionary, define dignity as the quality or state of being worthy, honored, or esteemed.[1]

Even though there is no concrete definition, it does not mean that the term should not be used, for the way the term is used can elucidate its meaning. For example, the Universal Declaration of Human Rights recognizes the inherent dignity of all humans and proclaims it as the basis for freedom and justice.[2] Indeed, "the post-1945 moral-political landscape, in the West and in the world generally, has been powerfully shaped by appeals to human dignity."[3] In medical care, doctors and nurses are enjoined to treat patients with dignity, and that same standard is expected in other areas in the treatment of other vulnerable groups, such as prisoners and refugees. We can understand the term when we consider situations when a person is not treated with dignity: for example, when a patient is roughly manhandled by nurses, when prisoners are tortured, or when a person with a disability is mocked. We recoil when we see these situations because the other person is not treated with dignity, as a human being. Our reaction in these cases is also because people are so treated because of their vulnerability, whether as poor and marginalized, or sick and infirm, or not looking like other people.

---

1. "Dignity" in https://www.merriam-webster.com/dictionary/dignity.
2. "Universal Declaration of Human Rights" in https://www.un.org/en/universal-declaration-human-rights/.
3. Thomas Albert Howard, "Introduction" in Thomas Albert Howard, ed., *Imago Dei: Human Dignity in Ecumenical Perspective* (Washington, DC: Catholic University of America Press, 2013), 2.

Hence unpacking the concept of human dignity is partly to discern what it means to be human, as it is related to or synonymous with terms such as human worth or human identity. Cicero defined dignity as the honorable authority of a person which merits attention and honor and is worthy of respect.[4] But this seems like going through a thesaurus for synonyms. As American political theorist George Kateb admits, human dignity is a difficult term to define from a non-religious perspective.[5]

In trying to unpack the term as Christians in the evangelical tradition, we shall draw from Scripture and the Christian tradition. In this regard, medical ethicist and Franciscan Daniel Sulmasy's description of human dignity is helpful because it can encompass both theological and cultural dimensions of the term; and we shall then modify it to encompass the fullness of meaning.[6]

Sulmasy suggests that there are three aspects of human dignity, namely the *attributed*, *intrinsic*, and *inflorescent*. Attributed dignity is the honor which other people or society confer upon a person: Asian societies would attribute dignity on those they admire or who have certain skills, for example professionals like accountants, or doctors; or people who have special powers such as priests. Intrinsic dignity is that which a person has because of his or her own humanity; this is not based on value to others or human excellence. This also follows a more Kantian way of looking at dignity.[7] For Christians, this understanding comes closest to the idea that all people are made in the image of God, have worth in themselves regardless of what they are, and should therefore be treated with respect and honor. We would then say that *all* persons have intrinsic dignity simply because they are human, no matter that they look different from us.

Inflorescent dignity, in Sulmasy's description, has a combination of both these meanings, as it refers to "individuals who are flourishing as human beings, living lives that are consistent with and expressive of the intrinsic dignity of the human."[8] Inflorescent dignity is what others may ascribe to someone who faces a particularly trying situation "with dignity." This dignity is not intrinsic to the person and is partly attributed by others depending on some objective

---

4. In Daniel P. Sulmasy, "Dignity and Bioethics: History, Theory and Selected Applications" in President's Council on Bioethics, *Human Dignity and Bioethics: Essays Commissioned by the President's Council on Bioethics*, March 2008, 1–13, https://bioethicsarchive.georgetown.edu/pcbe/reports/human_dignity/chapter18.html.
5. George Kateb, *Human Dignity* (Cambridge, MA; London, England: Belknap Press, 2011).
6. Sulmasy, 1.
7. Sulmasy, 2.
8. Sulmasy.

conception of human excellence. As we shall suggest, for Christians, that objective understanding of personhood would come from the belief that every person is made in the image of God. By granting them inflorescent dignity, they can be given worth which the culture does not. For Sulmasy, "while all three senses have moral relevance, the intrinsic sense of dignity is the most fundamental from a moral perspective."[9]

These several ways of perceiving human dignity will give us a sufficient framework as we discuss various ethical issues, but we shall refrain from having too tight a definition, so as not to sink into reductionism. After all, it has also been recognized that the way we understand human nature will differ depending on the purpose of that discussion.[10] Since human dignity is so broad, a full understanding should make a difference in a wide variety of fields, including but not limited to, caring for the sick and disabled, serving the marginalized, and providing education to all.

Outside the church, the concept of human dignity can be a public language, a way of engaging with others, for example, with Muslims in interfaith dialogue, because it is a term or concept which can be quite easily and meaningfully used. Few people outside the church would agree on Christian theological foundations, but many would agree that each person has a quality or humanity which translates to some form of dignity.

At the same time, Christians should seek to reflect upon the ways in which their conception of human dignity may be distinctive from, or even at odds with, culturally normative understandings of the term. We should be vigilant about cultural or social factors which undermine dignity in others. Similarly, we should consider how the church can be counter-cultural when the culture does not accord full dignity to others. When Christians fully grasp and apply the concept of human dignity in their theology and practice, what will the impact be on the life and ministry of the church?

---

9. Sulmasy.
10. See Nancey Murphy's "Introduction" in Nancey Murphy and Christopher Knight, *Human Identity at the Intersection of Science, Technology and Religion* (Abingdon, OX; New York, NY: Routledge, 2010).

BIBLICAL PERSPECTIVES: IMAGE OF GOD AND DIGNITY IN SCRIPTURE

For Christians, the basis of human dignity rests on the belief that human beings are made in the image of God, or *imago Dei*.[11] The Bible implies that because human beings are made in the image of God, they are unlike the animals and other created beings. In the beginning, God created all things, the cosmos, the flora and fauna of the world, and then God said, "Let us make humankind in our image, after our likeness, so that they may rule over the fish in the sea . . ." (Gen 1:26 NET).[12] The psalmist looks at humanity in the midst of all of creation and responds in worship to the Lord, "You have made them a little lower than the angels and crowned them with glory and honor" (Ps 8:5). Amid all of creation, human beings have been given special honor, and this leads the psalmist to worship God.

This means that every person, including the sick, the infirm, those of different socioeconomic classes, and the illegal immigrant, is worthy of respect because they are made in the image of the Creator God. The *imago Dei* rests so profoundly in every person that infirmities, including losing mental capacity for one with dementia, do not alter this identity. Since it is the *imago Dei* which grants a person inherent dignity, it is worth exploring this more closely.

There is a physical dimension to being in that image. However, beyond this, there is much scholarly discussion about what constitutes that image. It "has something to do with our humanness, and it is the whole complexity of being human, the diversities and distinctiveness of what it is to be a human being in this world."[13] Biblical scholars have posited at least two broad ways of understanding this image of God: the substantive, and the relational, though these are not uncontested.[14] The substantive refers to some feature of human nature – rationality, for example – which sets humankind apart from the rest of creation. In a relational understanding, as human beings are in God's image, they can live in right relationship with God.[15] The image or likeness is an ele-

---

11. Gilbert C. Meilaender, "Afterword" in Thomas Albert Howard, ed., *Imago Dei: Human Dignity in Ecumenical Perspective* (Washington, DC: Catholic University of America Press, 2013), 114.
12. Biblical references are from the New International Version (2011) unless otherwise stated. Scholars debate whether the terms "image" and "likeness" are the same or different, but we shall not discuss that here and will use the term "image." See for example, Gordon Wenham, *Genesis 1–15*, WBC (Dallas, TX: Word, 1991), 29–33.
13. David Atkinson, *The Message of Genesis 1–11* (England: Inter-Varsity Press, 1990), 36.
14. Meilaender, 115.
15. Wenham, 38.

ment of human personality and gives rise to moral or relational responsibility because humanity can relate with God in a special way, different from the animals.[16] In whichever way one defines that image, whether in a form of embodiment and creatureliness, mental and spiritual faculties including autonomy and freewill, or as God's representative on earth, "his life is sacred: every assault on man is an affront to the creator."[17]

The fall of humans did not destroy the image, though the image certainly has been distorted.[18] Because even so, God still considered humanity worth redeeming; after God pronounced judgment on Adam and Eve for disobedience, he took the initiative to make garments of skin for them and clothed them to hide their nakedness (Gen 3:21). Ultimately, God himself became man in Jesus Christ, taking upon himself the sin of humanity so as to restore the relationship between God and people "for God was pleased to have all his fullness dwell in him [Jesus Christ], and through him to reconcile to himself all things, whether things on earth or things in heaven, by making peace through his blood, shed on the cross" (Col 1:19–20). As Haack declares, "dignity is to be discovered, not in social convention, but in God's acts toward humankind, in particular the monumental act of salvation through the incarnation of his Son."[19]

It is important to bear in mind that those to whom society may attribute little dignity, such as the poor, are also human beings made in the image of God and have an intrinsic dignity. Indeed, the poor and marginalized are especially dear to God, because generally they do not have the means to care for themselves. Often depicted in the Old Testament by the phrase "widows and fatherless,"[20] God demands that the poor be given justice, and judged Israel and Judah severely for failing to do so.[21] Thus, by showing his justice to the marginalized, God gives them a dignity in a context where the society in which they lived did not. God, by caring for them and demanding that society does likewise, grants them an inflorescent dignity.

In the context of the Old Testament, God showed his care by putting in place laws and structures which provide such care. God's justice allows for each person in the community to live with dignity. One example is the gleaning laws

---

16. C. F. H. Henry "Image of God" in Walter Elwell, ed., *Evangelical Dictionary of Theology* (Grand Rapids: Baker, 2001), 591–94.
17. Wenham, 32. See also Susan Haack, "Christian Explorations in the Concept of Human Dignity," *Dignitas 19*, no. 3 (2012): 4–7, 10–13.
18. Henry, 591.
19. Haack, 7.
20. See for example, Psalm 68:5; Isaiah 9:17; Jeremiah 49:11; Malachi 3:5.
21. See for example Isaiah 1:16–25; Amos 2:6–7; 4:1–13.

in Leviticus 19:9–10. When the poor are allowed to glean, harvesting the grain for themselves, they are given the dignity of labor and not simply provided with a handout. Thus, Ruth, who was a widow, poor, and a Moabitess, was dignified by laws that were in place that allowed her to glean, thereby gathering sufficient grain to feed her mother-in-law Naomi and herself. Subsequently, through Boaz playing the role of the kinsman redeemer, Ruth could marry and be part of the genealogy of King David, Israel's greatest king. Ruth benefited from just social structures that gave her dignity.

Where the laws did not provide, as in the story of Zelophehad's daughters (Num 27:1–11; 36:1–13) the Lord, through Moses, was willing to make an exception to the law to ensure that the clan was not wiped out. This underscores the need for society and its laws to be just, for following these laws would grant inflorescent dignity to those on the margins.

Jesus, by showing particular concern and attention to the outcasts whom the rest of society ignored, also dignified them. He recognized their inherent dignity as human beings and responded to their cries for help or healing. For example, the Canaanite woman in Matthew 15:21–28 persistently begged Jesus for mercy and even his disciples urged him to send her away. But Jesus dignified her by speaking with her, allowing her to take "the crumbs that fall from their master's table," and healing her daughter. Likewise, when Jesus allowed the sinful woman to anoint him (John 12:1–8) he dignified her act of pouring expensive perfume at his feet, swiftly scolding Judas, who sought to monetize the perfume. Again, where the society attributed little dignity to the woman, Jesus saw her intrinsic worth and granted her an inflorescent dignity. These examples serve as models for Christians today as to how we can treat those we serve with grace and dignity.

The apostles' teaching about church life and relationships also add to the concept of human dignity. Their anthropology permeates the epistles and makes it clear that the church was counter-cultural and lived by an ethic different from the rest of Roman society. This was radical. For example, in 1 Corinthians 11, Paul corrects the abuse of the Lord's supper. At that time in Corinth, the practice was that those who came first ate their fill, so that there was little left for those who came later. It was likely that those who came later were manual workers who finished work later or had a longer way to travel to the home where the believers met, for they were lower on the socioeconomic ladder in this diverse body of believers. More than just not having enough to eat, their exclusion led to Paul's admonishment of the church: "Do you despise the church of God by humiliating those who have nothing?" he asks (1 Cor

Human Dignity

11:22). The word humiliate here is a strong word, denoting far more than dishonor or disrespect; they were degrading and humiliating the have-nots.[22] As Fee comments, "Paul's present concern is *not* with penury or gluttony but with their being truly together at the common table, with no class distinctions being allowed on the basis of the kind and amount of food eaten. . . . his primary concern here . . . is the meaning of the Table itself for their unity in Christ."[23]

When Paul urges both masters and slaves to treat each other as brothers, he was thereby elevating the status of slaves who were believers, granting them an inflorescent dignity.

> This injunction would have sounded extremely strange in the ears of those who first heard it as slaves were still popularly regarded as the property of their masters, who had absolute power over them. And of course, where there are thought to be no rights, there can be no justice. Justice for slaves was a revolutionary new concept. Essentially it was the gospel which insisted that slaves had rights.[24]

As he implored Philemon to receive back the runaway slave Onesimus "as a brother" (Phlm 6) Paul raised the status and dignity of the criminal runaway slave. This was in marked contrast to Roman society in general, where dignity was not distributed equally, and slaves had no attributed dignity.[25] The commands of Paul were thus a radical counter-cultural step for the New Testament church. Where society *does not* attribute to a group of people any dignity, the church *does*, by recognizing a person's inherent dignity. Christians today should follow in the same vein. Krause, in an illuminating few sentences, sums it up well:

> Throughout history God's people have been sustained by the knowledge that they are created in the image of God. In spite of the world's cruelty and pain, they know beauty and great joy. Although believers live in the flesh, they also live in the spirit in the presence and wisdom of God . . . As we see in the baptismal practice of Paul and his churches, these traditions encourage us to live in God's new creation in Jesus Christ – neither Jew nor

---

22. Fee, 544.
23. Fee, 544, emphasis in original.
24. John Stott, *God's New Society* (England: Inter-Varsity Press, 1979), 258.
25. Paulina Parhiala and Gorden Simango, "*Diakonia* and Human Dignity" in *The Ecumenical Review* 66, no.3, Oct 2014, 330–340, 331. DOI:10.1111/erev.12115.

Greek, slave or free, male or female – in the midst of a world where hierarchical and oppressive divisions are all too real.[26]

CULTURAL VALUES

We have seen how the nascent Christian faith, partly because of their anthropology which views all persons as made in the image of God and therefore with equal dignity, quietly challenged the prevailing Roman culture by their values and dignifying classes of people like slaves and women. Christians must thus be conscious of the ways our cultures fail to accord proper dignity to many persons, and so we are called to act counterculturally. As ethicist Christine Pohl notes, "many people who are not valued by the larger community are essentially invisible to it. When people are socially invisible, their needs and concerns are not acknowledged and no one even notices the injustices they suffer."[27] Therefore, to perceive who are those in the community we do not see, it is necessary to unpack our culture and its values. Bearing in mind that while culture is how things *are*, as with all products of human activity, all aspects of culture are affected by the fall. Many aspects of culture are not what they should be and fall short of the glory of God. Thus, Christians must be conscious of the ways their cultures fail to accord proper dignity to many persons and consider how they can act counterculturally in the light of their faith.

Cultures are integrated systems and complex wholes; the various parts are related to and influence other parts.[28] A value in one part of a culture often has repercussions in other parts of the culture. For example, the culture's view of gender, the roles for male and female in family and society, would have an economic impact, setting forth the types of jobs that men and women are expected to do. When a culture values work outside the home, those who work inside the home, often women, are given little worth; while men and those in the marketplace are valued and will be considered superior.

Cultures attribute dignity to people because of their achievements, positions, or even their physical looks. For example, in many Asian societies, fair skin and complexion is the high standard of beauty. For the Chinese,

---

26. Deborah Krause, "Keeping it Real, The Image of God in the New Testament," in *Interpretation*, Oct 2005, 358–68, 367.
27. Christine Pohl, *Making Room: Recovering Hospitality as a Christian Tradition* (Grand Rapids; Cambridge, UK: Eerdmans, 1999), 62.
28. Refer to Paul G. Hiebert, *Cultural Anthropology* (Grand Rapids: Baker, Second Edition, 1983) for a fuller understanding of culture generally. The focus here will be limited to those aspects of culture which will have an impact on human dignity.

fair skin is also connected with one's work – to have dark skin means one has become sunburnt from doing manual work out in the hot sun, whereas to be fair signified that one could sit indoors and not have to do such work. Thus, one cultural value of fairness of skin also judges the work that a person does.

Asian cultures are generally considered "face cultures" with a stable hierarchy.[29] Self-worth, which we shall equate to one's dignity for purposes of our discussion here, is based on other's assessments of whether the individual is fulfilling stable social role obligations; that is, one's self-worth arises from attributed dignity. That dignity is attributed through the social hierarchy in which "certain people have more face than do others, though everyone can have some face as long as they are fulfilling the expectations of their position. Worth is socially conferred in a face society."[30] These cultures would attribute dignity to those who perform their duty and place in society. In the Chinese hierarchical system, this would be first from the emperor, then to the nobleman, the merchant classes, and so on down to the farmers and slaves. Conversely, society can also "deface" a person which is to "deny them the respect and regard due to them by virtue of their full humanity."[31] Going against one's place in the system would be to act in an unworthy or undignified manner and would also lead to a loss of face and dignity.

Leaders are accorded high dignity; conversely, those from a lowly position have little honor and are given little dignity. The deeply entrenched Indian caste system, in which there are higher castes on the one hand and lower castes on the other, results in a culture where some people are perceived as having little worth and dignity simply because of their birth. They have little attributed dignity. Not only do these values affect a person's relationships and expectations, but they also affect how a person behaves in society and are closely related with a culture's views of honor and shame.

East Asian cultures influenced by Confucianism tend to accord dignity to leaders and those in prominent position. Coupled with the Confucian

---

29. See Young-Hoon Kim and Dov Coven, "The Jury and Abjury of My Peers: The Self in Face and Dignity Cultures" in *Journal of Personality and Social Psychology*, 2010, vol. 98, no. 6, 904–916; and Soroush Aslani, et al "Dignity, face and honour cultures" in *Journal of Organizational Behaviour*, 1178–1201 (2016), DOI:10.1002/job. While the contrast is drawn between "face" and "dignity" cultures, those terms would be confusing in this chapter, and we shall not refer to "dignity" cultures here.
30. Kim and Cohen, 904.
31. Beverley Eileen Mitchel, "The Struggle for Human Dignity in a Consumer-Oriented Culture" in *Anglican Theological Review*,98.1, 111–23 at 114 drawing from the work of Emanuel Levinas.

respect for education, these cultures also grant high dignity to people who are educated; and parents' desire for their children is to have good office and professional jobs in the city. This exacerbates the low views held of manual work, occupations such as farming, and living in rural areas. In Asian societies, those who do manual work, domestic helpers, and cleaners tend to be looked down upon. Often, they are not even seen or acknowledged, and therefore afforded little worth or dignity. While Asian cultures generally value elders, this is being eroded in fast-paced and globalized urban cities like Bangalore, Bangkok, or Beijing, where economic productivity and the young and technologically savvy are prized. Family units have become smaller, and the elderly are neglected and unseen. And yet, since people live longer, there are more old people present, though they may be unseen or hidden away.

Since harmony is prized in honor cultures, people are not encouraged to rock the boat or to act outside the prescribed notions and categories of behavior. "The nail that sticks out will be knocked down," a Japanese proverb which has echoes in other cultures, exemplifies this value. The church would need to be boldly counter-cultural in this aspect, granting dignity to those whom the culture does not.

HUMAN DIGNITY IN PRACTICE

Since people bear the *imago Dei*, every person should be treated with dignity. As Christine Pohl rightly notes, "[b]earing God's image establishes for every person a fundamental dignity which cannot be undermined either by wrongdoing or neediness."[32] She draws from Calvin, for whom the basis of recognition was the shared image of God and shared experience of suffering and vulnerability, and John Wesley who drew his theological understanding from the truth that every person, created by God for eternity and redeemed by Christ, was due fundamental respect regardless of his or her condition or position in the world. The ancient practice of hospitality, then, can be where human dignity is seen and lived out, for as Pohl observes, "respect cannot be sustained at the level of abstract claim or commitments. To have any meaning, they must be lived out in concrete everyday relations – in the family, church, community, and political sphere."[33] Asian Christians can rediscover the ancient practice of hospitality as they live out their belief in universal human dignity.

---

32. Pohl, *Making Room*, 63–72.
33. Pohl, *Making Room*, 63.

But as we have seen, aspects of Asian cultures may make it difficult for every person to receive and experience that dignity. Thus, when the church lives out this foundational doctrine, she will be counter-cultural. For Asian Christians, who are generally in the minority and not in positions of power, this can be a powerful testament to the Creator God who redeems and sanctifies people. The biblical story shows how this was done. If this is how Asian Christians can live out this profound truth, then they should be willing to endure the shame that such action brings.

Impact in the Wider Society

Christians can provide an environment where people are valued, granting them inflorescent dignity, and this could have a social impact. For example, in the nineteenth century in Malaysia and Singapore, missionaries set up schools for girls, at a time when this was generally considered a waste of effort. Many of these schools continue today and are well regarded by the community; and today, few people would question the necessity to educate girls. Healthserve in Singapore, an NGO started by Christians in 2006, has been providing medical care and advocacy for migrant workers and seeks to build a society "where every migrant worker lives a life of dignity."[34] Their consistent work has been recognized, and the government has invited them to be part of a taskforce to improve and address the mental health issues of among this group of generally overlooked residents.[35]

Indeed, issues of mental health are often neglected as it is generally a taboo subject, and society can be unsympathetic to those with depression, schizophrenia, and other similar disorders. The Mental Health Association of Hong Kong provides services for a wide range of children and adults who are mentally handicapped, such as education, training, rehabilitation, as well as residential services.[36] Here is an example of Christian ministry which recognizes the inherent dignity of those whom society shuns. These examples challenge Christians to see the unseen in their communities and provide holistic care because Christian anthropology recognizes the wholeness and complexities of human being.

---

34. https://www.healthserve.org.sg/about/.
35. See https://www.facebook.com/healthservesg.
36. http://www.mhahk.org.hk/chi/index.htm.

Caring for the Sick, the Disabled and Those with Dementia

Intrinsic dignity should be the basis of all medical care: the sick, infirm, and the dying always should be treated with dignity by both medical personnel and caregivers. Such care can be seen in hospitals set up by Christian missionaries in the early twentieth century which are scattered throughout Asia, such as the Yodogawa Christian Hospital in Osaka, Japan,[37] and the Kwangju Christian Hospital in Gwangju, South Korea.[38] These hospitals are not only places where patients are cured of their illness, but are also places where compassion, care, and concern are demonstrated, since sick people and their families are often vulnerable and afraid. Christians are also often at the forefront of hospice care where they help the terminally ill to die well. The Assisi Hospice in Singapore is one such example; there, volunteers ensure that the dying person does not die alone, even if they have no family or friends accompanying them.[39] Attending health care professionals, family members, and care givers, by recognizing these dignities in the other, especially the patient, "will dispose us to actions by which we show our respect for them."[40]

While not all of us are health care professionals, many of us will have to, at one time or another, care for family members or loved ones with illness. Often, providing that care will be long term, such as caring for a child with special needs, or aging parents. Jean Vanier and the L'Arche homes that he founded, popularized by Henri Nouwen in his later writings such as *Adam*, are inspirational as they show how to care for adults with disabilities with great dignity.[41] In Taiwan, the Taichung Rong Chung Chapel organizes yearly camps for children with special needs which not only provides a wide range of activities including drama and arts for them, but also trains volunteers to participate and care for these children. Their holistic approach to integrating the special needs children as well as to provide respite and resources for their families is an example of holistic ministry founded on the dignity of special needs children.[42]

---

37. http://www.ych.or.jp/en/.
38. http://www.kch.or.kr/eng/about.html.
39. https://www.assisihospice.org.sg/news/no-one-dies-alone/.
40. David Albert Jones, "Human Dignity in Healthcare: A Virtue Ethics Approach" in *The New Bioethics*, vol. 21, no. 1, 2015, 87–97, at 90.
41. After his death in 2019, it emerged that Vanier was involved in abusive relationships of women without disabilities (https://www.larcheusa.org/news_article/findings-of-larche-internationals-inquiry-into-jean-vanier/). While this raises questions about the man, it should not negate the work that he has done.
42. https://www.facebook.com/1474317262866130/posts/1687931851504669/.

Some Asian societies are aging, and while the healthy elderly are relatively easily cared for, those who are infirm and bedridden, who need help to be fed, bathed, and toileted, require more care and attention. Elderly parents with dementia are a particular challenge in this regard as the disease may have robbed them of those qualities which makes them relatable, such as their ability to recognize family members or to respond meaningfully. Disability and dementia are a challenge because, as theologian Amos Yong points out:

> Disability is not only an individualized, biological/medical experience but also a social phenomenon of oppression, marginalization, and exclusion. According to this definition, Jesus entered into the experience of disability fully in his suffering, persecution, and execution at the hands of others. Thus, he is able to identify with people who have disabilities as one who has shared in their ostracism "in every respect."[43]

Since disability also has socio-cultural dimensions, the broader community needs to come together to care for them. As Mitchel notes, "human dignity can be realised and protected only in community."[44] This could be an area for the church to reflect the rich relationships which can build up other people.

Yong also suggests that it is an epistemology of the cross and a theology of weakness which exults in the redemption of the blemished, defective, and impaired body, since it is precisely in the salvation, rather than the erasure or elimination, of such bodies that the wisdom, power, and glory of God are most clearly revealed.[45] This can be, ironically, a powerful message for Asian Christians where a message of weakness and suffering would not only be more real, but would be a better contextualization of the gospel.[46]

Extending long term care to family members with special needs can take a toll on the caregivers. This is where the larger community, the family of Christ, can provide support and encouragement and so live out gospel imperatives.

---

43. Amos Yong, *The Bible, Disability and the Church* (Grand Rapids; Cambridge, UK: Eerdmans, 2011), 126.
44. Mitchell, 115.
45. Yong, 130.
46. On contextualisation which reaches deeply into worldviews, see for example Hwa Yung, *Mangoes or Bananas, the Quest for an Authentic Asian Theology* (England: Regnum Books, 1997).

Development Work

An issue with Christian development work at the level of individualized person-centered support (where most Christian caring activity is focused) is that the challenges associated with such work can often create unintended impacts – slipping easily into being provider-centered and patronizing, and thus depriving the "other" of their dignity. While such a stance may "get the job done," it can hurt people in both the immediate and longer terms. This is increasingly being recognized and addressed. Corbett and Fikkert, for instance, have outlined some ways that Christians could be actively involved in development work, but without hurting the other. One example is by encouraging work instead of merely giving handouts.[47] This strategy of focusing on both the immediate and longer term circumstances of people is exemplified by organizations like Malaysian Care, which provides a wide range of care for the poor through education, empowerment, and advocacy, by aiming at long term sustainability, seeking to partner with the poor, and not merely running programs for them.[48]

Children are vulnerable and often bear the brunt of poverty and weakened social structures like education and health care. Malnourished, poorly educated children grow up with poor prospects for getting out of the poverty cycle. World Vision International is well known for their child sponsorship program in which donors around the world are invited to choose to sponsor a child from an underprivileged situation for about US$40 a month. By all accounts, this program has helped many children and communities. However, in 2019, World Vision changed a foundational aspect of this program: instead of the donors applying and choosing the child they wished to sponsor, each child now chooses whom he or she would like to be their sponsor.[49] The organization changed the older model of a patronizing way of sponsorship and, in doing so, gives each child a little dignity from choice.

These examples show that Christians have put into action Jesus's call to serve "the least of these" (Matt 25:40) with whom he personally identifies himself. These actions and ministries go against the grain of maintaining status, position, and privilege in our cultures, but seek to dignify every person because it is in them that we see Jesus.

---

47. Steve Corbett and Brian Fikkert, *When Helping Hurts: How to Alleviate Poverty without hurting the Poor . . . and Yourself* (Chicago, IL: Moody Publishers, 2012), 208–10.
48. https://www.malaysiancare.org/about.
49. https://www.worldvision.org/chosen.

Human Dignity and Technology

On deeper philosophical and wider societal levels, the impending artificial intelligence (AI) and robotics revolutions are raising many questions about what it means to be human and what characterizes human relationships; moreover, the use of these sophisticated technologies seems to threaten personal dignity. The issues here are wide and complex. For example, there are press reports of robots providing "care" to elderly with dementia in Japan, but to what extent can a machine replace human touch and care and show empathy?[50] Then there is surveillance technology which, while maintaining some level of security, is also deeply intrusive to human rights and freedoms. On the one hand, it can be said that robots can promote human dignity when they can perform mundane or even dangerous jobs which humans used to do, but on the other hand robots can also present a threat to human dignity when efficiency is linked to robotization, automation, and digitalization, and people lose jobs and are unable to find other means of livelihood.[51]

Governments are taking the initiative to manage the growth of AI, partly because it is technology, being developed mainly by independent companies, that has the potential to make state- and society-level impact. Thus, in April 2018, the European Union signed its *Declaration of Cooperation on Artificial Intelligence* which includes the formation of a High Level Expert Group on AI who are tasked with drafting AI ethics guidelines.[52] The church must also be aware and monitor these developments because, while AI may seem to provide solutions to some global challenges such as food scarcity and climate change, it may also exacerbate issues like personal data protection, and increase the digital divide between urban and rural communities and the older and younger generations, among other issues. All these issues have an impact on people and their dignity.

---

50. See, for example, https://www.bbc.com/worklife/article/20200205-what-the-world-can-learn-from-japans-robots.
51. Jason Thacker, "Why artificial intelligence can be a threat to human dignity," June 11, 2018 in https://erlc.com/resource-library/articles/why-articial-intelligence-can-be-a-threat-to-human-dignity/.
52. Berk Kocaman, "The rise of AI: Human Dignity in the age of Data," a news analysis from 4 February 2019, https://baslangicnoktasi.org/en/the-rise-of-ai-human-dignity-in-the-age-of-data/. See also, for example, Mathias Risse, "Human Rights and Artificial Intelligence" from the Carr Center of Harvard University, https://carrcenter.hks.harvard.edu/files/cchr/files/humanrightsai_designed.pdf.

PRACTICING HOSPITALITY

Having considered the multifarious challenges raised by the issues of human dignity, we suggest that the practice of hospitality can be one way of responding to some of these concerns. Jesus's acts of identification, recognition, and welcome of all humans, especially the needy, the marginalized, and the broken, forms the basis of the practice of Christian hospitality. While hospitality includes sharing meals together, it also encompasses a posture of "making room" for others.[53] Eating together is a valued Asian cultural practice and, when it is layered with the deep Christian tradition, this can be a rich way of recognizing human dignity in others.

Hospitality provides a context of recognizing the worth of a person who seems to have little when assessed by worldly standards and is a practice that integrates both respect and care.[54] As Pohl notes:

> When a person who is not valued by society is received by a socially respected person or group as a human being with dignity and worth, small transformations occur. The person's self-assessment, so often tied to societal assessment, is enhanced. Because such actions are countercultural they are a witness to the larger community, which is then challenged to reassess its standards and methods of valuing.[55]

These transformations are significant and can counter the accepted cultural practice of eating with friends, but not strangers, with a desire to impress. For example, the multi-generational family who eats together with their domestic helper is making a powerful statement about their value of all members of the household – and grants inflorescent dignity to their guests.

Shared meals often have hosts and guests, but as the disciples on the road to Emmaus discovered, the guest can also become the host and share precious gifts (Luke 24:28–32). As Pohl highlights, it included a posture of respect for the other as well as being proactive in reaching out to others, which is a deep recognition that guests bring gifts which can transform hosts.[56] She gives the example of the L'Arche communities where people with disabilities are at the centre of the community and are hosts to the many visitors, even though they

---

53. The title of a book on Christian hospitality by Christine Pohl. *Making Room: Recovering Hospitality as a Christian Tradition* (Grand Rapids: Eerdmans, 1999).
54. Pohl, 62, 69.
55. Pohl, 62.
56. Pohl, 69–75.

need to be cared for; and other places where guests and hosts share tasks of cooking and washing and in this way equalize some relationships.[57] Inherent human dignity is recognized in all persons.

Christians are a minority in most Asian societies and all these acts, though seemingly small and insignificant, can be counter-cultural and a witness to the gospel. Hospitality can also be the framework by which Christians reach out to people of other faiths, such as that developed by Amos Yong.[58] Echoing Pohl's concept of making room, he suggests that a "stranger-centered" theology of hospitality opens space where people of other faiths can enter and be transformed into friends, where hosts do not dictate how guests should change but rather provide a safe forum for changes to occur.[59] In these shared conversations about faith, much as Jesus engaged with others over meals (for example, Matt 9:10–13; Luke 19:1–10; 24:13–35), Christians can practice graceful evangelism.[60]

CONCLUSION

We have seen that a full understanding of the concept of human dignity in Christian anthropology can be a firm guide for Christians in life and ministry and this can have an impact on Christian witness in Asian society today. When all people are *seen*, and not part of the scenery and ignored, when they are valued for who they *are* and not what they can produce, the whole community is strengthened. By recognizing that every person is made in the image of God and therefore has intrinsic dignity, the church can give them inflorescent dignity, thereby allowing them to flourish and the community transformed. The Christian practice of hospitality, making room for others at home, in church, and the community especially around meals, is a powerful way of embodying this belief.

QUESTIONS FOR DISCUSSION

1. Read through the Gospels and find three examples of how Jesus acted counterculturally by granting others inflorescent dignity.

---

57. Pohl, 122–23.
58. Amos Yong, *Hospitality and the Other: Pentecost, Christian Practices, and the Neighbor*, (Maryknoll, NY: Orbis Books, 2008).
59. Yong, 132–33.
60. This is the title of a book by Frances S. Adeney, *Graceful Evangelism: Christian Witness in a Complex World* (Grand Rapids: Baker Academic, 2010).

2. The chapter quotes Christine Pohl saying "[b]earing God's image establishes for every person a fundamental dignity which cannot be undermined either by wrongdoing or neediness" and that, "respect cannot be sustained at the level of abstract claim or commitments. To have any meaning, they must be lived out in concrete everyday relations – in the family, church, community, and political sphere." How does this challenge your conceptions of people?
3. Some examples are given in the chapter of people who are often overlooked or treated with disdain, given little dignity, in society. Which groups are applicable in your context? Seek out positive examples of Christian ministries in your community which reach out to such groups with grace and dignity.
4. To whom does your culture attribute much dignity, and who are those who are attributed little dignity? How can the church live out passages such as Colossians 3:5–15 and grant inflorescent dignity to everyone?

BIBLIOGRAPHY

Adeney, Frances S. *Graceful Evangelism: Christian Witness in a Complex World.* Grand Rapids: Baker Academic, 2010.

Aslani Soroush, et al. "Dignity, Face and Honor Cultures" in *Journal of Organizational Behaviour* (2016): 1178–201. DOI:10.1002/job.2095.

Atkinson, David. *The Message of Genesis 1–11.* England: Inter-Varsity Press, 1990.

Corbett, Steve, and Brian Fikkert. *When Helping Hurts: How to Alleviate Poverty without Hurting the Poor . . . and Yourself.* Chicago, IL: Moody Publishers, 2012.

Henry, C. F. H. "Image of God" in *Evangelical Dictionary of Theology.* Edited by Walter Elwell, 591–94. Grand Rapids: Baker, 2001.

Hiebert, Paul G. *Cultural Anthropology.* Grand Rapids: Baker, Second Edition, 1983.

Howard, Thomas Albert, ed. *Imago Dei: Human Dignity in Ecumenical Perspective.* Washington, DC: Catholic University of America Press, 2013.

Jones, David Albert. "Human Dignity in Healthcare: A Virtue Ethics Approach" in *The New Bioethics* 21, no. 1 (2015): 87–97.

Kateb, George. *Human Dignity.* Cambridge, MA; London, England: Belknap Press, 2011.

Kim, Young-Hoon, and Dov Coven, "The Jury and Abjury of My Peers: The Self in Face and Dignity Cultures" in *Journal of Personality and Social Psychology* 98, no. 6 (2010): 904–16.

Kocaman, Berk. "The rise of AI: Human Dignity in the age of Data." 4 February 2019. https://baslangicnoktasi.org/en/the-rise-of-ai-human-dignity-in-the-age-of-data/.

Krause, Deborah. "Keeping it Real, The Image of God in the New Testament," in *Interpretation*, Oct (2005): 358–68.

Mitchel, Beverley Eileen. "The Struggle for Human Dignity in a Consumer-Oriented Culture" in *Anglican Theological Review* 98, no. 1 (2016): 111–23.

Murphy, Nancey, and Christopher Knight, eds. *Human Identity at the Intersection of Science, Technology and Religion.* Abingdon, Oxford: Routledge, 2010.

Parhiala, Paulina, and Gorden Simango. "*Diakonia* and Human Dignity" in *The Ecumenical Review* 66, no. 3, Oct (2014): 330–40. DOI:10.1111/erev.12115.

Pohl, Christine. *Making Room: Recovering Hospitality as a Christian Tradition.* Grand Rapids; Cambridge: Eerdmans, 1999.

Sulmasy, Daniel P. "Dignity and Bioethics: History, Theory and Selected Applications." In *Human Dignity and Bioethics: Essays Commissioned by the President's Council on Bioethics.* Ed. by The President's Council on BioEthics, March 2008. https://bioethicsarchive.georgetown.edu/pcbe/reports/human_dignity/chapter18.html.

Thacker, Jason. "Why artificial intelligence can be a threat to human dignity," June 11, 2018. https://erlc.com/resource-library/articles/why-articial-intelligence-can-be-a-threat-to-human-dignity/.

Yong, Amos. *The Bible, Disability and the Church*. Grand Rapids; Cambridge: Eerdmans, 2011.

———. *Hospitality and the Other: Pentecost, Christian Practices, and the Neighbor.* Maryknoll, NY: Orbis Books, 2008.

Yung, Hwa, *Mangoes or Bananas, the Quest for an Authentic Asian Theology.* England: Regnum Books, 1997.

CHAPTER 7

ETHICS OF SUFFERING FOR ASIAN RELIGIOSITY

Dick O. Eugenio

Doleo ergo sum: "I suffer, therefore I am." Unfortunately, this phrase represents the reality for many Asians – not because we actively pursue misfortune or find torment pleasurable – but because suffering is a part of our attempt to meet the exigencies of daily existence. A poor Filipino who wants to buy basic necessities cannot avoid sitting uncomfortably in a congested jeepney in traffic, walking in sweat through filthy roads and alleys under the unmerciful heat of the sun, wading through the overcrowded market while enduring an ever-present stink in the air, bargaining with vendors who wish to make good profit, carrying the purchased groceries with aching limbs and hands, and going home to a twenty square meter house with twelve family members. The illustration might not be applicable to all, but whatever the day has been, an amount of suffering – in various forms and means – would have been endured by anyone trying to get through the day in relationship to employment, social relationships, and even family expectations.

Anyone who studies Asian history, both past and present, would be struck by the amount and degree of misfortune that has befallen and continues to transpire in our nations – from the horrors of colonization to the heartlessness of politics and economics – affecting everyone, but especially implicating the poorest of our citizens. The suffering of Asians is neither a consequence of our undisciplined incompetence nor of our irresponsible slothfulness. Our suffering mostly comes from without and because of matters beyond our prerogative. Our multi-aspect poverty – which is the primary ground of much of our suffering – is the consequence of the actions or inaction of others, most of them predating our birth. The sufferer, to a large degree, is collateral damage of unwritten histories of persons and institutions.[1]

---

1. Andreas Anangguru Yewangoe, *Theologia Crucis in Asia: Asian Christian Views on Suffering in the Face of Overwhelming Poverty and Multifacted Religiosity in Asia* (Amsterdam: Rodopi, 1987), 3.

I cannot avoid treating suffering as a socio-political term. However, we must recognize that not all discussions related to suffering relate to questions of rights. Suffering may be weaponized for political gain. World history provides many instances of this and I will not argue in favor of this tactic. My concern for suffering as a socio-political term is its reality that must elicit a response from Christians. This is, after all, a book on ethics. Suffering is "an evocative term," M. Anne Brown states. She adds:

> Whereas the language of rights and abuse, of claim and obligation, can appear to offer a proper balance of settled equivalences and hoped-for justice, "suffering" can work as a reminder that the reality of pain, loss, and trauma, even within indisputably political exchanges, can pose dilemmas not easily contained within our moral languages.[2]

This chapter hopes to expand our social consciousness and theological vocabulary in relation to the reality of suffering in Asia.

The socio-political dimension of suffering, although pertinent and important, is approached here within the larger religious sphere. After all, although secularization is an increasing reality, the majority of Asians are still religious.[3] As will be seen, religious beliefs and commitments are crucial in understanding the reality of, and coping with, suffering in Asia. The chapter assumes that religious consciousness of Asians, no matter how variegated it is, is *the* foundation upon which people's conception and response to suffering are built. After all,

> Asians are religious people. Religious feeling is deeply embedded in their hearts so that the whole of their life, their attitudes, and their thinking, are enduringly inspired and directed by it. In other words, the activities of Asian people can only with difficulty be separated from their religious experiences. All human problems, including suffering, are viewed from a religious perspective. Through religion people try to understand the significance of life with all its ups and downs.[4]

---

2. M. Anne Brown, *Human Rights and the Borders of Suffering: The Promotion of Human Rights in International Politics* (Manchester: Manchester Univ. Press, 2002), 4.
3. Secularization prophecies in the mid-twentieth century have failed. See Peter Berger, ed., *The Desecularization of the World: Resurgent Religions and World Politics* (Grand Rapids: Eerdmans, 1999).
4. Yewangoe, *Theologia Crucis in Asia*, 7.

Ethics of Suffering for Asian Religiosity

This chapter presents the various considerations Christian ethicists must be familiar with when dealing with the reality of suffering in Asia, especially because of the enduring prevalence of religious commitments among its diverse citizens. It begins with an intentionally brief and broad definition of suffering, because although there is epistemological beauty in nuanced categorization, suffering is better perceived as an experience that affects the entire self. Any degree of discomfort is suffering, regardless of intensity or length. The complication is that, grounded in religious doctrines, suffering may be regarded as a just consequence of one's misbehavior or directly caused by divine action. This requires the appropriate response to be one of wholehearted resignation – because one's suffering is ultimately for one's own benefit, whether for here or in the afterlife. Given these responses, the ethicist is faced with a dilemma: If suffering has a redemptive significance for religious Asians, how can it be addressed in a way that is both religiously sensitive and compassionately responsive?

WHAT IS SUFFERING?

Suffering exists and persists as a universal and common human condition in the world. It may have unique forms contingent on geographical situatedness, vary in manifestations and degree, and perceptions and responses may be culturally conditioned, but its reality is universally indubitable. Suffering is pervasive and definitely uncomfortable, whether they are caused by harmful natural, ecological, political, economic, social, emotional, cognitive, or spiritual conditions.[5] People suffer as whole human beings; *shalom* is easily disrupted by any pain in one's physical, emotional, intellectual, or spiritual life.

External reality plays a crucial role in dictating a person's internal state of affairs. Sadly, most factors that cause suffering in Asia are outside the realm of our control. Asia has everything: (1) natural calamities such as typhoons, frequent earthquakes, landslides and floods, volcanic eruptions, and bad weather conditions; (2) political unrest such as civil wars, corrupt government, poor justice systems, underdeveloped human rights in civil laws, and prevalence of neighborhood crime; (3) socioeconomic challenges like underemployment and unemployment, inflation of cost of commodities, low income per capita for families, impoverished urban communities, and poor educational programs; (4) health-related issues like malnutrition, unhygienic living environment, lack

---

5. Ulrich Diehl, "Human Suffering as a Challenge for the Meaning of Life," *Existenz* 4.2 (2009), 37.

of sufficient medical establishments, expensive health care, and the spread of AIDS; and (5) social fragmentation realities like separated families because of employment migration (e.g. overseas Filipino workers), inhospitable homes because of parental discord, online exploitation of children, self-trafficking and prostitution, and loosening morals in the present generation. Statistical data about any of these can easily populate this chapter. Ulrich Diehl is right, and this is pertinent in Asia in particular:

> In a region of the world which is haunted by natural catastrophes or ecological damage, by dictatorship or anarchy, by wars or terrorism, by cultural or political crises, by bad economies or insufficient health care systems people normally get more and more frustrated emotionally, cognitively, and spiritually.[6]

Not all suffering, however, may be blamed on external factors. As complex entities with multi-faceted aspects of life, humans suffer because of malfunctions of the frail human body (e.g. an excruciating toothache), regardless whether they are ultimately consequences of our own culpable neglect or not. Our cognitive ability, prized by many since the Enlightenment, may lead us to feelings of frustration because of poor memory and perceived low deduction capability, bad judgments, and inability to understand many things. As affective beings, we can also suffer stress, loneliness, grief, guilt and shame, fear, and other gripping emotions. Related to this is our spiritual turmoil manifesting in existential anxiety, feeling of detachment, guilt and shame, and even fear of divine retribution.

RESPONSES TO SUFFERING

The experience of suffering is common to all, but perceptions and responses to it are diverse, influenced primarily by culture and location. It is henceforth that the Asian dimension will be particularly emphasized. Asian religiosity, more than geographical location, will be underscored. However, Asian religious diversity also entails complications that hinder us from making general statements applicable to all Asians. A continent-wide description of suffering is unrealistic, but providing a list of generic prescriptions is an even more impossible task. Hence, in this chapter, we can only discuss issues that deserve

---

6. Diehl, "Human Suffering as a Challenge for the Meaning of Life," 38.

consideration in relation to suffering and an ethical response to it that takes into account both Christian teachings and the reality of Asian religious plurality.[7]

It must be mentioned at the outset that, in response to suffering, we must avoid the hasty alleviation common in narcotics-based approaches. For Michael Stone, this is Western medicine's quick-fix mentality.[8] Suffering is a sign of disharmony and "there's an app for that." While this makes perfect sense to the secular mindset and in dealing with bodily illness, when applied to psychotherapy and counseling, problems emerge because Asian perceptions of suffering – its causes, symptoms, and treatment – are deeply prejudiced by religious affirmations. Therefore, to "medicalize human suffering"[9] is to potentially create a paradoxical dialectic in the sufferer's mind of a sense of satisfaction from receiving somatic pain alleviation while feeling guilt and shame because of violated religious commitments. This way, the physical suffering is only replaced by another form of suffering (e.g. psychological or emotional). Because of the communal nature of religion and the honor-shame culture of Asian societies, psychological suffering is probably more permanently damaging to the healed person.[10]

Responding to suffering in Asia requires deep penetration into the Asian psyche. Our shared experience of a particular suffering does not entail uniform interpretation. As hermeneutical beings, the same circumstance may be perceived in different ways. The words of the Stoic philosopher Epictetus are wise:

> When you see anyone weeping in grief because his son has gone abroad, or is dead, or because he has suffered in his affairs, be careful that the appearance may not misdirect you. Instead, distinguish within your own mind, and be prepared to say, "It is not the accident that distresses this person . . . , it is the judgment which he makes about it."[11]

Individuality and subjectivity – grounded in various presuppositions – are important elements of human conceptualizations. The observer's reflections

---

7. For a short presentation of how suffering is viewed in various Asian religions, see Yewangoe, *Theologia Crucis in Asia*, 6–11.
8. Michael Stone, "The Two Darts: Meeting Pain with Mindfulness Practice," *ReVision* 29 (2007), 3–9.
9. Elzbieta M. Gozdziak, "Training Refugee Mental Health Providers: Ethnography as a Bridge to Multicultural Practice," *Human Organization* 63 (2004): 206.
10. See Sam Louie's thought-provoking book on this, *Asian Shame and Addiction: Suffering in Silence* (Scotts Valley, CA: CreateSpace, 2013).
11. Epictetus, *Enchiridion*; available at http://classics.mit.edu/Epictetus/epicench.html.

on the suffering of others, although important, must not violate the integrity of the sufferers' own capacity to think, understand, and explain their own suffering. In the same way that we can choose an attitude with respect to the suffering of others (e.g., affirmation or denial, toleration or medication, minimization or magnification), sufferers are entitled to their perceived appropriate solutions, including paying their suffering no attention.

What follows, therefore, are important issues that merit consideration in constructing a Christian ethical response to suffering. No definite proposals or solutions are offered for each. I hope, however, that there is sufficient insight here to guide readers in making appropriate decisions that are culturally and religiously sensitive. The problem is that Asian religions are ambivalent about suffering. "On the one side," Yewangoe writes, "religions can preserve ways of release from suffering. On the other side, however, religions can lock people into suffering permanently."[12] The paradox of religions is found in its various faces experienced by people:

> In its *psychologically enslaving face*, religion becomes superstition, ritualism, dogmatism, transcendentalism, while in its *sociologically enslaving face*, it tends to legitimize an oppressive status quo. On the other hand, while the *psychologically liberating face* of religion can be seen in interior liberation from sin, its *sociologically liberating face* is seen in religion's potential for radical social change.[13]

SUFFERING AS APPROPRIATE CONSEQUENCE

There is consensus among major religions that human suffering does not arise solely because of causes external to us. Ultimately, we create our own suffering because we are accountable for our own actions. Whether in the form of divine punishment or naturalistic determinism, the established principle is that of just retribution. Human suffering is often interpreted as evidence of past misbehavior and must be deemed a consequence that needs to be experienced, either for the expiation of guilt or the liberation of the self from past ties. Hinduism, for instance, blames the mechanism of *karma* that dictates one's current favorable or unfavorable life in the world. One accumulates both *punya* (meritorious karma) and *papa* (demeritorious karma) in one's former existence and enters *samsara* (cycle of death and rebirth) in accordance with the just

---

12. Yewangoe, *Theologia Crucis in Asia*, 8.
13. Yewangoe, *Theologia Crucis in Asia*, 8–9 (italics mine).

weight of one's actions or inactions. The emphasis is on the responsibility of the moral agent for the suffering they are experiencing.

The same conception may be found in Islam and Christianity, although not as doctrinally emphasized in the latter. The commonality is found in the centrality of free will, which, when misused, can cause suffering to moral agents and the people around them. In Islam, when the *nafs amarra* or the lower state of the soul pursues its desires without regard of consequences, certain suffering follows.[14] We suffer because our God-given freedom may be used to choose unhealthy, harmful habits that produce negative short-term or long-term consequences. Although the official dogma of Christianity does not accept suffering as the manifestation of divine punishment, the thought lingers among Christians, particularly because this element of Jewish faith is found in the judgment of Job's three friends (Job 4:7–8; 8:20; 11:14–17) and in the question of Jesus's disciples (John 9:2). There is also biblical support (Gen 19:1–29).[15] The syllogistic reasoning is clear: wicked people suffer; one suffers; therefore, one is wicked. Liberation theologian Gustavo Gutierrez rejects this principle of divine retribution in his commentary on Job,[16] but based on my pastoral experience, popular Christian spirituality maintains an enduring although unverbalized affirmation of this.

While the conclusion that suffering is the consequence of misbehavior seems logical, it has serious ramifications on how sufferers understand their situation and how society responds to sufferers. On the one hand, a suffering person with persistent feelings of guilt because of wrongdoing may develop a masochistic tendency to welcome misfortunes of all kinds and even rejoice in them, all the while thinking of their redeeming value.[17] The underlying problem with this is that, in Asia, because of the prevalence of injustice and poverty, every person to a certain degree is a wrongdoer. For poor nations like the Philippines, in our attempt to maintain the mere fact of existing and in order to perform even the most basic tasks, the poor are constantly forced to

---

14. Emily Pimpinella, "Dealing with Suffering: A Comparison of Religious and Psychological Perspectives" (PsyD diss; Antioch University New England, 2011), 73.

15. While this is a generally accepted view in Judaism, this was challenged by Jesus himself as too deterministic and simplistic. Jesus rejects the presupposition of the disciples in John 9:2–3, and in Luke 14:2–4, he explicitly taught that one's misfortunes must not be conceived as commensurate punishments.

16. Gustavo Gutierrez, *On Job: God-Talk and the Suffering of the Innocent* (Maryknoll: Orbis, 1987).

17. Daniel Rancour-Laferriere, *The Slave Soul of Russia: Moral Masochism and the Cult of Suffering* (New York: New York Univ. Press, 1995), 112.

be illegally employed to meet their family's needs, give bribes to police officers and government officials in order to acquire legal documents, cheat in their small business to earn enough money, abandon their families to work abroad, or be engaged in the cheapest form of entertainment – drinking liquor with friends – in order to relieve stress. In the words of Nancy Condee and Vladimir Padunov, "from the lowest menial worker to the highest party official, everyone survives because everyone breaks the rules. Being alive is proof of guilt."[18] For a guilty person, suffering may be perceived as a deserved experience, a rightful exchange for the benefits accrued from necessary but dishonorable dealings. The sin-punishment cycle can be a numbing strategy and may perpetuate further injustice.

On the other hand, a society that accepts the reality of suffering as divine punishment may express a detached and judgmental attitude toward sufferers. Instead of showing empathy, the observer might show disdain toward those whose sufferings are great, since the degree of suffering may be commensurate to the degree of evil one has committed. Apathy fueled by religious concern is a paradoxically possible response. In Hindu societies, for instance, palliative care may not be desired by the sufferer and would not be provided by observing neighbors for fear of going against the divine will or the dictates of karma. Present temporary relief might delay or increase *papa* of another, resulting in even greater long-term suffering in the next rebirth.[19] From this perspective, it is much more merciful to let others suffer now in order not to harm their future.

FATALISM AND RESIGNATION

Resignation to the current situation – personally and communally – is another potential response to suffering. Since sinners are predestined to suffer, people must be accountable and responsible for their past actions and accept their current situation. This fatalistic tendency is not perceived as a destructive response, but an appropriate passivity informed by a recognition of greater workings that make society just. It is going against the established order of cause and effect that may be perceived as a threat to social stability. Hindu and Buddhist societies are generally more prone to this perspective. Christian ethics

---

18. Nancy Condee and Vladimir Padunov, "The Soiuz on Trial: Voinovic has Magistrate and Stage Manager," *Russian Review* 46 (1987), 316; quoted in Rancour-Laferriere, *The Slave Soul of Russia*, 113.
19. Pimpinella, "Dealing with Suffering," 171.

must take care to avoid a response to religious fatalism that involves negative assessments that depict sufferers as lazy, unconcerned, or generally pathetic. Alongside our attempt to alleviate suffering, we must learn to address the deep-seated religious worldviews concerned with principles of religious justice and retribution. Asian sufferers have two concerns, and temporary mitigation constitutes the lesser of these. What is at greater stake is people's mindset about the long-term harm they might receive from outside intervention.

Fear of contradicting the divine imperative (Islam and Christianity), accumulating more bad karma (Hinduism), or going against established reality may be reasons for a fatalistic response to suffering. In Buddhism, suffering is perceived as a natural mark of existence. This first Noble Truth states that *dukkha* (suffering) constitutes all existence, not only because of bad karma accumulated in previous planes of existence but also because of human craving and the inevitability of change in earthly life.[20] As long as humans exist, suffering follows. The three marks of existence are interrelated – *anicca* (impermanence), *dukkha* (suffering), and *anatta* (no-self) – and so long as anicca and anatta remain, dukkha in physical, emotional, and mental states is a person's inescapable reality.[21] Buddhism, however, does not end with the recognition of earthly suffering. The teachings of the Buddha underscore a means of escaping suffering. The problem is that nirvana, or salvation from the cycle of rebirth and therefore from suffering, is an unattainable goal while living.[22] Thus, although relief is available, its release is suspended until a later season. In the meantime, and closely related to Hinduism, the monk is called to abandon fleshly pleasures – even embrace material destitution – in order to seek salvation for the future. The paradox, therefore, is that the elimination of suffering in the future is dependent on the willingness to embrace suffering in the present.

The typical fatalistic response would be to exercise silent endurance and patience during suffering. It may even be said that the Buddhist practice of meditation is a coping mechanism that turns one's attention inward to forget the outward experiences of suffering. *Samadhi* (meditation) is the pre-requisite

---

20. Matthew Meghaprasara, *New Guide to the Tipitaka: A Complete Reference to the Pali Buddhist Canon* (Regina: Sangha of Books, 2013), 382.
21. Cing Sian Thawn, "The Concept of Self-Liberation in Theravada Burmese Buddhism" (MST thesis; Asia-Pacific Nazarene Theological Seminary, 2020), 39–40.
22. Rudi Maier, "Salvation in Buddhism," *Journal of Adventist Mission Studies* 10 (2014), 9–42.

to *panna* (wisdom) that recognizes suffering and the means to escape from it.[23] The Islamic response is even more passive. According to W. Montgomery Watt, the nomadic life of early Muslims, characterized by living under unpredictable and unforeseeable circumstances in the desert, planted an ethos of acceptance of difficulties in the Islamic psyche. "The fatalism of the nomadic Arab," he adds, "is not something to be regretted, but a quality which he must have if he is to make a success of life."[24] In the face of suffering, what is required are *sabr*, patience or patient endurance, and *tawakkul*, trust in Allah and his future deliverance.[25] This is applied to all misfortunes, including when facing opposition from unbelievers.

DIVINE INVOLVEMENT AND PREROGATIVE

The prescription for patience is grounded in another important religious element that we need to consider in thinking about our ethical response to suffering — in Asian religions, suffering happens within the scope of divine providence. While the Hindu perspective leans more toward a universal principle of justice, its plethora of gods are still involved in the affairs of mortals. In animistic societies, fortunes and misfortunes are explained through the existence of benevolent and malevolent gods and spirits that need to be pleased and appeased. Suffering, thus, is not merely a naturalistic consequence of actions toward oneself but is a divine prerogative. This is most explicitly found in Islam; it resonates with Christianity too.

Islam is a religion of absolute surrender or submission to the will of Allah. The sovereignty of Allah includes his involvement in the particularities of human life, including his just and wise decision to allow suffering for his followers. Suffering occurs only because God permits it. Everything is purposely willed by Allah as he forges people's destinies. If God inflicts suffering, "he obviously wills it for some reason, either to cure the sinner or to exact reparation for evil that has been done."[26] Thus, in the face of suffering, Muslims comfort and encourage others by saying *Alhamdulliah*, which means "All praises are due to Allah" or *Insha' Allah*, which means "Allah willing," or *Masha Allah*, which

---

23. Nanatiloka Thera, *The Buddha's Path to Deliverance: A Systematic Exposition in the Words of the Sutta Pitaka* (Seattle: BPS Pariyatti, 2002), 49.
24. W. Montgomery Watt, "Suffering in Sunnite Islam," *Studia Islamica* 50 (1979), 9.
25. Watt, "Suffering in Sunnite Islam," 11.
26. Avery Dulles, "Divine Providence and the Mystery of Human Suffering," in *Divine Impassibility and the Mystery of Human Suffering* (eds. J. F. Keating and T. J. White; Grand Rapids: Eerdmans, 2009), 331.

means "with the will of Allah."[27] Because Allah is involved in one's afflictions, the appropriate response would be repentance for whatever possible sin has been committed, followed by patience and gratitude. In addition, a Muslim must not fear the punishment and consider it as certain evidence of God's special attention upon him. Hope is birthed, and trust in Allah is kindled, thinking that as an object of divine attention and love, divine plans for him are perfect.[28]

Because God is involved, either in inflicting or allowing suffering, there is an awareness that suffering serves as a test that when passed will be rewarded. The story of Job becomes paradigmatic, particularly his response to his situation. When tempted by his wife to curse God for his misfortunes, Job replies: "You are talking like a foolish woman. Shall we accept good from God, and not trouble?" (Job 2:10). However, we must admit that this does not apply to all situations. Although there was indeed reward at the end of Job's suffering, he cannot be used as an example of silent patience in the face of adversities. Marilyn McCord-Adams is right:

> The book of Job is in the Bible to send the message that God doesn't expect us to meet disastrous emergencies with pious slogans, that God doesn't need to have his divine self-esteem propped up by insincere court flattery, that God is willing to hear the truth about what divine policies cost us, that horrors don't mean that God hates us; that the eclipse of God does not signal that God has abandoned us; that the only burden of making good on horrendous situations does not fall primarily on us. It is God's job to make good on God's boast about the human race, God's responsibility to make success of divine plans![29]

SILVER LINING IN SUFFERING

Patience is important in Islam because suffering is not only ordained; it is also temporary. Moreover, its purposes may be several. First, it may serve as just punishment of wrongdoing that believers need to accept wholeheartedly for their soul's eternal benefit. "No fatigue, nor disease, nor sorrow, nor sadness,

---

27. H. Hamid, "Basic Tenets of Islam," in *The Crescent and the Couch: Cross-Currents between Islam and Psychoanalysis* (ed. Salman Akhtar; Lanham, MD: Jason Aronson, 2008), 15.
28. Nour Loufty and George Berguno, "The Existential Thoughts of the Sufis," *Existential Analysis* 16 (2005), 150–51.
29. Marilyn McCord-Adams, "Death and Horrors," *The Expository Times* 120 (2009), 597.

nor hurt, nor distress befalls a Muslim, even if it were the prick he received from a thorn, but that Allah expiates some of his sins for that."[30] Suffering, thus, is a cleansing process. Afflictions come for the good of people: "If Allah wants to do good to somebody, He afflicts him with trials."[31] Second, suffering serves as a divine warning. For instance, children's suffering must be conceived as a test to their parents.[32] Third, suffering reinforces individual and communal responsibility. Muslim piety holds people accountable for their actions and recommends undertaking righteous acts to help others in their suffering. Finally, suffering is an opportunity for growth in religious piety and commitment:

> [Rumi] resorts to total submission to the ultimate and solitary source of power, intelligence, enlightenment, creativity, and absolute beauty. He advises yielding to the supreme will that governs the entirety of all that now exists, ever has, or ever will. Submitting to this will and surrendering to the empowering servitude of this power is the only viable course to salvation and the sole straight path to the destination of fulfillment, enlightenment, transcendent consciousness, and sustaining peace.[33]

Clearly, suffering may not be completely considered as a problem that needs to be hastily eased. In various Asian religions, including Christianity, suffering is considered valuable because it makes possible spiritual growth, connection, and transformation.[34] Paul writes: "We also glory in our sufferings, because we know that suffering produces perseverance; perseverance, character; and character, hope" (Rom 5:3–4). Even atheistic Buddhism emphasizes that the experience of dukkha helps humanity to acknowledge its reality, determine its causes, and be motivated to be freed from it. Suffering serves as a great teacher. Like medical science, suffering is a sign that something is not right; without it, we would not be alarmed to address a looming greater threat to our well-being. Christopher Tollefsen succinctly expresses it:

> Suffering involves an awareness on our part of a harmony that should exist, whether in our physical or mental being, or our

---

30. Muhammad Muksin Khan, trans. *Sahih Al-Bukhari*, vol. 7 (Riyadh: Darussalam, 1997), 307 (Book 75, Chapter 1, Number 5461, 5462).
31. Khan, *Sahih Al-Bukhari*, 308 (Book 75, Chapter 1, Number 5645).
32. Scott J. Fitzpatrick, et al., "Religious Perspectives on Human Suffering: Implications for Medicine and Bioethics," *Journal of Religion and Health* 55 (2016), 169.
33. M. Hossein Etezady, "Rapture and Poetry," in *The Crescent and the Couch*, 52.
34. Rebecca Sachs Norris, "The Paradox of Healing Pain," *Religion* 39 (2009), 22–33.

moral being, or between loved ones, or between ourselves and God, and a further awareness that that harmony is currently being damaged, rent asunder.[35]

This awareness of disharmony then serves "a salutary role in a moral agent's life, leading her to repair that which can be repaired, and to develop virtues that are necessary for that reparative work."[36]

For others, suffering affords the opportunity to reflect on life's meaning. This is not surprising, Yewangoe writes, because "the problem of suffering is very closely related to the question of human destiny."[37] Suffering disturbs routine, creating a pause in the busy-ness of work and the abuse of the psycho-somatic self, thus allowing a rare moment of serious self-introspection about what led to the unwelcome disruption and how it may be prevented in the future. In this sense, suffering is the gateway to a therapeutic journey toward self-betterment. It may be the impetus to understand the real meaning of free will and its exercise. It may serve as a wakeup call regarding destructive habits. It may lead to a recognition of the balance required in life, and that meaning is not found in wanton pursuit of fleshly pleasures.

In all these things, although suffering may not have an intrinsic value and may be perceived as essentially intrusive in a person's normal situation, it cannot be denied that in religious societies, suffering is afforded an instrumental value. It is all a matter of interpretation, guided by personal and communal belongingness. Indubitably, the religious Asian reflects upon his experience of suffering and finds silver linings. First, suffering provides an opportunity for consideration of one's actions and very existence. Second, it shapes humans to develop virtues such as patience, trust in God, and perseverance. Third, it serves as a stimulus for a person to engage in metaphysical deduction and spiritual reflection. Fourth, it births a resilience that inspires hope in oneself and others. Fifth, it forces a search for meaning in life.

OBSERVERS AND RESPONDENTS

Evidently, Christian ethics faces a dilemma in responding to sufferings in Asia. The root of the challenge is expressed by Diehl: "Since one's personal sense for the meaning of life is highly individualized people may cope, react and act in many different, unpredictable and even surprising ways toward

---

35. Fitzpatrick, et al. "Religious Perspectives on Human Suffering," 163.
36. Fitzpatrick, et al. "Religious Perspectives on Human Suffering," 163.
37. Yewangoe, *Theologia Crucis in Asia*, 8.

any external and personal conditions of human suffering."[38] Because Asians attach religious significance to suffering, hasty alleviation of the suffering of others may be ill-advised because it may come at the expense of robbing the religious person of the opportunity toward spiritual growth.[39] Since suffering is embraced as a part of life – including one's relationship with the divine – it may not be treated as a problem that needs eradication but a temporary state of affairs that needs to be endured. External help might even be considered unwelcome meddling. If not careful, medical practitioners and ministers of compassion may be construed as evil witches offering poisoned apples; they give temporary relief for hunger that bring long-term damage.

So, what can Christians do? The Bible certainly does not call us to petrified inaction because of religious differences. Humans share dignity as entities created in God's image (Gen 1:26–27) and are therefore equal recipients of God's concern. The objects of divine care and compassion transcend racial or religious differences. This is exceptionally evident in the numerous divine stipulations communicated to the Israelites in the covenant, particularly in how they should treat the *ger* (the other, the stranger, the non-Jew) and the poor. The *ger* who is suffering must be provided food and clothing (Deut 10:18–19), share in the harvest (Lev 19:9–10; Deut 24:19–22), enjoy the Jewish festivals (Deut 26:2, 11), and be part of the recipients of the third-year tithe (Deut 14:28–29; 26:12–13). The suffering poor among them must not be mistreated (Exod 22:21–23) and their rights must be maintained (Exod 23:6; Lev 19:15; Deut 24:17; 27:19). They should be given free loans (Exod 22:24–26; Lev 25:35–37). They must be provided food (Exod 23:11; Lev 19:10–11; Deut 14:28–29; 24:19–21) and be given maximum years of service for their debts (Exod 21:1–11; Deut 15:12–18). Paul summarizes the biblical principle well: "As God's chosen people, holy and dearly loved, clothe yourselves with compassion, kindness, humility, gentleness, and patience" (Col 3:12). The parable of the Good Samaritan (Luke 10:25–37) expresses our human responsibility to the suffering other. We are to imitate Jesus's compassion (Matt 14:14; 15:32; Mark 6:34; 8:2; Luke 7:13).[40]

Given these biblical principles, it is no wonder that the history of Christianity is characterized by social activism seeking to alleviate suffering

---

38. Diehl, "Human Suffering as a Challenge for the Meaning of Life," 43–44.
39. Fitzpatrick, et al. "Religious Perspectives on Human Suffering," 163.
40. For a great study of the biblical theme of justice, see Jeremiah Unterman, *Justice for All: How the Jewish Bible Revolutionized Ethics* (Philadelphia: Jewish Publication Society, 2017).

caused by poverty, challenge social ills and practices that demean human dignity, and create programs for the betterment of people in general. Christians of the early church were notable for their resolve and action to alleviate the suffering of the poor, the sick, and the lowly. Even the monastic era narrates stories of monks going out to pray for, and serve, people. Evangelism and missions in the last five centuries, although regrettably intertwined with colonialism, incorporated works of mercy in their agenda, evident in the rise of schools, medical centers, birthing homes, orphanages, and homes for girls in many Asian nations. Missionaries have been intentional in creating programs that minimize the suffering of the less fortunate. God's "preferential option for the poor," although first beautifully phrased by liberation theology, is a sentiment shared by all Christians. The alleviation of suffering is an integral part of our Christian character and mission.

The social involvement of Christians throughout history is guided by a soteriological holism and presentism. Although an escapist soteriology that advocates the soul's migration to a heavenly dimension has been plaguing Christianity since Augustine, the church has not diverged from its historico-theological ethos – inherited directly from Jesus Christ as the exemplar – of proclaiming a salvation that impacts the now in persons and communities. Christian mercy is there where there is suffering, whatever its cause. Heeding the proclamation of the Old Testament prophets for love, justice, and mercy, the church has done much effort, in the words of Fanny Crosby, to:

> Rescue the perishing, care for the dying,
> Snatch them in pity from sin and the grave;
> Weep o'er the erring one, lift up the fallen,
> Tell them of Jesus the mighty to save.

The chorus of the hymn reveals both Christian action and the simplistic theology that motivates it:

> Rescue the perishing, care for the dying;
> Jesus is merciful, Jesus will save.

Our compassionate measures that alleviate human suffering are grounded in the resolute affirmation that our savior is everyone's savior. Moreover, the salvation he offers is not merely ethereal and futuristic; it is holistic and present. Cohen says it well: "Religion, in this holy-ethical sense, would no longer be a miraculous or predetermined escape from nothingness, a flight from the utter worthlessness of creation, from its 'husks,' but rather the perfecting of a creation."[41]

Perhaps our starting point is to avoid romanticizing suffering. Although suffering is afforded religious instrumental value, such an optimism is not always realistic because not all suffering leads to good things. Here the importance of the medical and psychological sciences cannot be understated. Even the most religious person can give in to resentment, self-loathing, and destructive habits such as suicide in the face of suffering. Depression can easily overcome a person filled with anxiety and the comfort of religious wisdom may not be sufficient. The enlightened mind also does not necessarily negate the agonizing body. Furthermore, the envisioned benefit is mostly futuristic, so the present suffering still needs to be addressed. It may also be the case that the sufferer already repented, experienced enlightenment, or found meaning, so the lingering affliction possesses no religious value anymore.

In this sense, the importance of a companion cannot be underestimated. The social value of suffering is that it may generate sympathy and empathy for others and lead persons to compassionate actions. The companion as a fellow-sufferer must, at least, feel empathy and offer encouragement. There seems to be basic agreement even among the major religions about this. Islamic emphasis on patience is balanced by the "insistence on the duty of relieving unmerited suffering whenever possible."[42] This is why almsgiving is one the primary responsibilities of Muslims. Giving alms to monks is also an important Buddhist act of virtue. In Mahayana Buddhism *bodhisattvas* choose not to experience nirvana or remain in the cycle of rebirth in order to help others. Thus, while acts of mercy cannot eliminate suffering entirely, it can at least make life "more bearable and help people understand the nature of reality."[43] Hindus are not against the alleviation of suffering if it does not increase bad karma and produce greater suffering in future life.[44]

The openness to alleviating suffering is an important element in our Christian ethical response. Varied reaction because of religious commitments is not a good excuse to invalidate or belittle pain experienced in all forms of suffering. The Scylla of unmindful intervention and the Charybdis of unconcerned detachment must be avoided. Reasonable decisions must be made

---

41. Richard A. Cohen, *Levinasian Meditations* (Pittsburgh, PN: Duquesne Univ. Press, 2010), 223.
42. Watt, "Suffering in Sunnite Islam," 14.
43. Pimpinella, "Religion and Suffering," 98.
44. Fitzpatrick, et al. "Religious Perspectives on Human Suffering," 172.

when facing the reality of suffering while being mindful of people's religious constructs. Suffering, after all, is not merely a religious problem; it is a problem of ethics and response.[45] Suffering creates a sense of crisis to the observer which demands action. Christian conscience compels us to treat suffering as a thing not to be witnessed in callous resignation.

In responding to the suffering of others in Asia, a tension exists because of the inexorable clash of values between the sufferer and the respondent (anyone who responds to the suffering of others). Perspectives on benefits and timings are the points of contention. The sufferer might delay palliative solutions for the sake of anticipated greater fruits in the future while the respondent might stress immediate alleviation to ease present misery. Both are thinking of benefits gained in their preferred courses of action, but their emphases are different.

So, should the morphine be administered now or later? When we think that our options are limited to this question as a response to the suffering of others, we fail to grasp the complexity of suffering. It is here that a unique Christian response is appropriate, patterned after the incarnation of Jesus Christ. Jesus is Immanuel, "God with us," with the poor, the sinners, the outcasts. He became one of us and shared in our humanity with all its frailty, limitations, and suffering. As savior, teacher, and healer, he was one *of* us, *with* us, and *among* us. As followers of Jesus Christ called to Christlikeness, we imitate, mirror, or participate in the "incarnational realism of God's action"[46] in Jesus Christ. We can be like Christ, Karen V. Guth says, through "faithful presence" with the people and the community.[47] The examples of Toyohiko Kagawa of Japan (1888–1960) and Mother Theresa of Calcutta (1910–1997) immediately come to mind. They saw and responded to the suffering of the people by being in solidarity with them. Theirs were incarnational mission or ministry at its finest.

Especially in Asia, where poverty-stricken communities are the recipients of many evangelical missions, "faithful presence" is important, because it reminds us that compassionate ministries are not just a matter of handing out relief packs or medicine; it involves sustained relationship. We must construe healing as a conversive-participative endeavor in which the respondent might

---

45. Fitzpatrick, et al. "Religious Perspectives on Human Suffering," 161.
46. Anthony J. Kelly, "'The Body of Christ: Amen': The Expanding Incarnation," *Theological Studies* 71 (2010), 794.
47. Karen V. Guth, "To Change the World: James Davison Hunter's 'Faithful Presence' Meets Political Theologies on the Margins," *Theology Today* 69 (2013), 511–18.

serve primarily as friend to the sufferer.[48] The sufferer's preference for treatment and help is secondary – because receiving or delaying means to alleviate suffering is the prerogative of the sufferer – but the willingness of the respondent to engage in faithful presence with the sufferer *now* is in itself a helpful act, especially considering the relational nature of Asians. A physician-like approach of diagnosis-treatment in rapid succession makes the process too detached. The Christian respondent functions chiefly as a comforting companion than an anesthetic doctor. Richard A. Cohen writes that:

> The discourse of ethics . . . is not simply about morality, morality as a topic, morality "at a distance," as it were, for it is permeated by the morality it elucidates. Morality occurs in an exorbitant proximity, immediacy without escape, without excuse, without the self-sufficient refuge of substance or identity.[49]

The Christian "vocation of suffering,"[50] including engagement in biblical-theological discourses, is incarnationally accomplished. Proximal engagement with sufferers brings unexpected gains to the respondent as well. There is no substitute to personal contact with the sufferer in understanding suffering and its victims. Theodore Jennings's statement about visiting the poor applies to suffering: "In visiting the marginalized, we invite them to transform us, to transform our hearts, to transform our understanding, to transform us into instruments of the divine mercy and justice."[51]

"What is universal about the morality of the face-to-face," Cohen asks, "about the commanding alterity of the unique one who faces and the first person singular responsibility of the moral self?"[52] The power of proximity to suffering is its evocative effect on the observer-in-person, whose whole being is drawn into a contemplative cringe overflowing with dissatisfaction of the reality of the moment and desire for a better state of affairs. External reality stirs the internal self to address external reality. This is a basic human feature. Using John Wesley's understanding of the *imago Dei*, humans have a natural, political, and moral image.[53] We have the capacity to think critically about

---

48. Fitzpatrick, et al. "Religious Perspectives on Human Suffering," 162.
49. Cohen, *Levinasian Meditations*, 341.
50. Fitzpatrick, et al. "Religious Perspectives on Human Suffering," 164.
51. Theodore Jennings, *Good News to the Poor: John Wesley's Evangelical Economics* (Nashville: Abingdon, 1990), 57–58.
52. Cohen, *Levinasian Meditations*, 248.
53. John Wesley, "The New Birth," in *The Works of John Wesley*, vol. 2, Sermons II (Bicentennial ed., ed. Albert Outler; Nashville: Abingdon, 1985), 188.

reality as it is presented to us and to respond in freedom. We are socio-political beings able to relate and be related to – in the dynamic of ruling and submission – and are implicated by the social condition of others. Above all, we are moral beings able to discern the right from the wrong, the good from the bad, the beautiful from the ugly.

Nevertheless, universal moral stirrings do not get translated to individual action deterministically. Every moral agent must be responsible for his own responsibility. Because humans are autonomous entities, we cannot insist on the responsibility of anyone other than of ourselves. Here the paradoxical dialectic between the reality of the universal and the indispensability of the autonomous individual is clearly discernible. Cohen writes: "Despite the universality of the 'all,' responsibility inexorably can only begin with *each* self in its 'me, myself,' with an ego, that is to say, continually and never adequately denucleated of its own spontaneous vitality for the sake of a responsibility."[54] Even the collective "I" – in the form of a group or a church – is composed of individuals whose participation is volitional. It would be ideal if such shared consensus is pervasive among ecclesial bodies, so that we can say with pride that it is not just the isolated Christian but the whole congregation which is the respondent.

CONCLUSION

Questions about appropriate responses to suffering should consider the tension between the universal and the several particulars. We must recognize the individual and collective intuitions intrinsically bound to cultures, contexts, and places, and their relationship to the power of a universal moral imperative. The multiplicity of interpretations and reception of suffering across Asia must not lead to the implementation of principles of non-interference in the affairs of another state or members of a different religion. The idea of a universal moral imperative is mesmerizing to anyone because it reveals the triumph of compassion as a human value. As Brown beautifully asserts:

> The power of the idea of the universality of human rights draws strongly on the recognition across cultures that people are profoundly mistreated and that this should not happen. This response to the fact of abuse – persistent if hardly literally universal – is

---

54. Cohen, *Levinasian Meditations*, 249 (emphasis original).

itself an assertion of the value of people, or more simply a recognition of the pain of the victim.[55]

Although we take individuality and difference seriously, existential concern is an unstoppable motivation for anyone to get involved across cultural, racial, and religious boundaries. In fact, "to reject the possibility of a definitive answer to questions about how to live well together [or] to reject the motif of the universal," Brown adds, "is an assertion of relativism and therefore a declaration of non-interference or despair in the face of violence and debilitation."[56] Because of vast racial and religious differences in Asia, overemphasizing the unique particularities of Asian suffering might lead to inaction in order to prevent potential conflicts with religious groups. This must be avoided. Ultimately, it would be better to be misinterpreted while alleviating the suffering of others than to be known for being religiously sensitive while doing nothing.

When left to choose between religious sensitivity and social action, Christians, I suspect, would lean toward the latter. This is not necessarily bad. It highlights that Christian values of compassion and generosity are given greater precedence over other considerations. This does not mean, however, that Christians may engage in the alleviation of suffering without regard for the religious commitments of others. Dealing with suffering includes faithful presence and interpersonal relationships, so thoughtless social action may greatly damage Christian mission. Unfortunately, there is no universal solution to this tension. We can only pray and rely on the Holy Spirit to teach us how to respond to unique situations. This is good, because it leads us to the recognition that Christian ethics is not merely action; it involves prayerful reflection and Spirit-enabled discernment.

QUESTIONS FOR DISCUSSION

1. How do we respond to Buddhists, Hindus, or Muslims who refuse relief from suffering because of constraints grounded in their religious commitments?
2. How do we avoid both the Scylla of hasty intervention and the Charybdis of educated passivity? What is the narrow road between the two?

---

55. Brown, *Human Rights and the Borders of Suffering*, 9.
56. Brown, *Human Rights and the Borders of Suffering*, 21.

3. The parable of the good Samaritan reveals that the religious commitments of the Levite and the priest prevented them from helping the sufferer on the road. What Christian commitments do we have that may hinder us from seeing the suffering of others and extending them help?
4. What are the implications of Christian "faithful presence" with those who suffer? What are ways to be intentionally incarnational in our approach to suffering?

BIBLIOGRAPHY

Ashkar, Salman. ed. *The Crescent and the Couch: Cross-Currents between Islam and Psychoanalysis*. Lanham: Jason Aronson, 2008.

Berger, Peter. Editor. *The Desecularization of the World: Resurgent Religions and World Politics*. Grand Rapids: Eerdmans, 1999.

Brown, M. Anne. *Human Rights and the Borders of Suffering: The Promotion of Human Rights in International Politics*. Manchester: Manchester Univ. Press, 2002.

Cing Sian Thawn. "The Concept of Self-Liberation in Theravada Burmese Buddhism." MST Thesis. Asia-Pacific Nazarene Theological Seminary, 2020.

Cohen, Richard A. *Levinasian Meditations*. Pittsburgh: Duquesne Univ. Press, 2010.

Diehl, Ulrich. "Human Suffering as a Challenge for the Meaning of Life." *Existenz* 4.2 (2009): 36–44.

Dulles, Avery. "Divine Providence and the Mystery of Human Suffering," in *Divine Impassibility and the Mystery of Human Suffering*, edited. J. F. Keating and T. J. White, 324–35. Grand Rapids: Eerdmans, 2009.

Epictetus, *Enchiridion*; available at http://classics.mit.edu/Epictetus/epicench.html.

Fitzpatrick, Scott J., et al. "Religious Perspectives on Human Suffering: Implications for Medicine and Bioethics." *Journal of Religion and Health* 55 (2016): 159–73.

Gozdziak, Elzbieta M. "Training Refugee Mental Health Providers: Ethnography as a Bridge to Multicultural Practice." *Human Organization* 63 (2004): 203–10.

Guth, Karen V. "To Change the World: James Davison Hunter's 'Faithful Presence' Meets Political Theologies on the Margins." *Theology Today* 69 (2013): 511–18.

Gutierrez, Gustavo. *On Job: God-Talk and the Suffering of the Innocent*. Maryknoll: Orbis, 1987.

Jennings, Theodore. *Good News to the Poor: John Wesley's Evangelical Economics*. Nashville: Abingdon, 1990.

Kelly, Anthony J. "'The Body of Christ: Amen': The Expanding Incarnation." *Theological Studies* 71 (2010): 792–816.

Khan, Muhammad Muksin. Translator. *Sahih Al-Bukhari*, vol. 7. Riyadh: Darussalam, 1997.

Loufty, Nour, and George Berguno. "The Existential Thoughts of the Sufis." *Existential Analysis* 16 (2005): 144–55.

Louie, Sam. *Asian Shame and Addiction: Suffering in Silence*. Scotts Valley: CreateSpace, 2013.

Maier, Rudi. "Salvation in Buddhism." *Journal of Adventist Mission Studies* 10 (2014): 9–42.

McCord-Adams, Marilyn. "Death and Horrors." *The Expository Times* 120 (2009): 596–98.

Meghaprasara, Matthew. *New Guide to the Tipitaka: A Complete Reference to the Pali Buddhist Canon*. Regina: Sangha of Books, 2013.

Norris, Rebecca Sachs. "The Paradox of Healing Pain." *Religion* 39 (2009): 22–33.

Pimpinella, Emily. "Dealing with Suffering: A Comparison of Religious and Psychological Perspectives." PsyD diss., Antioch University New England, 2011.

Rancour-Laferriere, Daniel. *The Slave Soul of Russia: Moral Masochism and the Cult of Suffering*. New York: New York Univ. Press, 1995.

Stone, Michael. "The Two Darts: Meeting Pain with Mindfulness Practice." *ReVision* 29 (2007): 3–9.

Thera, Nanatiloka. *The Buddha's Path to Deliverance: A Systematic Exposition in the Words of the Sutta Pitaka*. Seattle: BPS Pariyatti, 2002.

Unterman, Jeremiah. *Justice for All: How the Jewish Bible Revolutionized Ethics*. Philadelphia: Jewish Publication Society, 2017.

Watt, W. Montgomery. "Suffering in Sunnite Islam." *Studia Islamica* 50 (1979): 5–19.

Wesley, John. *The Works of John Wesley*, vol. 2, Sermons II. Edited by Albert Outler. Bicentennial edition. Nashville: Abingdon, 1985.

Yewangoe, Andreas Anangguru. *Theologia Crucis in Asia: Asian Christian Views on Suffering in the Face of Overwhelming Poverty and Multifaceted Religiosity in Asia*. Amsterdam: Rodopi, 1987.

CHAPTER 8

THE WAY OF THE CROSS AND THE GOOD LIFE

Evangelical Virtue Ethics in Asia

Aldrin M. Peñamora

INTRODUCTION

"What is the good life?" The Greek philosopher, Aristotle, says all actions aim at some good, that every activity has an end (*telos*). The end which is desired for its own sake is the chief good, *eudaimonia*, often translated as "happiness" or "human flourishing."[1] In our pluralistic society, the shape and content of eudaimonia vary from one society or tradition to another, which prompts us to ask what human flourishing looks like from an evangelical perspective in the Asian context, a context marked by immense suffering and oppression.

To arrive at such an understanding, let us first look at some salient features of the ethical teachings of two great Asian figures who addressed suffering and oppression in their own contexts – the Chinese philosopher, Confucius, and the Indian nationalist leader, Mahatma Gandhi. While the constitutive virtues and practices in their ethics vary, they share the idea of a moral exemplar who opposes social oppression and injustice, and who seeks the moral and political transformation of society. Such ideals resonate with an evangelical perspective that sees Jesus not only as the exemplar of the Christian moral life, but humanity's savior as well. Hence, this essay proposes an evangelical notion of human flourishing in the Asian context, which is grounded in the believer's participation in Christ whose "way of the cross" reveals that the good life is formed by cruciform virtues and practices for the purpose of existing for others.[2]

---

1. Aristotle, *Nicomachean Ethics* in *The Basic Works of Aristotle*, ed. Richard McKeon (New York: Random House, 1941), 935. Hereafter *NE*. I.1.1094.1–3; I.2.1094.3–8, 21–24.
2. Dietrich Bonhoeffer, *Letters and Papers from Prison*, ed. Eberhard Bethge (New York: MacMillan, 1972), 381–83.

VIRTUE ETHICS

The recent revival of virtue ethics owes much to G. E. M. Anscombe, as well as to Alasdair MacIntyre and Stanley Hauerwas, among others. Virtue ethics seek to address the inadequacies of the two other main ethical approaches, namely deontology and consequentialism, which emphasize, respectively, the rightness of an action in terms of performing one's moral duty, or whether such action produces the greatest amount of happiness.

Historically, virtue ethics can be traced to the ancient Greek thinkers. It is mainly concerned with a person's virtuous character, as shown in Plato's *Protagoras* and *Gorgias*, which reject equating virtue (*arete*) with rhetorical skills to persuade people, as the Sophists held.[3] For Socrates, Sophists were like merchants who only cared for profit and not for the genuine good of a person or society.[4]

Aristotle gave a more systematic account of virtue ethics in *Nicomachean Ethics*. Essentially, "character virtue" or *ethike arete* refers to permanent states (*hexis*) of character that have been embedded in a person due to habitual actions.[5] The focus of virtue ethics is the entirety of a person's life. In this sense, "virtues (and your vices) are a matter of what sort of adult you are."[6] What determines character are the actions we make in the normal course of our life, and not just individual actions or decisions. Hence, it is by a lifelong pattern of *doing* that we *become* a person who is good, wise, just, and so forth.[7]

VIRTUE ETHICS IN ASIA
Confucius and the Way (Dao) of Virtuous Relations

Confucius's concept of flourishing or eudaimonia is expressed by the notion of "great harmony" (*datong*). A datong society is one where virtues are followed; where all goods "under heaven" are not kept for private use but are public in nature; where the people treat others as family members, caring for each other, including the sick and the helpless; and where power is used to benefit everyone.[8] In a narrower sense, harmony (*he*) refers to the relational nature

---

3. Plato, *Gorgias*, 452.
4. Plato, *Protagoras*, 313.
5. Raymond J. Devettere, *Introduction to Virtue Ethics: Insights of the Ancient Greeks* (Washington, D.C.: Georgetown University, 2002), 66–67. See *NE*, II.1.1103a.16–19.
6. Rosalind Hursthouse, "Are Virtues the Proper Starting Point for Morality?" in *Contemporary Debates in Moral Theory*, ed. James Dreier (Malden, MA: Blackwell, 2006), 101.
7. *NE* II.1.1103b.14–15.
8. Bart Dessein, "Yearning for the Lost Paradise: The Great Unity (*datong*) and its Philosophical Interpretations," *Asian Studies* 5, no. 1 (2017): 84.

of the self and the condition where individuals exist and coexist, mandating living, learning, and flourishing together in mutual recognition and respect.[9]

Human Being as Human Becoming

The Confucian moral life is based on a particular understanding of the self. Unlike the ancient Greeks who held to an other-worldly conception of an immortal soul, the Confucian self is basically social and this-worldly.[10] Hence, self-cultivation for Confucius is basically a "person-making" (*zuo ren*), with the moral person viewed as the foundation of a good society.[11] In this sense, human *being* is a human *becoming*; a person "becomes human by cultivating those thick, intrinsic relations that constitute one's initial conditions and that locate the trajectory of one's life-force within family, community, and cosmos."[12] Having its origin in one's immediate family, virtuous relations radiate toward other social relationships, which ultimately affect the entire universe.

Confucius developed his ethical teachings as a response to the social-political and moral disintegration of Zhou society seeing that the rulers of his time failed to follow the mandate of "Heaven" (*tian*), which the Zhou people believed to bestow the authority to rule only upon virtuous persons. Thus, Confucius sought to revive the ethically correct "Way" (*dao*) of the ancient traditions for the promotion of the people's welfare through proper governance.[13] He believed that government exists to benefit the people, a conviction that was revolutionary in those times.[14]

The Junzi *and the Virtues*

The goal of Confucian self-cultivation is becoming a *junzi*. Historically, junzi ("son of a lord") refers to ancient China's class who lived according to the

---

9. Chenyu Wang, "Confucian Selfhood and the Idea of Multicultural Education," in *Confucianism Reconsidered*, ed. Xiufeng Liu and Wen Ma (Albany: SUNY, 2018), 191.
10. Tu Wei-Ming, *Confucian Thought: Selfhood as Creative Transformation* (New York: SUNY, 1985), 51.
11. Chenyang Li, "The Philosophy of Harmony in Classical Confucianism," *Philosophy Compass* 3, no. 3 (2008): 428.
12. Roger T. Ames, *Confucian Role Ethics: A Vocabulary* (Hong Kong: Chinese University Press, 2011), 87.
13. Bryan W. Van Norden, *Virtue Ethics and Consequentialism in Early Chinese Philosophy* (Cambridge: Cambridge University, 2007), 66–67. See Joseph Chan, "Territorial Boundaries and Confucianism," in *Confucian Political Ethics*, ed. Daniel A. Bell (Princeton: Princeton University, 2008), 63.
14. Lee Dian Rainey, *Confucius and Confucianism* (Oxford: Wiley-Blackwell, 2010), 45–46, 48–49.

principle of *wu* or military skills. Confucius refashioned it to signify an exemplar of moral self-cultivation that is accessible to everyone.[15] The junzi can be understood as one who in following the "Way" fosters "human and cosmic musicality."[16] Thus, moral excellence can only be learned with and through others, particularly by fulfilling "role specific duties . . . located within a specific and familial context."[17] Three virtues are crucial: *ren, li* and *yi*.

Ren refers to the cultivated disposition of benevolence.[18] This must be seen in the context of interdependent social relationships wherein the advancement of one's moral self and those of others are interconnected. As Confucius remarks, "The humane person wants standing, and so he helps others to gain standing. He wants achievement, and so he helps others to achieve" (6:30).[19] Ren is therefore essential for a harmonious community, and attaining it is considered the "fullest realization of one's capacities as a human being."[20]

Li (ritual propriety) is crucial in cultivating ren, for all social interactions are mediated through ritual observance. Central to li is the family, the foundation of citizenship. The virtues in filial relations are therefore not merely private, they are also translatable to the public sphere.[21] As May Sim explains:

> Li dictates the proper behavior for all roles: in the family toward relatives, and in the larger community . . . li enables the extension of love for family members, in a graduated manner, to everyone else in the community. When accomplished, one will have the highest Confucian virtue of humaneness (ren).[22]

---

15. Jinhua Song and Xiaomin Jao, "Confucius' Junzi: The Conceptions of Self in Confucian," *Educational Philosophy and Theory* 50, no. 6 (November 2017): 6; Charlene Tan, "Understanding Creativity in East Asia: Insights from Confucius' Concept of Junzi," *International Journal of Design Creativity and Innovation* 4, no. 1 (2016): 54.
16. Charlene Tan, *Confucius* (London: Bloomsbury, 2013), 106; Ames, *Confucian Role Ethics*, 169.
17. Edward Slingerland, "Virtue Ethics, the *Analects*, and the Problem of Commensurability," *Journal of Religious Ethics* 29, no. 1 (2001): 105.
18. Jiyuan Yu, *The Ethics of Confucius and Aristotle: Mirrors of Virtue* (New York: Routledge, 2007), 34–35.
19. Sim, *Remastering Morals*, 27.
20. Song and Jao, "Confucius' Junzi": 4–5.
21. Sang-Im Lee, "The Unity of the Virtues in Aristotle and Confucius," *Journal of Chinese Philosophy* 26, no. 2 (June 1999): 216. There are five central filial relationships (*wunlu*): father-son, ruler-subject, husband-wife, elder-younger brothers, and friend-friend.
22. May Sim, "Rethinking Virtue Ethics and Social Justice with Aristotle and Confucius," *Asian Philosophy: An International Journal of the Philosophical Traditions of the East* 20, no. 2 (July 2010): 198.

Indeed, for Confucius it is through li that the manifold relationships among people are humanized.[23] The virtue, yi, is similarly vital for the junzi. It refers to discerning the most appropriate conduct in human relations based on one's role and status as specified by ritual activities. Yi enables the moral person to consider what is the optimally appropriate action in specific situations.[24] This underlies Confucius's statement in 12:11 of the *Analects*, "Let the ruler be ruler, ministers ministers, fathers fathers, sons sons." As a virtue, yi is similar to distributive justice or giving others their due.[25]

In such a manner, with the family as the starting point and with li guiding and cultivating the virtues reflecting the "Way" (dao), Confucius envisioned harmony in all social relations which is the mark of human flourishing. What such flourishing means for Mahatma Gandhi is the focus of the following section.

Gandhi's Way of Ascetic Social Action

Gandhi's account of eudaimonia is related to India's struggle for independence from British colonization. For Gandhi, modern European civilization was spiritually and morally bankrupt due to its irreligious and materialistic nature. He perceived that its institutions did not lead to human flourishing, but brought about a deep sense of anxiety, meaninglessness, and poverty.[26] It also perpetuated imperialism and created a culture of fear among the colonized people, as India experienced. Gandhi thus conceived of self-rule (*swaraj*) as freeing oneself from the "diseases" of modern civilization masquerading as bodily pleasures. Freedom from such egoistic and materialistic tendencies is also called *moksha* in Hinduism, which can be equated with Gandhi's view of eudaimonia.[27] It is attained through efforts directed for the moral transformation of people and

---

23. Herbert Fingarette, "Human Community as Holy Rite: An Interpretation of Confucius' Analects," *Harvard Theological Review* 59, no. 1 (January 1966): 58–59.
24. Ames, *Confucian Role Ethics*, 201, 203–204; Hui-chieh Loy, "Classical Confucianism as Virtue Ethics," in *The Handbook of Virtue Ethics*, ed. Stan van Hooft (Durham: Acumen, 2014), 290.
25. Joseph Chan, "Is There a Confucian Perspective on Social Justice?" in *Western Political Thought in Dialogue with Asia*, ed. Takashi Shogimen and Cary J. Nederman (New York: Lexington, 2009), 263–64.
26. Mahatma Gandhi, "Hind Swaraj" in *The Collected Works of Mahatma Gandhi*, vol. 10 (E-Book) (New Delhi: Publications Division of the Government of India, 1999), 259–61, accessed on February 9, 2021, available from http://www.gandhiashramsevagram.org/gandhi-literature/collected-works-of-mahatma-gandhi-volume-1-to-98.php.
27. Alexander Livingston, "Fidelity to Truth: Gandhi and the Genealogy of Civil Disobedience," *Political Theory* 46, no. 4 (2017): 522–23; Veena R. Howard, Gandhi's Ascetic Activism: Renunciation and Social Action (Albany: SUNY, 2013), 40.

society that includes transforming the nature of politics itself.[28] For Gandhi, *Satyagraha* is the means toward eudaimonia.

Satyagraha *and the Virtues*

Satyagraha came from the Sanskrit words, *satya* (truth) and *agraha* (firmness), which was "Gandhi's supreme invention, discovery, or creation."[29] Initially called "passive resistance," Gandhi later rejected it for denoting passivity and weakness. Satyagraha, on the other hand, demonstrates strength, truth, and love. As Gandhi pointed out, "Truth (satya) implies love and firmness (agraha) engenders and, therefore, serves as a synonym for force. I thus began to call the Indian movement Satyagraha, that is, the force which is born of truth and love or nonviolence."[30]

As the main principle for nonviolent political strategy, Satyagraha is grounded on three spiritual pillars or virtues: satya (truth), *ahimsa* (nonviolence or love), and *tapasya* (suffering for the sake of truth).[31] Satya is the ultimate foundation of the moral life, for as Gandhi says, "Truth is God." One who holds on to truth can do great things by witnessing to the power of Truth-as-God.[32] This can only be done through ahimsa, an ethical discipline characterized by humility, selflessness, and non-injury. It is the way of love that includes loving enemies. According to Gandhi, "To see the universal and all-pervading Spirit of Truth face-to-face one must be able to love the meanest of creation as myself."[33] This form of love entails suffering or tapasya, Satyagraha's third pillar. One cannot attain to "truth" by inflicting violence on others, but only by tapasya or voluntary self-suffering, especially in the public realm.[34] Indeed, for Gandhi a nation's progress and character can only be measured by the amount of suffering the nation and its people have willingly undergone.[35]

---

28. Faisal Devji, *The Impossible Indian: Gandhi and the Temptation of Violence* (Cambridge: Harvard University, 2012), 3.
29. Anil Dutta Mishra, *Reading Gandhi* (Delhi: Pearson, 2012), 65–66.
30. Mishra, *Reading Gandhi*, 65–66.
31. Uma Majmudar, *Gandhi and Rajchandra: The Making of the Mahatma* (London: Lexington, 2020), 85.
32. Howard, *Gandhi's Ascetic Activism*, 52; Gandhi, *Collected Works*, vol. 91, 59. Gandhi earlier believed that "God is Truth" but later revised it saying, "Truth is God" to emphasize that "God" is only one of the designations of "Truth."
33. Mohandas K. Gandhi, *An Autobiography or the Story of My Experiments with Truth*, trans. Mahadev Desai (New Haven: Yale University, 2018), 769.
34. V. K. Kool and Rita Agrawal, *Gandhi and the Psychology of Nonviolence*, vol. 1 (Cham, Switzerland: Palgrave, 2020), 102–103; Puri, *The Tagore-Gandhi Debate*, 57–59.
35. Mohandas K. Gandhi, *Non-Violent Resistance (Satyagraha)* (Mineola, New York: Dover, 2001), 113.

The Way of the Cross and the Good Life

Gandhian Moral Exemplar: The Sthitaprajna

Gandhi's moral exemplar comes from the *Bhagavad-Gita*, which extols the *Sthitaprajna* as a person who attains to the fullness of self-realization.[36] Traditional readings concur that the *Gita* seeks to resolve the dichotomy between action (*pravrtti*) and inaction (*nivrtti*) through cultivating the virtue of non-attachment. Most commentators, however, do not situate such actions in the political sphere. It is here that Gandhi made a significant and radical contribution in reading the Gita by integrating the virtues of non-attachment and nonviolence to political action.[37]

The Sthitaprajna is one who has attained perfect mastery over all feelings and attachments of the inner self. Such a person embodies the Gita's main message of renunciation, which Gandhi considers to be the very essence of all religions.[38] This rendering of the Gita was partly influenced by the Sermon on the Mount.[39] But in contrast to Hindu notions of ascetic withdrawal as an expression of renunciation, Gandhi believed that self-denial should be demonstrated in every aspect of life. By fusing renunciation and action, he was able to justify his political involvements from a religious perspective, seeking to attain self-realization by immersion in political activities in an unattached or disinterested manner.[40]

The Gandhian moral exemplar is therefore a person of action. As Gandhi recounted, he chose the Gita as his primary Hindu text because it concentrated on action, on ethics, and not on other-worldly abstractions.[41] Along with political actions, equally important for Gandhi are the embodied ascetic practices in the public sphere, which cultivated the character and virtues of self-control and renunciation. These public practices included fasting, wearing of loincloth, staying in the colonies of *harijans* (untouchables), and others.[42] It is because of his "practices of austerities, his performance as an ascetic, his devotion to public service" that Gandhi came to be known as *Mahatma* (great souled).[43]

---

36. K. C. Chacko, *Metaphysical Implications of Gandhian Thought* (Delhi: Mittal, 1986), 35.
37. Howard, *Gandhi's Ascetic Activism*, 42, 48–49. Many Hindu scholars objected to Gandhi's nonviolent view of the Gita. J. T. F. Jordens, *Gandhi's Religion: A Homespun Shawl* (London: Macmillan, 1998), 130.
38. Jordens, *Gandhi's Religion*, 135–36.
39. Uma Majmudar, *Gandhi's Pilgrimage of Faith: From Darkness to Light* (Albany: SUNY, 2005), 86–87; Howard, *Gandhi's Ascetic Activism*, 47.
40. Chacko, *Metaphysical Implications of Gandhian Thought*, 35, 39.
41. Jordens, *Gandhi's Religion*, 134; Gandhi, *Collected Works*, vol. 90, 1.
42. Howard, *Gandhi's Ascetic Activism*, 196.
43. Howard, *Gandhi's Ascetic Activism*, 193–94.

JESUS'S WAY OF THE CROSS AND *EUDAIMONIA*

Confucius and Gandhi's ethical accounts, as we have seen, are ethico-political in nature. Like Aristotelian ethics, their accounts are embedded within the particularities of their respective societies. As Asian evangelicals who hope to contribute toward a relevant and transformative understanding of virtue ethics, it is vital to have an adequate awareness of Asian realities. Central to such realities, which Confucius and Gandhi also addressed in their own context, is the anguish of the peoples of Asia.

Asia's Suffering as Context for Evangelical Virtue Ethics

In 1988, Aloysius Pieris made an insightful observation about doing theology in Asia – that poverty and religious diversity mainly constitute the Asian context as the matrix of any truly Asian theology.[44] While the challenges in Asia are multidimensional,[45] Pieris's observation is still valid to this day: one cannot meaningfully do theology and ethics in Asia without adequately dealing with the concrete issues and causes of suffering, poverty, and oppression in the social-political sphere.

Suffering is indeed an enduring reality in Asia. For a majority of Asia's people, suffering is what makes Asian history truly historical and contextual.[46] Sadly, in many Asian countries this history has often been imposed through a lasting legacy of "past and often multiple iterations of political, economic, social, and religious colonization from the West."[47] Various expressions of the *culture of violence* have also led to Asia's suffering: first, in the negative effects of economic globalization that has led to widening the gap between the "haves" and the "have-nots"; second, in the structural violence of tyrannical governments, which often breed abuse of power and violence toward the people as exemplified by the recent killings of thousands of alleged drug users in the Philippines' "War on Drugs";[48] third, structural violence that

---

44. Aloysius Pieris, *An Asian Theology of Liberation* (New York: Orbis, 1988), 69.
45. See Clive S. Chin, "Challenges in Asia," *Journal of Asian Evangelical Theology* 20, no. 2 (2016): 5–24.
46. C. S. Song, *Jesus, the Crucified People* (Minneapolis: Fortress, 1996), 8–9.
47. Aldrin M. Peñamora, "Asia and God's Cruciform Eschatological Reign," in *All Things New: Eschatology in the Majority Word*, eds. Gene Green, Stephen Pardue, and K. K. Yeo (Carlisle: Langham, 2019). See also the insightful analysis of Peter C. Phan in "Jesus Christ with an Asian Face," *Theological Studies* 57, no. 3 (1996): 401.
48. According to human rights groups, around 27,000 have been killed from 2016 to 2019 in the "War on Drugs." The government gives a much lesser figure of 5,526. Matthew Tostevin and Neil Jerome Morales (July 2019); accessed from https://www.reuters.com/article/us-philippines-drugs-idUSKCN1UD1CJ.

results in discrimination based on gender, people with disabilities, race, caste, or class; fourth, violence against our environment;[49] and finally, persecution and suffering because of religious affiliation.[50] Theologies have thus emerged in Asia seeking to grapple with injustice, poverty, and oppression in order to give justice and voice to people who have fallen through the cracks of Asia's societies, such as the Dalits of India, the Minjung of Korea, and the Moros and Lumads of the Philippines.[51]

But while Asia's anguish and the Asian perspective are important in doing Asian theological and ethical reflections, it does not mean that Asian Christian ethics can be construed and constructed using only Asian lenses and resources. It is important to have in view the connectedness of evangelical communities worldwide in addressing such ethical concerns. For indeed – amending what Simon Chan said – a truly Asian evangelical ethics must not only be *from* and *for* Asia, it must also be done *with* and *for* the universal body of Christ.[52]

Ecce Homo! The Suffering God as Moral Exemplar

What would be the shape of an evangelical virtue ethics, then, given the above-mentioned situation in Asia? In his work, *Metaphysics*, Aristotle speaks of a "stone-faced" God, an Unmoved Mover who is eternally solitary, immutable, self-absorbed, and apathetic.[53] A similar posture of apathy can be discerned in Aristotle's notion of *eudaimonia*, for in Aristotle's Greek *polis*, "citizen-class women, all slaves, for the most part all foreigners, and perhaps landless laborers are all excluded . . . successful sociality can be exclusive sociality. The flourishing of one does not require the flourishing of all; it just requires the flourishing of some particular others."[54] In this version of eudaimonia, "unqualified" persons can be treated without regard for their well-being, which is compatible with living virtuously.

---

49. James Haire, "Public Theology – A Latin Captivity of the Church: Violence and Public Theology in the Asian Pacific Context," (2007): 457.
50. Kar Yong Lim, "A Theology of Suffering and Mission for the Asian Church," in *Asian Christian Theology: Evangelical Perspectives*, eds. Timoteo D. Gener and Stephen T. Pardue (Carlisle: Langham, 2019), 181.
51. Dalits are India's lowest caste; the Minjungs are the oppressed of Korea; the Moros and the Lumads are the Muslims and indigenous people of the Philippines.
52. Simon Chan, *Grassroots Asian Theology: Thinking the Faith from the Ground Up* (Downers Grove: InterVarsity Press, 2014), 7.
53. Metaphysics XII.7.5–12, 1074b.33–34.
54. Lisa Tessman, *Burdened Virtues: Virtue Ethics for Liberatory Struggles* (Oxford: Oxford University, 2005), 74.

In the same way, some aspects of Confucian and Gandhian ethics have been criticized for engendering and perpetuating oppressive practices. It is commonly held that Confucianism directly influenced the oppression of Chinese women and horrific practices toward them such as the "binding of feet, female infanticide, loveless marriages, second wives, the widow's obedience to the eldest son, widow suicide, and concubinage."[55] Gandhi, on the other hand, was criticized especially by B. R. Ambedkar for supposedly championing the oppressive caste system or system of the four *varnas*, which excludes the *avarnas* or "untouchables."[56] Christianity is not exempted, for it has also shown that the cross can be as oppressive as the sword, as many Asians have experienced under Western colonizers.

Such a "stone-faced" God and an ethics based on it cannot speak adequately to the suffering people of Asia. Rather, as the Apostle Paul recognized, what gives humanity hope is the fact that Jesus suffered and died for creation's redemption, so that Paul "resolved to know nothing . . . except Jesus Christ and him crucified" (1 Cor 2:2). Dietrich Bonhoeffer's description of Jesus's way of the cross gives hope to suffering and oppressed people: "God lets himself be pushed out of the world on to the cross. . . . Christ helps us, not by virtue of his omnipotence, but by virtue of his weakness and suffering. . . . *only the suffering God can help.*"[57]

Jesus's suffering and death, nonetheless, are usually interpreted by evangelical Christians only in terms of the atonement, having no relevance to social ethics. But as Eben Scheffler remarks, Jesus suffered because he also addressed social and material suffering, which are "part of . . . a *comprehensive view of suffering* in which different types of suffering feature equally."[58] In the Nazareth episode (Luke 4:16–31) where Jesus quoted from Isaiah 61, we thus see Jesus inaugurating his ministry of serving the poor, the prisoners, the blind, and the captives.[59]

---

55. Kelly J. Clark and Robin R. Wang, "A Confucian Defense of Gender Equity," in *Journal of the American Academy of Religion* 72, no. 2 (2004): 395. See "Women Existing for Men: Confucianism and Social Injustice Against Women in China," *Race, Gender and Class* 10, no. 3 (2003): 114–25.
56. Arundhati Roy, "The Doctor and the Saint," Introduction to B. R. Ambedkar, *Annihilation of Caste: Annotated Critical Edition* (London: Verso, 2014), 24.
57. Bonhoeffer, *Letters and Papers from Prison*, 360–61. Italics added.
58. Eben Scheffler, *Suffering in Luke's Gospel* (Zurich: Theologischer Verlag, 1993), 12. Italics in the original. See also Jurie le Roux, "The Different Manifestations of Suffering and the Lukan Jesus," *HTS Theological Studies* 75, no. 3 (2019).
59. Scheffler, *Suffering in Luke*, 41.

The Way of the Cross and the Good Life

Another important feature of Jesus's suffering is its redemptive dimension, a notion that is basically absent in the ethical teachings of Confucius and Gandhi. As K. K. Yeo points out, for Confucius "Heaven" or *tian* was a naturalistic being that does not have a redemptive purpose; it communicates and cares for creation without being directly involved in human affairs.[60] Gandhi gives great importance to suffering (*tapas*) as a key virtue toward attaining Truth (God) in the context of Satyagraha which locates suffering in the action of the person who perseveres and accepts suffering as part of the quest for Truth.[61] Christian Scripture, however, tells us that suffering finds meaning in God's redemptive initiative through Christ, who suffered and died for the redemption of human beings and all creation (John 3:16; Rom 8:22–23).

In the Old Testament, the prophet Isaiah clearly foretold of the Messiah's sufferings as represented by the Suffering Servant (*ebed Yahweh*).[62] Indeed, the Servant's redemptive and vicarious suffering for others is "the most prominent and revolutionary aspect of that figure" (e.g. Luke 22:37; Mark 10:45; 14:24).[63] Throughout his ministry, especially on the cross, Jesus became the embodiment of the Suffering Servant which is the epitome of the Old Testament prophetic paradigm.[64] In the New Testament, Jesus's suffering is linked to the "royal messianic figure," who as Israel's ideal king embodied and fulfilled in a new way, through his death on the cross, the Torah's requirement to "love your neighbor" (Lev 19:18; Gal 5:14), which sets him forth as the central figure for Christian imitation.[65]

Jesus's call to follow his way of the cross, however, is often neglected, if not entirely rejected, as only the biblical teachings on prosperity and triumphalism are recognized. But as Emily M. Townes reflectively observes, Christian triumphalism "gets away from being Christian so quickly. The goal is to win, dominate, conquer, convert – at all costs – even if that cost means lying, stealing, killing, and subverting justice."[66] Similarly, the early church struggled to

---

60. K. K. Yeo, *Musing with Confucius and Paul* (Eugene: Cascade, 2008), 116, 119–20.
61. William Borman, *Gandhi and Non-Violence* (Albany: SUNY, 1986), 78.
62. Stephen Pardue gives an excellent discussion of the arguments surrounding the nature and identity of the Suffering Servant in *The Mind of Christ: Humility and the Intellect in Early Christian Theology* (London: Bloomsbury, 2013), 39–65.
63. R. T. France, *Jesus and the Old Testament: His Application of Old Testament Passages to Himself and His Mission* (Vancouver: Regent, 2000), 130–31.
64. Waldemar Janzen, *Old Testament Ethics: A Paradigmatic Approach* (Lousville: Westminster, 1994), 199–200.
65. Joshua W. Jipp, *Christ is King: Paul's Royal Ideology* (Minneapolis: Fortress, 2015), 60–61.
66. Emily M. Townes, *Womanist Ethics and the Cultural Production of Evil* (New York: Palgrave, 2006), 92.

accept Jesus's suffering as essential to God's plan. As the two disciples on the Emmaus Road said about Jesus: "they crucified him; but we had hoped that he was the one who was going to redeem Israel" (Luke 24:20–21).

Like many Christians today, the two disciples were looking for a kingdom of glory on earth, therefore they failed to discern how Jesus's suffering was crucial to the inauguration of God's kingdom. John H. Yoder's remark is certainly incisive: "The cross is not a detour or a hurdle on the way to the kingdom, nor is it even the way to the kingdom; *it is the kingdom come.*"[67]

Eudaimonia and the Kingdom of God

Indeed, the notion of God's kingdom (*basileia tou theou*) provides us with an evangelical vision of eudaimonia. While awaiting its eschatological consummation, the blessings and righteousness of God's kingdom can already be experienced substantially "in part if not in perfection, in the present order."[68] God's kingdom thus serves as an ethical horizon in view of which our present lives can be ordered,[69] with Jesus's life and teachings unveiling its cruciform shape. Especially through Jesus, we can see that the vision of the kingdom consists of reciprocal well-being, justice, and boundless love, which call us to live in the hope of the transformation of all creation.[70] Ellen Ott Marshall aptly calls God's *basileia* vision the *summum bonum* or the highest good, pointing to God's presence which we experience in acts of love, solidarity, and resistance for others.[71] The vision of God's basileia therefore does not encourage passivity nor is it only descriptive; but it is participative and also *intensely transformative*.

The Gandhian and Confucian notions of eudaimonia, too, seek moral and social transformation, which is premised on the notion that human flourishing is the result mainly of human activities and practices that express the progressive development of human nature. Without nullifying the human side of moral action, the eudaimonia of the kingdom, however, is essentially

---

67. John Howard Yoder, *The Politics of Jesus*, 2nd ed. (Cambridge: Eerdmans, 1994), 51. Italics added.
68. George E. Ladd, *A Theology of the New Testament*, rev. ed. (Grand Rapids: Eerdmans, 1993), 127.
69. Daniel J. Harrington and James F. Keenan, *Jesus and Virtue Ethics* (Chicago: Sheed & Ward, 2002), 44.
70. Marjorie Hewitt Suchocki, *The Fall to Violence* (New York: Continuum, 1994), 160.
71. Ellen Ott Marshall, *Though the Fig Tree Does Not Blossom: Toward a Responsible Christian Theology of Hope* (Eugene: Wipf & Stock, 2015), 70.

a gift from God.[72] The beatitudes (Matt 5:3–12) – considered a treatise on the "good life" – emphasize the divine origin of human flourishing through the use of the Greek term *makarios* (often translated as "blessed") instead of its more philosophical synonym, eudaimonia.[73] In contrast with the virtues of the world, the kingdom virtues in the beatitudes are revolutionary and even paradoxical, for they speak of a happiness that only God can bestow.

Cross-Shaped Virtues of Discipleship

We saw earlier that for Confucius, virtues are cultivated by following the Way (dao) as prescribed through the li or ritual propriety, while for Gandhi it is through the nonviolent way of the Satyagraha. For evangelical Christians, virtues are cultivated through discipleship, through following and participating in the crucified Christ.[74] Bonhoeffer thus defined discipleship as "being bound to the suffering Christ."[75] As such, the virtues of discipleship are necessarily *cruciform*.

This does not mean that suffering is a virtue. It can, however, be virtuous. For as a disposition, virtues require the proper motive to bring an action toward a valuable end, so that if suffering will be virtuous it will depend on the motive of the action and the end for which it is endured.[76] Hence, Augustine defined the virtue of fortitude as "love readily bearing all things for the sake of the loved object."[77] In a similar manner, 1 Peter 2:19 says, "For it is commendable if someone bears up under the pain of unjust suffering because they are conscious of God." In both cases, suffering *by itself* is not "commendable" (Gk. *charis*, grace); it becomes charis only in light of its motive together with its object ("the loved"; "conscious of God"). As Lewis Donelson is correct to

---

72. Carl G. Vaught, *The Sermon on the Mount: A Theological Investigation*, rev. ed. (Waco: Baylor, 2001), 13.
73. Vaught, *Sermon on the Mount*, 12. For a good exposition of the term "makarios," see Jonathan T. Pennington, *The Sermon on the Mount and Human Flourishing* (Grand Rapids: Baker, 2017), 41–68.
74. Pieter Vos insightfully situates the concept of "imitating Christ" as external exemplar within the broader and internal concept of "participating in Christ." Chapter 6 of Vos, *Longing for God: Virtue Ethics After Protestantism* (London: Bloomsbury, 2020), https://ereader.perlego.com/1/book/1811264/15.
75. Dietrich Bonhoeffer, *Discipleship* in *Dietrich Bonhoeffer Works*, vol. 4, eds. Geffrey B. Kelly and John D. Godsey (Minneapolis: Fortress, 2003), 89.
76. Michael S. Brady, *Suffering and Virtue* (Oxford: Oxford University, 2018), 65.
77. Augustine, *The Writings Against the Manichaeans and Against the Donatists* in NPFS 1–04, ed. Philip Schaff (Grand Rapids: Eerdmans, 1925), 74.

point out: "Doing good and suffering for it, out of consciousness of God, in the pattern of Jesus Christ – this is the core of the Christian life."[78]

In view of the suffering and oppression in Asia, cross-shaped virtues can therefore be defined as dispositions that are cultivated by participating in Christ, which are marked by some form of suffering as a result of identifying with oppressed others. Three features express the shape of cruciform virtues: first, they are produced and cultivated through unity or participation in Christ; second, they are self-other regarding; and third, they are characterized by concreteness.

Unity or Participation in Christ

The concept of unity or harmony is a vital element of Asian philosophical and religious traditions. The Confucian and Gandhian ethical project exemplified it in the quest for communal harmony, which coheres with the broader Asian vision of unity as "an undifferentiated spiritual unity or harmony of nature, man, spirits, and gods."[79] In this schema, the moral life is one of *self*-cultivation that is aimed at attaining harmony, which differs substantially from an evangelical perspective that sees the moral life mainly in terms of *discipleship as participation in Christ*.

From this perspective, the moral life does not have "self" as its starting point; it is initiated and propelled from a Christological center, in and through Christ.[80] What makes the Christian moral life possible, says Jordan Wessling, is the fact that Jesus became incarnate. For it was Jesus's way of the cross that enables God, through the work of the Holy Spirit, to share intimately with believers the life and the virtues that Christ perfectly attained, which in turn empowers believers to fully manifest love for God and neighbors.[81] The primacy of divine action does not negate the believer's agency, for they actively partake in God's act of "gift-giving" through their acts of service for others as a mark

---

78. Lewis R. Donelson, *I & II Peter and Jude* (Louisville: Westminster John Knox Press, 2010), 82–83.
79. M. M. Thomas, *Man and the Universe of Faiths* (Madras: CLS, 1975), 33–34.
80. Autumn Alcott Ridenour, "Union with Christ: Participation as the Ground of Christian Ethics in Augustine and Reformed Augustinianisms," in *Scripture, Tradition, and Reason in Christian Ethics*, eds. Bharat Ranganathan and Derek Alan Woodard-Lehman (Cham, Switzerland: Springer, 2019), 199.
81. Jordan Wessling, *Love Divine: A Systematic Account of God's Love for Humanity* (Oxford: Oxford University, 2020), 241–42.

of their "gift-receiving."[82] Jürgen Moltmann describes this mutual indwelling this way: "God is in Christ – Christ is in God; Christ is for us – we are in Christ; God's Spirit dwells in us – we live in the Holy Spirit."[83] Discipleship as participation in Christ therefore means hearing and following God's call to suffer with and to be in solidarity with the suffering God and with those for whom he suffers.

"SelfOther" Regarding

Cross-shaped virtues are other regarding. They are self-regarding as well. Or more creatively, "SelfOther"-regarding.[84] This intertwined SelfOther relation can be seen in the biblical command to "love your neighbor as yourself" (Lev 19:18; Matt 22:39; cf. Luke 6:31). The Confucian "golden/silver rule" similarly states, "What you do not want others to do to you, do not do to others" (*Analects* 12.2; 15.24).[85] Both "rules" certainly specify acting for the well-being of others who are extensions of oneself. In Confucius's ren (humaneness), however, concern for others is strongest toward family members, whereas Jesus's "golden rule" requires radically going beyond filial and social differentiations in fulfilling our moral obligations to others.[86]

It is this "going beyond," as exemplified by the "good Samaritan" (Luke 10:25–37), that defines cruciform virtues as dispositions marked by sensitivity to other people's sufferings, and solidarity toward the excluded, oppressed, and even the enemy. Such virtues, says Lisa Tessman, are "burdened virtues," because they are cultivated in liberatory struggles against injustice and oppression that often detract from the agent's own flourishing.[87] In faithfully following Jesus in discipleship, however, believers can only flourish by taking on other people's burdens as if they are one's own. A Christian view of

---

82. Vos, *Longing for God*; John M. G. Barclay, *Paul and the Gift* (Grand Rapids: Eerdmans, 2015), 4, 361.
83. Jürgen Moltmann, *Arise! God's Future for Humanity and the Earth* (Minneapolis: Fortress, 2010), 112.
84. Merlinda Bobis, "Weeping is Singing": After the War, a Transnational Lament" in *At the Limits of Justice: Women of Colour on Terror*, ed. Suvendrini Perera and Sherene H. Razack (Toronto: University of Toronto, 2014), 243. SelfOther describes the Filipino concept of kapwa, or the identity of the Self with the Other.
85. Confucius, *The Analects of Confucius*, trans. Burton Watson (New York: Columbia University Press, 2007), 80, 109. The "Golden Rule" is the positive form of ethical conduct, while the "Silver Rule" is the negative.
86. K. K. Yeo, *Musing with Confucius and Paul: Toward a Chinese Christian Theology* (Eugene: Cascade, 2008), 300. See also Alan Kirk, "'Love Your Enemies,' the Golden Rule, and Ancient Reciprocity (Luke 6:27–35)," *Journal of Biblical Literature* 122, no. 4 (Winter 2003): 684–86.
87. Tessman, *Burdened Virtues*, 95–96; 116 ff.

eudaimonia therefore consists of living responsibly for others, which is marked by the cruciform virtue of compassion or the disposition of identifying with the suffering of oppressed others, and by the willingness to bear with the oppressed the burdens of their oppression.[88] Maureen O'Connell aptly remarks that "[c]ompassion is not comfortable and private but rather dangerous and political."[89] Thus, in demonstrating compassion Christians may themselves be seen as members of the "community of the guilty," but as Bonhoeffer points out, genuinely loving others entails entering such a community for their sake.[90]

In the Philippines, part of the community of the guilty are those suffering from drug addiction. Since 2016, thousands of alleged drug addicts have been killed without the benefit of due process under the Philippine government's "War on Drugs" program.[91] Sadly, very few Christians in the country voiced out their concern against this terrible bloodshed. Many believe that the brutal killings are justified, and anyway Scripture mandates Christians to simply submit to the governing authorities. Similar postures can also be discerned in many Christian circles toward the Muslim "other," even toward those experiencing severe oppression such as the Rohingyas of Myanmar. Dalit Christian thinkers thus aptly emphasize an ethic of solidarity and identification with the oppressed, calling on the church in India to join Jesus "outside the camp" and bear the disgrace with him as portrayed in Hebrews 13:11–13. Such an ethic, says Peniel Rajkumar, is what gives the church its "Christian character."[92]

Concreteness

In one of his works, C. S. Song recounts how a youth exposure trip in the slums of Bangalore, India, opened the eyes of the participants to the realities of poverty and suffering, and shattered their theological innocence.[93] Indeed, as Jesus became incarnate, the cultivation of cruciform virtues requires

---

88. C. Leonard Allen, *The Cruciform Church* (Abilene: ACU Press, 2016), 272–273; https://play.google.com/books/reader?id=261YDwAAQBAJ&pg=GBS.PT271.w.0.0.0.0.1_97&printsec=frontcover.
89. Maureen H. O'Connell, *Compassion: Loving Our Neighbor in an Age of Globalization* (Maryknoll: Orbis, 2009), 3.
90. Dietrich Bonhoeffer, *Ethics* in *Dietrich Bonhoeffer Works*, Vol. 6, ed. Clifford J. Green, Geffrey B. Kelly, and John D. Godsey (Minneapolis: Fortress, 2005), 234–35.
91. See Peter Bouckaert, "License to Kill," *Human Rights Watch*, March 2017, accessed August 8, 2021, https://www.hrw.org/report/2017/03/02/license-kill/philippine-police-killings-dutertes-war-drugs.
92. Peniel Rajkumar, "Christian Ethics in Asia," in *The Cambridge Companion to Christian Ethics*, 2nd ed., ed. Robin Gill (Cambridge: Cambridge University, 2012), 138.
93. C. S. Song, *Jesus and the Reign of God* (Minneapolis: Fortress, 1993), 80–81, 85.

concreteness; it requires coming face-to-face with the "frightening" realities of life. For cruciform virtues cannot be habituated *only* by academic abstractions, theological concepts, or philosophical frameworks.[94] Gandhi's emphasis on concrete practices in fighting oppression is therefore highly instructive for the foundational virtues of Satyagraha can be cultivated only by facing the enemy. Martin Luther King Jr. also valued concreteness in his ethical approach, and reflectively said:

> Living through the actual experience of the protest, . . . [m]any of the things that I had not cleared up intellectually concerning nonviolence were now solved in the sphere of practical action.[95]

In Asia's multicultural and religiously pluriform context, one tangible practice that aids in fostering a deeper understanding of religious "others" is interreligious dialogue[96] for religious prejudice and violence have been common features of the Asian landscape. Many religious minorities, including Christians, suffer religious and political prejudice and persecution, especially in the Southeast where Christianity is often viewed with distrust due to its association with the checkered history of Western colonialism in the region.[97] Dialogue in its various forms can help build bridges that can lead to cooperation and reconciliation, and essential to this are the cruciform virtues of peacemaking, remorse, and forgiveness.

Peacemaking, says Stanley Hauerwas, is "the very form of the church insofar as the church is the form of the one who 'is our peace,'" as Paul writes in Ephesians 2:13. Having its origin in the church, the virtue of peacemaking is community-specific, nurtured, and cultivated within the church as a truthful and forgiven community. From within the church, it is then extended toward other persons and communities as a way of confronting injustice and

---

94. Phil Zylla, *Virtue as Consent to Being* (Eugene: Pickwick, 2011), 117.
95. Martin Luther King, Jr., *Stride Toward Freedom* (Boston: Beacon, 2010), 89.
96. On the various forms of dialogue see Aemy Elyani Mat Zain et al., "Inter-Religious Dialogue: The Perspective of Malaysian Contemporary Muslim Thinkers," *International Journal of Islamic Thought* 5 (June 2014): 1–9. For a Christian perspective see S. Wesley Ariarajah, *Strangers or Co-Pilgrims? The Impact of Interfaith Dialogue on Christian Faith and Practice* (Minneapolis: Fortress, 2017).
97. Robbie B. H. Goh, *Christianity in Southeast Asia* (Singapore: ISEAS, 2005), 74–76. See also Patrick Ziltener and Daniel Kunzler, "Impacts of Colonialism – A Research Survey," *American Sociological Association* 19, no. 2 (2013): 290–311; Karen Vallgarda, "Were Christian Missionaries Colonizers?" *Interventions* (2016): 1–22.

offenses with the offer of reconciliation.[98] As such, the virtue of peacemaking is intertwined and further elaborated by the virtues of remorse and forgiveness.

In contrast to the Christian view, the ancient Greek philosophers had no place for an ethic of remorse or repentance, for they saw virtues as stable dispositions, and remorse expresses inconsistency that originates from a flawed character.[99] Gandhi gives repentance an important place in his ethics, which he demonstrated through fasting, even fasting unto death to atone for wrongs especially done by others.[100] While Gandhi's "death fast" from a biblical view violates the sanctity of life, his outlook that remorse is not a deficiency resonates with evangelical convictions. As a virtue, remorse expresses a person's moral resolve not to repeat the act of wrongdoing, and to sincerely carry out the necessary reparation,[101] which Peter exemplified after betraying Jesus (John 21:15–19).

Equally important is the cruciform and political virtue of forgiveness. But who is responsible for crimes committed by nations? Can a collective entity like a nation forgive and be forgiven? Can nations extend forgiveness to an individual, and vice versa? Such questions probe whether forgiveness can truly be a "political virtue."[102] The Jewish philosopher Hannah Arendt believes forgiveness is necessary in the sphere of political action, and that its discoverer is Jesus Christ.[103] But while forgiveness may not come from every member of the group, collective forgiveness is still possible through the vicarious actions of authorized representatives, for example, in 1970 West German Chancellor Willy Brandt knelt in repentance in Poland for the crimes committed by Nazi Germany against the Polish people during the Second World War. Such actions help create "a liberating, compassionate politics . . . for greater mutual

---

98. Stanley Hauerwas, "Peacemaking," *The Furrow* 36, no. 10 (1985): 605–7, 611–12.
99. Anthony Bash, *Remorse: A Christian Perspective* (Eugene: Cascade, 2020), 54, 80; *NE* IX.4.1166.19, 29.
100. Anupama Rao, *The Caste Question: Dalits and the Politics of Modern India* (Berkley: University of California, 2009), 163–65.
101. Jacob Neusner, *The Theology of the Oral Torah: Revealing the Justice of God* (London: McGill-Queen's University, 1999), 511.
102. Anthony Bash, *Forgiveness and Christian Ethics* (Cambridge: Cambridge University, 2007), 111–140. Although he did not elaborate in terms of virtue ethics, Donald W. Shriver considers forgiveness a political virtue. Shriver, *An Ethic for Enemies: Forgiveness in Politics* (New York: Oxford, 1998), 7, 11. L. Gregory Jones considers forgiveness as a "craft," which is similar to Alasdair MacIntyre's concept of "practice." In Jones, *Embodying Forgiveness: A Theological Analysis* (Grand Rapids: Eerdmans, 1995), 226 ff.
103. Hannah Arendt, *The Human Condition*, 2nd ed. (Chicago: University of Chicago, 1958), 238–39, 241.

understanding and political reconciliation."[104] As a Christian political virtue, forgiveness means foregoing vengeful acts, for its goal is not punishment or restitution, but a restored community based on the recognition that all of us are in need of God's forgiveness and mercy.[105]

The virtues of peacemaking, remorse, and forgiveness expressed through dialogue thus play an important part in Christian–Muslim relations in the Philippines. It has also shaped political discourses in the recently established autonomous Bangsamoro government, which created an important mechanism to address historical injustices.[106] These virtues therefore do not lead to forgetting the past; they direct people to remember the concreteness of oppression and injustice, to recognize deeply that they take place in time, to real people in actual situations. As God's cruciform people in Asia, we are thus called to address the injustices of the past toward a healed and transformed future concretely and in no other way.

CONCLUSION

We asked at the beginning of this essay: What is the good life? Perhaps we could also add, "What is the way to it?" We have seen how both Confucius and Gandhi sought the moral-political transformation of their respective societies. With Jesus as our Lord, Savior, and moral exemplar, evangelical Christians in Asia also cannot afford to be unmoved by the iterations of injustice, oppression, and suffering in their own contexts. As Alasdair MacIntyre reminds us, moral traditions are for the most part strengthened, weakened, or even destroyed by the exercise or non-exercise of the virtues.[107] Of course, it is not just our particular faith tradition, important though it may be, which is our main concern in living a virtuous life. What we are most concerned with is our obedience in discipleship, in hearing and heeding the call to responsible action for the sake of others within the limits, values, and goals determined by Jesus as the one who calls.[108] For the central point of evangelical virtue ethics

---

104. Mark R. Amstutz, *The Healing of Nations: The Promise and Limits of Political Forgiveness* (New York: Rowman & Littlefield, 2005), 73–74, 79.
105. Jeffrie G. Murphy, "Forgiveness and Resentment," in Jeffrie G. Murphy, *Forgiveness and Mercy* (Cambridge: Cambridge University, 1988), 29–32.
106. The Bangsamoro Autonomous Region in Muslim Mindanao (BARMM) was officially established in January 2019. A few years earlier, the Transitional Justice and Reconciliation Commission was formed.
107. Alasdair MacIntyre, *After Virtue*, 3rd ed. (Notre Dame: University of Notre Dame, 2007), 223.
108. Bonhoeffer, *Ethics*, 259.

is about participating in the "Way" (Acts 24:14). Only by abiding in him are we able to fully grasp that it is when we live our lives helping secure the good life of others – even suffering for them that we can truly attain ours.

QUESTIONS FOR DISCUSSION

1. How does your Christian faith help in shaping your view of the good life?
2. Can you identify urgent ethical issues your community or nation are facing that require an adequate biblical response from your country's evangelical leaders?
3. Name the virtues that you consider essential for the moral-political transformation of your country. What practices can help inculcate those virtues?

BIBLIOGRAPHY

Ames, Roger T. *Confucian Role Ethics: A Vocabulary*. Hong Kong: Chinese University Press, 2011.

Aristotle. *Nicomachean Ethics*. In *The Basic Works of Aristotle*. Edited by Richard McKeon. New York: Random House, 1941.

Barclay, John M. G. *Paul and the Gift*. Grand Rapids: Eerdmans, 2015.

Bash, Anthony. *Remorse: A Christian Perspective*. Eugene: Cascade Books, 2020.

Bobis, Merlinda. "Weeping is Singing": After the War, a Transnational Lament." In *At the Limits of Justice: Women of Colour on Terror*. Edited by Suvendrini Perera and Sherene H. Razack, 237–262. Toronto: University of Toronto Press, 2014.

Bonhoeffer, Dietrich. *Ethics*. In *Dietrich Bonhoeffer Works*, Vol. 6. Edited by Clifford J. Green. Minneapolis: Fortress Press, 2005.

———. *Letters and Papers from Prison*. Edited by Eberhard Bethge. New York: Macmillan, 1972.

Borman, William. *Gandhi and Non-Violence*. Albany: State of University of New York Press, 1986.

Brady, Michael S. *Suffering and Virtue*. Oxford: Oxford University Press, 2018.

Chacko, K. C. *Metaphysical Implications of Gandhian Thought*. Delhi: Mittal, 1986.

Chan, Joseph. "Is There a Confucian Perspective on Social Justice?" In *Western Political Thought in Dialogue with Asia*. Edited by Takashi Shogimen and Cary J. Nederman, 261–278. New York: Lexington Books, 2009.

Chan, Simon. *Grassroots Asian Theology: Thinking the Faith from the Ground Up*. Downers Grove: InterVarsity Press, 2014.

Clark, Kelly J., and Robin R. Wang. "A Confucian Defense of Gender Equity." *Journal of the American Academy of Religion* 72, no. 2 (2004): 395–422.

Confucius. *The Analects of Confucius*. Translated by Burton Watson. New York: Columbia University Press, 2007.

Cua, Antonio S. "The Conceptual Framework of Confucian Ethical Thought." *Journal of Chinese Philosophy* 23, no. 2 (1996): 153–74.

Devji, Faisal. *The Impossible Indian: Gandhi and the Temptation of Violence*. Cambridge: Harvard University Press, 2012.

Donelson, Lewis R. *I & II Peter and Jude*. Louisville: Westminster John Knox Press, 2010.

Fingarette, Herbert. "Human Community as Holy Rite: An Interpretation of Confucius' Analects." *Harvard Theological Review* 59, no. 1 (January 1966): 53–67.

France, R. T. *Jesus and the Old Testament: His Application of Old Testament Passages to Himself and His Mission*. Vancouver: Regent College Publishing, 2000.

Gandhi, Mohandas K. *An Autobiography or the Story of My Experiments with Truth*. Translated by Mahadev Desai. New Haven: Yale University Press, 2018.

———. *Non-Violent Resistance (Satyagraha)*. Mineola, New York: Dover Publications, 2001.

Gao, Xiongya. "Women Existing for Men: Confucianism and Social Injustice Against Women in China." *Race, Gender and Class* 10, no. 3 (2003): 114–25.

Goh, Robbie B. H. *Christianity in Southeast Asia*. Singapore: ISEAS Publications, 2005.

Haire, James. "Public Theology – A Latin Captivity of the Church: Violence and Public Theology in the Asian Pacific Context." *International Journal of Public Theology* (2007): 455–70.

Harrington, Daniel J., and James F. Keenan. *Jesus and Virtue Ethics: Building Bridges Between New Testament Studies and Moral Theology*. Lanham: Rowman & Littlefield Publishers, 2002.

Hauerwas, Stanley. *The Hauerwas Reader*. Edited by John Berkman and Michael Cartwright. Durham: Duke University Press, 2001.

Howard, Veena R. *Gandhi's Ascetic Activism: Renunciation and Social Action*. Albany: State University of New York Press, 2013.

Janzen, Waldemar. *Old Testament Ethics: A Paradigmatic Approach*. Louisville: Westminster/John Knox Press, 1994.

Jipp, Joshua W. *Christ is King: Paul's Royal Ideology*. Minneapolis: Fortress Press, 2015.

Jordens, J. T. F. *Gandhi's Religion: A Homespun Shawl*. London: Macmillan, 1998.

Kirk, Alan. "'Love Your Enemies,' the Golden Rule, and Ancient Reciprocity (Luke 6:27–35)." *Journal of Biblical Literature* 122, no. 4 (Winter 2003): 667–86.

Kool, V. K., and Rita Agrawal. *Gandhi and the Psychology of Nonviolence*, vol. 1. Cham, Switzerland: Palgrave Macmillan, 2020.

Ladd, George E. *A Theology of the New Testament*, rev. ed. Grand Rapids: Eerdmans, 1993.
le Roux, Jurie. "The Different Manifestations of Suffering and the Lukan Jesus." *HTS Theological Studies* 75, no. 3 (2019). https://hts.org.za/index.php/hts/article/view/5662/13855.
Li, Chenyang. "The Philosophy of Harmony in Classical Confucianism." *Philosophy Compass* 3, no. 3 (2008): 423–35.
Lim, Kar Yong. "A Theology of Suffering and Mission for the Asian Church." In *Asian Christian Theology: Evangelical Perspectives*. Edited by Timoteo D. Gener and Stephen T. Pardue, 181–198. Carlisle: Langham Global Library, 2019.
Loy, Hui-chieh. "Classical Confucianism as Virtue Ethics." In *The Handbook of Virtue Ethics*. Edited by Stan van Hooft, 285–93. Durham: Acumen Press, 2014.
MacIntyre, Alasdair. *After Virtue*, 3rd ed. Notre Dame: University of Notre Dame Press, 2007.
Majmudar, Uma. *Gandhi and Rajchandra: The Making of the Mahatma*. London: Lexington Books, 2020.
Marshal, Ellen Ott. *Though the Fig Tree Does Not Blossom: Toward a Responsible Christian Theology of Hope*. Eugene: Wipf & Stock Publishers, 2015.
Moltmann, Jürgen. *Arise! God's Future for Humanity and the Earth*. Minneapolis: Fortress Press, 2010.
Morimoto, Anri. "Contextualised and Cumulative: Tradition, Orthodoxy, and Identity from the Perspective of Asian Theology." *Studies in World Christianity* 15, no. 1 (2009): 65–80.
O'Connell, Maureen H. *Compassion: Loving Our Neighbor in an Age of Globalization*. Maryknoll: Orbis Books, 2009.
Pardue, Stephen. *The Mind of Christ: Humility and the Intellect in Early Christian Theology*. London: Bloomsbury T&T Clark, 2013.
Peñamora, Aldrin M. "God's *Basileia* in Asia's *Res Publica*: Situating the Sacred in the Public Sphere." In *Asian Christian Theology: Evangelical Perspectives*. Edited by Timoteo D. Gener and Stephen T. Pardue, 245–264. Carlisle: Langham Global Library, 2019.
Pennington, Jonathan T. *The Sermon on the Mount and Human Flourishing*. Grand Rapids: Baker Academic, 2017.
Phan, Peter C. "Jesus Christ with an Asian Face." *Theological Studies* 57, no. 3 (1996): 399–430.
Pieris, Aloysius. *An Asian Theology of Liberation*. New York: Orbis Books, 1988.
Plato. *Protagoras*. In *Plato: Complete Works*. Edited by John Cooper, 746–90. Indianapolis: Hackett Publishing Company, 1997.

Rainey, Lee Dian. *Confucius and Confucianism: The Essentials*. Oxford: Wiley-Blackwell, 2010.

Rajkumar, Peniel. "Christian Ethics in Asia." In *The Cambridge Companion to Christian Ethics*, 2nd ed. Edited by Robin Gill. Cambridge: Cambridge University Press, 2012.

Ridenour, Autumn Alcott. "Union with Christ: Participation as the Ground of Christian Ethics in Augustine and Reformed Augustinianisms." In *Scripture, Tradition, and Reason in Christian Ethics*. Edited by Bharat Ranganathan and Derek Alan Woodard-Lehman, 187–206. Cham, Switzerland: Springer Nature, 2019.

Roy, Arundhati Roy. "The Doctor and the Saint." In B. R. Ambedkar, *Annihilation of Caste: Annotated Critical Edition*. London: Verso Books, 2014.

Scheffler, Eben. *Suffering in Luke's Gospel*. Zurich: Theologischer Verlag, 1993.

Sim, May. "Rethinking Virtue Ethics and Social Justice with Aristotle and Confucius." *Asian Philosophy: An International Journal of the Philosophical Traditions of the East* 20, no. 2 (July 2010): 195–213.

Slingerland, Edward. "Virtue Ethics, the *Analects*, and the Problem of Commensurability." *Journal of Religious Ethics* 29, no. 1 (2001): 97–125.

Song, C. S. *Jesus and the Reign of God*. Minneapolis: Fortress Press, 1993.

Song, Jinhua Song, and Xiaomin Jao. "Confucius' *Junzi*: The Conceptions of Self in Confucian," *Educational Philosophy and Theory* 50, no. 6 (November 2017): 1–9.

Sonnleitner, Michael W. "Gandhian Satyagraha and Swaraj: A Hierarchical Perspective." *Peace and Change* 14, no. 1 (January 1989): 3–24.

Suchocki, Marjorie Hewitt. *The Fall to Violence*. New York: Continuum, 1994.

Tan, Charlene. "Understanding Creativity in East Asia: Insights from Confucius' Concept of Junzi." *International Journal of Design Creativity and Innovation* 4, no. 1 (2016): 51–61.

———. *Confucius*. London: Bloomsbury Academic, 2013.

Tessman, Lisa. *Burdened Virtues: Virtue Ethics for Liberatory Struggles*. Oxford: Oxford University Press, 2005.

Tostevin, Matthew, and Neil Jerome Morales. "War on Numbers," *Reuters* (July 2019), https://www.reuters.com/article/us-philippines-drugs-idUSKCN1UD1CJ.

Townes, Emily M. *Womanist Ethics and the Cultural Production of Evil*. New York: Palgrave Macmillan, 2006.

Vallgarda, Karen. "Were Christian Missionaries Colonizers?" *Interventions* (2016): 1–22.

Vaught, Carl G. *The Sermon on the Mount: A Theological Investigation*, rev. ed. Waco: Baylor University Press, 2001.

Wei-Ming, Tu. *Confucian Thought: Selfhood as Creative Transformation*. New York: State University of New York Press, 1985.
Wessling, Jordan. *Love Divine: A Systematic Account of God's Love for Humanity*. Oxford: Oxford University Press, 2020.
Yeo, K. K. *Musing with Confucius and Paul*. Eugene: Cascade Books, 2008.
Yoder, John Howard. *The Politics of Jesus*, 2nd ed. Cambridge: Eerdmans, 1994.
Yu, Jiyuan. *The Ethics of Confucius and Aristotle: Mirrors of Virtue*. New York: Routledge, 2007.
Ziltener, Patrick, and Daniel Kunzler. "Impacts of Colonialism – A Research Survey." *American Sociological Association* 19, no. 2 (2013): 290–311.

PART 2

ETHICS IN THE WORLD

CHAPTER 9
GOD'S STORY OF LIFE

Themes for an Asian Creation Care Ethics

Athena E. Gorospe

This essay will focus on the biblical story that shapes the moral vision of God's people and undergirds their actions in relation to the environment. In making the case for the value of narrative in ethics, Alasdair McIntyre asserts, "I can only answer the question 'What am I to do?' if I can answer the prior question 'Of what story or stories do I find myself a part?'"[1] In the same way, Stanley Hauerwas contends that moral vision, and hence, character, is formed by stories and metaphors because they suggest ways of seeing the world.[2]

However, it is important to tell the biblical story in ways that resonate with the plurality of contexts in Asia and the shared challenges that the region faces. In an earlier article, I proposed that the theme of life may be a major theme that resonates best with the Asian psyché because a reverence for life is characteristic of many Asian religions and cultures;[3] moreover, life in many parts of Asia is often under threat.

The following story is focused on the creation stories in Genesis, and thus incomplete. But even a partial telling already opens perspectives that show the importance of creation care in living out the gospel in Asia today. Ultimately, story must shape our "walk" – our way of life as individuals and communities – and how this is embodied in our corporate practices and structures.

GOD AND THE STORY OF LIFE

The story of life begins in the two creation accounts of Genesis (chapters 1–2). But unlike the story of life in science documentaries, life is connected with

---
1. Alasdair McIntyre, *After Virtue: A Study in Moral Theory* (Notre Dame: University of Notre Dame Press, 1981), 201.
2. Stanley Hauerwas, *Vision and Virtue: Essays in Christian Ethical Reflection* (Notre Dame: Fides Publishers, 1974), 36, 71.
3. Athena Gorospe, "Evangelicals and the Environment: Beyond Stewardship," *Evangelical Review of Theology* 37 (Jul 2013): 264–66.

the central character – God – who creates life and then puts up structures that would sustain, preserve, and renew life.

God as the Source of Life

The source of life is God; it is by God's intention, word, and work that the world and its inhabitants come into being. Life is not a product of impersonal elements that coincidentally interacted with each other.

However, the Christian tradition regards creation as a trinitarian process, "God the Father creates through the Son in the power of the Holy Spirit."[4] Hence, the book of John identifies the Word with Jesus, by whom all things were made, and the one that gives life and light to all (John 1:1–4). In the same way, the Spirit (*ruah*) is present in creation (Gen 1:2) and it is by God's Spirit that life is given to all. "When you send your Spirit, they are created, and you renew the face of the ground" (Ps 104:30; see also Gen 1:30; 2:7).

Sustainability and Diversity

Prior to creating earth's inhabitants, God sets up an environment that would be conducive to sustaining life. God calls forth light and separates it from darkness (Gen 1:3–4). God also creates the greater and lesser lights (i.e., the sun and moon) (Gen 1:14–19). While living creatures need sunlight to survive, their metabolic processes continue in darkness, which is as important to their growth and well-being as daylight.

God also puts up an abode (Gen 1:6–10) – the sky, land, and sea – even before creating the ones who were going to live in them. God puts as much careful thought and care in creating the environment as in the creatures themselves, for the latter need to live in a habitat that would enable them not only to survive, but to thrive. In Genesis 2, the home of God's creatures is a garden, and God is pictured as a gardener who gets his hands dirty planting fruit trees, which are pleasant to the sight and good for food (2:8–9).[5] By planting the garden in a place of many rivers, God ensures that the trees will have adequate water to sustain them.[6]

God populates the environment – first with vegetation (Gen 1:11–12), then with sea creatures and birds (1:20–22), followed by domestic and wild

---

4. Jürgen Moltmann, *The Source of Life: The Holy Spirit and the Theology of Life* (Minneapolis: Fortress, 1997), 115.
5. John Goldingay, *Old Testament Theology, vol. 1: Israel's Gospel* (Downers Grove; InterVarsity Press 2003), 117–18.
6. Cf. Ps 66:9.

animals – after which God creates human beings (1:25–27). There are notable features of this creative process. First, God includes a self-reproducing and self-perpetuating dynamic in the act of creation. Then God said, "Let the land produce vegetation: seed-bearing plants and trees on the land that bear fruit with seed in it, according to their various kinds." And it was so (Gen 1:11). Plants and trees have seed and fruit so that they carry within themselves the stamp of their species to the next generation, ensuring that their species would not die out.

For birds, sea, and land creatures, including humans, there is the blessing to "be fruitful and multiply" (Gen 1:22, 28). Blessing has to do with the "bestowal of a life-force, related to generativity, birth, and reproduction," "an act in which the power-for-life is transmitted."[7] Human beings and animals have the capacity to reproduce life, so that their "kind" would not become extinct. This implies a limit to overgrowth of one species that could result in an unsustainable environment that threatens the existence of others.

The theme of blessing continues in the rest of the Old Testament as life goes on with its ebbs and flows. In the patriarchal narratives, God's blessing is seen in the promise to Abraham, which is worked out in relation to his family, as their offspring multiply and are saved from threats to the continuity of life, such as barrenness and famine. In the life of Israel, blessing is associated with keeping the covenant, which results not only in the blessing of progeny, but also in the blessing of the land, with its crops and flocks (Deut 7:13–16; 28:1–14). Nevertheless, the scope of blessing is not just the people of God or humanity. Blessing is God's means of preserving the world through its various rhythms, not only in the cycles of nature and seasons, but in the quiet, continuous process of birth, growth, maturity, weakening and renewal, decline, and eventual death.[8] The universality of blessing is reiterated in what Jesus said about God's providence extended to all, causing "his sun to rise on the evil and the good, and sends rain on the righteous and the unrighteous" (Matt 5:45).

Genesis 1 also emphasizes the variety and specificity in the earth's inhabitants. A repeated phrase is "according to its kind" (*l'mino*).[9] The phrase indicates the way God deliberately creates a multiplicity of life forms. However, it is not only diversity and specificity that is being accentuated, but fecundity.

---

7. Walter Brueggemann, *Theology of the Old Testament* (Minneapolis: Fortress, 1997), 165.
8. Claus Westermann, *Elements of Old Testament Theology* (Atlanta: John Knox, 1978), 88, 103, 112.
9. Gen 1:11, 12, 21, 24, 25.

The picture is one of fullness, abundance – "Let the water teem with living creatures . . ." (Gen 1:20). God does not stint in creating the world. Like a master painter who is generous with color yet puts in a lot of distinctive features, we see a world of all sorts of hue, intricate details, and dynamism that conveys liveliness and vibrancy. This is seen particularly in God's last speech in the book of Job (Job 40:6–41:34) in which God names and describes in detail the non-human creation, showing clearly how the Maker delights in them. Thus, the psalmist exclaims, "O LORD, how manifold are your works! In wisdom you have made them all; the earth is full of your creatures" (Ps 104:24 NRSV).

Death that Leads to New Life

But all great paintings have darkness and shadows, and the world which God has created has shadows too. Even though not explicitly stated, death is assumed to be taking place. For the seeds to sprout new life, they need to be buried into the ground and "die." In order to have the nourishment to continue living, animals and human beings eat herbage, so that "the life of the world is dependent on death."[10] However, the function of death in the initial creation is to produce new life; it is not a judgment or a terminal event. Thus, in the genealogies, we see the continuity of life; there are deaths, but life begins again in new birth.

The pre-sin world which God has created, although "good," according to Fretheim, is not perfect, in the sense that it is complete and needs no further work. It continues to develop through a creative process in which new landscapes can only be formed through natural activities that may involve destruction. Thus, natural disasters like earthquakes, volcanic eruptions, and storms are all part of the "good" world that God has made – they are integral to the cycle of life.[11] When human beings inhabit the space where a natural process is occurring (e.g. an earthquake), there is potential for harm and death, which are unrelated to sin and judgment.

That the initial creation was intended by God to improve further is implied in the command to human beings to "be fruitful and increase in number" and "to fill the earth and subdue it" (Gen 1:28a). There is to be continued growth and human beings are given a key role in an earth that is still becoming, even

---

10. Goldingay, *Old Testament Theology*, vol 1, 95.
11. Terence Fretheim, *Creation Untamed: The Bible, God, and Natural Disasters* (Grand Rapids: Baker Academic, 2010), 9–37.

as the initial foundation and structures have been put in place. As Fretheim argues, the command "to subdue" implies a world still in process, in which human beings play a part in bringing God's creation to its full potential.[12] However, the command "to rule" and "to subdue" has been construed in more than one way.

The Role of the Human

The command "to subdue" and "to rule" ("have dominion") (Gen 1:26, 28) has become controversial due to it being used as a license for human beings to exploit nature in whatever way they please. Because of this, Christianity has been blamed for being the root of the ecological crisis because the above passage seems to justify humanity's superiority and control over nature.[13] Indeed, Christian theology, as developed in the West, imbued by Greek philosophy and shaped by modernity's optimism in regard to the advancement of science and technology, has espoused a "dominion theology" that supports the unbridled utilization of nature for the sake of human progress.[14]

Certainly, the Hebrew terms have forceful meanings. The word for "rule" (*radah*; 1:26, 28) can refer to the general governance of the king over his subjects (Ps 72:8), but in some instances has the nuance of oppressive control (Lev 26:17, cf. 25:53; Neh 9:28), or the sense of "to prevail over" (Isa 14:2; Ps 49:14). On the other hand, "to subdue" (*kavash*) also has the same forceful sense of "bringing something into subjection" and has been used in the context of subjecting people to slavery (Jer 34:11, 16; Neh 5:5; 2 Chr 28:10), mastering sin (Mic 7:19), and imposing oneself on another (Esth 7:8). Thus, it is not surprising that some see legitimacy in the unbridled dominance of human beings over the non-human creation, if one were to look at the role of the human based on Genesis 1:26–28 alone.

In reaction, other Christians have argued that the mandate to rule over creation in Genesis 1:26–28 does not mean domination but responsible stewardship.[15] Thus, "to rule" and "subdue" have the sense of "to manage with care" on God's behalf who has entrusted to human beings the stewardship of God's creation. Indeed, in contrast to Genesis 1:26–28, the verbs in the responsibility

---

12. Fretheim, *Creation Untamed*, 13–15.
13. Lynn White, Jr., "The Historical Roots of our Ecologic Crisis," *Science* 155 (1967), 1205–207.
14. Richard Bauckham, "Dominion Interpreted – A Historical Account," in *Living with Other Creatures: Green Exegesis and Theology* (Milton Keynes, UK: Paternoster, 2012).
15. Douglas Hall, *Imaging God: Dominion as Stewardship* (Grand Rapids: Eerdmans,1986).

given to human beings in Genesis 2:15 have the sense of "to serve" (*'abad*) and "to protect" (*shamar*).

Nevertheless, there have been criticisms of the stewardship framework,[16] which will be discussed more fully later. One main objection is that it is too focused on the human as one who is set above non-human creation. The mutuality and interdependence between the human and non-human are not emphasized, so that nature is portrayed as wholly dependent on the human for its care and well-being.[17]

Hence, it is important to give another nuance to the mandate "to rule" and to "subdue." Because human beings are made in God's image (what constitutes this image is not explicitly defined in the text), they have the capacity to represent God in the same way that the king represents God in fulfilling God's intentions for creation. God's actions in creation are intended to create, reproduce, and sustain life. Even with the presence of death and natural processes of disintegration and formation, the whole movement is toward order and not disorder.

Moreover, the king is portrayed as a shepherd whose task is to nurture, heal, and strengthen; it is not to oppress, exploit, and abuse (cf. Ezek 34).[18] The king in Israel ensures the practice of righteousness and justice throughout his realm. Psalm 72 speaks of the ideal king as one who defends the vulnerable leading to shalom in the land.[19] In the same way, human beings, as God's representatives, need to reflect God's righteousness and justice and be nurturing in their relationships to both human and non-human creation.[20]

The object of the verb "subdue" is the earth and not the creatures themselves. Since the earth is created good but not perfect, it needs more work.[21] The responsibility "to cultivate [the garden] and take care of it" (Gen 2:15) is given to human beings who are fed and nurtured by the garden's plant life. This work may involve cutting back overgrowth and working the soil so

---

16. Clare Palmer, "Stewardship: A Case Study in Environmental Ethics," in *Environmental Stewardship: Critical Perspectives – Past and Present*, ed. R. J. Berry (London: T&T Clark, 2006), 65–66.
17. Richard Bauckham, *Bible and Ecology: Rediscovering the Community of Creation* (London: Darton, Longman, and Todd, 2010), 10–11.
18. Christopher J. H. Wright, *Old Testament Ethics for the People of God* (Downers Grove: InterVarsity Press 2004), 122–26.
19. Steven Bouma-Prediger, *For the Beauty of the Earth: A Christian Vision for Creation Care* (Grand Rapids: Baker Academic, 2001), 74.
20. Wright, *Old Testament Ethics*, 123–25.
21. Fretheim, *Creation Untamed*, 33.

that it is able to produce more – actions that involve force and labor but are necessary to sustain life. In this context, "to subdue" means "to bring order out of the disorder"[22] because the garden may deteriorate if no work is done to make it flourish.

Sharing Life with God's Creation

The creation accounts emphasize how much human beings have in common with the rest of God's creation. The term used for human beings and animals – *nephesh haya* ("living beings") (Gen 1:20–21, 24, 30; 2:7, 19) – shows our continuity with other creatures of the earth. We – the creatures of the sky, sea, and land – all receive life from God and are dependent on God for our life. We are not inert objects – we are alive because of God's breath, and when this is withdrawn, we die. Moreover, it is not only human beings that God considers "good' but all creation, valuing and appreciating all, even though it is humanity's peculiar task to harness and enhance this goodness.[23]

In addition, the earth is the home of all; hence, human beings do not have exclusive rights to this home. All the other inhabitants have the right to breathe, find food, and reproduce their own kind. Respect for other inhabitants of the shared space is fundamental, unless the life and well-being of others are being threatened, and part of the unique role of human beings is to exercise leadership in this area.

But not only this, we all share in the call to praise God, the creator. "Let everything that has breath praise the LORD" (Ps 150:6). "This orientation toward the creator is something the creatures and creations, people, animals, and the others have in common. Praise is the joy of existence turned toward God, and this joy of existence inheres in the creation as a whole."[24]

While the non-human creation praise God by being and functioning how God has created them to be (Ps 19:1–4), human beings give expression to praise through verbal and bodily expressions and by how they live their lives for God. Each in its own way give praise, with no hierarchy or anthropocentricity.[25]

---

22. Terence Fretheim, *God and World in the Old Testament: A Relational Theology of Creation* (Nashville, TN: Abingdon, 2005), 52.
23. Bauckham, *Living with Other Creatures*, 5.
24. Westermann, *Elements of Old Testament Theology*, 93.
25. Bauckham, *Living with Other Creatures*, 150. The view that human beings are "priests of creation," in that they mediate the praise of the non-human creation to God, shows the same anthropocentric pitfall as stewardship, according to Bauckham, because it excludes non-human creation's own unique relationship to and praise of God (Bauckham, *Bible and Ecology*, 84–86; Bauckham, *Living with Other Creatures*, 151–53).

But it is not only commonality but also relationality that characterizes God's creation – a relationality that is an expression of who God is. God discerns and provides man's need for a companion (Gen 2:18–24) and walks in the garden where human beings and animals live (3:8a). There is interaction and interdependence among human and non-human creation. The animals provide a form of companionship to man, while the man names the animals, placing them in relation to him and his world. And while human beings till the garden (2:15), they also come from and return to the ground (2:7; 3:19), in the same way as trees and animals (2:9, 19).[26]

Our commonality, interdependence, and bond with the rest of God's living creatures should fill us human beings with humility. The non-human creation has a vocation to fulfill – as do human beings – all of us receiving from God's hands our own peculiar tasks and the capacity to do them.[27] We are mortal, as they are mortal – so that human beings are metaphorically compared to grass in temporality – and we are grateful to God for the gift of life.

SABBATH AND LIFE

While the presence of activity seems to connote that there is life, God pauses in the flurry of creative doings, showing that there is more to life than working all the time. On the seventh day, God had finished his work and thus, "ceased . . . all the work that he had been doing" (Gen 2:2 NET). This means that God withdrew from initiating action and intervention and allowed creation to run its own course and fulfill its created function.[28] Involvement is replaced by disengagement. Time flows in a period set apart and sacred, but not marked by the flow of motion and productive labor.

Other parts of the Scripture show that God's creatures follow the Creator in a God-mandated rhythm of work and rest – "remember the Sabbath day by keeping it holy. Six days you shall labor and do all your work, but the seventh day is a Sabbath to the LORD your God. On it you shall not do any work" (Exod 20:8–10; Deut 5:12–15). The seventh day and the sabbatical year is described as "a Sabbath to the Lord" (Exod 20:10; Lev 25:2, 4) – when, in a moment of reflection and celebration, the "completed work" and the land

---

26. A word play on the Hebrew word for a human being (*'adam*) and ground (*'adamah*) emphasizes their bond.
27. Fretheim (*God and World*, 270, 278–84) argues that non-human creation has a vocation as well.
28. Fretheim, *God and World*, 62.

are offered to God as the creator of all and the owner of the land.[29] "Sabbath rest . . . is work's fulfillment. Rather than saying, 'no,' to work, Sabbath says, 'enough for now.'"[30]

The command is meant not only for landowners and their families but also for their servants, foreigners living with them, and their domestic animals (see Exod 23:12).[31] But the Sabbath imperative is also for the land. In the seventh year, the land is to rest and lie fallow, that is, it should not be worked on, sown, or harvested. In Exodus, the reason for this practice is humanitarian; whatever the unsown land yields on the seventh year is reserved for the poor and the resident alien (23:10–11). In Leviticus, however, the intention of the sabbatical year is for the land itself, so that it can rest from being worked on for human consumption (Lev 25:1–7). It is the land that observes the Sabbath, and human beings are enjoined to give the land its right to do so. Thus, the land is portrayed as "a living reality with rights to be respected."[32]

This connects Sabbath consciousness with a simpler lifestyle that sets limits to human effort, consumption, and economic growth. The story of the manna illustrates this. Each day, for six days, they are to gather sufficient for the day, but on the seventh they are to stop. Since the sixth day provision is good for two days, they have enough for their daily needs (Exod 16:13–30). When the Sabbath command is respected, the land yields its produce (Lev 25:18–22), but if it is disregarded, the fruit of the land dries up.

Perhaps, it is in this sense that the seventh day was blessed by God (Gen 2:3), in that even without putting in any more effort, the life of the world that God created is sustained. Hence, there is no need to be anxious about the future (Matt 6:25–34), or to hoard wealth in the face of other people's need (Luke 12:15–21), or to overexploit the earth's resources to fuel unrestrained economic growth.

But how come Jesus allowed his disciples to pick grain when they were hungry? Jesus also healed on a Sabbath; hence, his detractors accused him of

---

29. God is likened to a landowner and the Israelites to tenants (Lev 25:23).
30. Richard Lowery, "Sabbath and Survival: Abundance and Self-Restraint in a Culture of Excess," *Encounter* 54, no. 2 (Spring 1993): 155.
31. This concern for the well-being of those who do not have the choice to rest is motivated by the other reason given for the Sabbath: "Remember that you were slaves in Egypt and that the LORD your God brought you out of there with a mighty hand and an outstretched arm" (Deut 5:15a).
32. Norman Habel, *The Land is Mine: Six Biblical Ideologies* (Minneapolis: Fortress, 1995), 103–4.

being unlawful.[33] Jesus's response to his detractors shows how he interprets the meaning of the Sabbath: "I ask you, which is lawful on the Sabbath: to do good or to do evil, to save life or to destroy it?" (Luke 6:9). Here he alludes to the meaning of the Sabbath as a day which God has blessed, in that it has to do with the continuity and sustenance of life. Thus, the Sabbath is not intended to destroy or impede life-giving efforts, such as getting daily food or bestowing and receiving healing. Moreover, the Sabbath is a liberating action, especially for the vulnerable (Deut 5:12–15). Thus, to heal a woman who has been crippled by ailment for eighteen years is the right thing to do, as much as providing life-giving water to domestic animals (Luke 13:15–16).

Choosing Life; Losing Life

Ethics implies the moral agency of human beings – as individuals or as part of a collective – who have the freedom to choose what is good or not good, what is right or wrong, or what kind of character they would embody. In the garden, the power of choice is given to human beings, as represented by the two trees in the garden: the tree of the knowledge of good and evil, of which eating the fruit would lead to death (Gen 2:17), and the tree of life, whose fruit offers life that transcends mortality (Gen 3:22). The choice is between gaining knowledge apart from God, leading to self-sufficiency and autonomy that do not recognize the limitations of creaturely existence, or a life within the boundaries set by God,[34] but experiencing the presence of God and the fullness of life that it brings, including an immortal existence, as symbolized by the tree of life.[35]

As the story goes, man and woman chose self-autonomy to gain superior knowledge and be "like God," thus separating themselves from their Creator, from each other, and the community of creation (Gen 3:1–7). From then on, the natural processes of creation became marked by increased pain and struggle, and the harmony between human and non-human creation increasingly fractured (3:14–19). Finally, with the barring of the entrance to the garden and the tree of life, the fullness of life in the presence of God was withheld (3:22–24).

---

33. Luke 6:1–11 (cf. Mark 2:23–3:6; Matt 12:1–14;); Luke 13:10–17; 14:1–6; John 5:1–18; 9:13–17.
34. Walter Brueggemann, *Genesis, Interpretation* (Atlanta: John Knox, 1982), 51–52.
35. The tree of life is used to refer to "anything which enhances and celebrates life," (Brueggemann, *Genesis*, 45). The tree of life is used as a metaphor for wisdom (Prov 3:18), life for others (Prov 11:30), attained desire (Prov 13:2), the healing balm of soothing speech (Prov 15:4), healing in general (Rev 22:2, 14; cf. Rev 2:7; Ezek 47:12) and immortality (Goldingay, *Old Testament Theology*, vol 1, 119).

The amplification and consequences of this overstepping of boundaries are seen in the story of humankind and Israel in Genesis 4–11 and in the rest of the Old Testament. Choosing death, rather than life in the will of God, results in increasing violence in family and community relationships (Gen 4) and in the whole earth: "Now the earth was corrupt in God's sight and was full of violence" (Gen 6:11). The ensuing flood and the return to chaos is just a reflection of the corruption that has taken place, as human beings violate God's good purposes for creation.

Likewise, Israel is presented a choice: "I have set before you today life and prosperity, death and adversity. . . . Now choose life, so that you and your children may live" (Deut 30:15, 19). Choosing life means keeping the covenant and leads to the promise: "then you will live and increase, and the LORD your God will bless you in the land you are entering to possess" (30:16).

However, Israel violates the covenant, resulting in the increasing withdrawal of God's active presence, escalating violence in society, a land subjected to conflicts, and the disintegration of the social fabric, as the book of Judges shows. Even when a king is chosen to lead them, peace and prosperity do not endure, as both people and king choose the way of injustice and death. The choices of people and leaders result in suffering not only for the community, but also for the land.[36] In Jeremiah, the land as God's gift is the place of God's provision and blessing to Israel, which cares for, sustains, and protects the land. However, Israel's idolatry and social injustice have polluted it, and a reversal happens – the fruitful land becomes a desert,[37] showing how "human conduct matters for the well-being of creation."[38]

As previously, God steps in to end the idolatry and injustice – not only for the sake of the people, but also for the sake of the land, which has been wounded and traumatized because of the bloodshed and violence. The people go into exile for their own discipline, as well as to allow the land to have a Sabbath (see 2 Chr 36:21).

In the New Testament, people are also given a choice: to believe and accept life with Christ, which means living in the sphere of God's rule, with its potentials and limits; or to reject Christ's lordship and live autonomously outside of God's will and community, a path that leads to death, in all its facets.

---

36. The land is affected when human beings violate God's laws (Gen 3:17–19; 4:10–12; 6:11–13; Hos 4:1–3).
37. Noli P. Mendoza, "The Threat of Chaos: Jeremiah's Vision of a Suffering Earth," in *Phronesis* 16 (2012): 91–96.
38. Mendoza, "The Threat of Chaos," 104.

However, Christ offers life that encompasses the whole cosmos. Through the cross, Christ reconciles to himself all created things, human and non-human (Col 1:15–20). Thus, choosing Christ is not just a choice for one's self, but a choice for the redemption of all creation, which is portrayed as groaning in bondage because of humankind's sin (Rom 8:21–22).[39]

New Covenant, New Creation, and the Renewal of Life

Nevertheless, the disastrous consequences of sin are not the last words in God's story with humanity and the world. God's character, which is rooted in mercy and grace, means that there is always the possibility for restoration and renewal.

We see this after the great flood, when God renews the blessing of creation to be fruitful and multiply (Gen 9:1, 7). God establishes a covenant not only with Noah and his descendants, but "with every living creature that is with you, the birds, the domestic animals, and every animal of the earth with you" (9:10) – that God will not allow another flood to destroy the whole earth again" (9:11–17). While in the post-flood world, killing animals for food is allowed (9:2–3) – which may be the reason for the stronger language in Genesis 1:26, 28 when referring to humankind's rule over the animals – respect for the life of living creatures is affirmed with the prohibition not to eat "meat that has its lifeblood still in it" (Gen 9:4), for blood represents life (Deut 12:23). However, shedding human blood (murder) merits the death penalty. Because human beings are made in the image of God, their lives are invaluable. Thus, one must pay account by another life because that is the only value commensurate to the loss of a human being (9:5–6).

In terms of Israel's broken covenant with God, with its effects on social relationships and the land, there is hope of restoration and a new covenant. In Jeremiah 31–33, God promises to Israel the rebuilding of ruins, recovery and healing, mutual commitment with God, and a return to and renewed blessing of the land, which will become fruitful again so that "their life shall become like a watered garden" (31:12 NRSV). The same vision can be seen in Isaiah 40–66, in which God's salvation and restoration include a land that resembles Eden, not a wilderness.[40]

---

39. Gilbert Soo Hoo, "Implications of Creation's Present Suffering and Future Glory in Romans 8:17–25," *Journal of Asian Evangelical Theology* 21, nos. 1–2 (2017): 76–79.
40. Walter McConnell, "From Creation to New Creation: Missions and the Natural World," in *Mission Round Table: The Occasional Bulletin of OMF Mission Research* 9, no. 1 (2014): 20.

Finally, the vision of renewed life culminates in "the new heaven and the earth" (Rev 21:1), in which God comes to dwell among the people. Some believe that everything will eventually be destroyed, hence justifying inaction toward the deteriorating state of the earth and other societal problems.[41] The language in the New Testament, however, is one of both continuity and discontinuity.[42] Thus, what will happen is more of a purging rather than obliteration, with the goodness that God created being retained and transformed, while the evil is purged.[43] In this transformed creation, suffering and death will cease (Rev 21:4) and fullness of life will be experienced, as expressed in nature metaphors – spring of life, river of the water of life, and the tree of life, with its leaves for the healing of the nations (Rev 21:6; 22:1–2). But it is God's presence that will animate all. This glorious vision of where the story is leading should shape our values and ethical actions, especially in working for the fullness of life for human beings and the rest of creation.

EVANGELICAL ECOLOGICAL ENGAGEMENT IN ASIA
Nature in Asian Cultures and Religions

Even before the introduction of Christianity to Asia, indigenous cultures and Asian religions had already shaped the worldview of Asians in relation to the world around them. Because of the multiplicity of religions and geographical landscapes in this vast region, the perspectives, attitudes, and conduct toward nature are widely diverse. The influences of globalization and free-market economy have also produced a mixture of attitudes and actions, depending on their impact on the local culture and worldview.

For example, a major precept of early Buddhism is to kill no sentient beings – those possessing consciousness and capable of suffering and rebirth, such as human beings and animals. Thus, there is an attitude of compassion and benevolence toward animals which is not motivated by concern for biodiversity and conservation of ecosystems.[44] On the other hand, in Hinduism,

---

41. Katsuomi Shimasaki, "The New Heavens and the New Earth: Our Hope and Motive for Stewardship," in *The Earth is the Lord's: Reflections on Stewardship in the Asian Context*, eds. Timoteo Gener and Adonis Gorospe (Manila: OMF Literature, 2011), 7–8, 18.
42. Douglas Moo, "Eschatology and Environmental Ethics," In *Keeping God's Earth: The Global Environment in Biblical Perspective*, eds. Noly J. Toly and Daniel I. Block (Downers Grove: InterVarsity Press, 2010), 23–43.
43. Christopher J. H. Wright, *The Mission of God: Unlocking the Bible's Grand Narrative* (Downers Grove: InterVarsity Press, 2006), 409.
44. Lambert Schmithausen, "Buddhism," in *The Encyclopedia of Religion and Nature*, ed. Bron Raymond Taylor; Oxford Reference (London: Continuum, 2005; published online 2010). All

God and nature are equated, with human and non-human creatures having equal value and rights to protection and care.[45] The Japanese love for nature, portrayed in artwork, poetry, and gardens, were shaped by Zen Buddhism, Shintoism, and Daoism, which see the unification of humanity with nature as the religious and aesthetic ideal.[46] The Chinese concept of yin–yang sees the whole cosmos as whole, continuous, and dynamic, with the part and the whole interconnected and interdependent.[47]

The view that nature is sacred – whether the whole cosmos or the earth is considered divine (e.g. the earth goddess), or different natural phenomena or elements are identified with or seen as being inhabited by spirits or deities (e.g. the mountain as god) – is shared by many Asian religions, including indigenous ones. Although predominantly Catholic, Filipinos have an underlying animistic orientation, in which spirits are believed to live in trees, rocks, and rivers.[48] An Indonesian evangelical shares how pre-Hindu Balinese regard nature: "Balinese consider nature as being very powerful. It is beyond their control, and it is very important for their well-being. They look at nature as power or spirit. They depend upon it. They respect nature and express their gratitude to it."[49] There is also a shared view among Asians about the interconnectedness of life in the cosmos as an integrated whole. The role of human beings, on this view, is to discern and enter harmony with creation – a more contemplative position rather than an active interventionist one.

In some ways, the introduction of religions in the Abrahamic tradition, such as Islam and Christianity, challenged these worldviews. Both religions see the deity as transcendent over nature; not part of or equivalent to nature. Second, both see a more active role for human beings. In Islam, human beings are *khalifa* on this Earth, the guardian or vicegerent of nature,

---

references are from the online version.
45. Jo Yong-Hun, "A Christian Environmental Perspective on the View of Nature in Asian Thought," *Asia Journal of Theology* 16, no. 2 (2002): 398–99. "Hindus value nature, think of the universe as the body of God, pray for peace between all the elements of the universe, urge non-violence to all beings on Earth, and personify nature and the Earth as goddesses." Vasudha Narayanan, "Hinduism," in *Encyclopedia of Religion and Nature*.
46. Yotaro Miyamoto, "Japanese Religions," in *Encyclopedia of Religion and Nature*.
47. Yong-Hun, "Nature in Asian Thought," 403.
48. Rodney Henry, *Filipino Spirit Word: A Challenge to the Church* (Manila: OMF Literature, 1986), 7.
49. Wayan Mistra, "Environment and the Christian Faith: A Holistic Approach from Bali," *Evangelical Review of Theology* 17, no. 2 (Apr 1993): 96.

whose responsibility is to protect and ensure the earth's continued bounties.[50] Nevertheless, the focus of Islamic scholars is on the relationship between Allah and the believer. Thus, ecological concerns are neglected, as seen in predominantly Muslim countries in Asia, in which environmental policies are often not given priority.[51]

In the same way, the dominant form of Western Christianity that reached Asia through Catholic and Protestant missionaries had for its goals the spreading of Christianity and Western civilization, with no thought for the ecological impact. Moreover, the unilateral rejection of other religions as pagan has resulted in the negation of beliefs that see the inherent value of nature and the interconnection and interdependence of life.[52]

The evangelical view of creation care clearly sets it apart from the pantheistic view of some Asian religions. God is not equated, identified with, or regarded as part of creation or any of its elements. Nevertheless, there may be something to be learned from engaging the religious worldviews of most Asians that can soften the over-transcendent, anthropocentric, over-interventionist approach toward creation that characterize much of Christian history. Asian theologian Hwa Yung notices that "evangelical thinking toward other faiths has been preoccupied with the negative, weak, and sinful in these traditions, and thereby has failed to see the good in them," leading to a negative view, "preventing us from taking seriously their challenge both in theology and in life."[53]

Asia's Ecological Landscape

Regardless of religions and worldviews, environmental degradation in Asia has not been prevented,[54] revealing that other factors are involved. For instance, even though the Asia-Pacific region has twenty percent of the world's biodiversity, fourteen percent of the world's tropical forests, and thirty-four percent

---

50. Mohammad Aslam Parvaiz, "Islam on Man and Nature," in *Encyclopedia of Religion and Nature*.
51. Richard C. Foltz, "Islam," *Encyclopedia of Religion and Nature*. In the World Ranking in the Environmental Performance Index for 2018, Pakistan, Indonesia, and Bangladesh are numbered 169, 133, and 179, respectively. See Bihong Huang and Yining Xu, "Environmental Performance in Asia: Overview, Drivers, and Policy Implications," *ADBI Working Paper Series*, No. 990, Asian Development Bank Institute Tokyo, August 2019, https://www.adb.org/sites/default/files/publication/521606/adbi-wp990.pdf.
52. Dana L. Robert, "Historical Trends in Missions and Earth Care," in *Creation Care in Christian Mission*, ed. Kapya J. Kaoma (Oxford: Regnum Books International, 2015), 71–73.
53. Hwa Yung, "A Christian Apologetic – In Dialogue with Asian Religions and Cultures," in *Naming the Unknown God* (Manila: OMF Literature, 2006), 9, 10.
54. Yong-Hun, "Nature in Asian Thought," 397.

of the world's coral reef, the rapid loss of forest lands and natural habitats due to agricultural expansion, urbanization, and trade globalization plus climate change have impacted ecosystems, resulting in the decline, and even near extinction, of endemic wildlife and plant species.[55] While Southeast Asia has the most extensive and diverse coral reefs in the world, these are also the most threatened, with ninety-five percent at high risk from threats,[56] which include overfishing and destructive fishing, global warming that leads to reef bleaching, and pollution of the watershed and marine waters. The damage to natural habitats and coral reefs affects the livelihood, food security, and well-being of vulnerable coastal populations with limited resources.[57]

Asia is also a region of great economic disparities. While it has three of the world's largest economies – China, Japan, and India – with some of the world's wealthiest nations such as Singapore and South Korea, it is also home to half of the world's poor. Overconsumption may characterize the wealthy, but materialism – which puts prime value on material possessions and accumulating wealth – can be seen in both rich and poor nations alike, especially if the latter transitions too quickly to commercialization and urbanization after years of deprivation.[58]

It has long been recognized that poverty and the environment are interrelated issues.[59] While the poor bear the brunt of climate change and environmental degradation they also contribute to the damage impacting their daily survival, thus leading to a downward spiral, in which the further depletion of resources leads to increasing poverty. Hence, to address one without addressing the other fails in providing long-term solutions.

Many Asian countries are in the "Ring of Fire" – a rim along the Pacific Ocean where most active volcanoes are located and the majority of earthquakes occur – and in the path of the most powerful typhoons. Floods, tsunamis, and droughts wreak havoc on people's lives and livelihoods. The high population

---

55. Suneetha M. Subramanian et al., "Unraveling the Drivers of Southeast Asia's Biodiversity Loss," (United Nations University, 2011), https://unu.edu/publications/articles/unraveling-the-drivers-of-southeast-asia-biodiversity-loss.html#info; https://esajournals.onlinelibrary.wiley.com/doi/10.1002/ecs2.1624.
56. Lauretta Burke et al., *Reefs at Risk Revisited* (Washington, DC: World Resources Institute, 2011), 53–56; https://reefresilience.org/pdf/Reefs_at_Risk_Revisited.pdf.
57. *Reefs at Risk*, 38–46, 86–87.
58. Helen I. Duh, "Antecedents and Consequences of Materialism: An Integrated Theoretical Framework," *Journal of Economics and Behavioral Studies* 7/1 (Feb 2015), 27–28, https://core.ac.uk/download/pdf/288022832.pdf.
59. See Ken Gnanakan, "Environment, Poverty, and Justice," in *Inheriting the Earth: Poor Communities and Environmental Renewal* (Monrovia, CA: World Vision, 2004), 41–50, 73–87.

density of some of these areas, many of whom are inhabited by the poor, means that the disaster is magnified a hundredfold. Global warming has intensified these disasters.[60] So even if some disasters are not of human origin, they are aggravated by harmful human activities.

Public sector governance is crucial in pushing for policies and regulatory mechanisms that can lessen the environmental impact, and in providing funding for research, education, and innovative ecofriendly technologies. However, many countries in Asia have strong central governments so that environmental policies are dependent on the inclinations of those in power.

This brings up the issue of geopolitics and how geographical factors influence power relationships on the international stage. The South China Sea – home to numerous species of coral reefs, fish, sponges, mangroves, and seagrass – is being claimed by several nations, but China's activities have the greatest ecological impact. Clam excavations and dredging operations to construct artificial islands have damaged the reefs and depleted fish stocks. Overfishing by all claimants has resulted in the rapid decline of fish, threatening the food security and livelihood of small fisher folks and the communities they supply.[61]

Asian Evangelicals and Creation Care

Despite these threats, the majority of Asian evangelical churches do not see creation care as an integral part of the mission of the church or as part of their Christian discipleship. This is out of step with popular culture and media, which do put more emphasis on environmental issues even though in some countries there is generally no consistent follow-through in terms of government policy and actual daily practice.

Asian evangelical involvement in creation care follows the contours of worldwide evangelicals, especially in the areas of stewardship and integral mission. Even though the *Lausanne Covenant* (1974) is a landmark in terms of evangelical social engagement, ecological concerns are not mentioned in the document.[62] Nevertheless, the Lausanne Covenant paved the way for a

---

60. UNESCAP, *Asia-Pacific Disaster Report 2019*, 7, https://www.unescap.org/publications/asia-pacific-disaster-report-2019.
61. Pratnashree Basu and Aadya Chaturvedi, *In Deep Water: Current Threats to the Marine Ecology of the South China Sea*, Observer Research Foundation Issue Brief 449 (March 2021), 11–12, 5–10, https://www.orfonline.org/research/in-deep-water-current-threats-to-the-marine-ecology-of-the-south-china-sea/.
62. Lausanne Movement, *Lausanne Covenant*, https://lausanne.org/content/covenant/lausanne-covenant#cov; likewise, with the *Manila Manifesto* (1989), https://lausanne.org/content/manifesto/the-manila-manifesto.

broader understanding of mission as transformation.[63] After the Cape Town Congress (2010), creation care increasingly became mainstream through the Lausanne Movement and the World Evangelical Alliance.[64]

An important theme in evangelical ecological engagement is the emphasis on God's ownership of all things and the stewardship role of human beings – "The earth is the LORD's and all that is in it" (Ps 24:1). This implies that human beings cannot do what they please with the earth; they are entrusted with the unique responsibility of being stewards.[65]

The concept of the steward was originally drawn from the English caretaker of a household or an estate. In Christian circles, the concept of stewardship was first employed in relation to financial matters, then to one's talents, and then applied to the preservation and care of natural resources. However, the association of stewardship with business has perpetuated the thinking that creation is a "natural resource"[66] – its value is only instrumental, derived from how it contributes to the well-being and progress of humankind. This can easily lead to exploitative environmental practices for human profit.[67] Thus, the Cornwall Alliance for the Stewardship of Creation uses "wise-stewardship" as its framework, but its members are skeptical about climate change, see exercising dominion as simply using resources for human betterment, and put no intrinsic value in the non-human creation.[68]

In Asia, Ken Gnanakan from India takes stewardship further in *Responsible Stewardship of God's Creation*,[69] dealing with biblical themes such as creation, covenant, land, and justice. The book's strength is the inclusion of questions for reflection and practical tips for beginners in creation care. In addition, the book features excerpts from diverse religious and cultural traditions and

---

63. Al Tizon, *Transformation After Lausanne: Radical Evangelical Mission in Global–Local Perspective* (Eugene, OR: Wipf & Stock, 2008), 37–52.
64. Dave Bookless, "Jesus is Lord . . . of All? Evangelicals, Earth Care, and the Scope of the Gospel," in Kaoma, *Creation Care in Christian Mission*, 113–16.
65. Calvin Dewitt, *Caring for Creation: Responsible Stewardship of God's Handiwork* (Grand Rapids: Baker Books, 1998).
66. Palmer, "Stewardship: A Case Study," 66–68, 72.
67. H. Paul Santmire, "From Consumerism to Stewardship: The Troublesome Ambiguities of an Attractive Option," *Dialog* 49, no. 4 (2010): 336.
68. Laurel Kearns, "Green Evangelicals," in *The New Evangelical Social Engagement*, eds. Brian Steensland and Philip Goff (New York: Oxford University Press, 2014), 163. Cf. Cornwall Alliance, "The Cornwall Declaration on Environmental Stewardship," https://cornwallalliance.org/landmark-documents/the-cornwall-declaration-on-environmental-stewardship/.
69. Ken Gnanakan, *Responsible Stewardship of God's Creation* (Bonn: Culture and Science Publishing, 2014), which is a revised version of *God's World: A Biblical Theology of the Environment* (London: SPCK, 1999).

engages other ecological frameworks, such as deep ecology, ecofeminism, social ecology, and eco-justice. Nevertheless, the book fails to integrate all these under the overall concept of stewardship.

The Cape Town Commitment (2011) emphasizes another important theme in evangelical ecological engagement, which is integral mission.

> Integral mission means discerning, proclaiming, and living out, the biblical truth that the gospel is God's good news, through the cross and resurrection of Jesus Christ, for individual persons, *and* for society, *and* for creation. All three are broken and suffering because of sin; all three are included in the redeeming love and mission of God; all three must be part of the comprehensive mission of God's people.[70]

Creation care is seen as an expression of love for the Lord who owns the earth. Because Christ is Lord over all creation, the gospel is not just for people, but for society and the whole creation.[71] This idea is reiterated in *Creation Care and The Gospel: Jamaica Call to Action* (2012), which reaffirms "that creation care is an issue that must be included in our response to the gospel, proclaiming and acting upon the good news of what God has done and will complete for the salvation of the world."[72] Thus, creation care is not a temporary addition to the task of the church but an indispensable component of proclaiming and living out the gospel.

The practical implications of this are spelled out in the Cape Town Commitment. These include: (1) repentance for ecological irresponsibility; (2) lifestyle change in terms of forsaking habits of consumption that pollute or destroy the earth; (3) advocacy for government policies that address climate change and environmental degradation; and (4) affirmation of creation care advocates (e.g. those involved in protecting and restoring natural habitats) as part of their missional calling.[73]

A mission organization based in Singapore, OMF International, has incorporated creation care as part of its church-planting efforts among the indigenous in Asia, stressing the importance of integral mission. Thus, sustainable

---

70. Lausanne Movement, *The Cape Town Commitment*, Part 1, Sec. 7a, http://www.lausanne.org/en/documents/ctcommitment.html#pl-l.
71. *Cape Town Commitment*, Part 1, Sec. 10, A.
72. "Creation Care and the Gospel: Jamaica Call to Action," https://lausanne.org/content/statement/creation-care-call-to-action.
73. *Cape Town Commitment*, Part 2, Sec. 6.

agriculture, the management of waste, water, and flood, as well as restoration of ecosystems are all seen as part of God's mission, along with evangelism.[74] OMF grounds its theological basis for creation care on the triune God – God the creator is glorified through creation and values creation; Christ is lord, redeemer, and sustainer of creation; the Spirit gives life to creation. However, this structure rooted in the Trinity is not followed through and is only briefly mentioned in relation to the human response: "Being made in God's image implies that our lives should reflect the character and will of the triune God, creator, king, redeemer, and life giver."[75]

While the theme of integral mission provides a unifying umbrella that encompasses the whole creation, it is too abstract for most Asian Christians and needs to be explained further using conceptual categories. What is needed are in-life metaphors that are oriented by the biblical story and easily grasped by the ordinary lay person. In addition, these theological metaphors should lead to ethical reflection that addresses the value and role of human beings in relation to the non-human creation, the importance of sustainability for future generations, and the lifestyle of materialism and overconsumption as harmful to human and non-human creation.[76]

Trajectories for Asian Ecological Engagement

One proposal that resonates with Filipinos is *Kapwa* Ethics by Aldrin Peñamora. *Kapwa* is a Filipino term that connotes a sense of kinship and shared identity that motivates compassion and responsibility for the other. Peñamora argues that *pakikipagkapwa* (treating others as oneself) should be extended not only to fellow human beings but to the rest of God's creation. The basis for this is Christ's example who, as the center of creation (Col 1:15–23), is a person-for-others. The strength of Peñamora's Kapwa Ethics is that it has both a reflective element (a recognition of one's relationship with non-human

---

74. David Gould, "Creation Care in the Mission of CIM and OMF: People and Places," in *Mission Round Table* 9, no. 1, 2–3.
75. OMF Mission Research, "OMF International's Theological Basis for Creation Care," in *Mission Round Table* 9, no. 1, 4–6.
76. Young Seok Cha, "Theological and Ethical Implications of Creation Care," *The Journal of Applied Christian Leadership* 6, no. 2 (2012), 95–104, https://digitalcommons.andrews.edu/jacl/vol6/iss2/.

creation) and an active one, in that this recognition leads to being responsible for them.[77]

My proposition is along a theology and ethic of life that is informed by the biblical story, as partially expounded in the first part. In the future, I would like to develop this further using the trinitarian framework: God and life, Jesus as life, the Spirit and life. Here "life" covers the whole creation – human and non-human – and encompasses all aspects of life, as captured in the idea of the biblical shalom. The role of the human is to affirm God's value for creation, and to work toward preserving, sustaining, and enhancing life by identifying and helping to resolve threats, and by exerting effort to make life flourish for all creation – as individuals, as people of God, as co-dwellers of a planet in peril.

QUESTIONS FOR DISCUSSION

1. In what ways do stories form our beliefs and actions?
2. What themes in God's story of life in Scripture are significant for creation care?
3. Reflect on your relationship and role as a human being in regard to God's non-human creation. What do you have in common with it? What is your responsibility toward the rest of God's creation?
4. How do you understand the concepts of stewardship and integral mission? How are they related to the care of creation?
5. Discuss the ecological challenges in your own country or community. What can you do to respond to these challenges, as an individual or as part of a faith community?

BIBLIOGRAPHY

Basu, Pratnashree and Aadya Chaturvedi. *In Deep Water: Current Threats to the Marine Ecology of the South China Sea*, Observer Research Foundation Issue Brief 449. March 2021. https://www.orfonline.org/research/in-deep-water-current-threats-to-the-marine-ecology-of-the-south-china-sea/.

Bauckham, Richard. *Bible and Ecology: Rediscovering the Community of Creation.* London: Darton, Longman, and Todd, 2010.

———. *Living with Other Creatures: Green Exegesis and Theology.* Milton Keynes: Paternoster, 2012.

---

[77]. Aldrin M. Peñamora, "*Kapwa* Ethics: Christ-Centered Ethics of Responsibility Towards the Earth, Our Neighbor," in *Why, O God: Disaster, Resiliency, and the People of God*, eds. Athena E. Gorospe et al (Manila: OMF Literature, 2017), 133–36.

Bell, Colin Roy, and Robert S. White, eds. *Creation Care and the Gospel: Reconsidering the Mission of the Church*. Lausanne Library. Peabody: Hendrickson, 2016.

Bookless, Dave. "Jesus Is Lord . . . of All? Evangelicals, Earth Care, and the Scope of the Gospel." In *Creation Care in Christian Mission*, edited by Kapya J. Kaoma, 105–120. Regnum Edinburgh Centenary Series 29. Oxford: Regnum Books International, 2015.

Bouma-Prediger, Steven. *For the Beauty of the Earth: A Christian Vision for Creation Care*. Grand Rapids: Baker Academic, 2001.

Bruggemann, Walter. *Genesis*. Interpretation. Atlanta: John Knox, 1982.

———. *Theology of the Old Testament*. Minneapolis: Fortress, 1997.

Burke, Lauretta, Kathleen Reytar, Mark Spalding, and Allison Perry. *Reefs at Risk Revisited*. Washington, DC: World Resources Institute, 2011. https://reefresilience.org/pdf/Reefs_at_Risk_Revisited.pdf.

Cha, Young Seok. "Theological and Ethical Implications of Creation Care." *The Journal of Applied Christian Leadership* 6, no. 2 Fall (2012): 88–106. https://digitalcommons.andrews.edu/jacl/vol6/iss2/.

Cornwall Alliance. *The Cornwall Declaration on Environmental Stewardship*. 8 April 2014. https://cornwallalliance.org/landmark-documents/the-cornwall-declaration-on-environmental-stewardship/.

Dewitt, Calvin. *Caring for Creation: Responsible Stewardship of God's Handiwork*. Grand Rapids: Baker Books, 1998.

Duh, Helen I. "Antecedents and Consequences of Materialism: An Integrated Theoretical Framework." *Journal of Economics and Behavioral Studies* 7, no. 1 (2015): 21–35. https://core.ac.uk/reader/288022832.

Evangelical Environmental Network. "An Evangelical Declaration on the Care of Creation." https://creationcare.org/what-we-do/an-evangelical-declaration-on-the-care-of-creation.html.

Foltz, Richard C. "Islam." In *Encyclopedia of Religion and Nature*, edited by Bron Raymond Taylor. 2 vols. Oxford Reference. London: Continuum, 2006; online, 2010.

Fowler, Robert. *The Greening of Protestant Thought*. Chapel Hill: University of North Carolina Press, 1995.

Frame, Randy. "Greening of the Gospel?" *Christianity Today* 40, no. 13 (1996): 82–86. https://www.christianitytoday.com/ct/1996/november11/6td082.html.

Fretheim, Terence. *Creation Untamed: The Bible, God, and Natural Disasters*. Grand Rapids: Baker Academic, 2010.

———. *God and the World in the Old Testament: A Relational Theology of Creation*. Nashville: Abingdon, 2005.

Gnanakan, Ken. "Environment, Poverty, and Justice." *Inheriting the Earth: Poor Communities and Environmental Renewal.* Monrovia: World Vision, 2004.

———. *God's World: A Biblical Theology of the Environment.* London: SPCK, 1999.

———. *Responsible Stewardship of God's Creation*, edited by Thomas K. Johnson. Rev. ed. The WEA Global Issues Series 11. Bonn: Culture and Science Publishing, 2014.

Goldingay, John. *Old Testament Theology, volume one: Israel's Gospel.* Downers Grove: InterVarsity Press, 2003.

Gorospe, Athena. "Evangelicals and the Environment: Beyond Stewardship." *Evangelical Review of Theology* 37, no. 3 July (2013): 256–66.

Gould, David. "Creation Care in the Mission of CIM and OMF: People and Places." *Mission Round Table: The Occasional Bulletin of OMF Mission Research* 9, no. 1 May (2014): 2–3.

Habel, Norman. *The Land is Mine: Six Biblical Ideologies.* Minneapolis: Fortress, 1995.

Hall, Douglas. *Imaging God: Dominion as Stewardship.* Grand Rapids: Eerdmans, 1986.

Hauerwas, Stanley. *Vision and Virtue: Essays in Christian Ethical Reflection.* Notre Dame: Fides Publishers, 1974.

Henry, Rodney. *Filipino Spirit Word: A Challenge to the Church.* Manila: OMF Literature, 1986.

Huang, Bihong, and Yining Xu. "Environmental Performance in Asia: Overview, Drivers, and Policy Implications." *ADBI Working Paper Series*, no. 990, Asian Development Bank Institute, Tokyo, Aug 2019. https://www.adb.org/sites/default/files/publication/521606/adbi-wp990.pdf.

Hughes, Alice C. "Understanding the Drivers of Southeast Asian Biodiversity Loss." *Ecosphere* 8, no. 1 January (2017): https://doi.org/10.1002/ecs2.1624.

Kaoma, Kapya J. *Creation Care in Christian Mission.* Regnum Edinburgh Centenary Series 29. Oxford: Regnum Books International, 2015.

Kearns, Laurel. "Green Evangelicals." In *The New Evangelical Social Engagement*, edited by Brian Steensland and Philip Goff, 157–78. New York: Oxford University Press, 2013; online, 2014.

Lausanne Movement. *The Cape Town Commitment.* Jan 25, 2011. https://lausanne.org/content/ctcommitment.

———. "An Evangelical Commitment to Simple Lifestyle." *Lausanne Occasional Papers* 20. Jun 20, 1980. https://lausanne.org/content/lop/lop-20.

———. *The Lausanne Covenant.* 1 Aug 1974. https://lausanne.org/content/covenant/lausanne-covenant.

———. *The Manila Manifesto.* 20 Jul 1989. https://lausanne.org/content/manifesto/the-manila-manifesto.

Lowery, Richard. "Sabbath and Survival: Abundance and Self-Restraint in a Culture of Excess." *Encounter* 54, no. 2 Spring (1993): 143–67.

MacIntyre, Alasdair. *After Virtue: A Study in Moral Theory.* Notre Dame: University of Notre Dame Press, 1981.

McConnell, Walter. "From Creation to New Creation: Missions and the Natural World." *Mission Round Table* 9, no. 1 May (2014): 17–22.

Mendoza, Noli P. "The Threat of Chaos: Jeremiah's Vision of a Suffering Earth." *Phronesis* 16 (2012): 83–109.

Micah Network. "Declaration on Creation Stewardship and Climate Change." *International Bulletin of Missionary Research* 33, no. 4 Oct (2009): 182–84. http://www.internationalbulletin.org/issues/2009-04/2009-04-182-network.html.

Mistra, Wayan. "Environment and the Christian Faith: A Holistic Approach from Bali." *Evangelical Review of Theology* 17, no. 2 Apr (1993): 94–101.

Miyamoto, Yotaro. "Japanese Religions." In *Encyclopedia of Religion and Nature*, edited by Bron Raymond Taylor. 2 vols. Oxford Reference. London: Continuum, 2006; online, 2010.

Moltmann, Jürgen. *The Source of Life: The Holy Spirit and the Theology of Life.* Minneapolis: Fortress, 1997.

Moo, Douglas. "Eschatology and Environmental Ethics." In *Keeping God's Earth: The Global Environment in Biblical Perspective*, edited by Noly J. Toly and Daniel I. Block, 23–43. Downers Grove, IL: InterVarsity Press, 2010.

Narayanan, Vasudha. "Hinduism." In *Encyclopedia of Religion and Nature*, edited by Bron Raymond Taylor. 2 vols. Oxford Reference. London: Continuum, 2006; online, 2010.

OMF Mission Research. "OMF International's Theological Basis for Creation Care." *Mission Round Table* 9, no. 1 May (2014): 4–6.

Palmer, Clare. "Stewardship: A Case Study in Environmental Ethics." In *Environmental Stewardship: Critical Perspectives – Past and Present*, edited by R. J. Berry, 63–75. London: T&T Clark, 2006.

Parvaiz, Mohammad Aslam. "Islam on Man and Nature." In Taylor, *Encyclopedia of Religion and Nature*.

Peñamora, Aldrin M. "*Kapwa* Ethics: Christ-Centered Ethics of Responsibility Towards the Earth, Our Neighbor." In *Why, O God? Disaster, Resiliency, and the People of God*, edited by Athena E. Gorospe, Charles Ringma, and Karen Hollenbeck-Wuest, 119–37. Manila: OMF Literature, 2017.

Robert, Dana L. "Historical Trends in Missions and Earth Care." In Kaoma, *Creation Care in Christian Mission*, 71–84.

Santmire, H. Paul. "From Consumerism to Stewardship: The Troublesome Ambiguities of an Attractive Option." *Dialog* 49, no. 4 (Winter 2010): 332–39.

Schmithausen, Lambert. "Buddhism." In Taylor, *Encyclopedia of Religion and Nature.*

Shimasaki, Katsuomi. "The New Heavens and the New Earth: Our Hope and Motive for Stewardship." In *The Earth is the Lord's: Reflections on Stewardship in the Asian Context,* edited by Timoteo Gener and Adonis Gorospe, 5–19. Manila: OMF Literature, 2011.

Soo Hoo, Gilbert. "Implications of Creation's Present Suffering and Future Glory in Romans 8:17–25," *Journal of Asian Evangelical Theology* 21, nos. 1–2 (Mar-Sept 2017): 73–89.

Subramanian, Suneetha M., Alexandros Gasparatos, Ademola K. Braimoh, and Wendy Elliott. *Unraveling the Drivers of Southeast Asia's Biodiversity Loss.* United Nations University Institute of Advanced Studies Policy Report, Nov 8, 2011. https://unu.edu/publications/articles/unraveling-the-drivers-of-southeast-asia-biodiversity-loss.html#info.

Taylor, Bron Raymond, ed. *Encyclopedia of Religion and Nature.* 2 vols. Oxford Reference. London: Continuum, 2006; online, 2010.

Tizon, Al. *Transformation After Lausanne: Radical Evangelical Mission in Global-Local Perspective.* Eugene: Wipf & Stock, 2008.

UNESCAP. *Asia-Pacific Disaster Report 2019.* United Nations ESCAP. Aug 22, 2019. https://www.unescap.org/publications/asia-pacific-disaster-report-2019.

WEA Creation Care Task Force. "Evangelical Call to Action on Biodiversity." WEA Creation Care. Sept 2020. https://www.weacreationcare.org/call-to-action-on-biodiversity.

Westermann, Claus. *Elements of Old Testament Theology.* Atlanta: John Knox/Edinburgh: T&T Clark, 1982.

White, Lynn, Jr. "The Historical Roots of our Ecologic Crisis." *Science* 155 (1967): 1203–207.

Wilkinson, Loren. *Earthkeeping in the 90's: Stewardship of Creation.* Rev. ed. Grand Rapids: Eerdmans, 1998.

Wright, Christopher J. H. *The Mission of God: Unlocking the Bible's Grand Narrative.* Downers Grove, IL: InterVarsity Press, 2006.

———. *Old Testament Ethics for the People of God.* Downers Grove, IL: InterVarsity Press, 2004.

Yong-Hun, Jo. "A Christian Environmental Perspective on the View of Nature in Asian Thought." *Asian Journal of Theology* 16, no. 2 (2002): 396–408.

Yung, Hwa. "A Christian Apologetic – In Dialogue with Asian Religions and Cultures." In *Naming the Unknown God,* 5–25. Manila: OMF Literature, 2006.

CHAPTER 10

A PROPHETIC VOICE IN THE WILDERNESS

Church, Political Engagement, and Public Theology

Agnes Chiu

INTRODUCTION

What role should the church[1] have in its respective historical context in witnessing the Christian faith? When faced with diverse cultural and political challenges, how can the church continue with the bold proclamation of the Gospel? Public theology provides a viable platform for this engagement. Public theology ties theology to its context in which the church situates itself and examines theology's relevance to current social issues. Ecclesiology and public theology go together.

This chapter explores the biblical role of the church in doing public theology, its duty to provide the moral vision for society and the state, and its role as a new family sphere – a home for new relationships among believers, particularly in its engagement with the state. In practicing public theology, the church needs to maintain an openness to pluralistic views, be willing to be scrutinized, and take advantage of shared values as the common language to conduct dialogue. To provide concrete examples of public theology and political engagement, the chapter will survey two case studies: (1) Korea's democratization process and (2) the Iraq War. It examines the church's engagement in the government's policy and decisions in both cases. Finally, the chapter posits a pragmatic approach to prepare and assist the church in engaging the political government of its local area using the tools of communication technology and social media platforms to share the needed vision of God's values.

---

1. The term "church" used in this chapter refers to the Christian body and Christian churches collectively. It does not signify an organization or denomination.

Theology is public and should apply to more than a defined community. One of theology's tasks is to mediate in public practice, using reason, to discover the truth for the contribution to the broader society's good.[2] Public theology helps the church relate to society at large. This duty to relate is not only an aspect of the divine mandate to cultivate and keep God's creation order, but is critical to keep the Christian faith relevant in a culture of secularization. To prosper, people and government, regardless of their faith orientation, need God's moral vision. Where and how do people and governments seek this moral vision? The church is the channel.

THE THEOLOGICAL BASIS OF PUBLIC THEOLOGY

Abraham Kuyper was a nineteenth century Dutch theologian, journalist, educator, and politician. In a famous speech, *The Social Question*, delivered in 1891 at the First Christian Social Congress in Holland, Kuyper opened with a provocative and convicting question: What should we, as confessors of Christ, do about the social needs of our time?[3] Kuyper vehemently argued for an affirmative duty of Christians to respond to the social needs of their time. Their identity as "confessors of Christ" demands no less.

This mandate to respond to social needs has a biblical foundation. When God created humans, God gave a task to Adam before the fall: to cultivate and keep the land. "Then the LORD God took the man and put him into the garden of Eden to work it **and take care of it**." (Gen 2:15 , emphasis added) The word, "work" is also translated as "cultivate," and in Hebrews is עָבַד (*abad*) and means to work and to serve, to the point that humans are to be "slaves" or under a bond to work.[4] The covenantal nature of work is to endure all circumstances and cultivate the land to production. The word, "keep," שָׁמַר (*shamar*) means to keep, watch, and preserve. God enables the land to become productive, and humans are obligated to maintain and protect it carefully. This ongoing duty to keep the creation order is the "cultural mandate" given to humans.

---

2. Sebastian Kim, *Theology in the Public Sphere* (London: SCM Press, 2011), 26.
3. Abraham Kuyper, *The Problem of Poverty*. Translated by James W. Skillen (Sioux Center: Dordt College Press, 2011), 13.
4. God gave the work mandate before the fall. Work is thus a calling, not slavery. Nevertheless, the Hebrew word עָבַד (*abad*) was used repeatedly in the context of slavery in the Old Testament. Ironically, God foresaw the fall and the punishment he subsequently rendered to man.

The Cultural Mandate: A Public Faith and Public Theology

This cultural mandate features several characteristics. First, as this mandate is a command from God, humans must fulfill this responsibility to cultivate. Second, the work mandate is a covenant requiring a lifetime of devotion. Even after the fall, the duty to cultivate continues. Yet sin changed the nature of work into toil as God said that "through painful toil, you will eat of it all the days of your life" (Gen 3:17). Third, it takes effort to cultivate and keep the environment. The task is not easy and takes effort. Finally, the object of this mandate is the garden or the public domain of God's creation. Humans are to be concerned for not just their internal spiritual being, but also the needs of the society at large. This task is to benefit God's creation, including humans, and maintain God's creation order. In short, God desires humans to work. It is a lifetime of satisfaction amid toil. It takes effort. And the final beneficiary is God's creation order.

This cultural mandate forms the biblical foundation for public theology. The term, public theology, was coined by Martin Marty in the 1960s.[5] Marty defines public theology as "an effort to interpret the life of a people in the light of a transcendent reference."[6] Engaging in public theology is the effort to relate one's private faith to the public order.[7] Thus, public theology involves the definition of the public sphere. What are the public issues in which we need to be involved? What are the private matters from which we need to be protected? The exact meanings of public spheres are not specific. Sebastian Kim, a scholar of public theology and editor of the International Journal of Public Theology, defines the public sphere in six major bodies: state, media, religious communities, academics, civil society, and market.[8] Each body has its sub-groups. These six bodies represent the different natures of the public sphere and the contexts in which public theology can engage. Doing public theology is an effort to engage theology in dialogue with these bodies. Take the state body as an example; this body deals with politics, policymaking, governments, judiciary, and legislatures that impact society. Public theology that engages the state body would dialogue on the issues involving the above aspects. Indeed, these bodies do not stand alone by themselves but inter-relate

---

5. Martin Marty, "Reinhold Niebuhr: Public Theology and the American Experience," *The Journal of Religion* 54, no. 4 October (1974).
6. Martin Marty, *Public Church: Mainline-Evangelical-Catholic* (New York: Crossroad, 1981), 9–11.
7. Marty, 9.
8. Kim, *Public Sphere*, 12–13.

to each other. For example, in non-democratic countries, the state controls the other bodies, such as the media and economy.[9] Doing public theology would require engagement in multiple discourses with different issues and seek to understand the relationships among the different bodies.

The Role of the Church in Doing Public Theology

While we affirm the role of individual Christians in doing public theology, what is the role of the church? The first time the word, "church," appears in the New Testament is in Matthew 16:18, when Jesus said to Peter, "on this rock I will build my church." The Greek word for church, ἐκκλησία (*ekklesia*), means an assembly or congregation. The word does not limit the church to an established organization or a building. Instead, it refers to a group of believers. Similarly, the book of Acts uses the term to describe the group of believers at that time. For example, the text says that fear descended upon the church and speaks of persecution against the church, referring to believers (Acts 5:11; 8:1). Saul ravaged the church, which again means the group of believers (Acts 8:3). There was no "registration" of the church group. As Paul, the converted Saul explicated the cultural mandate for all Christians in the book of Romans. He urged the believers to "live at peace with everyone" and to "overcome evil with good" (Rom 12:18, 21). Believers are the "salt" and "light" of the world as Jesus taught in the Sermon on the Mount in Matthew chapter 6. With this understanding, the cultural mandate that God gave to Adam, representing humans, is also applicable to the collective body of believers in the form of a church.

The church, as a collective body of believers, has a unique advantage. Together, Christians encourage one another and build one another up (1 Thess 5:11). Hebrews 10:24–25 thus urges believers to "consider how to spur one another on toward love and good deeds. Let us not give up meeting together . . . but let us encourage one another. . . ." This is an echo of the principle taught in Ecclesiastes 4:9–10 that "two are better than one because they have a good return for their work. If one falls down, his friend can help him up." In the good works of caring for the social needs, the church, as a collective body, can build up the Christian body and encourage each other to continue with the effort. In the effectiveness of good work, the church becomes a healthier body, a catalyst for the permeation of gospel value into society.[10]

---

9. Kim, *Public Sphere*, 12.
10. Kim, 230.

In this unique role, the church can not only be fruitful, but can also reflect God's values. It points out the biblical values that can speak to society. It welcomes and invites dialogue with non-believers. The church can engage in open discourse with the non-believing world to seek the common goal of public good. Contrary to the worry of some, when the church maintains its core Christian values and belief, it does not lose its Christian identity. Instead, as Sebastian Kim points out, public theology extends Christian concerns for human well-being, justice, and community life into the wider public sphere.[11] This open communal dialogue engages the church on public issues. Dialogues draw the broader community of non-believers to understand how Christianity is relevant to social concerns.

The Church's Duty to Provide Moral Vision

The church takes up the priestly function in modern culture. The Apostle Paul refers to rulers and the governing authorities as ministers and servants ordained by God (Rom 13:1, 3–4, 6). The state is obligated to uphold justice and avenge evil. In assisting the state to fulfill this function, the church, as God's representative, performs a priestly function by conveying God's message and vision. Unfortunately, some countries do not always seek to advance the freedom of the people they govern. Religious freedom and personal freedom could be restricted. The World Council of Churches, after its conference in 1948, stated the criteria of a responsible society:

> A modern society can be a responsible society if "people have the freedom to control, to criticize, and to change their governments" and the power is distributed "as widely as possible through the whole community."[12]

When society goes astray, the church bears the responsibility to bring back the moral vision it needs. Without moral vision, the government and its people will conduct themselves according to their fleshy desires. The recognition and fulfillment of such responsibility upon the church is the critical first step to do public theology, especially when society is in unrest and turmoil.

---

11. Kim, 231.
12. Odair Pedroso Mateus, *World Council of Churches, WCC70 Amsterdam 1948 (4): Covenanting in Study: Communism, Capitalism, and the Responsible Society.* September 4, 2018. https://www.oikoumene.org/en/press-centre/news/wcc70-amsterdam-1948-4-covenanting-in-study-communism-capitalism-and-the-responsible-society. Accessed August 14, 2020.

In his book, *Asian Public Theology*, Felix Wilfred, a liberation theologian, points out three concerns that the church needs to address to live out the faith: political freedom, freedom from economic oppression, and creation of a harmonious and non-exclusive community.[13] The church needs to join people in their struggles for justice and freedom, rather than limiting its functions to the traditional ecclesiological framework and traditions. Wilfred, using the context of India, connects conversions to the rejection of social-economic discrimination. This recognition of discrimination is particularly crucial for Asian cultures because the cultural content favors a hierarchical structure that is prone to exploitation. The church pays attention to the cultural context and needs to relate theology to the cultural challenge.

When a government does not allow criticism or abuses its power to control its people's freedoms, the church is obligated to voice concern and participate in freedom struggles. One example of this courage in speaking up is the church is India. India has a rigid and discriminating caste system. It originated in the Hindu law as early as 1000 BC and divided people into distinct categories; within this system a segment of the entire population is banned and restricted from full social participation based solely on family origins. Although India abolished the caste system in 1950 in the Independence Constitution, the practice lives on. The church can provide governments and people with the moral vision needed to understand the injustice associated with the caste system. However, the church in India, has historically enjoyed a privileged status due to its connection with the ruling class during India's colonial past. The church needs to connect with and show compassion to the oppressed, and especially needs to engage with the oppressed in their fight for freedom. Wilfred, in another article, *Action Groups and the Struggle for Justice in India: Ecclesiological Implications*, explains the Christian involvement in these struggles. Individual Christians in India began to form action groups to fight for freedoms and succeeded in the fight. However, they also conflicted with the established church's leadership, which considered activism as being outside the traditional church business framework. Wilfred points out that the church must reflect on the political and cultural context in which it exists and witness

---

13. Felix Wilfred, *Asian Public Theology: Critical Concerns in Challenging Times*. Delhi: Allianz Enterprise, 2010), xi–xiv.

to society universally.¹⁴ If the people suffer, the church is obligated to respond. If the government fails its people, the church must cry out.

The action groups in India also align themselves with other religious communities to form alliances to fight for freedoms. According to Wilfred, this type of inter-religious communion is a kind of "kingdom-community" and a part of God's plan.¹⁵ Traditional church leadership does not accept this type of community and activism, nor do they regard it as a type of the traditional church practices. However, this activism effort is crucial to keep the church relevant to people, especially in the plights of people's suffering. Mission and theology do not exist in a vacuum but are lived out in real lives. The Asian cultural context calls for the church's intervention for good governance and the pursuit of society's common good. This responsibility is the essence of public theology.

The Church as a New Family Sphere

In his book, *Chinese Public Theology: Generational Shifts and Confucian Imagination in Chinese Christianity*, Alexander Chow explores the significance of the church as a public body in twenty-first century China. In Chinese tradition, the family unit is vital. The Cultural Revolution in the 1960s when children were encouraged to report on their parents severely marred this tradition. The subsequent One Child Policy in the 1980s eradicated the extended family structure. Finally, the ill effects of globalization separating parents and children broke down the nuclear family unit in modern Chinese society.

Chow argues that the church has taken the place of the traditional family as a new surrogate family.¹⁶ This interpretation of the church's surrogate function may be valid for those who migrate to other cities for education and work, and who treat the church as their new family. The church provides support to individuals with the pastors as the patriarchs. The church also replaces the family to engage in key functions such as charity work. Chow attributes such involvement to the Confucian imagination of "inward sageliness, outward kingliness" (*nei sheng wai wang*). This phrase originates from the Daoist text, *Zhuangzi*. It refers to the unfortunate reality of those who seek to change the world (outward kingliness), but inevitably forget the true beauty of Heaven

---

14. Felix Wilfred, "Action Groups and the Struggle for Justice in India: Ecclesiological Implications." *The Ecumenical Review* 39.3 (2010): 303.
15. Wilfred, 306.
16. Alexander Chow, *Chinese Public Theology: Generational Shifts and Confucian Imagination in Chinese Christianity* (Oxford: Oxford University Press, 2018), 150.

and Earth ("inward sageliness"). Internal transformation must take place before the transformation of the world.[17]

Chow also utilizes an ancient Confucian concept of "managing the world" (*jing shi*). Contemporary Confucian scholar, Tu Wei-Ming, prominently uses the jing shi concept as a bridge to connect public theology with the Chinese Confucian culture as the foundation for public theology. The Confucian concept of managing the world is analogous to Christians' obligation to engage theology with public issues. Chow's usage of Confucianism and the churches' role in arguing for public theology might be too optimistic. The restrictions placed on the church, both the government churches and the underground family churches, limit a wide scale of social involvement. Nevertheless, the church, especially the underground family churches, is a tight niche supportive community and has proven to be a strong network for support. Chow also observes that some of the urban churches embrace the cultural mandate, which includes understanding the church as a non-governmental organization that can engage in the Chinese civil society.[18] Churches begin to engage in charitable activities, whether officially or unofficially, addressing social needs. This engagement is indeed a positive development among the Chinese churches in mainland China. Christians in China form circles around their fields such as universities and workplaces, and these circles become the new "reorientation" of familiar structures.[19] They collectively developed various media such as the academic field of Sino-Christian theology and several academic periodicals to speak into the Chinese public space. The church plays a crucial role in the study and methods of doing public theology.

However, the challenges of doing public theology in China remain strong. In his article on public theology in China, Xie Zhibin, a professor at Tongji University, Shanghai, cited other theologians such as Qingbao Zeng and reiterated the importance of the church in public theology. "The serving as a witness to God, a real public theology can be solely produced by the church," Xie quoted Qingbao Zeng.[20] Indeed, the church bears the task of bearing witness to the public domain. However, the church is under many restrictions and much pressure, Xie reasoned. In contemporary Chinese context, the state penetrates or influences the religious sphere. One of the challenges of doing

---

17. Chow, 150.
18. Chow, 150.
19. Chow, 149.
20. Zhibin Xie, "Why Public and Theological? The Problem of Public Theology in the Chinese Context." *International Journal of Public Theology* 2 (2017): 392–93.

public theology in China, as Xie observed, lies in the limited public social space apart from the government and the relatively unclear identity of the religious organizations engaging in charitable activities.[21] Yet these challenges are not surprising. In the case study of South Korea which will be addressed later, the church remained strong and courageous. Despite these obvious challenges, the church in China continues to flourish and enables the development of public theology in China.

PRACTICING PUBLIC THEOLOGY

Public theology involves the church engaging in discourses on social issues. The ability to carry this discourse is crucial for the church to remain relevant to Christian social witnessing. Several essential pointers would be helpful in practicing public theology.

Openness to Pluralism

The church must be ready to receive and be open to criticism from within the church body and outside. Discourses with a broad spectrum of groups and people navigate among differences in opinion. Disagreement is inevitable. The temptation is to keep silent to avoid confrontation and disagreement. Yet, the result can be devastating. Uniformity in opinions is not necessarily a sign of unity for the church. Instead of viewing differences in opinion negatively, the church can view this pluralism as a complementary check and balance, and a means to keep it humble. The church speaks up, teaches the Lord's expectations, and calls out injustice. At the same time, the church remains humble to consider all opposing views. The church submissively seeks God's vision, and then faithfully delivers the message in boldness.

Openness to Scrutiny

The church, naturally, is under strict scrutiny in its actions as a witness for God, as the community observes whether they are consistent with what the church preaches or believes. The church must be genuine in its actions and beliefs. Individual believers are also judged by their actions. This openness to critical scrutiny helps the church to remain genuine and faithful.[22] Regrettably, there have been too many incidents in which the church has lost its ability to be a trusted witness. The child abuse scandals of the Catholic Church and

---

21. Xie, "Why Public and Theological," 395–98.
22. Kim, *Public Sphere*, 232.

the Boy Scouts organization are just the tips of an iceberg. When the church has the priestly role to deliver God's message, the church must be ready to be scrutinized.

Common Language

In discussing social issues, participants might not share the same Christian faith. Non-believing participants might not submit to the authority of the Bible. While Christians should stand firm in their religious beliefs and convictions, the methodology in engaging open discourses should utilize humans' shared values. Indeed, when God created humans, they were given a special place in the creation order. There are unique values common to all, regardless of religious convictions. Christians should be conversant in this language of shared values. By holding firm to one's Christian belief without wavering, one would not be compromising on the Christian conviction. By speaking in a language that others can understand, one can achieve the goal of doing public theology – engaging others to view the different social issues with theology.

God has instilled the spirit of conscience and a sense of humanity's common good. This common good concept is also common in Catholic teaching, particularly in the modern encyclical teachings of Pope John Paul II. Similarly, Protestant Christians also utilize this concept of common good to promote social dialogue and public theology. Sebastian Kim encourages churches to utilize the common good objectives and useful public insights as resources for the discourses.[23] This openness to other insights does not diminish Christian values. Instead, it is a recognition of God's sovereignty over all realms and the creation order. This openness begins a discussion that can embrace Christian and biblical authorities.

TWO CASE STUDIES

How should the church react to injustice and thus engage the government in combating the injustice? Two cases, one from South Korea and one from the West, help us understand and appreciate churches' government engagement.

Korea – the Church's Role in the Democratization Process

Churches in South Korea have been through various stages of theological development since the 1950s. After the Second World War, the theology of *kibock sinang* or "faith for seeking blessings" to deliver them from poverty gained

---

23. Kim, *Public Sphere*, 17–18.

ground in South Korea. With the backdrop of economic growth that began in the 1950s and 1960s, economic injustice and industrial abuse incidents were common. At the same time, church membership grew and mega-churches emerged.[24] The church generally interpreted material rewards such as wealth and healing as God's spiritual blessings.[25] The church in South Korea and their pastors simply accepted injustice as a necessary part of the economic development that the country enjoyed.

As the economy grew, so did the level of social injustice associated with industrialization. The incident where a sewing factory worker named Jun Tae-Ill set himself on fire to protest workplace abuse awoke the South Korean churches. Christian leaders were shaken by this and began to align themselves with the poor. The Minjung Movement began. Minjung means "people," and Minjung theology represented the ideology of standing with the people. The church felt the need to respond to the needs of the poor. Christian leaders in South Korea realized the structural and systematic injustice that caused the urban poverty problem. The *Korean Christian Manifesto* was authored in 1973; it identified those who oppressed people as having "evil power," and declared that Jesus the Messiah would one day destroy them. Two years later, another well-known Minjung theologian named Suh Nam-Dong, argued that the liberation of the poor involves communal and political changes.[26] This call for social justice caused a paradigm shift – from merely caring for the poor to making concrete changes with a particular political vision.

Another important political backdrop for the rise of Minjung theology was the political dictatorship of General Park Chung-hee. Park seized power in South Korea with a coup in 1961. From 1961 to the 1980s, different dictators controlled the economic power of the country. In the meantime, Christian activists emerged and defied the authoritarian government's rule. Korean Christians organized different grassroots organizations such as the Korean Student Christian Federation. The National Council of Churches of Korea and the Catholic Church joined in the democracy movement.[27] They held prayer meetings, all-night vigils, fasting, and mass demonstrations. They called for reforms to end the autocratic regime and to call for a new democratic

---

24. Kim, 116.
25. Kim, 110–111.
26. Kim, 117.
27. Yun-Shik Chang, The Progressive Christian Church and Democracy in South Korea, *Oxford Journal of Church and State* 40, no. 2 (1998): 438.

constitution. The church took advantage of its privileged position to continue the movement and never was timid with their position on this social issue.

The authoritarian government arrested religious leaders for their support of the democracy movement. The church suffered persecution from the government for decades. The church chose to be visible and influential. It refused to yield to the government's pressure to limit its activities to solely religious matters.[28] The authoritarian government used many tactics to deter the church. It monitored and harassed the church's activities, exerted economic pressures, expelled foreign missionaries, and prevented dissidents from getting visas to go abroad. Nevertheless, the church stood firm.

Some religious leaders supported the authoritarian government. Kim Jong-Pil, prime minister at the time, used the Bible to criticize church leaders for their political involvement, which he considered a worldly matter. Some held that Christians should just support and submit to their government.[29] Others organized groups to oppose any democratic movement effort and attributed the rising crime rate to the activists' protests. It was only in hindsight that they regretted such a position.[30] It took a long time to educate and build unity in the call for democracy.

The Christian activists received support from overseas Korean Christians and churches. Democratic Korean Christians formed different coalitions with overseas Christian organizations such as the Documentation Center for Action Group in Asia in Japan, the North America Coalition of Human Rights in New York, and the World Council of Churches to raise awareness of the oppression and to initiate changes.[31] Overseas Koreans formed groups to lobby international entities such as the United States Congress. Over the years, Christian activists were persistent in raising awareness of the condition in South Korea and pressured the government to change. These efforts also stimulated Christian groups in other countries and led to the social justice movement in South Korea.

Finally, in 1993, a genuine election took place to elect Kim Young Sam, the first civilian president in South Korea.[32] The free election marked the end of

---

28. Chang, 444.
29. Chang, 456.
30. Chang, 440.
31. Misook Lee, "South Korea's Democratization Movement of the 1970s and 80s and Communicative Interaction in Transnational Ecumenical Networks," *International Journal of Korean History* 19, no. 2 (2004).
32. *South Korea – Timeline*, BBC News. May 1, 2008. https://www.bbc.com/news/world-asia-pacific-15292674. Accessed on July 5, 2020.

authoritarian rulers in the country. The effort of the church in Korea to engage in these democratization efforts in these last few decades was crucial. Although the church had its many shortcomings, the church fulfilled its prophetic voice to call out the injustice and engage in political changes.

War and Peace – A Case Study of the Church's Advocacy in the Iraq War

The Iraq War in 2003 was controversial. On 15 February 2003, massive demonstrations against the war happened in sixty different countries and 800 cities.[33] Millions of people participated in the protest, including many Christians. The United Nations' Security Council rejected the call to go to war. But in March 2003, the US and the United Kingdom decided to wage war against Iraq, claiming Iraqi possession of weapons of mass destruction.

Facing such a political dilemma, should the church get involved? How should it engage amid diverging and polarizing opinions, even among Christians? First, the church engaged in discourses, formal and informal. For example, Richard Neuhaus, the editor of *First Things*, a religious journal, was among the advocates to support the war, seeking to prevent more significant harm.[34] Others, such as those from the Mennonite tradition of nonviolence, opposed the conflict. Despite this difference in opinions, the church in their respective platforms engaged with the issue. Conducting discourse on the issue was an essential step of discernment, a necessary step to understand the reasoning behind different positions.

Second, different religious denominations put together documents and analysis arguments. About one year before the actual invasion of Iraq, the Archbishop's Council of the Church of England put out the document, *Evaluating the Threat of Military Action Against Iraq*, to oppose the war based upon an analysis of the just war theory.[35] Just war theory is an ethical theory used to determine whether a country can legitimately go into war. The analysis result was that there were options other than war. Moreover, it noted that the war option had a critical flaw in lacking a viable plan to rebuild the Iraqi government after the toppling of Saddam Hussein. The criticism proved

---

33. Kim, *Public Sphere*, 158.
34. John Ydstie and Robert Siegel. "Issue of War with Iraq from Theological, Political and Military Perspectives," *All Things Considered*, USA: National Public Radio. 27 September 2002. https://legacy.npr.org/programs/atc/transcripts/2002/sep/020927.siegel.html. Accessed on July 5, 2020.
35. Kim, *Public Sphere*, 159.

insightful. Even today, in 2022, the US still struggles with the rebuilding of a new Iraqi government, leaving Iraq vulnerable to division and chaos, and hampering the task of rebuilding the country constructively.

Third, the church built coalitions to invite other churches and denominations to join in. The common language of human rights can be a useful tool for this coalition. Diverse groups, regardless of religious convictions, came together to argue against the impending war.

Fourth, the different groups within the church offered options other than war. They tried to analyze the situation and present other options, putting together documents such as *Disarm Iraq without War*. The World Council of Churches organized a Berlin conference on 5 February 2003, seeking to warn against the impending war. Even the Catholic Church joined in. Pope John Paul II made clear his opposition to military action in his address on 13 January 2003, saying "No to War!"[36] The churches tried but to no avail.

Years later, in retrospect, did the church do the right things? Did the church fail because it was unable to prevent the war? Sebastian Kim attributes the failure to the mistake in using the just war theory as it was too vague. The same theory can very well lead to different conclusions depending on how the arguments are arranged.[37] Although Kim's criticism of the just war theory has merits, there was no other theory available for discussion.

In addition to critiquing the use of just war theory, Kim also argues that the church lacked sufficient passion in opposing the war. He argues that the church's message was generally weak. "The Church was without sufficient courage, and the option plan was not sufficiently concrete," Kim criticized.[38] Kim's criticism might be a bit too harsh. The US and the UK were determined to go to war; no theory or public opinion could have altered their decision. The church did raise its prophetic voice and deliver the message in good faith.

When evaluating the effectiveness of public engagement, one should refrain from judging the effectiveness based on the immediate result. With a strong government, engagement takes a long time. The example of the democratic movement of South Korea should give hope to Christians and the church. Remain faithful, endure hardship, and be patient. If the church is faithful, God, as the sovereign lord of all, will bring justice at the end.

---

36. Pope John Paul II, Address of His Holiness Pope John Paul II to the Diplomatic Corps. 13 January 2003. http://www.vatican.va/content/john-paul-ii/en/speeches/2003/january/documents/hf_jp-ii_spe_20030113_diplomatic-corps.html. Accessed on July 5, 2020.
37. Kim, *Public Sphere*, 166–67.
38. Kim, 67–169.

A Prophetic Voice in the Wilderness

A PRAGMATIC APPROACH

If we are convinced that it is the duty for the church to do public theology, the question remains: what would this mean in practice, especially as the social context of the church continues to evolve and change? We can make several observations that can help bring clarity.

First, technology has developed so rapidly that many options are now available to continue the effort to raise awareness. China has tried for decades to confine religious practice within church buildings through registration requirements, restrictive laws, and imprisonment. However, the newest generation of Chinese intellectual and elite Christians have defied such restrictions. These Christian intellectuals are referred to as the third generation of Chinese Christian intellectuals. They make excellent use of technologies such as Weibo, blogs, microblogs, and online and print magazines to discuss social issues.[39] The third generation of public theologians in China demonstrates that no authoritarian rule can stop freedom of thought and speech. South Korean churches' example attests to the importance of building a coalition with like-minded groups within and without, at home or abroad. These types of coalitions would be helpful in building consensus and bring about change.

Second, doing public theology requires a willingness to pay a price and to cultivate the character needed to endure. The Bible contains many narratives of authoritarian governments such as the Egyptian government during Moses's time and the Roman Empire during the early church period. Yet the Bible attests that oppression cannot suppress the people's voice. The pharisees did their best to silence the disciples about Jesus's resurrection and to stop his teaching from spreading. But the disciples did the opposite. The question is whether the church is willing to pay the price of obedient and faithful witness. Such willingness does not suddenly happen. It takes time to educate believers and nurture the character to endure. When the church is ready to suffer on this journey, the message can be delivered.

Violence risks the loss of witnessing. What is the role of using violence in the process of voicing one's concern? Violence can be useful in the short term to voice frustration. However, in the long run, violence is not preferred. That is why Jesus's ministry never resorted to violence (except the incidents at the temple). Reinhold Niebuhr, in his famous book, *Moral Man and Immoral*

---

39. Chow, *Chinese Public Theology*, 112.

Society, considers nonviolence a strategic tool.[40] Niebuhr rightly points out that violence tends to make the opposing side more stubborn. Because people would be so concerned about the effect of violence, they lose sight of the real issues. One should be beware of the blind spots of ideology. Violence might lead to the loss of a message in violence. Nonviolence, on the contrary, reduces the dangers of conflict to the minimum. It preserves moral, rational, and cooperative attitudes within an area of conflict and augments the moral forces without destroying them.[41] Gandhi of India and Martin Luther King Jr. of America are good examples of nonviolent social activists. Violence very easily distracts the discussion and gives opponents a foothold in their resistance to change. The church, as the messenger of moral vision, should be wise in its approach.

CONCLUSION

God chose his people to be his channels and to convey his message to the world. The church, which includes all believers, continues to fulfill this priestly role in providing God's moral vision to the society. Public theology has a unique role as the means to guide and protect the moral quality of a society. When the wider society or the government go astray and lose their morality, history reminds us that Christians who live out their faith and engage their theological beliefs publicly can benefit their society. The relationship between the church and the greater society and state can be tense, especially when the social culture considers Christian morals and character offensive. The church and its members reflect the higher calling from God and serve as a check on the decline of social morality. The church collectively serves as a body to fulfill the mandate of God.

Nevertheless, this mandate requires the church to nurture and instruct believers and society of what the Lord has asked of them. Engaging both the social culture and governments requires engaging in dialogue with diverse groups, addressing public concerns, being open to scrutiny and criticism, developing a common language, seeking the common good, and risking all in being faithful to God's call in the prophetic voice. Although the church might be inadequate in fulfilling the challenges, its faithfulness is what God demands. The example of the church in South Korea gives hope that changes are possible

---

40. Reinhold Niebuhr, *Moral Man, and Immoral Society: A Study in Ethics and Politics* (Louisville: Westminster John Knox Press, 1932), 251.
41. Niebuhr, 251.

with perseverance and faithfulness. Although the church was unable to prevent the Iraq War, it changed public opinion toward the war. Despite any immediate setbacks, history has also repeatedly proved that the church succeeded in its role to bring about common good and human rights. Nevertheless, the judgment of its success might not be readily apparent. With the eschatological view, this hope of cultivating and keeping the creation order does not die.

QUESTIONS FOR DISCUSSION

1. Identify the cultural ethe that are threatening your society, such as individualism, consumerism, relativism, and nationalism. How do these cultural ethe affect morality of the people?
2. Can you think of examples of how Jesus engaged his cultures and participated in his community, socially, racially, and politically?
3. How can the church cultivate among Christians the passion to engage with culture and society?
4. Identify a particular social issue and discuss how the church can provide the moral norms to guide the society at large.
5. What are the personal and structural barriers to the practice of public theology? Identify ways to overcome these barriers.

BIBLIOGRAPHY

BBC News. *South Korea – Timeline*, May 1, 2008. https://www.bbc.com/news/world-asia-pacific-15292674.

Chang, Yun-Shik. "The Progressive Christian Church and Democracy in South Korea," *Oxford Journal of Church and State* 40, no. 2 (1998): 437–65.

Chow, Alexander. *Chinese Public Theology: Generational Shifts and Confucian Imagination in Chinese Christianity*. Oxford: Oxford University Press, 2018.

Kim, Sebastian. *Theology in the Public Sphere*. London: SCM Press, 2011.

Kuyper, Abraham. "Sphere Sovereignty", in *Abraham Kuyper, A Centennial Reader*, edited by James D. Bratt. Grand Rapids: Eerdmans, 1998.

———. *The Problem of Poverty*. Translated by James W. Skillen. Sioux Center: Dordt College Press, 2011.

John Paul II (pope). Address of His Holiness Pope John Paul II to the Diplomatic Corps. 13 January 2003. http://www.vatican.va/content/john-paul-ii/en/speeches/2003/january/documents/hf_jp-ii_spe_20030113_diplomatic-corps.html.

Lee, Misook. "South Korea's Democratization Movement of the 1970s and 80s and Communicative Interaction in Transnational Ecumenical Networks."

International Journal of Korean History 19, no. 2 (2004). https://ijkh.khistory.org/journal/view.php?doi=10.22372/ijkh.2014.19.2.241.

Marty, Martin. "Reinhold Niebuhr: Public Theology and the American Experience," *The Journal of Religion* 54, no. 4 (1974): 332–59.

———. *Public Church: Mainline-Evangelical-Catholic.* New York: Crossroad, 1981.

Mateus, Odair Pedroso. *World Council of Churches, WCC70 Amsterdam 1948 (4): Covenanting in Study: Communism, Capitalism, and the Responsible Society.* 4 September 2018. https://www.oikoumene.org/en/press-centre/news/wcc70-amsterdam-1948-4-covenanting-in-study-communism-capitalism-and-the-responsible-society. Accessed 14 August 2020.

Niebuhr, Reinhold. *Moral Man, and Immoral Society: A Study in Ethics and Politics.* Louisville: Westminster John Knox Press, 1932.

United Nations, High Commissioner for Human Rights, Press Briefing Note on Hong Kong, China. 13 August 2019. https://www.ohchr.org/EN/NewsEvents/Pages/DisplayNews.aspx?NewsID=24888&LangID=E.

Wilfred, Felix. "Action Groups and the Struggle for Justice in India: Ecclesiological Implications." *The Ecumenical Review* 39, no. 3 (2010): 291–309.

———, *Asian Public Theology: Critical Concerns in Challenging Times.* Delhi: Allianz Enterprise, 2010.

Xie, Zhibin. "Why Public and Theological? The Problem of Public Theology in the Chinese Context," *International Journal of Public Theology* 2 (2017): 381–404.

Ydstie, John, and Robert Siegel. "Issue of War with Iraq from Theological, Political and Military Perspectives." *All Things Considered*, USA: National Public Radio. 27 September 2002. https://legacy.npr.org/programs/atc/transcripts/2002/sep/020927.siegel.html.

CHAPTER 11

HOMOSEXUALITY IN TWENTY-FIRST CENTURY ASIA

The Case of Taiwan

Shang-Jen Chen

In the past decades, homosexuality has been one of the most controversial issues in Western societies as well as the church. Lesbian, gay, bisexual, and transgender (LGBT) social movements advocate for moral approval and LGBT peoples' rights. These social movements challenge the reproach of homosexual acts in the Bible and accuse the church of discrimination against LGBT minorities. These social movements have caused tremendous changes in legislation, cultural norms, and social practices in the West. They have also had an impact on some Asian societies and Asian churches. This chapter will explore different passages in the Bible which are essential to teachings regarding homosexual acts. Arguments in favor of homosexuality will be brought under scrutiny. In addition, since Taiwan is the first Asian country to provide legal recognition for homosexual partnerships, the current situation in Taiwan will be discussed. In the end, the chapter will provide a retrospection and prospection of the church in Taiwan.

HOMOSEXUALITY IN THE BIBLE

Evangelical churches insist that the Bible is an essential resource for contemplating ethical issues. Church tradition, reason, and experience are also important, but they do not override the Bible's supremacy.[1] Therefore, it is essential to carefully read and interpret the passages which relate to homosexuality.

The Bible only has a few passages which directly relate to homosexuality. Unlike themes such as justice, care of the poor, respect of human life, which frequently and consistently appear in the Bible, texts which relate to homosexual

---

1. P. C. Lo, *Hei bai Fen Ming* [*Distinction between Black and White*] (Hong Kong: China Alliance Press, 1992), 230–31.

issues occur sporadically. In addition, the meaning of some of these verses is not as clear as we used to think. Therefore, we need to mindfully read these passages with particular attention to what they can teach Christians regarding homosexuality today. The verses which directly relate to homosexual themes are (a) Genesis 19:1–29, (b) Leviticus 18:22; 20:13, (c) 1 Corinthians 6:9–11; 1 Timothy 1:10; Acts 15:28–29, and (d) Romans 1:18–32.

Genesis 19:1–29

The church has interpreted the story taking place in Sodom as being pertinent to homosexuality. The English word "sodomy," meaning anal sex between men, is derived from the name of the city, Sodom. However, many contemporary biblical scholars indicate that the sin and crime of the story is gang-rape. Richard B. Hays says, "The gang-rape scenario exemplifies the wickedness of the city, but there is nothing in the passage pertinent to a judgment about the morality of consensual homosexual intercourse."[2] Choon-Leong Seow states, "Rather, it is a story about wickedness in general, violence, and the violation of a sacrosanct code of hospitality. Gang rape is at issue in the passage, not same-sex love."[3] Some other verses mention the wickedness of Sodom, including Isaiah 1:10 and 3:9; Jeremiah 23:14; Ezekiel 16:49; Matthew 10:12–15; and Luke 10:12–12. In these verses, the sins in view seem to be injustice, adultery, lying, pride, gluttony, excess wealth, indifference to the poor, and their inhospitality. None of these texts mention homosexuality. The only exception is Jude 7, ". . . Sodom and Gomorrah and the surrounding towns gave themselves up to sexual immorality and perversion." Even though this passage is concerning sexual immorality, it does not clearly state whether it is a heterosexual or homosexual act.

Leviticus 18:22 & 20:13

Leviticus 18:22 states, "Do not have sexual relations with a man as one does with a woman; that is detestable." Similarly, Leviticus 20:13 later reiterates the point, saying, "If a man has sexual relations with a man as one does with a woman, both of them have done what is detestable. They are to be put to death; their blood will be on their own heads." These two passages clearly and

---

2. Richard B. Hays, *The Moral Vision of the New Testament: Community, Cross, New Creation: A Contemporary Introduction to New Testament Ethics* (New York: HarperOne, 1996), 381.
3. Choon-Leong Seow, "A Heterosexual Perspective." In Choon-Leong Seow ed. *Homosexuality and Christian Community* (Louisville: Westminster John Knox Press, 1996), 14–27, 15.

directly address homosexual acts. The prohibition of the man–man homosexual act in Leviticus is unambiguous, and punishment is death. Clearly, the moral judgment on such acts is negative.

Reading these passages in context suggests that Leviticus 18 and 20 not only warn against such acts, but explicitly prohibit them. First, these passages categorize homosexual acts alongside other clearly prohibited behaviors such as adultery, incest, and bestiality. Second, God instructs the Israelites not to follow the immoral sexual practices of the gentiles, "You must not do as they do in Egypt, where you used to live, and you must not do as they do in the land of Canaan, where I am bringing you. Do not follow their practices" (Lev 18:3). Third, the passages make clear that God has set apart the Israelites as chosen people, and that as a result, they must be holy because God is holy (Lev 19:2; 20:26). The prohibition of homosexual acts in Leviticus is the foundation for the subsequent repudiation of homosexual acts between men within Judaism.[4]

Some interpreters argue that the regulations of Leviticus 17–26 are part of the holiness code – an element of the Mosaic law that was abandoned by early Christians in light of the law's fulfillment in Christ. The many distinctions related to ceremonially clean food and behavior was intended to highlight the Israelites' unique status and identity. The Israelites were holy, and the gentiles were not.

Yet since the first century, Christians stopped complying with the holiness code of Leviticus, asserting that they need not follow the commandments regarding circumcision and kosher foods. Thus, some interpreters suggest that if Christians, the new Israelites, are not bound by the ritual codes of Leviticus, the prohibition of homosexual acts, a part of the holiness code in Leviticus, should be lifted at once.[5]

For evangelical Christians, this argument is not convincing. Most of the prohibitions in Leviticus 18 and 20 are clearly connected not only to ceremonial purity, but fundamental morality. The acts forbidden here – adultery, incest, bestiality – are seen as impure and unholy precisely because they are immoral. It is no surprise, as a result, that these acts continued to be deemed as immoral even in the New Testament. The apostles did not regard the Levitical prohibitions on sexuality to be analogous to the abolition of circumcision,

---

4. Hays, *The Moral Vision of the New Testament*, 381.
5. Yang-en Cheng and Tsong-sheng Tsan, ed. *Wo men he ju zhi you? Ji du xin yang yu tong zhi qun ti de hui yu* [*What Do We Fear? The Encounter of Christian Belief and the Homosexual Community*] (HuaLian: Taiwan hao shi xie hui, 2019), 69.

which is clearly stated in Acts and Pauline epistles. Instead, the repudiation of homosexual acts occurs several times in the New Testament.

1 Corinthians 6:9–11 & 1 Timothy 1:10

Although gentile Christians do not comply with the ceremonial rituals and regulations of kosher food of the Old Testament, Hays insists that, "The early church did, in fact, consistently adopt the Old Testament's teaching on matters of sexual morality, including homosexual acts."[6] In 1 Corinthians 6:9 and 1 Timothy 1:10, Paul gives a list of evil deeds; both of the lists include homosexual acts.

> Or do you not know that wrongdoers will not inherit the kingdom of God? Do not be deceived: Neither the sexually immoral nor idolaters nor adulterers nor men who have sex with men nor thieves nor the greedy nor drunkards nor slanderers nor swindlers will inherit the kingdom of God. (1 Cor 6:9–10)

The NIV translation of "have sex with men" in verse nine actually translates two different words in Greek, *malakoi* and *arsenokoitai*. Malakoi means being the passive partners – often young boys – in homosexual activity. Arsenokiotai refers generally to homosexual intercourse.[7] Arsenokiotai is also used in 1 Timothy 1:10. Robin Scroggs, a New Testament scholar, notes that the Septuagint, the Greek version of the Old Testament, uses arsenokoitai in Leviticus 20:13. He suggests that Paul takes the word from Leviticus 20:13 of the Septuagint and uses it in 1 Timothy 1:10, indicating that Paul reaffirms the prohibitions of homosexual acts in the Old Testament.[8] What concerns Paul here is not the ceremonial ritual of the Old Testament at all. It is the idolatry and immoral behaviors committed by the Corinthian Christians that worried Paul. He reminds the Corinthians that some of them had committed these sins and now since they are sanctified in the name of the Lord Jesus Christ and by the Spirit of our God (6:11), they should not continue in these acts. Homosexual acts are clearly one of the sinful behaviors in Paul's list.

---

6. Hays, *The Moral Vision of the New Testament*, 382.
7. Hays, *The Moral Vision of the New Testament*, 382.
8. Robin Scroggs, *The New Testament and Homosexuality* (Philadelphia: Fortress, 1983), 106–8.

Romans 1:18–32

This passage is the essential text in the New Testament to understand when we are seeking to explore the moral assessment of homosexual acts. Unlike 1 Corinthians 6:9 or 1 Timothy 1:10 which could be taken to suggest that homosexual acts are merely one vice in a list of evils, Romans 1:18–32 is an integrated passage setting out an important theological argument.

To understand what role homosexual acts play in the passage, we need to understand the main theme in Romans 1:18–32. Before this passage, in Romans 1:16–17 Paul presents a thesis regarding the gospel:

> For I am not ashamed of the gospel, because it is the power of God that brings salvation to everyone who believes: first to the Jew, then to the Gentile. For in the gospel, the righteousness of God is revealed – a righteousness that is by faith from first to last, just as it is written: "The righteous will live by faith."

In Romans 1:18–23 Paul articulates that the fall of human beings stems from the consequences of idolatry and sinful desires. That "women exchanged natural sexual relations for unnatural ones" and that "men also abandoned natural relations with women and were inflamed with lust for one another" are given as examples to illustrate the sinful desires caused by the fall of human beings. In addition to unnatural homosexual acts, Paul provides a long series of wicked acts in Romans 1:29–31.

In chapter one of the book of Romans, Paul's central subject is God's creation of human beings and the world, human idolatry, God's wrath, and the miserable consequences of sin. Although Christian sexual ethics is not the main theme here, Paul considers homosexual desires and acts offensive to God.

Agreement between Old and New Testaments

After these passages are explored, one observation and one clarification need to be made. Although there are only some biblical texts that address homosexuality, they unanimously convey strong repudiation of homosexual acts. The attitude toward homosexuality in the New Testament agrees with the Old Testament. It is important to clarify that neither the Old Testament nor the New Testament says that homosexuality is the worst sin. When Leviticus 18:26 says, "The native-born and the foreigners residing among you must not do any of these detestable things," these "detestable things" include all unethical sexual acts. Most of them are related to incest. As noted previously, in 1 Corinthians 6:9–10 and 1 Timothy 1:10, Paul provides a list of wrongs, and lists homosexual acts as just one among many. In Romans chapter one, homosexuality is given as the primary example to illustrate the miserable consequences of human rebellion to God, but Paul also mentions more than twenty other transgressions (vv. 29–31).

LIBERAL THEOLOGY ON HOMOSEXUALITY

Some liberal theologians argue for the approbation of homosexual acts, gay marriage, and ordination for practicing homosexual persons.[9] Although liberal theologians rightly indicate that the Bible's interpretation is closely correlated with church tradition, reason, and human experience, most liberal arguments do not give the same weight to the Bible as evangelical arguments do. Rather, liberal theologians who defend homosexuality tend to challenge the traditional interpretations of the related passages or even the Bible's authority, justifying homosexuality using four common reasons.[10]

First, according to the liberals' interpretation, the Bible does not repudiate homosexual acts. They say that the church has misunderstood these relevant passages for the last two thousand years and that this misunderstanding needs to be corrected now. The liberal interpretation of the passages in Leviticus is that the passages condemn prostitution and male-prostitution found in the temple cults of the pagan religion.[11] Liberal theologians cite Deuteronomy 23:18 when interpreting Leviticus 18:22 and 20:13. In an analogous way, liberal theologians claim that the New Testament does not disallow homosexual acts and homosexual relationships between two adults. Rather, they state that what Paul cites as an example of human sinfulness in Romans is the exploitative relationship between men and young boys often seen in Greek culture in his time.[12] They insist that the relationship between men and young boys is unjust and, therefore, sinful because the relationship is exploitative. However, the exploitive relationship between young boys and men is different from the equal relationship between two consensual adults who "love" each other.

Second, the impact of feminist theology has played an essential role in the justification of homosexuality. Feminist theology has developed for more than a

---

9. Yang-en Cheng and Tsong-sheng Tsan, ed. *Wo men he ju zhi you? Ji du xin yang yu tong zhi qun ti de hui yu* [*What Do We Fear? The Encounter of Christian Belief and the Homosexual Community*] (HuaLian: Taiwan hao shi xie hui), 2019.
10. L. Y. Kung, "Response to Lo C. P. in chapter 1," 25 and 27. C. P. Lo, and L. Y. Kung, *Tong Xing Lian de Shi zi Jian* [*The Cross of the Homosexuality*] (Hong Kong: Hong Kong Christian Institute, 2013).
11. Yang-en Cheng and Tsong-sheng Tsan, ed., *What Do We Fear?*, 71.
12. Yang-en Cheng and Tsong-sheng Tsan, ed., *What Do We Fear?*, 97.

half-century. It emphasizes that justice is the core value of Christianity, and that women are suppressed in patriarchal societies. Therefore, Christians must read and interpret the Bible from the eyes of the oppressed, and from the female perspective to counterbalance male bias. Elisabeth Schüssler Fiorenza, a leading feminist theologian says, "Only when theology is on the side of the outcast and oppressed, as Jesus was, can it become incarnational and Christian. Christian theology, therefore, must be rooted in emancipatory praxis and solidarity."[13]

Feminist theology makes a significant contribution to drawing Christian attention to female roles in the Bible and church history, critiquing the injustice of the patriarchy of societies, in order to improve female social status, especially in the church. However, feminist theology goes far beyond that. Feminist theology insists that the experiences of oppressed women are essential for criticizing and challenging the authority of the Bible. Schüssler Fiorenza argues New Testament texts are to some extent, "androcentric codification of patriarchal power and ideology that cannot claim to be the revelatory Word of God."[14]

Some liberal theologians use the argument of patriarchic and androcentric ideology to justify homosexual relationships and acts. Using the feminist argument, liberal theologians claim that historically human societies have been hetero-hegemonic; therefore, people that are attracted to their same-sex are the minority and often misunderstood and oppressed. Since the Bible was written some two thousand years ago, liberal theologians argue that the authors would have no way of understanding same-sex relationships or their emotional and sexual needs. Liberal theologians thus believe that based on our contemporary understanding of social and behavioral science, homosexuals should be treated justly and equally. In addition, biblical scripture with patriarchal, male-centric, and hetero-hegemonic ideology should be reinterpreted.

The third reason, one of most common justifications of homosexuality, is that sexual orientation is genetic, not simply a life choice. People should not be admonished for their natural orientation and the acts induced by nature. However, "I was born this way" is an over-simplified and misleading argument in validating homosexuality. There are at least two points that need to be clarified. One is scientific; the other is theological. First, the American

---

13. Elisabeth Schüssler Fiorenza, "Feminist Theology as a Critical Theology of Liberation," *Theological Studies* 36, no. 4 (1975): 616.
14. Elisabeth Schüssler Fiorenza, *In Memory of Her: A Feminist Theological Reconstruction of Christian Origins* (New York: Crossroad, 1983), 32.

Psychiatric Association, which in 1973 ceased to list homosexuality as a psychiatric disorder, recognizes that "there are biological, psychological, social, and cultural influences at play in gender and sexual developmental trajectories. Social factors, such as family and peer relationships, robustly shape behavior during preschool and school-age years."[15] There is no conclusive evidence that genes determine homosexual orientation. Therefore, the claim that a person is born as homosexual has no scientific proof. Second, the Bible does not teach that human beings are the measure of all things. Neither does the Bible say that human beings take responsibility only when they have free will to choose. Since Adam's fall, human beings have had no choice but to sin against God. Human beings are slaves of sin (Rom 5:14; 6:16; 7:15). As Hays puts it, sin distorts perceptions of human beings in a corrupted world and overpowers the human will. The human inclination is to sin, not to do good.[16] The criteria of what is lawful and sinful for Christians is given as a revelation from God through the Scripture, not human reason nor inclinations. Sinful human inclinations do not justify human behaviors. Biblical standards and teachings from the Bible are true both for heterosexuals and homosexuals.

The fourth argument is that all human beings are sinners, whether heterosexual or homosexual. Therefore, the church should not admonish only homosexual acts. This argument intends to confuse and take focus away from the main point of the discussion. To clarify, it is important to point out that the church does not approve all kinds of heterosexual acts, but only consensual sex in marriage, which is between one man and one woman. This standard is given by scripture and has been recognized by the church. In the West, some liberal churches have gradually become more laxed regarding compliance with the moral standards of Scripture. Evangelical churches consistently require ordained ministers to be faithful to their spouse if married or adopt a celibate lifestyle when single. The LGBT movement demands the recognition and blessing of same-sex marriage and the ordination of practicing homosexual persons. In a way, the LGBT movement asks the church to change the definition of marriage and overlook the moral criteria contained in the Bible.

---

15. American Psychiatric Association website, https://www.psychiatry.org/psychiatrists/cultural-competency/education/best-practice-highlights/working-with-lgbtq-patients.
16. Richard Hays, *The Moral Vision of the New Testament*, 390.

Avoiding the Bipolar Interpretations of Genders

While the pitfalls of LGBT theology must be recognized, the opposite extreme, namely an extreme form of complementarianism, should also be avoided. Some complementarians advocate a very conservative interpretation of genders, believing that women are to submit themselves to the leadership of men because it is the order ordained by God. They do not take into consideration the different examples shown in Scripture and the social and historical differences between the biblical ages and contemporary society. Although these complementarians proclaim that men and women are created with equal dignity, they insist on certain fixed gender expressions and a kind of patriarchy unjust to women, claiming that they stem from a God-ordained created order.

LGBT theology is on the other extreme, saying that all the gender differences are cultural constructions and open to continuous change. LGBT theology does not respect the theological understandings of the created order derived from Genesis 1 and 2. Namely, God creates men and women with biophysical differences and commends them to "be fruitful and increase in number, fill the earth, and subdue it" (1: 28). Marriage is God's ordained institution in which heterosexual intercourse and procreation are blessed. Therefore, marriage, sexual acts, and procreation are interconnected for the welfare of individuals and the community. They ought not to be arbitrarily disjoined. Contrasted to the potentially procreative heterosexual act in a committed marriage, homosexual acts and relationships serve, at most, the satisfaction of individuals' sexual desire and the expression of mutual affection.

THE LGBT MOVEMENT IN TAIWAN

Attitudes toward LGBT people and their homosexual acts have been influenced by religious, legal, social, political, and cultural heritage. Most Asian countries do not recognize same-sex marriage. Taiwan is the only exception. The secular government has generally tolerated homosexuality to varying degrees, while countries that have established Islam as their state religion prohibit homosexuality and impose penalties for homosexual acts.[17] The countries which culturally share the Confucian heritage, such as China, Japan, South Korea, and Singapore, traditionally disapprove of homosexuality. Still,

---

17. Daniel Ottosson, *State-Sponsored Homophobia – A World Survey of Laws Prohibiting Same-Sex Activity Between Consenting Adults*, 2010 ILGA. http://old.ilga.org/Statehomophobia/ILGA_State_Sponsored_Homophobia_2010.pdf.

people's attitudes toward homosexuality are constantly being challenged by the LGBT movement.

The evolution of legislature regarding homosexual acceptance can be categorized into five phases. The first phase is to remove the sodomy law that penalizes consensual same-sex sexual activity. Second, advocates for the LGBT movement push states to legitimatize the so-called "gender equality educational law" and impose it on schools in order to eliminate any kind of gender discrimination. In the law, lesbians, gays, bisexuals, and transgenders are considered gender minorities. All sorts of sexual inclinations should be treated as equal, and all kinds of sex between consensual adults should be protected by law. School teachers who express their opinions against "gender equality" are subject to prosecution with possible permanent deprivation of their teaching positions. LGBT advocates know very well that it is easier to indoctrinate school children with "progressive" moral ideas than change the attitudes of mature adults. Third, when school children indoctrinated by LGBT teachings grow old and have the right to vote, LGBT advocates think that they can then run for election so that they have the power to pass same-sex marriage laws in State Congress. Fourth, once same-sex marriage law has been passed, people become desensitized and are more inclined to grant adoption rights to same-sex couples. Fifth, when most of society does not oppose LGBT behaviors, LGBT advocates can champion the so-called anti-discrimination law to criminalize those who have different moral attitudes, speeches, and acts. Christian clergy and the church are often the targets of these anti-discrimination law.

A notable introductory point of the LGBT movement in Taiwan was the establishment of sexology, or sex studies, in universities in the 1990s. Sexology is the study of human sexuality, including human sexual interests, behaviors, sexual orientation, gender identity, and atypical sexual interests. To protect freedom of speech and academic studies, professors of sexology advocated for sexual liberation, de-stigmatization of sex workers, legalization of the sex industry, LGBT rights, etc., though these issues were seen as morally controversial by the public. These advocates try to influence the thoughts of the younger generation through education, publishing journals and books, holding international and domestic symposia, public speaking, and mobilizing social movements.[18]

Since 2001, the LGBT Pride Parades have been held annually in Taipei and other major cities in Taiwan. The parades gathered more and more of the

---

18. http://sex.ncu.edu.tw/history/index.html.

young generation to uphold the LGBT rights. In 2004, the Gender Equity Education Act was promoted. This Act was promoted to "advance genuine gender equality, eliminate gender discrimination, safeguard human dignity, and soundly establish education resources and environments that epitomized gender equality."[19] The Act defines "gender identity" as an individual's awareness and acceptance of their particular gender category. In practice, it includes lesbian, gay, bisexual, transgender, etc. Those who provide negative commentary on gender traits, sexual orientation, and gender identity are seen as sexual bullies or engaging in harassment and are subject to removal from teaching positions. In a way, the Act secures the legitimacy of the LGBT ideology in educational institutes of all levels. It silences schoolteachers who have oppositional opinions. The LGBT ideology has been indoctrinated in students fully. Ironically, most parents are not aware of the impact this Act has on their children.[20]

Some Christian scholars have responded to the LGBT movement and argued that the moral value of the same-sex relationship is not equivalent to the moral value of the husband–wife relationship; therefore, homosexual union ought not to be seen as marriage. In 2006, *Solitudo*, a Taiwanese Christian journal, published a special issue to describe the case against the legalization of homosexual union. It contained articles by theologians, philosophers, and legal scholars.[21]

The moral concept of natural law was used as an argument to make the case against LGBT unions to the public. Monogamy has attained its status as the primary marital institution in major civilizations because it provides a structure that may fulfill three basic human needs. They are (1) sexual satisfaction, (2) a long-term, intimate, and stable emotional bond between a couple, and (3) an ideal environment for raising children. Homosexual acts and relationships are not able to contribute to the society by procreation which is an essential common good of marriage. Therefore, the homosexual relationship does not have equal moral value to the husband-and-wife relationship.[22]

---

19. https://law.moj.gov.tw/ENG/LawClass/LawAll.aspx?pcode=H0080067.
20. Zhang Wenhang, "Zheng shi xing ping jiao yu de zheng yi yu kun jing" [An Investigation to the Controversies and Dilemmas of Gender Equity Education] in Daowei, Wang et al., *Dang Ye Su yu Jian Tong Zhi* [*When Jesus Meets Homosexuals*], (Taipei: Zhen na da, 2020), 170–98.
21. Immanuel Chih-Ming Ke, editor-in-Chief, "Solitudo – A Meditative Journal of Taiwan Christian Thought," *Theology of Sex, Love, and Marriage.* no. 12, Special Issue Dec (2008).
22. Shang-Jen Chen, "A Moral Evaluation of Homosexual Acts," *Journal of Life Education* 3, no. 1 June (2011): 67–91.

The natural law argument was not well received by the public for three reasons. First, the public paid little attention to Christian scholars. Second, the public was not familiar with the moral concept of natural law. Third, the younger members of Taiwanese society have lower marriage and fertility rates and are less sympathetic to the emphasis on procreation. In 2005, the total fertility rate in Taiwan was 1.1 children per woman over a lifetime on average. Taiwan has had among the lowest fertility rate in births per woman among the world since 2005.[23] [24] The majority of younger people do not recognize that there is a direct connection between marriage and procreation.

In 2011, the Ministry of Education in Taiwan included LGBT education and "the variety of sexual desires" in the guidelines of gender equality education for the primary and high school students. Textbooks of gender equality education were edited accordingly.[25] Through quoting and posting the controversial contents found in school textbooks, a group of Christian parents and schoolteachers intended to raise public awareness and appeal to the Ministry of Education. The authors of the textbooks sued the six Christians for slander for criticizing textbook contents. Up to this event, the church and Christians had only slowly started to realize the rapidly changing legislation and ethos of the younger generation on LGBT issues.

The Taiwan Alliance to Promote Civil Partnership Rights drafted three bills of diversified family formation in 2012. The draft bills aimed to allow same-sex marriage, legal recognition of cohabitation without sexual fidelity to partners, and a multiple-person family system.[26] Some legislators upheld the draft bills and brought them to be discussed in the second readings in the Legislative Yuan. At this critical moment, the church and people who held conventional family values, joined together to hold a huge demonstration to oppose the draft bills at the end of 2013. The protest had approximately 300,000 people. Thus, the legislators laid the controversial draft bills aside.

Although the opponents set back the LGBT legislation, the proponents simultaneously took another route. Two gay partners asked the Constitutional Courts for interpretation of marriage laws. They claimed that the Civil Code

---

23. National Development Council, Taiwan, https://pop-proj.ndc.gov.tw/dataSearch2.aspx?r=2&uid=2104&pid=59.
24. https://www.statista.com/statistics/1112676/taiwan-total-fertility-rate/.
25. The Ministry of Education of Taiwan. *Ren shi tong zhi: jiao you zi yuan shou ce* [*To Know Homosexuals: A Handbook of Educational Resource*] (Taipei: The Ministry of Education of Taiwan, 2008).
26. https://tapcpr.org/english/about-us.

provisions on the family that do not allow same-sex marriage violate Article 7 and Article 22 of the Constitution. Article 7 guarantees the people's right to equality. Article 22 guarantees the people's right to marry. The 24 May 2017 Court Constitutional ruling, *Interpretation No. 748*, declared that family provisions which do not allow same-sex partners to create a permanent union of intimate and exclusive nature for the committed purpose of managing a life together are a gross legislative flaw. In addition, they concluded that the current provisions of the Civil Code violate the right to marriage and the rights of equality. Therefore, the Legislative Yuan decided that it shall amend or enact new laws following the ruling of the interpretation within two years.[27] The ruling of the Interpretation of the Constitutional Court has equal status to the Constitution. That means people's opinions and the representatives of the Legislative Yuan cannot overwrite the ruling. Thus, the LGBT movement won a decisive war through the Interpretation of the Constitutional Court.

The church and the conventionalists did not give up on their efforts to defend the traditional values of the family. They proposed three clauses to be voted directly by the people in the referendum and the legislators and mayoral elections of 2018. Clause 10 insisted that the Civil Code should define "marriage" as the union between one man and one woman. Same-sex union should not be defined using the word marriage. Clause 11 opposed the Ministry of Education implementing the *Enforcement Rules of the Gender Equity Education Act* in primary and middle schools. Clause 12 responded to the ruling of *Interpretation No. 748* of the Constitutional Court. Clause 12 insisted that same-sex union is to be enacted as a new law and not as an amendment to existing provisions regarding the family in the Civil Code. These clauses were attempts to preserve the traditional understanding of the family and marriage prescribed in the Civil Code. These three referendum clauses had seventy-two percent, sixty-seven percent, and sixty-one percent of the valid ballots and the referendum was passed.[28] The referendum results expressed that the Constitutional Court opposed the opinions of the majority in Taiwan regarding same-sex marriage.

Nevertheless, referendum results do not confer power to challenge interpretations of Constitutional Court rulings. As a result of the decade long struggle between progressive and conventional groups, the *Act for Implementation of Interpretation No. 748* passed in May 2019. "Two persons of the same-sex may

---

27. https://cons.judicial.gov.tw/jcc/en-us/jep03/show?expno=748.
28. https://en.wikipedia.org/wiki/2018_Taiwanese_referendum.

form a permanent union of intimate and exclusive nature for the purpose of living a common life." Although same-sex union is not marriage de jure, the obligations and rights between same-sex couples are almost the same as married couple de facto, except same-sex couples have no right to adopt children.[29]

THE PASTORAL DILEMMA

Generally speaking, most congregations in Taiwan have been friendly to all kinds of people, including divorcées, the remarried, addicts, and people with homosexual orientation. However, the enthusiasm to evangelize to the marginalized and disadvantaged varies from church to church. The churches preach that God's salvation is for all and all need to repent and accept God's redemption, regardless of ethnicity, nationality, marital status, gender, and sexual orientation. However, those who fear reproach by Christian teachings may either hide their identities or shy away from Christian communities.

Taiwan's LGBT movement, the ruling of the *Interpretation* of the Constitutional Court in favor of homosexual union, and the referendum voting against the legalization of gay marriage intensified the tension between the two sides. Meanwhile, the position of pastors and church members on the homosexual issues became more public. Congregational conflicts also sporadically occur. LGBT congregants feel more pressure. Some of them choose to leave Christian communities, even though their pastors and church members do not push the issue.

The evangelical churches in Taiwan hold positions that are similar to their allies in the West. The churches stress that the gospel is the power of God for salvation to everyone who has faith (Rom 1:16). The power of God will eventually liberate all from the oppression of sin, sexual or other.[30]

In 2013, more than 100 congregations and around 10,000 Christians in Hong Kong declared a joint declaration, *Walking Together in True Love*, which encouraged pastoral care for gay Christians while rejecting same-sex relationships. It states that "we encourage churches to care for and pastor those struggling with same-sex orientation with gentleness and patience." It "encourages churches to establish a respectful atmosphere and a safe environment, to teach brothers and sisters to be accepting to those struggling with same-sex orientation." The declaration also makes clear that "we believe that believers

---

29. https://law.moj.gov.tw/ENG/LawClass/LawAll.aspx?pcode=B0000008.
30. Thomas W. Gillespie, "The Pastoral Dilemma," 113–122, 121, in Choon-Leong Seow ed. *Homosexuality and Christian Community* (Louisville: Westminster John Knox Press, 1996).

who continue to engage in same-sex activity, and refuse to pursue a holy life, are not walking in truth."[31] In 2014, the General Assembly of the Presbyterian Church in Taiwan, the denomination which has had the widest diversity of opinions on homosexuality, also promulgated a *Pastoral Letter on Homosexual Marriage Issue* signed by the moderator and general secretary.[32]

Only a few independent churches in Taiwan unambivalently state their revisionist position that God gives alternative sexual orientations. In these churches, people are to make peace with God and continue in their way of life. These churches emphasize God's unconditional love and Christian inclusiveness. Sin is not understood in terms of individual behaviors such as homosexual activity, but oppression and social injustice.

RETROSPECT AND PROSPECT FOR THE CHURCH IN TAIWAN

After the *Act for Implementation of Interpretation No. 748* was enacted, the church leaders of the Evangelical wing reviewed why Christians and those who oppose same-sex marriage were unsuccessful in blocking legislation that approved it.

The reasons can be divided into two categories. The first set of factors is theological, while the other is structural. First, the theological factors. Most evangelical churches and Christians in Taiwan pay more attention to internal affairs of the church and neglect social issues. They care about church growth and church-planting much more than policies related to school education and law-making. Many Christian parents who had elementary and middle school aged children were not aware that their children, since 2004, had been indoctrinated by the Gender Education Act. The result of the Gender Education Act's implementation is that the younger generation overwhelmingly believes that homosexual orientation is as normal as heterosexual orientation, and that same-sex marriage is a characteristic of a liberal and progressive society.

In evangelical churches, congregations view pastors as the opinion leaders and speakers of the churches, but because of the narrow vision of pastors, this made sensible recognition of social changes and discussion on political issues nearly impossible. Therefore, most evangelical churches in Taiwan have not paid attention to, and expressed criticism about, education policy, law-making, and social issues.

---

31. http://www.sexculture.org.hk/b5_press_details.php?press_id=24.
32. http://www.pct.org.tw/ab_doc.aspx?DocID=118.

Some very conservative Christians are very reluctant to openly discuss homosexual and same-sex marriage issues because they do not want to "mix religion and politics." They consider that "separation of church and state principle" means Christians should not bring faith into the public square. Even though they strongly oppose same-sex marriage and believe it is immoral, they still think that Christians should not be involved in social advocacy or openly oppose the Act. The other reason that makes evangelical churches hesitant to react to the LGBT movement is that theologians and pastors in the evangelical wing have little skills and tools to engage in public discussion on homosexual issues due to their negligence of public theology. Most evangelical theologians and pastors are only experienced in communicating exclusively to Christians. They do not know how to debate homosexual issues using non-Christian language in public. All they know is that it is morally wrong according to biblical teaching. While the LGBT advocates proclaim that homosexuals have equal rights to marriage and that same-sex marriage is a human right, and that assertions against these rights are discrimination, very few Christians who are professionals in ethics, law, and politics dare to publicly challenge these human rights discourses. This phenomenon shows that even Christian professionals are not prepared to defend Christian convictions on man–woman marriage in the secular world, and that pastors do not make effective use of Christian professionals.

Aside from theological factors, structural factors must be considered as well. Evangelical churches in Taiwan are loosely organized. They belong to a couple of dozen denominations, and there is no national council of churches. Even though these churches generally oppose same-sex marriage, it is not easy for them to unite to form a campaign. The first organization supporting the LGBT movement was formed in 2000.[33] Christian organizations to oppose same-sex marriage were not formed until the 2010s. They were ten years behind.

Since evangelical churches rarely paid attention to social, political, and legislative issues in the past, they were not familiar with social advocacy. The only exception is one mainline church that has experience in democratic and social justice movements in Taiwan. However, this particular denomination had no consensus on issues related to homosexuality, so they were not able

---

33. Taiwan LGBTQ+ Hotline Association was the first organization in Taiwan to support the LGBTQ people and to mobilize them to the LGBT movements. It was established in 2000. https://hotline.org.tw/aboutus.

to assist the church to oppose the legislation of same-sex marriage. In general, evangelical churches did not know how to formulate advocacy goals and objectives. In the 2010s, the evangelical church gradually realized that they needed to form associations, mobilize people, and identify allies to counter the LGBT movement. However, the learning pace was not fast enough to catch up with the lost time.

Evangelical organizations have little experience working with the decision-making bodies, such as the Ministry of Education and the Ministry of Justice. Evangelical organizations had lobbied legislators, but the results were not satisfactory. Most of the media were sympathetic to the LGBT movement. Their positions made media reports one-sided and unfair to the conventional campaign.

The LGBT movement, on the contrary, has been strategically flexible. Advocates of the LGBT movement are social activists and often involved in other social movements that plead on behalf of the socially disadvantaged minorities, such as laborers, the physically disadvantaged, and victims of environmental pollution. They allied together and eventually many socially disadvantaged minorities became important comrades in the LGBT movement.

WHAT CAN THE CHURCH LEARN FROM THIS SOCIAL ENGAGEMENT?

Christians can learn several key lessons from close observation of these events. First, to counter the LGBT movement and the legislation for same-sex marriage, evangelical churches gradually united together in the late 2010s. They realized that the church needs to be united to be a witness to society. Second, evangelical churches realized that they did not understand or care enough for people with same-sex attraction. In general, in fact, evangelical churches did not care enough for society's socially disadvantaged minorities. Third, some evangelical churches reconsidered their stance on the principle of separation of church and state. They became more attentive to social, legislative, and social issues while they did not lose their passion for spreading the gospel. For example, in 2015 a new website funded by evangelical churches, Kairos, came into being. Its mission is to make effective use of the internet and to promote traditional family values.[34] Unlike much previous Christian media, its target viewers are the public, especially those who are concerned with children's education, parenting, and marital relationships. Fourth, churches and

---

34. https://kairos.news/5726.

Christian parents began paying more attention to primary and middle school education. Last, but not least, Christians were shocked when *Interpretation No. 748* of the Constitutional Court was announced. They eventually realized that the Christian worldview is very different from the worldview of secular society. The differences are most evident in the realms of sex, marriage, and family. Christian values are usually not in accord with the values and laws of secular society.

Although legislation supporting homosexual unions has passed, the culture war does not end there. LGBT activists are advocating for the right to adopt children, artificial reproduction, and surrogate pregnancy for the LGBT couples. The churches in a secular and liberal society encounter perpetual challenges and they need to discern how to respond.

QUESTIONS FOR DISCUSSION

1. Does your church have any roles or positions that are restricted to men? Such as pastors, elders, deacons? What are the theological explanations behind these restrictions?
2. Has your church ever discussed homosexual issues? Is there anyone who challenges the biblical teachings on homosexual acts in Romans 1:18–32? Are you able to defend the positions that you hold?
3. Does your church provide the congregation with theological perspectives to evaluate different social movements (such as the environmental protection movement, labor movement, or LGBT movement)?
4. Do the Christian denominations in your country have an organization to bind them together, such as a national council of churches? If they have, what kind of social witness do they provide to society?
5. Does your church communicate their Christian viewpoints of some social issues to the public in a way that non-Christians understand? Could you give an example and assess its effectiveness in communicating with non-Christians?

BIBLIOGRAPHY

American Psychiatric Association website, https://www.psychiatry.org/psychiatrists/cultural-competency/education/best-practice-highlights/working-with-lgbtq-patients.

Brooten, Bernadette Brooten. "Junia . . . Outstanding among the Apostles' (Romans 16:7)," http://www.womenpriests.org/classic/brooten.asp.

Campbell-Reed, Eileen R. "Report Details Trends for U.S. Women Clergy." *The Christian Century* 135, no. 23 November (2018): 16–17.

Chen, Shang-Jen. "A Moral Evaluation of Homosexual Acts." *Journal of Life Education* 3, no. 1 June (2011): 67–91.

Cheng, Yang-en, and Tsong-shen Tsan, ed. *Wo men he ju zhi you? Ji du xin yang yu tong zhi qun ti de hui yu* [What Do We Fear? The Encounter of Christian Belief and the Homosexual Community]. HuaLian: Taiwan hao shi xie hui, 2019.

Council on Biblical Manhood and Womanhood, "Our History," https://cbmw.org/about/history/.

Council on Biblical Manhood and Womanhood, "Affirmations," https://cbmw.org/about/affirmations/.

Duff, Nancy J. "The Ordination of Women: Biblical Perspective," *Theology Today* 73, no. 2 (2016): 94–104.

Hays, Richard B. *The Moral Vision of the New Testament: Community, Cross, New Creation: A Contemporary Introduction to New Testament Ethics*. New York: HarperOne, 1996.

Families in a Changing World. United Nations Entity for Gender Equality and the Empowerment of Women, 2019, 57. https://reliefweb.int/sites/reliefweb.int/files/resources/Progress-of-the-worlds-women-2019-2020-en.pdf.

Ke, Immanuel Chih-Ming, editor-in-Chief, "Solitudo – A Meditative Journal of Taiwan Christian Though," *Theology of Sex, Love, and Marriage*. Special Issue, 12 December (2008).

Lo, C. P., and L. Y. Kung. *Tong Xing Lian de Shi zi Jian* [*The Cross of the Homosexuality*]. Hong Kong: Hong Kong Christian Institute, 2013.

Lo, P. C. *Hei bai Fen Ming* [*Distinction between Black and White*]. Hong Kong: China Alliance Press, 1992.

Maxwell, Melody. "A Winding and Widening Path: American Women's Roles in Twentieth-Century Baptist Life," *Baptist History and Heritage* 53 no. 2, Sum (2018): 8–22.

National Development Council, Taiwan, https://pop-proj.ndc.gov.tw/dataSearch2.aspx?r=2&uid=2104&pid=59

Ottosson, Daniel. *State-Sponsored Homophobia – A World Survey of Laws Prohibiting Same-Sex Activity between Consenting Adults*, 2010 ILGA. http://old.ilga.org/Statehomophobia/ILGA_State_Sponsored_Homophobia_2010.pdf

Schüssler Fiorenza, Elisabeth. "Feminist Theology as a Critical Theology of Liberation," *Theological Studies* 36, no. 4 (1975): 605–626.

———. *In Memory of Her: A Feminist Theological Reconstruction of Christian Origins*. New York: Crossroad, 1983.

Scroggs, Robin. *The New Testament and Homosexuality*. Philadelphia: Fortress, 1983.

Smith, Susan. "Women's Human, Ecclesial and Missionary Identity: What Insights Does the Pauline Correspondence Offer the Contemporary Woman?" *Mission Studies* 27 (2010): 145–59.

Seow, Choon-Leong, ed. *Homosexuality and Christian Community*. Louisville: Westminster John Knox Press, 1996.

The Ministry of Education of Taiwan. *Ren shi tong zhi: jiao you zi yuan shou ce* [*To Know Homosexuals: A Handbook of Educational Resource*]. Taipei: The Ministry of Education of Taiwan, 2008.

Zhang, Wenhang,. "Zheng shi xing ping jiao yu de zheng yi yu kun jing" [An Investigation to the Controversies and Dilemmas of Gender Equity Education]. In Wang, Daowei et al. *Dang Ye Su yu Jian Tong Zhi* [*When Jesus Meets Homosexuals*]. Taipei: Zhen na da, 2020.

Websites

https://cons.judicial.gov.tw/jcc/en-us/jep03/show?expno=748
https://en.wikipedia.org/wiki/2018_Taiwanese_referendum
https://tapcpr.org/english/about-us
https://hotline.org.tw/aboutus
https://kairos.news/5726
https://law.moj.gov.tw/ENG/LawClass/LawAll.aspx?pcode=B0000008
http://www.pct.org.tw/ab_doc.aspx?DocID=118
http://sex.ncu.edu.tw/history/index.html
http://www.sexculture.org.hk/b5_press_details.php?press_id=24
https://www.statista.com/statistics/1112676/taiwan-total-fertility-rate/

CHAPTER 12

THE EYE OF THE NEEDLE

Wealth and Poverty

Vinoth Ramachandra

On a visit to Delhi one freezing winter, I watched construction workers as they erected an office tower that would house one of the famous companies in the global computer industry. The workers were inadequately clothed, and their accommodation took the form of flimsy canvas tents. I found myself musing: What will this company do for these workers, most of whom have been drawn as casual labor from surrounding villages? Will they slap copyright laws on their software products so that the children of these workers, even if fortunate enough to go to school, could never afford them? And what justice is there in the concept of intellectual property rights when it is the general public (both in the rich world and the poor) whose taxes are subsidizing these corporations and their global operations?

The Oscar-winning film *Slumdog Millionaire* movingly depicted the casual brutality that haunts the lives of the urban poor. India's social elites regard the latter as a national embarrassment, while depending on them for their daily chores. Politicians, filmmakers, and the mass media ignore them until the next round of elections. It has often been said that India encapsulates the paradoxes of the human condition, for instance, cutting-edge medical technology and aerospace industries deployed in centers a walking distance away from open sewers and fetid hovels in which lice-ridden children offer their bodies in exchange for food. *Slumdog*, while presenting the "underbelly" of Indian society, also brings out the humor amid the heartache, the simple dignity and resilience of people, however destitute and in the most hopeless of situations.

Writing in *The Times of India* three decades ago, the eminent sociologist Rajni Kothari lamented:

> As I talk to my friends, my relatives, my professional colleagues today, I get a feeling of total ignorance of the other India. When in fact they are forced to take note, such as when they walk

through the pavements on which people are sleeping, there is a feeling of revulsion, of rejection, of contempt, not of compassion, empathy, and least of all of any sense of guilt.[1]

Little has changed since Kothari wrote these chilling words. Such lament, of course, is not limited to India – it applies worldwide. Pope Francis raises a similar passionate cry over distorted priorities and middle class difference:

> How can it be that it is not a news item when an elderly homeless person dies of exposure, but it is news when the stock market loses two points? This is a case of exclusion. Can we continue to stand by when food is thrown away while people are starving? This is a case of inequality . . . Exclusion ultimately has to do with what it means to be a part of the society in which we live; those excluded are no longer society's underside or its fringes or its disenfranchised – they are no longer even a part of it. The excluded are not the "exploited" but the outcast, the "leftovers."[2]

LEARNING A COUNTER-CULTURAL VISION

"We have, for once, learnt to see the great events of history from below, from the perspective of the outcast, the suspects, the maltreated, the powerless, the oppressed, the reviled – in short, from the perspective of those who suffer."[3] We must "learn," another perspective, says Dietrich Bonhoeffer. This is because it goes against the dominant perspectives in all our societies where news reporting, the education system, and economic priorities revolve around the lives of the rich and the powerful. Nor does "enlightened self-interest" get us very far. The moral demand placed on us by the victims of our political or economic order often goes against our individual interests. Somewhere along the line we must invoke the notion of justice. And justice rests on certain convictions we have about the worth and, therefore, the intrinsic rights of all human beings.

My learning, like Bonhoeffer's, occurred through prolonged immersion in the world of the biblical narrative. At the heart of the historic Christian message is the conviction that we see the human face of God in the person of

---

1. Rajni Kothari, *The Times of India*, 27 April 1986, quoted in Braj Ranjan Mani, *Debrahmanising History: Dominance and Resistance in Indian Society* (New Delhi: Manohar Publishers, 2005), 408.
2. Pope Francis, *Evangelii Gaudium*, English Trans. *The Joy of the Gospel* (London: Catholic Truth Society, 2013), 32.
3. Dietrich Bonhoeffer, *Letters and Papers from Prison* (SCM, 1953; Macmillan expanded edition, 1973), 17.

Jesus of Nazareth. In showing who God is, Jesus also shows indirectly what human beings are: we are those creatures who put God on a Roman cross. Here is a God who suffers *at our hands*, as well as *for* us and *with* us. And, in freely doing so, he exposes the depths of human sin as well as affirms our unique human worth. He heals our human brokenness and in his bodily resurrection Jesus draws the human into his own divine life forever. This is a unique vision; there is nothing comparable in any of the world's religious literature or philosophies.

The God who suffers as the ultimate human victim is also the God of justice. Justice is at the heart of the biblical vision of life: "I, the Lord, love justice" (Is 61:8; Ps 37:28) is repeated throughout the Old Testament.

> Of course, it is not the abstract entity *justice as such* that God loves. What God loves is the *presence* of justice in society. And God loves the presence of justice in society simply because God desires that each and every human being in that society shall flourish, that each and every one shall experience what the Old Testament writers call *shalom*. Injustice is the impairment of shalom. That is why God loves justice. God desires the flourishing of each and every one of God's human creatures; justice is indispensable to that. Love and justice are not pitted against each other but intertwined.[4]

The biblical narrative speaks of God not simply as a God of justice but one whose demand for justice takes the concrete form of solidarity with the "widow, the orphan, and the resident foreigner." The widows, the orphans, the resident foreigners, and the impoverished were the vulnerable people, those at the bottom of the social hierarchy. They were those who were pushed to the wall in times of economic hardship. The rich and the powerful walked all over them, trampled them down. Rendering justice to such people is often described as "lifting them up."

Wolterstorff points out that the biblical prophets and psalmists do not give us a philosophical theory of justice that requires alleviating the plight of the downtrodden, they simply assume it. Whenever they speak of God's justice, when they urge their hearers to practice justice, when they complain to God about the absence of justice, they take for granted that justice requires lifting

---

4. Nicholas Wolterstorff, *Justice: Rights and Wrongs* (Princeton, NJ: Princeton University Press, 2008), 82.

those at the bottom: "Seek justice, rescue the oppressed, defend the orphan, plead for the widow." (Isa 1:17) And, addressing the wider world of nations and their rulers: "Give justice to the weak and the orphan; maintain the right of the lowly and the destitute, rescue the weak and the needy; deliver them from the hand of the wicked." (Ps 82:3–4) And elsewhere: "Speak out for those who cannot speak, for the rights of all the destitute; speak out, judge righteously, defend the rights of the poor and needy." (Prov 31:8–9)

While we cannot directly transpose the subsistence agrarian economy of ancient Israel into today's complex debates about global market economies, institutions such as the Sabbath and the jubilee (Lev 25) exemplify God's unchanging concern for human societies based on *equal* respect and concern. He calls his covenant people to ensure that economic inequalities do not exceed a level where social solidarity is undermined through a few accumulating all the land for themselves and turning the rest into wage-laborers on their land. That would be to return to the slave economy of Egypt and spurn the egalitarian economy of Israel's God. It is significant that the jubilee was announced in Israel on the Day of Atonement – freedom from sin entailed that we released others from their economic indebtedness.

The Hebrew Sabbath (a kind of weekly jubilee) was intended to protect men, women, and animals from both *addiction* and *exploitation*. It reminded the people of God that their identity came not from their work of "cultivating the earth and caring for it" (Gen 2:15), however important that was, but from the worship of the God who alone gives meaning to human work. "When we work, we are most god-like," observes Eugene Peterson, "which means that it is in our work that it is easiest to develop God-pretensions. Un-Sabbathed, our work becomes the entire context in which we define our lives. We lose God-consciousness, God-awareness, sightings of resurrection."[5] At the same time, the Sabbath decreed the protection of workers and domestic animals from economic exploitation and provided rest for the land on a regular basis, so that it did not lose its productivity.

Jesus greatly expanded the category of the downtrodden to include not only the victims of social structures and practices – widows, orphans, aliens, the poor, the imprisoned – but also those excluded from full participation in society because they are defective, malformed, or seen as religiously inferior. The in-breaking of God's just reign through the Christ-event requires that

---

5. Eugene H. Peterson, *Christ Plays in Ten Thousand Places: A Conversation in Spiritual Theology* (Grand Rapids: Eerdmans, and London: Hodder & Stoughton, 2005), 117.

these, too, be lifted up. Jesus denounced the way God-given institutions such as the Torah, the Sabbath, and the temple had been subverted by the ruling class to become institutions that exploited the poor and oppressed the vulnerable (e.g. Luke 11:42–53; 13:10–16; 20:45–21:6).

In the primitive church, "remembering the poor" (Gal 2:10) was an Old Testament practice that was accepted, without controversy, by gentile and Jewish Christians alike. In the Apostle Paul's ministry this took tangible, concrete form in the shape of "the collection" which he took to Jerusalem at risk of imprisonment and death (2 Cor 8–9) and for which he was even willing to postpone his missionary ambition to reach the outermost Western edge of the Roman world (Rom 15:23–28). That collection:

> was both the expression of Christian solidarity and love, and a visible sign that the new world was breaking into the harsh social and economic realities of the old one, destroying ethnic and racial barriers and demonstrating the power of the Cross to break the idolatrous hold of Mammon and heal the fractures which divided the human family.[6]

The American legal scholar, Frank Alexander, reminds us that property is about identity, power, and control. Property is that which defines relationships between persons with respect to a thing:

> Property is identity because we use it to symbolize, define, and express who we are as individuals and as communities. Property is power because it lies at the essence of survival (consumption) and is the subject matter of exchange. Property is control because it allows the property "owner" the right to consume it, dispose of it, and – more importantly – to exclude others from it.[7]

The church fathers viewed property as essentially a means of fostering living community. The reason they were suspicious of the notion of "private property" was because, as Charles Avila explains:

> it imposed the impersonal character of things themselves on social relations, especially between owners and those whom the owners

---

6. David W. Smith, *Stumbling Towards Zion: Recovering the Biblical Tradition of Lament in the Era of World Christianity* (Carlisle, UK: Langham Publishing, 2020), 70.
7. Frank S. Alexander, "Property and Christian Theology," in John Witte, Jr., and Frank S. Alexander (eds.), *Christianity and Law* (Cambridge, UK: Cambridge University Press, 2008), 207–8.

excluded from their wealth. Thus, in order to cement *koinonia*, people would now have to renounce their private ownership of the natural productive elements so that all could share them in common.[8]

The words of Ambrose of Milan (c.333–397) are typical of this instrumental attitude to property:

> A possession ought to belong to the possessor, not the possessor to the possession. Whosoever, therefore, does not use his patrimony as a possession, who does not know how to give and distribute to the poor, he is the servant of his wealth, not its master; because like a servant he watches over the wealth of another and not like a master does he use it of his own. Hence, in a disposition of this kind we say that the man belongs to his riches, not the riches to the man.[9]

This vision of human solidarity and well-being was carried forward in the early church. Christian theologians challenged the absolutist and exclusivist understandings of wealth and property that undergirded Roman law. Here are some representative quotations from some of the great leaders of the church:

> Need alone is the poor man's worthiness; if anyone at all ever comes to us with this recommendation, let us not meddle any further . . . I beg you remember this without fail, that not to share our own wealth with the poor is theft from the poor and deprivation of their means of life; we do not possess our own wealth but theirs.[10] (John Chrysostom c.347–407)

> Will not one be called a thief who steals the garment of one already clothed, and is one deserving of any other title who will not clothe the naked if he is able to do so? That bread which you keep belongs to the hungry; that coat which you preserve in your wardrobe, to the naked; those shoes which are rotting in your possession, to the shoeless; that gold which you have hidden in the ground, to the needy. Wherefore, as often as you were able

---
8. Charles Avila, *Ownership: Early Christian Teaching* (Maryknoll: Orbis, 1983), 146.
9. Quoted in Avila, 67.
10. John Chrysostom, *On Wealth and Poverty*, trans. Catherine Roth (New York: St. Vladimir's Seminary Press, 1984), 55.

to help others, and refused, so often did you do them wrong.[11]
(Basil of Caesarea c.329–c.379)

To say that need alone constitutes the poor man's right to food or medical treatment has profound personal and political implications. If I have food in my house that I do not need for my survival, but my neighbor is starving, then the food in my house belongs to my neighbor and his family, not to me. I commit theft when I refuse to share it with them. The right to life trumps the right to private property. Similarly, if a few farmers own all the arable land in an area and are using it not to grow food for the hungry but cash crops for wealthy businessmen, then the starving rural poor have a God-given right to take over those farms to grow food necessary for their survival.

Wherever modern capitalism encourages a view of absolute property rights, or an instrumental approach to nature, and indeed to human beings (cf. the reduction of the natural world to "natural resources" and of human beings to "human resources"), it is surely to be resisted by Christians as expressions of idolatry. So, too, when market thinking encroaches on areas which nurture the sources of a culture's countervailing moral values, such as families, religious communities, and schools. This is what has been happening in recent decades, and hence the growing "anti-globalization" sentiments around the world.

Modern liberal theorists proclaim their belief in equal opportunity. For "equality of opportunity" to make any sense, the factors over which we have no control in our decision-making must be the same for all. Possessing a wealthy nation's passport, merely because of birth, gives one an automatic advantage over billions of others. Disadvantages are also cumulative. Positions in the social hierarchy tend to be inherited. We can predict that the child of professional parents is likely to occupy a higher position as an adult than the child of high-school dropouts. Better-educated parents make for healthier as well as better-educated children. A society in which the quality of education or health care one receives depends on one's ability to pay is one that perpetuates inequality into successive generations. If opportunities are to be equalized, high-quality care for every child, from as early an age as possible and sustained over several generations, is indispensable.

The eighteenth-century Scottish moral philosopher Rev. Adam Smith (often but misleadingly called the father of modern capitalism) pointed out that the ability to appear in public without shame requires more in a wealthy

---

11. Quoted in Avila, 50.

society than an overall poor one: at a certain point, he suggested, a man needs a linen shirt to be respectably dressed.[12] Today, to impress at a job interview, one needs not only the relevant ability or skill but also the right clothing and means of transport, perhaps the right accent and social mannerisms. The whole idea of a standard of poverty unrelated to the incomes of others is false. Becoming relatively worse off can actually make a person absolutely worse off, in terms of opportunities and social standing.

With a nod toward Adam Smith, the late economist and US ambassador to India, John Kenneth Galbraith proposed that:

> People are poverty-stricken whenever their income, even if adequate for survival, falls markedly behind that of the community. Then they cannot have what the larger community regards as the minimum necessary for decency; and they cannot wholly escape, therefore, the judgement of the larger community that they are indecent.[13]

STEALING FROM THE POOR

Economic inequality is largely driven by the unequal ownership of capital, which can be either privately or public owned. A global study of wealth inequality between 1980 and 2016 showed that as countries get richer, their governments get poorer; for public wealth is transferred increasingly into private wealth: "While national wealth has substantially increased, public wealth is now negative or close to zero in rich countries. Arguably this limits the ability of governments to tackle inequality; certainly, it has important implications for wealth inequality among individuals."[14] If we assume the world trend to be captured by the combined experience of China, Europe, and the United States, the wealth share of the world's top one percent of the wealthiest people increased from twenty-eight percent to thirty-three percent while the share commanded by the bottom seventy-five percent oscillated around ten percent between 1980 and 2016.[15]

---

12. Quoted in Alain De Botton, *Status Anxiety* (London: Penguin, 2005), 195.
13. *The Affluent Society* (1958), quoted in Alain De Botton, *Status Anxiety* (2004; Penguin edition, 2005), 196.
14. "World Inequality Report 2018," https://wir2018.wid.world/files/download/wir2018-full-report-english.pdf, 14.
15. "World Inequality Report," 17.

Despite all the rhetoric about market efficiency and foreign aid, the net financial flows in the world economy every year are not from the rich to the poor but from the poor to the rich. Debt repayments, tariffs on exports, and falling prices of agricultural goods caused by rich nations' farm subsidies mean that the low income nations transfer to the rich nations every year far more than what they receive in so-called aid. There is also the cost to poor nations of the export to rich nations of engineers, scientists, doctors, and accountants – most of whom have been trained in state institutions at local taxpayers' expense – and who are actively recruited by rich governments and corporations.

Moreover, corruption in poor countries would not be possible without the tacit support, and often active involvement, of rich corporations, banks, and governments in the North as well as in countries like China, Japan, Malaysia, Indonesia, Dubai, and Singapore. For every bribe taken, there is a bribe offered. These bribes are stored, not in local banks, but in the banking system owned and controlled by the rich nations. Offshore tax havens (most of which are the playgrounds of super-rich tourists in places like the Caribbean, Monaco, and Switzerland) are major means of tax evasion and money laundering and are homes to vast pools of speculative capital that destabilize poor economies. The wealth held in tax havens has increased considerably since the 1970s and currently represents more than ten percent of global Gross Domestic Product (GDP). Trillions of dollars, enough to pay for the entire health and education needs of the world's developing countries, are being siphoned off through offshore companies and tax havens.[16]

China's 100 richest men are collectively worth over $300 billion, while an estimated 300m people in the country still live on less than $2 a day. In January 2014, Xu Zhiyong, a legal scholar and prominent human rights activist, was jailed for four years by a Beijing court (in a closed-door trial) simply for calling on Chinese officials to declare their assets. A two-year reporting effort led by the International Consortium of Investigative Journalists has revealed that more than a dozen family members of China's top political and military leaders are making use of offshore companies based in the British Virgin Islands. The documents also reveal the central role of major Western banks and accountancy firms, including PricewaterhouseCoopers, Credit Suisse, and UBS in the offshore world, acting as middlemen in the establishing of such companies. Between $1 trillion and $4 trillion in untraced assets have left China since 2000, according to estimates. The Chinese government has blocked foreign

---

16. "World Inequality Report," 263.

news sites that revealed details of offshore holdings by the relatives of China's political leaders and internet service providers were ordered to target and report any users posting on the subject.[17]

The uncomfortable truth about Southeast Asia, home to some of the world's fastest expanding economies, with a combined economy of US$2.6 trillion (about the size of the United Kingdom's economy), is that the wealth gap between the "haves" and the "have-nots" is steadily widening. The richest one percent in Thailand controls fifty-eight percent of the country's wealth and the top ten percent earned thirty-five times more than the bottom ten percent. In Indonesia, the four richest men there have more wealth than the poorest 100 million people, and about fifty percent of the country's wealth is in the hands of the top one percent. In Vietnam, 210 of the country's super-rich earn more than enough in a year to lift more than 3,200,000 people out of poverty. The country's richest man earns more in a day than the poorest person earns in ten years. In Malaysia, while only point six of a percent of its thirty-one million people are living under the poverty line, thirty-four percent of the country's indigenous people and seven percent of children in urban low-cost housing projects live in poverty. In the Philippines, the average annual family income of the top ten percent is estimated at US$14,708 in 2015, nine times more than the lowest ten percent at US$1,609.[18] All these figures were reported before the economic impact of COVID-19 on the region could be estimated. They are bound to deteriorate because of the pandemic.

In Sri Lanka, where I live, the backbone of the economy comprises small farmers, tea plantation workers, textile factory workers, and migrant workers in the Gulf states and elsewhere who remit foreign exchange back to the country. A disproportionate number of these are women. The nouveau riche use this foreign exchange to send their children to international schools and foreign universities. Education and healthcare services are starved of funding, resulting in hundreds of rural schools being forced to shut down, and state-run hospitals (the only medical services accessible to the poor) regularly running out of basic drugs.

In the more affluent world, the men and women who clean the rooms of the rich, and wait on their tables, are drawn from the global "underclass" and

---

17. James Ball, "China's Princelings Storing Riches in Caribbean Haven," *Guardian Weekly*, 31 January 2014, 12.
18. These figures are from the UNESCAP Report given in the *ASEAN Post* of 20 April 2020, https://theaseanpost.com/article/southeast-asias-widening-inequalities.

paid minimum wages or less than the minimum. Barbara Ehrenreich, in her best-seller *Nickel and Dimed*,[19] took an undercover job as a New York hotel maid and showed how the wages were less than live-able and the working conditions subhuman. Many are often undocumented – that is, "illegal" workers – and unsurprisingly, some are forced to turn to prostitution to complement their meagre incomes. Yet without such people, the hotel and restaurant industries in the US and Western Europe, not to mention agriculture in states like California and Texas, would collapse.

In the city-state of Singapore, one of the ten richest countries in the world, companies recruit workers from the poorer Asian countries on short-term contracts. They do work, usually in the construction industry and as domestic helpers, that most Singaporeans would shun. Singapore has over a million such workers, forty percent of the total population. Some are decently housed and well-treated by their companies. But others live in abysmal conditions, such as disused containers which have been turned into shelters and in which fifteen workers may be put up in a small cubicle on three-tiered bunk beds. Indeed, their presence is resented when some companies have sought to house their workers nearer those neighborhoods where the rich live. These workers are needed for Singapore's survival, they are everywhere visible, but they need to be made invisible to the rich. Depression and loneliness are the biggest emotional problem they face. And hordes of Chinese, Thai, and Malaysian women are trafficked into Singapore by criminal gangs to provide "sexual services" for these workers separated from wives and families for the whole duration of their contracts.

I have spoken with workers from India and Bangladesh who have paid enormous amounts of money to unscrupulous local agents to get these unskilled or semiskilled jobs in Singapore. Their families back home are plunged into massive debt as a result. On a daily salary of $16–20, it will take two years for the principal, let alone the interest, on the debt to be repaid. Most of the temporary jobs do not last that long. So, once their contracts are over, they must scramble to find another job. Only then can they hope to start earning.

The injustice in the global labor market needs to be tackled at both ends. Governments in poorer Asian countries need to regulate these local recruitment agencies and negotiate fair wages and legal safeguards with the foreign governments that want their labor. Some economists have argued cogently for

---

19. Barbara Ehrenreich, *Nickel and Dimed: On (Not) Getting by in America* (New York: Henry Holt, 2001).

a global minimum wage. Why can't the arguments used by Lord Shaftsbury and others in early industrial Britain against the sacrifice of men, women, and children to the idols of profit and economic growth be marshaled on an international scale by Christians and others with a moral sensitivity?

Work and housing conditions in Singapore for migrants are probably better than in many other countries. (I have seen worse conditions in Dubai, another darling of the West.) But given the affluence of Singapore, it is inexcusable that there is no minimum wage in the country. (There are many poor Singaporeans, and not only migrant workers.) The answer usually given by politicians is that it will make Singapore "less competitive" in the global market. That is the identical argument given to justify slavery in eighteenth-century Britain and the nineteenth-century American south.

There is a small group of volunteer Christian doctors who offer free medical clinics to migrant workers. They also recruit volunteers, including students, to give English classes, and provide legal aid and counseling.[20] Given the wealth of the Christian church in Singapore, and the huge numbers of Christians serving in government, the judicial system, and medical professions, it is tragic that these doctors and helpers struggle to find financial support and people willing to advocate for the rights of these workers on whose backs the rich make their money. Churches raise millions of dollars to send their members on so-called "mission trips" to poor Asian countries but seem indifferent to the suffering and injustices on their doorsteps.

Recognizing the rights of migrant workers cannot be separated from the need to recognize the rights of workers in their home countries. And this would mean bringing morality and political responsibility back into the heart of economic policy.

QUESTIONING CONVENTIONAL ECONOMICS

One week before the Great Crash of October 1929 – which precipitated the Great Depression in the United States – Irving Fisher of Yale University, perhaps the most distinguished US economist of his time, claimed that the American economy had attained a "permanently high plateau."[21] Three years later, the national income had fallen by more than fifty percent. No one, not a single economist, had seen it coming. The usefulness of economics, once

---

20. See https://www.healthserve.org.sg.
21. Quoted in Robert Heilbroner, *The Worldly Philosophers*, 7th ed. (London: Penguin, 2000), 251.

observed that wittiest of economists, John Kenneth Galbraith, is that it provides employment for economists.

Standard economics textbooks continue to assert, as if it were a scientifically established truth, that people make rational economic choices which can be captured in formal mathematical models. Such rational actors are motivated exclusively by self-interest, they know exactly what they want, never change their minds, and have complete access to all relevant pricing information. This allows economists to make precise, predictive equations of exactly how individuals are expected to act. The influence of public policy, religious beliefs, cultural norms, the behavior or economic position of others around us, and even advertising in shaping and constraining individuals' choices are discounted. The result is an increasing theoretical abstraction that is out of touch with economic realities on the ground. Once it is recognized that individuals are unaware of some of the forces shaping their choices, it can no longer be argued that they will successfully maximize their well-being.

Furthermore, in the typical mode of thought of economists and businesspeople, as long as production is increased, little concern is given to whether it is at the cost of future resources or the health of the environment; as long as the clearing of a forest increases production, no one calculates the losses entailed in the desertification of the land, the harm done to biodiversity, or the increased pollution. In a word, the true costs of an enterprise, and the way the costs are distributed, rarely enter the calculation of economists. Businesses profit by paying only a fraction of the costs involved.

Moreover, standard texts in economics do not help students think about what are called meta-externalities – the unintended consequences of economic outcomes for social, political, and cultural values and activities. For instance, how do gambling and currency speculation affect the work-ethic and the moral fabric of a society?

Two American Nobel laureates in economics, George Akerlof and Robert Shiller, have argued that modern economics inherently fails to grapple with deception and trickery. We should be a lot more worried about the harmful effects of competition. In their view, companies exploit human weaknesses not necessarily because they are malicious or venal, but because the market makes them do it. If businesspeople behave in the purely self-serving way that economic theory assumes, the system tends to spawn manipulation and deception.

> The problem is not that there are a lot of evil people. Most people play by the rules and are just trying to make a good living. But,

inevitably, the competitive pressures for businessmen to practice deception and manipulation in free markets leads us to buy, and to pay too much for, products that we do not need; to work at jobs that give us little sense of purpose; and to wonder why our lives have gone amiss.[22]

Therefore, a Christian student or professor of economics will seek to re-locate her discipline within a wider Christian understanding of what makes for human *shalom*. This would involve, at least, the following: a) a richer anthropology, one that stresses the complexity of human motivations and the embedding of rationality in historical and social relationships; b) an incarnational commitment to "bottom-up" rather than "top-down" ("one-size-fits-all") solutions to economic problems; c) an ecological sensitivity that situates economic exchanges within the energy flows of the earth; d) bringing social justice, particularly the rights of the poor, into the heart of the discipline (e.g. by looking at distributions of costs and benefits, and not being content with merely aggregate indices); e) exploring the role that spiritual and religious capital plays in generating economic outcomes.

Public debates on how the economy is doing generally focus on the growth of GDP. However, this measure is of only limited use in measuring national welfare. The GDP measures the value of all goods and services sold in an economy, after having subtracted the costs of materials or services incurred in production processes. It does not properly account for capital depreciation, or for environmental degradation, rising crime, or illnesses because these lead to expenditures that contribute to GDP. Indeed, when the social and environmental costs of growth are considered, a completely different picture of development emerges. India and China are expected to spend hundreds of billions of dollars annually to address the crises generated by pollution and climate change.[23] GDP conveniently disregards these costs, but they are real.

A relational approach to economics will focus on the *means* we use to generate wealth. Wealth creation from the outset needs to have built into it such values as egalitarianism, grassroots participation, environmental sustainability, the dignity of work, transparency about who benefits, and respect for the family (so reducing the need, as much as possible, for breadwinners to leave their families to seek work). Otherwise, we end up sacrificing whole

---

22. George A. Akerlof and Robert J. Shiller, *Phishing for Phools: The Economics of Manipulation and Deception* (Princeton: Princeton University Press, 2015), vii.
23. See https://www.ft.com/content/0a89f3a8-eeca-11e2-98dd-00144feabdc0.

generations on the altar of economic growth. The means and processes we adopt determine what kind of society we have.

One of the myths about capitalism that was popular during the Cold War was that it was the handmaid of democracy. Economic freedom would usher in political freedom. This has not proved to be the case in China. But, even in the history of Western nations, the truth was the very opposite. It was the spread of adult suffrage and the maturing of democracy that curbed the excesses of capitalism and protected men, women, and children from the worst forms of exploitation.

The average human today lives longer, travels further, burns more carbon, and eats more food than in any generation before us. The unsustainable consumption habits of Europe, the USA, and Japan have been promoted worldwide and are now being emulated by hundreds of millions in China, India, Brazil, and Indonesia. The carbon-fueled, capital-intensive approach to economic development has gathered so much momentum that, however much the world's leaders may pay lip-service to caring for the planet, very few have the imagination and courage to envision alternative pathways.

HOW (NOT) TO HELP THE POOR

The poor really do not need us. Unless, of course, they are utterly destitute, severely disabled, or the victims of disasters such as war or earthquakes. What they want is not our charity, but a recognition by us of their *rights*. They want us to remove the barriers that the rich have erected, locally and globally, that prevent them from participating in their own sustainable development. On the global level, this would mean such things as removing the massive subsidies given by rich nations to their agribusinesses, ending the discriminatory practices of taxes (tariffs) on imports from poor nations, access to the life-saving pharmaceuticals stolen from their forests, and a stop to the destruction of their water-sources, soil, wetlands, and atmosphere by the greenhouse emissions of the well-to-do.

A *waiapi* Indian in the Amazon rainforest once told a UN consultant:

> Please stop calling us poor. Our only poverty consists of our lack of legal entitlements to our land (rich rain forest). Without legal rights to this land, we cannot defend it from invading timber

companies and others (including landless farmers). Could you instead help us obtain these documents?[24]

When small farmers depend on unscrupulous moneylenders because they have no access to bank credit, they are vulnerable when monsoon rains fail. In India, about 200,000 such farmers have committed suicide over the past decade because of heavy debt. They borrowed money to buy genetically modified cotton seed and the necessary inputs to grow it, believing erroneously they would become better off.

An area where poor nations need international help is in building effective institutions and collective, entrepreneurial organizations. There are severe limits to developing individual talents alone. The Cambridge-based economic historian, Ha-Joon Chang, argues persuasively that people in poor countries are generally more entrepreneurial than those in rich countries. Most citizens of rich countries work for a company doing highly specialized jobs. As a result, they spend their working lives implementing somebody else's entrepreneurial vision, and not their own. According to an OECD study, in most developing countries thirty to fifty percent of the non-agricultural workforce is self-employed (the ratio tends to be even higher in agriculture). In some of the poorest countries the ratio of people working as one-person entrepreneurs can be way above that: sixty-seven percent in Ghana, seventy-five percent in Bangladesh and a staggering eighty-nine percent in Benin. In contrast, only thirteen per cent of the non-agricultural workforce in developed countries is self-employed.[25]

For developing-country entrepreneurs, however, things go wrong all the time: power cuts, delivery delays due to bureaucratic red-tape, bribery, and transport breakdowns. Coping with all these obstacles, Chang observes, requires agile thinking and improvisation. An average American businessman would not last a week if he had to manage a small company in Maputo or Phnom Penh. Why then do these entrepreneurs remain poor?

Recognizing the entrepreneurial energy of the poor has led many secular and Christian NGOs to leap on the micro-credit bandwagon in the past couple of decades. The main idea behind microcredit is that the poor lack the necessary capital to realize their entrepreneurial potential. Regular banks ignore

---

24. Michael Taylor, *Christianity, Poverty and Wealth: The Findings of "Project 21"* (London: SPCK and Geneva: WCC, 2003), 10.
25. These are rounded figures. These figures, as well as the following discussion on entrepreneurship and the failure of microcredit, are taken from Ha-Joon Chang, *23 Things They Don't Tell You About Capitalism* (London: Allen Lane, 2010), 157–66.

them, and local money sharks charge exorbitant interest on loans. Enter the microcredit (or, more broadly, the microfinance) industry which gives poor people, especially poor women, small loans at reasonable interest rates to set up a food stall, buy a mobile phone to rent calls, or buy a cow or chickens and sell their produce.

This was seen as the magic formula to end poverty. It proved immensely popular among American donor agencies who saw it as a way of making every poor person a capitalist, no longer depending on government handouts. Governments, in turn, could simply forget the poor and leave their welfare in the hands of foreign and local development agencies who would distribute microcredit loans far and wide. The popularity of microcredit reached fever pitch in 2005, which the UN declared the International Year of Microcredit. The following year Muhammad Yunus and his Grameen Bank in Bangladesh, widely hailed as the pioneers of microcredit, received the Nobel Peace Prize.

Unfortunately, the cracks in the microcredit industry began to appear before this. And they have widened. Several books have questioned the claims that microfinance has significantly improved the lives of its clients. The problems are too numerous to mention. But just consider the woman who initially makes good money by renting out a mobile phone in her village. As soon as more "telephone ladies" appear on the scene, the incomes fall dramatically. The answer to such overcrowding of the market is to start manufacturing the phones yourself or writing software to develop applications for the phones. But this is a major step up and the telephone ladies do not have the education or wherewithal to move into manufacturing or software design. The problem is that there is only an extremely limited range of simple businesses that the poor in developing countries can take on, given their limited skills, lack of education, lack of access to technologies, and the limited amount of funds that they can mobilize through microfinance.

What really made rich countries rich, argues Ha-Joon Chang, was their ability to channel individual entrepreneurial energy into *collective, productive enterprises*. Exceptional individuals like Thomas Alva Edison or Bill Gates were supported by a host of collective institutions:

> the scientific infrastructure that enabled them to acquire their knowledge and to experiment with it; the company law and other commercial laws that made it possible for them subsequently to build companies with large and complex organizations; the educational system that supplied highly trained scientists, engineers,

managers and technicians to man those companies; the financial system that enabled them to raise large amounts of capital when they wanted to expand; the patent and copyright laws that protected their inventions; easily accessible markets for their products, and so on.[26]

PRACTICING INTEGRITY

I asked an African friend of mine who once worked with a UN development agency in Sri Lanka, "Have any of your colleagues chosen to work in the United Nations because they care about the poor in Sri Lanka?" He looked at me as if I had come from another planet: "Of course not," he said, "it is a good career move to spend a few years in a place like Sri Lanka." Now I am sure that there are many who are motivated by genuine compassion to work among war victims, abused women, or the economic poor. But it is easy to become cynical of the "development game" (yet another high-priced "foreign consultant" being flown in for yet another seminar on poverty held in a luxury hotel; yet another "think-tank" or "policy centre" on poverty alleviation or conflict resolution; yet another doctoral thesis or paper on these topics because the funds are readily available, but none of the results of the research ever circulating down to help the people who were interviewed, measured, or categorized, and on whose hospitality the researcher depended). Poverty, almost as much as war, has become big business. It is easy to be cynical when those who suffer are so often exploited, when they become stepping-stones to academic honor or personal fortune.

We have seen that the redemption that the gospel announces is contradicted by a global economy that persuades persons and nations to live beyond their means. Poor nations are pressurized by the rich into selling their rights to their "commons" as partial repayment of national debts. (Would this be a contemporary equivalent of the taking of a poor man's millstone as security for a debt [cf. Deut 24:6?]) Moreover, many poor nations are governed by incompetent and corrupt politicians who are willing to sell off their nation's natural inheritance in exchange for large armies and wasteful, grandiose development projects. Thereby, whole generations live under the shadow of crippling debts which require extraordinary and sustained levels of economic growth to offset. The more indebted we are, the less control we have over our own lives.

---

26. Ha-Joon Chang, 165–66.

Unthinking, unbridled consumerism has become a global religion. Personal debt is now a pandemic among the world's middle-classes. On a personal level, we can stop using credit cards to buy things we cannot afford. (There are numerous studies that show that we are more likely to spend more when using credit cards than cash.) Living beyond our means leads to enslavement and ecological disaster. In this regard, the ninety-nine percent whom groups such as the "Occupying" movement claim to represent (against the one percent super-rich) are not blameless, for they have encouraged a financial system whose short-term benefits they have reaped. But, on a political level, church leaders, economists, businessmen, journalists, artists, lawyers, and social activists need to come together with the poor to claim the rights of the marginalized, the exploited, and the economically vulnerable.

Let me conclude with these stirring words from Martin Luther King Jr.'s Nobel Prize acceptance speech:

> I have the audacity to believe that people everywhere can have three meals a day for their bodies, education and culture for their minds, and dignity, equality, and freedom for their spirits. I believe that what self-centered men have torn down other-centred men can build up. I still believe that one day mankind will bow down before the altars of God and be crowned triumphant over war and bloodshed, and nonviolent redemptive goodwill will proclaim the land. And the lion and the lamb shall lie down together, and every man shall sit under his own vine and fig tree and none shall be afraid. I still believe that we shall overcome.[27]

QUESTIONS FOR DISCUSSION

1. What changes in your personal lifestyle will follow from your reading of this essay?
2. How will you get your local church, and the denomination to which your church belongs, to come together to explore what can be done, individually and collectively, to tackle corruption, tax evasion, and other ways that the rich steal from the poor?
3. How are theological institutions and curricula shaped by the worldviews of the rich and powerful?

---

27. Quoted in Sheila Cassidy, *Audacity to Believe* (London: Collins, 1977), dedication page.

BIBLIOGRAPHY

Akerlof, George A., and Robert J. Shiller. *Phishing for Phools: The Economics of Manipulation and Deception*. Princeton: Princeton University Press, 2015.

ASEAN Post Team, "Southeast Asia's Widening Inequalities," *ASEAN Post,* 20 April 2020, https://theaseanpost.com/article/southeast-asias-widening-inequalities

Avila, Charles. *Ownership: Early Christian Teaching*. Maryknoll: Orbis, 1983.

Ball, James. "China's Princelings Storing Riches in Caribbean Haven," *Guardian Weekly*, January 31, 2014.

Bonhoeffer, Dietrich. *Letters and Papers from Prison*. New York: Macmillan, 1973.

Cassidy, Sheila. *Audacity to Believe*. London: Collins, 1977.

Chang, Ha-Joon. *23 Things They Don't Tell You About Capitalism*. London: Allen Lane, 2010.

Chrysostom, John. *On Wealth and Poverty*, trans. Catherine Roth. New York: St. Vladimir's Seminary Press, 1984.

De Botton, Alain. *Status Anxiety*. New York: Penguin Publishing, 2005.

Ehrenreich, Barbara. *Nickel and Dimed: On (Not) Getting by in America*. New York: Henry Holt, 2001.

Heilbroner, Robert. *The Worldly Philosophers*, 7th ed. London: Penguin Publishing, 2000.

Mani, Braj Ranjan. *Debrahmanising History: Dominance and Resistance in Indian Society*. New Delhi: Manohar Publishers, 2005.

Pope Francis. *Evangelii Gaudium: Apostolic Exhortation on the Proclamation of the Gospel in Today's World*, English Trans. *The Joy of the Gospel*. London: Catholic Truth Society, 2013.

Peterson, Eugene H. *Christ Plays in Ten Thousand Places: A Conversation in Spiritual Theology*. Grand Rapids: Eerdmans, 2005.

Smith, David W. *Stumbling Towards Zion: Recovering the Biblical Tradition of Lament in the Era of World Christianity*. Carlisle: Langham Publishing, 2020.

Taylor, Michael. *Christianity, Poverty and Wealth: The Findings of "Project 21."* London: SPCK, 2003.

Wolterstorff, Nicholas. *Justice: Rights and Wrongs*. Princeton, NJ: Princeton University Press, 2008.

CHAPTER 13

RENEWED ACTION FOR AGE-OLD CONCERNS

Caste and Indian Christian Ethics

Nigel Ajay Kumar

INTRODUCTION

For most of us, the year, 2020, was the year of the pandemic. However, even as the Indian government enforced one of the largest national lockdowns in the world, achieving almost a complete standstill, the Dalit Human Rights Defenders Network (DHRDNet) documented at least sixty horrific stories of violence against the "outcasts" of India during that time.[1] According to DHRDNet, these stories were recorded to bring to light the atrocities that low caste communities of India constantly suffer, made all the worse because victims were now further isolated and alone.

The stories ranged from a man who was beaten to death for daring to ask the upper caste community for protection during floods,[2] a brutal rape of a Dalit minor that left her paralyzed,[3] a man killed for trying to marry outside his caste,[4] or of a similar fate for declining to do menial work when demanded.[5]

But these were just those reported by DHRDNet during 2020. From friends working in rural and semi-rural churches, we regularly hear stories about religious persecution. However, when we dig a little deeper, inter-caste tensions often come to light. One story stands out. A pastor's son, who had recently returned to his home village after getting a bachelor's degree, was looking to serve his own lower caste community. Instead, only a few weeks

---

1. Salma Veeraraghav, *No Lockdown on Caste Atrocities: Stories of Caste Crimes During the COVID-19 Pandemic* (Dalit Human Rights Defenders Network [DHRDNet], 2020).
2. The story of Pintu, in Veeraraghav, *No Lockdown on Caste Atrocities*, 12–17.
3. The story of Pooja, in Veeraraghav, *No Lockdown on Caste Atrocities*, 22–25.
4. The story of Sudhakar, in Veeraraghav, *No Lockdown on Caste Atrocities*, 40–43.
5. The story of Haribhai, in Veeraraghav, *No Lockdown on Caste Atrocities*, 167.

ago, this son was lynched by an upper caste mob. Before the police could investigate the body was cremated, leaving no evidence. The pastor was, and is, devastated. Onlookers note how the upper caste community in the region will not allow any of the lower caste to rise in education or influence.

Today, most will be aware that Hindu society is divided into several birth-determined hierarchies that affect social standing, access to religious and educational institutions, and determine professions and trade for generations on end. Western anthropologists have called this ancient social ordering practice the "caste system." This practice is often called evil and corrupt. Ancient Hindu texts are blamed as its cause, while the priests are named as the ones who enforce its power.

Many may not be aware that this concept of the caste system is being problematized in India today. Scholars are asserting that it was British colonialism and Christian missionaries that caused much of the modern-day caste problems as we currently see them. This problematization is discussed in this paper to help Christians a) become aware of the trends and b) develop new sensibilities and strategies for discourse and ethical practice.

What remains true is that currently there are lower caste communities who are forced to comply with upper caste rules, which leaves them disadvantaged and filled with fear. And if the lower caste community falls out of line (or even if not), as is evident through the stories mentioned earlier, they are brutally assaulted with little recourse for justice. Violence and discrimination against the lower castes has become so common that we, as a nation, may have become desensitized to it.

Sadly, caste hierarchies are also being exposed in the Indian church as well. In some churches, especially in rural and semi-urban India, lower caste Christians do not attend the same services with upper caste Christians. And even if they do attend the same service, they certainly do not share the same communion cup. In urban contexts, some upper caste Christians refuse to allow their children to marry outside their caste. And some Christians even continue to hold on to their caste identities to continue in good social standing with their previous community. This is not to say that all Christians in India are caste-oriented, but caste in Indian Christianity is more common than we would like to admit.

The Indian church, as a result, needs a clearer vision of what the caste system is, why it is contrary to the gospel, and what we need to do, to address its unique ethical challenges.[6] To achieve this, I will first provide a recent history of the caste system in India, especially in terms of the shifting trends regarding the understanding of caste. Next, I will develop a Christian response to caste discrimination, drawing out practical ethical steps from theological rethinking.

UNDERSTANDING CASTE AMID CHANGING TRENDS

According to the Indian state-sponsored National Council of Educational Research and Training (NCERT) syllabus on social institutions, caste is a foreign word used to denote an ancient Indian practice of social stratification, namely *varna* and *jati*.[7] Varna, literally meaning "color," refers to the broad four-fold classification in Indic society; *Brahmins*, the priestly class, on top; next, *kshatriyas*, the warriors; then *vaishyas*, the merchants and traders; and the *shudras*, those who do manual work. There are several who fall outside this four-fold category, like the hill and tribal people, foreigners, slaves, and others, who are termed as outcastes or *panchamas* (the fifth category). These are often assigned the most menial of jobs. The other word, jati (which means "group" or "classification"), has been used to designate the sub-groups within these broad categories that differ from region to region. There can be hundreds of jatis – each with a hierarchical relation with others.

The NCERT text further notes that the caste distinctions in society are determined by two principles; separation based on purity, and wholism based on unity. The separation principle determines that the higher castes are purer than the lower castes, and thus warrant more privilege and status. The wholism principle views all society as working together, where no one community is independent from others, regardless of their status.

Using these two principles, the NCERT text highlights six distinctives to the caste system. First, caste is determined by birth and not choice, so that no one can leave their caste (though someone can get expelled from their caste). Second, caste membership requires strict rules that govern marriage (only intra-caste marriages are acceptable). Third, laws around eating and

---

6. While this chapter focuses only on issues related to caste, the Indian church must also be mindful of tribal communities and other poorer sections who face similar discrimination and ostracization from mainstream society.
7. National Council of Educational Research & Training (NCERT), *Indian Society: Textbook in Sociology for Class XII*, Chapter 3, "Social Institutions: Continuity and Change," 2022–23, https://ncert.nic.in/textbook/pdf/lesy103.pdf. This information in this section is adapted from this NCERT text. I am aware of the politics of official textbooks, especially ones that come from a government that has been accused of undermining lower caste rights. But the NCERT syllabus still represents what a large section of Indians are currently taught about this complex concept.

"food sharing" are strictly to be adhered to (eating food with the upper caste is considered unacceptable). Fourth, a hierarchical system must be followed, where each community must know its place in relation to others. Fifth, the social hierarchy extends beyond the caste to sub-castes (jatis). Finally, caste is often (loosely) linked to occupation, where a family trade is passed down from generation to generation.[8]

Alternative Narratives

While the above information may be considered general knowledge to those aware of Indian culture, it is important to keep in mind that the study of caste in India is going through a paradigm shift. Previously held narratives about India and caste are being dismantled, and alternative narratives that are more consistent with the nation's current ideology are being asserted. Three such narratives stand out. First, a stronger link is being made between the current caste structures and the British colonial occupation. Second, it is asserted that the Christian missionary interest in lower caste communities is governed not by a conviction for equality, but their failure to convert the higher castes. Third, the use of ancient religious texts to justify current caste structures is being rejected.

Caste and Colonial Powers

There are a growing number of voices that assert that the British colonial occupation damaged the core of India, even the caste system. The narrative is that the caste system was loosely applied in precolonial days with people being able to shift castes. The proponents go on to say that it was the British governing methodology that established a more rigid caste structure in India.

For instance, the NCERT textbook states that in ancient times, roughly during the Vedic period of 900–500 BC, the varna system was not rigid, was not always determined by birth, and, significantly, movement across varnas was common.[9] The NCERT text then goes on to say that "what we know today as caste is more a product of colonialism than of ancient Indian tradition."[10]

This idea of colonialism uniquely influencing the Indian caste system is also supported by an anthropologist, Susan Bayly, who argues that "caste as we

---

8. As an example, there is a lower caste village in the northern hills of India, whose only job is to make alcohol for the surrounding upper caste villages.
9. The politics of this assertion is important to note because some Hindu movements are calling for the rejection of the rigid caste system, but not entirely dismantling the Vedic *varna* system.
10. NCERT, "Social Institutions."

now recognize it has been engendered, shaped, and perpetuated by comparatively recent political and social developments."[11] Bayly notes that while Indians were party to the process, it was the British rule that "significantly expanded and sharpened these norms and conventions, building many manifestations of caste language and ideology into its structures of authoritative government."[12]

The main criticism is directed against three colonial acts. One, having a caste-based census that hardened the lines of a community's self-definition, using categories that were not dominant before.[13] Two, allowing upper caste members to lay claim to land that was earlier not possessed in the economic sense. This led the lower caste community to become landless and further marginalized.[14] Three, by providing special privileges to lower caste communities so that caste politics and caste-based reservations became an acceptable governing model.[15]

Caste and Christian Missionaries

A second alternative narrative being promoted is that Christian missionaries focused on converting the lower castes only after facing failure when trying to convert the higher castes, which led to their further criticism of the caste system. The mass lower caste conversions by those who were eager to raise their status ironically led Christianity to be regarded as a lower caste religion. This, in turn, led Christians to criticize caste as one of the main obstacles stopping the progress of the gospel.

S. N. Balagangadhara, a social theorist whose work argues that categories like "Hinduism" and "religion" must also be problematized, supports this critical narrative.[16] He argues that, since missionaries were unable to make a significant impact in the upper caste communities, they "had to rest content with the induction of lower 'caste' groups."[17] As a result, "this meant that Christianity was identified with the lower 'caste' groups and began to be

---

11. Susan Bayly, *The New Cambridge History of India*, vol. 4, pt. 3, *Caste, Society and Politics in India from the Eighteenth Century to the Modern Age* (Cambridge: Cambridge University Press, 1999), 18.
12. Bayly, 18.
13. Bayly, 119–22.
14. Bayly, 205–9.
15. Bayly, 239–43.
16. S. N. Balagangadhara, *"The Heathen in His Blindness...": Asia, the West and the Dynamic of Religion* (Leiden: Brill, 1994). See also my book, *What is Religion? A Theological Answer*, South Asian ed. (Bengaluru: SAIACS Press, 2013), where I discuss Balagangadhara's criticism of the category of religion in more detail.
17. Balagangadhara, *Heathen in His Blindness*, 112.

socially marginalized."[18] In fact, even when a few Brahmins became converts, these Brahmins were isolated. Making matters worse for missionaries, the Christian converts "continued their old practices of 'caste' discrimination."[19] It was not surprising, then, that missionaries believed that the "penetration and the acceptance of Christianity were stifled by the 'caste system.'"[20] He goes on to say, "Unable or impotent to bring God's word to the heathens in a successful manner . . . the rage and fury of the Europeans turned against the two things, which appeared impermeable to the Christian message: the 'caste' system and its 'priests', viz. the Brahmins."[21]

Additionally, Rupa Vishwanath traces some of the missionary struggles with caste, and proposes that a disappointment with the lack of higher caste converts led to their lower caste focus.[22] She states that initially Protestant missionaries had little interest in the lower caste Pariah community. The missionary interest was "almost entirely on the high caste elites, an interest stemming from the widely held presumption that religious change must begin with those at the top of the social order, whose actions would then naturally be imitated by their social inferiors."[23] In addition, Vishwanath notes that though Protestant missionaries were known to be opposed to caste, they believed in its "slow eradication" and in fact, continued to promote "rational concepts and practices of class hierarchy."[24] However, the missionaries faced much resistance and several obstacles when trying to convert members of the high caste community. One of the most common objections to Christianity was that becoming a Christian would not only spoil caste, but also make a person a Pariah.[25] Vishwanath notes that a shift in missionary strategy occurred when Wesleyan missionaries saw promise in the numbers of the Pariah community who expressed great interest in becoming Christians and even "demanded" to be baptized.

The missionaries suspected that the lower caste community's motives to convert was "not purely spiritual," because they were "poor, hungry, and oppressed."[26] But rather than address their social conditions, the missionaries

---

18. Balagangadhara, 112.
19. Balagangadhara, 112.
20. Balagangadhara, 112.
21. Balagangadhara, 112.
22. Rupa Vishwanath, *The Pariah Problem: Caste, Religion, and the Social in Modern India* (New York: Columbia University Press, 2014), eBook.
23. Vishwanath, 67.
24. Vishwanath, 70.
25. Vishwanath, 67–68.
26. Vishwanath, 70.

continued to stress the need for "spiritual salvation," and signaled that "the spiritual realm was their only rightful remit."[27] The missionary focus was on "inner transformation" and their involvement with the Pariahs was geared toward self-improvement and the "development of new personal habits."[28]

Caste and Ancient Texts

Another alternative narrative pertains to the rejection of ancient texts to determine what caste was or should be today. This is another way of saying that the doctrinal basis of caste is less of an interest in favor of a more sociological or political view of caste.

Traditionally, the *Manusmriti*, a text referred to also as the *Laws of Manu*, has been credited as the religious basis (authority) for caste differentiations in India. The Manusmriti suggested that the four major varnas represented different body parts of the Lord Brahma, the creator of the world. According to the text, the Brahmins came from the head, the kshatriyas came from the arms, the vaishyas came from the thighs, and the shudras came out of the legs. The Manusmriti seemed to both legitimize caste and caste discrimination, and became the basis of much criticism about the caste system. However, the value of Manusmriti as an authoritative text has been challenged. The NCERT text does not even mention the Manusmriti when teaching about caste.

Balagangadhara argues that it was the missionaries and Christianity-influenced anthropologists who brought in Christian views about normative texts and doctrines to observe Indian phenomena.[29] He notes that the missionaries were confused by the caste system, especially in how it did not seem to emanate out of a valid authority (much like how the Bible is authoritative for Christians). So, they looked for ancient texts, like the Manusmriti, as the foundation of the system and thought it to be the normative document for current culture. Balagangadhara observes that the missionaries were not fully aware of the irony of trying to understand current practices through an ancient text that had little sway on the Indian ground realities:

> Consider just how ridiculous this really is . . . what could one say about European culture and its people of the eighteenth century by studying The Bible? How could one understand even the Middle Ages by reading the Gospel of St. Matthew? Just

---

27. Vishwanath, 70.
28. Vishwanath, 71.
29. See especially, Kumar, *What is Religion?*, 17–25.

imagine a group of "scholars" in India, none of whom know either the classical or modern languages of Europe, studying the Bible only to make pronouncements about, say, fifteenth-century Europe. . . . Yes, this happened in Europe with respect to India for over two hundred years. What makes the absurdity a total farce is its continuation today. How many treatises do not refer to The Laws of Manu in order to talk about Hindu ethics? How many "ethno-graphic" . . . works talk about the "caste system" without solemnly mentioning the four Varna's? How many Brahmins have ever read the laws of Manu?[30]

Bayly interacts more deeply with the textual question and disassociates the Manusmriti from caste realities, saying that neither it nor other ancient texts were sufficiently influential to create caste or even to affect Indic culture universally.[31] Bayly notes that caste norms were not absolutes, but rather functioned as "reference points to be negotiated, challenged, or reshaped to fit changing circumstances."[32] Bayly also reveals that "there are many widely revered sacred texts and doctrines which devalue or condemn caste principles."[33] These texts emerge from "casteless" and anti-Brahmanical sections of Indic society, including the spiritual traditions associated with *bhakti* (devotion) movements.[34]

The point being made by these and similar social theorists is that our understanding, and even rejection of caste, must not be based on simplistic studies by anthropologists (and missionaries) that prioritized one or two key religious texts to study caste in India. Also, caste is less about religion, and more about society/culture.

Lower Caste Struggles: The Channar Revolt

I do want to note that we should not enter this revision of history with our eyes closed. While the revision of history is inevitable, one must certainly not ignore when there is caste imbalance and discrimination in history. So, rather than simplistically assert that caste conflict was a foreign invention, it

---

30. Balagangadhara, 139.
31. Bayly, 29.
32. Bayly, 30.
33. Bayly, 9.
34. Bayly, 47–48.

is important to remember that the oppression of lower caste communities in India is not a recent invention.

To get a glimpse of some of the struggles of lower caste communities, one can look at the Channar Revolt in the early to mid-1800s.[35] A low caste community, the Parayans, in South India, were not just untouchables but were "unseeables," in that they were not allowed to be seen near members of the upper caste community. The Parayan community faced tremendous discrimination. They were not allowed to enter temples, they were not allowed to cover their dwellings with a roof, and the women were not allowed to cover their breasts. Restakis notes how, "Exposed breasts were a humiliating mark of subservience . . . all lower caste women were subject to a breast tax . . . An official would go from door to door collecting a tax on any woman past the age of puberty who wanted to cover her breasts."[36]

A group of Nadar women, a large subcaste among the Parayan community, decided to protest. Some of the Nadar women who had converted to Christianity had begun to wear upper garments called the channar, which was similar to what upper caste women wore. In fact, in 1813, a British judicial officer of the region decreed that "Nadar women could cover their breasts only if they had converted to Christianity first."[37] However, many of the Nadar women who did not want to convert to Christianity argued that they should be allowed to dress as they liked, and they began to wear the channar. This caused an uproar and upper caste men were seen tearing the cloth from the women's bodies, exposing them publicly. The Nadar women retaliated with violent protests, and a revolt spread across the region. Eventually, in 1859, the Maharaja of Travancore decreed that Nadar women be allowed to dress like their upper caste counterparts.

This story shows that, in the nineteenth century, caste disparity and discrimination was rampant. While it may not have been simply a spiritual or doctrinal issue, it was still a serious issue that affected the lives of the religious

---

35. To provide a glimpse on this event, I will be using two sources. Avni Singh, "The Channar Revolt: The Fight For A Dignified Existence," *Feminism in India*, 5 August 2019, https://feminisminindia.com/2019/08/05/the-channar-revolt-dignified-existence/ and John Restakis, *Civilizing the State: Reclaiming Politics for the Common Good* (Gabriola Island, Canada: New Society Publishers, 2021), eBook.
36. Restakis, *Civilizing the State*.
37. Singh, "The Channar Revolt."

communities. The irony must not be lost that this story about caste revolt has been removed from the NCERT textbooks.[38]

Independent India and Caste Reform

The problem of caste, especially untouchability, was also keenly felt by nationalist freedom fighters who knew that even as they fought for freedom from the British, the nation needed reform.

Reformers: Ambedkar and Gandhi

One of the champions against the caste system was B. R. Ambedkar, an educated lower caste social reformer who fought for the political identity and protection of the oppressed castes. His was a radical approach in that he rejected caste altogether, and he appealed for a utopia where there would be no religion, and hence no caste.[39]

This was different from M. K. Gandhi, known to Indians as the father of the nation, who wanted to uplift the plight of the lower castes, while still allowing for the caste system to prevail. Gandhi urged that the outcastes not be called "untouchables" but be called (children of God). Ambedkar, in contrast, took on the name of Dalit, which means the oppressed ones, to highlight their suffering. Ambedkar was one of the key thinkers who helped draft the Constitution of free India (Article 17 of the Indian Constitution abolishes the practice of untouchability), and all caste discrimination was outlawed through the Untouchability (Offences) Act of 1955. These were significant victories.

New India

However, caste reform was not automatically achieved. The NCERT document criticizes post-independence caste reforms that did not entirely rid India of the problems of colonialism.[40] On one side, caste-based discrimination was officially abolished in the new Indian Constitution, with a provision to allow for special privileges to the lower castes. However, prevalent inequality was not adequately addressed.

---

38. The Wire Staff, "NCERT to Drop Chapters on Caste Struggles, Colonialism from Class 9 History Book," *The Wire*, 18 March 2019, https://thewire.in/education/ncert-history-textbook-caste-struggles-colonialsm.
39. See the speech by B. R. Ambedkar, "Annihilation of Caste," published as B. R. Ambedkar, *Annihilation of Caste: The Annotated Critical Edition*, edited by S. Anand (Navayana Publishing, 2014).
40. This is political because the current government is open of its criticism of the initial post-independent government and differentiates its views on almost all its policies.

Renewed Action for Age-Old Concerns

The NCERT text notes four such problems. First, with the rise of urbanization and industrialization, it seemed as if it was possible that Indian society would function without caste. However, caste was still always present – jobs still went to caste-based communities, urban dwellings were determined by caste-based allegiances, and there was no support for inter-caste marriages which remained rare and prone to violent disapproval.

Second, there was a rise of the middle "caste." Post-independence land reforms took away some agricultural lands from upper caste absentee landlords and gave it to local middle-caste communities. These middle-caste communities grew in power and influence in their regions. However, the lower caste communities did not benefit from this change, as they continued to be exploited as laborers. Similarly, "Sanskritization" became common among some middle-caste communities. As the middle-castes moved up the economic ladder to a higher class, they took on upper caste traditions, like wearing a sacred thread, vegetarianism, and even changing which gods they worshipped. This move helped those communities gain access to privileges previously reserved for the higher castes.

Third, with economic growth, the upper castes could exist in casteless states while continuing to receive the privileges of status, education, and access. It was not that the upper castes were all rich, but those who did well did so because they reaped the benefits of their ancestral station. As a result, the rich–poor divide increased, and class divisions became even more pronounced along with caste divisions.

Fourth, in view of their lack of privilege, the lower caste communities found more security in maintaining their caste identities. They opted for strategies of self-preservation through communal identity and political influence. This led to political parties targeting the lower caste communities for votes, and in turn, the lower caste communities trying to leverage this influence for their upliftment. This has not always been successful because true upliftment has not been achieved.

Current Scenario

In the current scenario, the lower castes, known as scheduled castes or Dalits, have been recipients of some state-sanctioned benefits like reserved places (or reservations) in educational institutions and in government workplaces. There are other social assistance programs as well, though their value in actually helping the Dalits is called into question. Some of these reservations, particularly in education, have been met with violent protests from higher caste students, which have further entrenched the caste divide. According to Bayly, some of these provisions to advance or uplift the "backward" castes has ironically "played an important role in perpetuating rather than eliminating the claims of caste for many Indians."[41]

An additional challenge facing Dalits when they become Christians is that they lose the privileges of caste-based reservations. The government argues that because Christianity is a casteless religion, they cannot claim these benefits. However, Christians argue that it takes time to remove the caste disadvantage and other communities like Sikhs and Buddhists, which are also theoretically casteless, continue to receive benefits for the lower caste members in their community.

In terms of ideology, the current ruling government is influenced by its parent religious body, the Rashtriya Swayamsevak Sangh (RSS), whose official position is that they are "caste neutral."[42] And yet, during the ground-breaking ceremony of the controversial Ayodhya temple, the RSS Chief Mohan Bhagawat quoted the Manusmriti saying, "That all the human beings on this Earth should learn from the firstborn (i.e. Brahmins) of this country about developing their own character."[43] This evident contradiction makes many from the lower caste community continue to distrust politicians and especially those from the ruling government.

Positively, there is an increasing sense that criticism of caste discrimination, at least publicly, is acceptable. The NCERT asserts that Hindu society need not be beholden to its past as it can construct new paradigms for contemporary society: "Just because something happened in the past or is part of our tradition, it is not necessarily right or wrong forever. Every age has to think afresh about such questions and come to its own collective decision about its social institutions."[44] This is encouraging for lower caste communities, if the powers that be are genuine in eradicating caste-based discrimination for good. There are also several movements that have emerged to protect the rights of the Dalits, including Christian circles that promote Dalit Liberation and Dalit theology.

---

41. Bayly, 21.
42. Vasudha Venugopal, "New book on RSS looks into its approach to caste and women's participation," *The Economic Times*, 13 September 2019.
43. Suresh Khairnar, "Glorification of Manu-Smriti at Ram Temple's consecration event in Ayodhya," *Mainstream Weekly*, 14 August 2020.
44. NCERT, "Social Institutions."

Nevertheless, while all this is happening, caste-based discrimination and violence continues to be rampant in certain parts of India as the DHRDNet book (as seen above) reveals. And there remains an urgent need for change.

CHRISTIAN ETHICAL RESPONSE

Having established that caste realities in India are complex, we move now to the Christian ethical response. Due to limitation of space, I will be briefly noting some ethical imperatives – aware that a stronger theological basis must also be constructed when there is more time and space. This is developed in four parts. First, through an ethical re-reading of history without missing the victims. Second, through an ethical self-reflection where, as Christians, we are called to introspect on our role in caste dynamics to especially challenge the caste system in our churches. Third, by developing a theological basis using the "rethinking model" that does not simply refer to biblical texts but asks difficult questions of the text and also explores how Scripture can inform a life without caste discrimination. And fourth, through practical suggestions of how we can engage, aware of our theological warrant and the current caste dynamics.

Ethical Re-Reading of History without Missing the Victims

One of the lessons we can derive from the above study is that, as Christians, we need to adopt an ethical reading of other cultures – being willing to recover the truth of the past even if it makes us look bad. We can be alert to how Christians have misused power or misunderstood events and be willing to call out negative action as abusive or misguided. Ethical readers also aspire to be neutral and not overly critical of the past. This means we must understand past actions in their context. While past actions may have had negative present consequences, the past actors did not necessarily have the negative motives that we may ascribe to them. We should be cautious about applying anachronistic standards of morality and ethics.

At the same time, we need to avoid simplistically blaming Hindu religious culture and doctrines for the caste system as some of our predecessors have done. The caste system has similarities with other flawed systems of social ordering, such as the class system, family hierarchies, or even gender roles. There are several religious, sociological, and political factors that have made caste uniquely what it is today.

We can assert that what makes the caste system particularly wrong is that it is deterministic and linked with dehumanization, discrimination, and violence. However, Christians must remember that we are not the only ones speaking against caste and asking for reform. Many Hindus, both in the past and present, have sought to move away from the caste system, particularly fighting against its inequality and discrimination. Some of the present reformers do not feel that past realities will shape the future. Thus, we also need to be careful about using past narratives to discredit current religious and political institutions.

Nevertheless, an ethical re-reading of history must not ignore caste discrimination in history and even extend toward the recovery of minority and oppressed voices today. Events like the Channar Revolt must not be forgotten. What is happening today must be exposed. Even if such stories make early Christians or others look bad, the stories of the sufferings of the oppressed must still be highlighted to ensure that the "unseen" are seen.

Ethical Self-Reflection

In addition to an ethical re-reading of history, we must have an ethical self-reflection, where we confess that caste has influenced Indian Christianity and collectively express a desire to act rightly.

When one speaks of caste and Christianity, we must remind ourselves that there are many Christianities in India, and hence many approaches. The Catholic Church, for instance, has its own history of dealing with caste. According to David Mosse, for the Catholic Church, caste is an external matter having no spiritual significance. Thus, the Catholic Church, especially in Tamil Nadu, is able to integrate caste into its services, festivals, and rituals.[45]

Protestant missionaries have held on to a strong anti-caste rhetoric, theologically emphasizing the equal value of all people. So, when caste hierarchies are manifest among Protestant churches, the contradiction is all the more stark. Pandita Ramabai (1858–1922), one of the most prominent high caste converts in early India, and a woman who devoted her life to help oppressed women, noted how the Roman Catholic churches are "more or less ruled by caste," but now even Protestant "clergymen were compelled to use different cups for each separate caste when they celebrated the Lord's supper."[46]

---

45. David Mosse, "Caste and Christianity," *India-Seminar*, 2012. https://www.india-seminar.com/2012/633/633_david_mosse.htm. This is not to say that the Catholic Church has not spoken out against caste, it's just that they have been able to integrate it more intentionally into their services.
46. (Pandita) Ramabai Saraswati, *The High-Caste Hindu Woman*, originally published in 1887, new edition (New York: Fleming H. Revell Company, 1901), 37–38.

Renewed Action for Age-Old Concerns

Sadly, even 100 years later, such divisions continue. Just recently, I saw for myself how some churches in Maharashtra (a state in western India) catered to the elite upper caste Christians, while the lower caste Christians had separate congregations. Then, in a village in Northern India, I just heard of how Brahmin Christians stopped attending church with the lower caste Christians who ate eggs. Similarly, in some areas in Karnataka (a state in southern India), there are cases where lower caste Christians do not even dare to see eye-to-eye with higher caste Christians, even if those upper caste Christians are trying to break the caste (and class) barrier. These, and many such stories, force us to admit that there are still caste issues that need to be addressed in Protestant churches in India.

A good start toward collective action is to adopt a "confession and repentance" model, as the Asia Theological Association and Evangelical Fellowship of India Theological Commission attempted in 1984. The Commission stated, "We confess and repent that on occasions and places we have permitted the evils of caste to influence the Church and to mar the beauty and unity of the body of Christ."[47] Similarly, in a more recent statement from the National Council of Churches in India (NCCI), Bishop Dr. D. K. Sahu stated:

> The Indian church has to make a confession first. We tell them [Dalits] . . . "if you become Christian then there is no discrimination," but once they become Christian they are looked down upon by Christians of higher castes. A higher caste Christian will never marry a Dalit Christian, yet we say we are all one.[48]

Another example is how the World Council of Churches Central Committee called Indian churches to "recognize that the continued discrimination and exclusion of millions of people on the basis of caste" and see it as a "serious challenge to the credibility of their witness to their faith in God."[49] Public statements such as these highlight that Indian Christians do not occupy any sort of "high-ground" when rejecting caste discrimination and are together with others in trying to find a solution to this problem.

---

47. Asia Theological Association and Evangelical Fellowship of India Theological Commission, "Editorial: Declaration on Caste and the Church," 9–12 February 1984. https://journals.sagepub.com/doi/pdf/10.1177/026537888500200201.
48. WCC, "Indian Christian leaders call for an end to caste-based discrimination, also within churches," *Oikoumene*, 30 September 2009. https://www.oikoumene.org/news/indian-christian-leaders-call-for-an-end-to-caste-based-discrimination-also-within-churches.
49. WCC, "Indian Christian leaders."

Ethical Rethinking of Theology: Beyond *Imago Dei*

Beyond ethical reflection is the need to formulate how we are to engage with the caste discrimination around us. This we do via theological rethinking. Theological rethinking is a way of doing theology that is inspired by the Rethinking Movement in India during the 1930s and 40s. The Rethinking Movement's goal was not to simply correspond to what some call orthodoxy, but rather to engage with Scripture authentically in view of a genuine Christ experience and in view of contextual realities. For Indian evangelicals to adopt this method, Rethinking Movement would need to differ from the original Rethinking Movement by having faith in the whole of Scripture, rather than only in the words of Christ. In addition, we would need to work more intentionally within the church. Nevertheless, a healthy skepticism of traditional interpretations and theological answers would remain appropriate. It is through such rethinking that we would be able to distinguish ourselves from naïve missionaries or the colonial oppressors.

The caste system discriminates in a way that many modern-day people, regardless of religious persuasion, believe is wrong. So, what does the Bible, the voice of God, uniquely say to society that is already aware of its evils? The answer must provide both a basis for explaining why caste discrimination is wrong and a way for overcoming caste discrimination. The traditional and useful starting point is to emphasize that all humans are created equally as the image of God (*imago Dei*), and so they have equal value. However, there is a problem if we only emphasize the image of God as the basis for equality – especially if we think that simply by being created equal, we are automatically equal. The traditional image of God concept must be supplemented by a deeper engagement with Scripture to find ways to work equality and develop right relations.

To build on the *imago Dei*, we need to do five things. First, we need to come to terms with difficult passages in Scripture. Second, we need to recognize how Indian theology has not always done well in addressing the caste system. Third, we must reinterpret the image of God concept in a more exegetically appropriate way. Fourth, we should draw attention to the more significant concept of being "in Christ" in the New Testament.

Discrimination in Scripture?

We need to be careful not to simplistically portray the Bible as a clear champion for equality. In fact, after the formation of Israel, several places in the Old Testament narrative are devoted to emphasizing the separateness of the people of God, and even to the point that the Old Testament people of God were required to stay away from being defiled by others. See, for instance, the "problem" raised in Nehemiah 13 and Ezra 9–10, where the Jews repented of their sin of inter-cultural marriages and cast away the people who defiled the community for not marrying within the pure Jewish lineage.

The challenge of this story is raised by Gethzi Kamala in her doctoral study on Ezra 9–10 from a Dalit perspective. Kamala uses her Dalit experience to identify with the "disenfranchised characters in the text . . . who are pronounced impure and who faced injustice" in a world that was similar to what Dalits live in today. She asserts that the narrator and interpreters of Ezra have had "elite perspectives" and they have not just ignored the "unjust rejection of the women of the land as outcasts" but also silenced them.[50]

Of course, there are alternative studies that defend the Ezra (and Nehemiah) narratives.[51] But it is not easy to ignore Kamala's point. Note, also that there was no mention of the people who were expelled as being made in the image of God or having had the same value as the faithful Israelites. So, contemporary arguments based on *imago Dei* are only part of the scriptural narrative. How can we reject the caste system in India, when some biblical narratives sound like they could support it?

There is no space to develop a complete answer to that here, but the problem must be felt truly by Christians who want to oppose caste discrimination and violence by also being biblical. Constructively, we must strive to interpret (and reinterpret) Scripture authentically in view of complex realities that we see.

Discrimination in Theology?

We also need to improve our theological effort. Lower caste (Dalit) Christian theologians have pointed out how early Indian Christian theology was more interested in engaging with higher caste Hindu religion and philosophy. Peniel Rajkumar notes how Christian Dalit Theology emerged partly because of "the insensitivity of the church and Indian Christian theology to Dalit concerns and the deeper dimensions of their struggle and aspirations for fuller humanity,

---

50. Gethzi Chella Kamala, "The Expulsion of the Outcaste Women of the Land: Re-reading of Ezra 9–10 from a Dalit Perspective" (PhD diss., Flinders University, Adelaide, 2014).
51. And several scholars have looked at that text to interpret it in our context, like Pieter M. Venter, "The dissolving of marriages in Ezra 9–10 and Nehemiah 13 revisited." *HTS Theological Studies* 74 (2018): 1–13. https://dx.doi.org/10.4102/hts.v74i4.4854.

despite the majority of Christians being of Dalit origin."⁵² Rajkumar notes an overall apathy and lack of pastoral focus on Dalits, caused by a preference for urban and elite leaders, institutionalization without empowerment, and a theological fascination with the Sanskrit Hindu religion (that has historically oppressed Dalits).⁵³ This, in turn, alienated Indian Christian Dalit theologians from both western theologians and Indian theologians.

There is currently a shift with many more Indian scholars attempting to address the struggles of Dalits and other oppressed communities. However, not all such scholars hold on strongly to the traditional orthodox theologies of the priority of Scripture or even the exclusivity of Jesus Christ, leading to further confusion in Indian theology.⁵⁴ A clear theological effort is needed that holds on to faith in Jesus, while also addressing the ills of caste discrimination.

The Function of the Image of God

In the spirit of rethinking, we also need to recognize that the *imago Dei* concept goes beyond the idea of what humans possess, toward an operative concept that requires action. The dominant stream of Christian thought has viewed the *imago Dei* as something that we possess, like an ontological reality. Some have argued that God's image in humanity was our reason, while others have asserted it was our religious feelings. However, exegetically, a case can be made that the image of God in Genesis 1:27 was meant as a sign that humanity represents God on Earth, and that sign entailed a task – a function – to be fulfilled.⁵⁵ In that sense, while some ontological significance may be present, the image of God is still a call to action.

This way of looking at the image of God is reflected in how John Stott portrays it as the theological basis of human rights,⁵⁶ and how Vinoth Ramachandra sees it as the basis for global responsibility.⁵⁷ I also mean that

---

52. Peniel Rajkumar, *Dalit Theology and Dalit Liberation: Problems, Paradigms and Possibilities* (Farnham, Surrey: Ashgate Publishing, 2010), 25.
53. Rajkumar, 31.
54. For instance, see Anderson Jeremiah, "Dalits and Religion: Towards a Synergetic Proposal," *Black Theology* 17, no. 1 (2019): 40–51.
55. See E. H. Merrill, "Image of God," in *Dictionary of Old Testament: Pentateuch*, edited by T. Desmond Alexander and David W. Baker (Downers Grove: InterVarsity Press, 2003), 441–45.
56. John Stott, *Human Rights and Human Wrongs: Major Issues For A New Century* (Grand Rapids: Baker Books, 1999).
57. Vinoth Ramachandra, "Globalisation: Towards a Theological Perspective and Critique," *Queretaro* (September 2003).

it is relevant on a personal relational level, where the image of God concept must impact how different humans relate with one another.

"In Christ" as the Unity Principle: Lessons from Galatians 3:28 and Communion

Next, we need to embrace the New Testament concept of being "in Christ." To the Galatian church, Paul declares, "There is neither Jew nor Greek, slave nor free, male nor female, for you are all one in Christ Jesus" (Gal 3:28). Note that the image of God is not the normative basis for oneness in this passage. Paul clearly sees unity only "in Christ," and that is the key. However, here too, rather than think of "in Christ" as a static doctrinal position, Paul's "in Christ" is an active assertion related to how people should behave.

We see this principle most clearly in the communion passage (1 Cor 11:17–34). Sadly, when serving the elements, most churches today only read 1 Corinthians 11:23 onwards. Many also interpret "unworthy manner" to mean either hidden sin or something that the text does not suggest. However, if we are to read the passage from verse 17, Paul is clearly upset with the Corinthian church for taking communion in an unworthy manner. The context suggests that the rich (upper class) Christians were taking the communion before the poor (presumably lower class Christians). Those who were delayed had very little, and yet those who did not wait could eat in their homes but did not. Paul asks for discipline and understanding from the upper class Christians, urging them to take the communion in remembrance of Jesus, which is another way of saying to remember the manner in which Jesus would have behaved/acted (rather than a more modern mental remembering).

The point being made is that Paul was concerned with a division in the church, and actively asked the Christians to be sensitive to the poor and weak. In doing so, the Christians were to be "in Christ," which in effect meant to act so that there would no longer be any division. As a result, the Christian community must see "in Christ" as a new way of being the people of God, and a new way of inviting others into fellowship, a new way of existing in love.

But what about the defilement between Jews and gentiles, as suggested in Ezra and Nehemiah? To answer, the New Testament vision of Jews and gentiles eating together, and worshiping together, is a radical sign of how the new covenant is different from the old. It is true that the narratives of defilement exist in Scripture. But, in Christ, this is no longer normative. The barriers between Jews and gentiles, and all peoples, have been broken. And this is the foundation of one of the largest inter-cultural communities on Earth – the church.

We can still use the image of God concept as a basis for equality, especially to assert that all people have equal value. But, in reality, Paul's call for unity is more appropriate for our times. We need to be aware that equality is not automatically apparent, and it must be achieved through work and love, in the church and in society. This can only happen in Jesus, through the Spirit.

It remains true that there are no hierarchical differentiations in humanity because we are made in the image of God. In addition, we must say that even if there are hierarchical differentiations in society, these can be overcome by acting as our Lord Jesus would like us to act. It is not enough to say, "caste is wrong," because we are created equal. Rather, we must add that, even though a person comes from another caste, we should see how we can work together to remove those barriers as Jesus would have done. We must ask ourselves, "What must I do to remove caste/class barriers?" Or even, "What can I do to help the other overcome any barriers?"

Ethical Caste-Aware Action

Finally, having done theological rethinking, we need to formulate a practical ethical proposal to engage with caste realities. We need to be aware that caste discrimination is a socioeconomic (not just religious) problem that affects societies and individuals uniquely. As a result, Christians must be aware that denying caste will not be enough. We need to address the economic, social, even psychological divisions that have been embedded for generations. Similarly, we need to have an authentic concern for the poor, defined in both social and spiritual terms. In addition, we need to be aware that a casteless society is an ideal that is not immediately achieved, even in the church. As a result, realistic and long-term goals need to be set.

For practical action, in the 1984 document referred to earlier, the Asia Theological Association and Evangelical Fellowship of India Theological Commission listed six proposals to address caste discrimination. These were:

- We preach more openly against the caste system and seek to include this teaching in our constitutions, articles of faith, and doctrinal statements of all our churches and related bodies.
- Systematic teaching be prepared to educate all ages of men, women and children.
- The importance of teaching these issues at home be emphasized and definite attempts be made to encourage families to discuss

these issues and to seek to implement and inculcate these teachings in all areas of life, particularly in marriage.
- Local Churches, theological institutions, organizations, leaders, families and individuals presently and periodically evaluate the influence of caste-ism in their lives and take corrective measures to eradicate this evil.
- Wherever the evil of caste system has permeated the church's worship and witness we seek corrective measures in the light of biblical teaching through the empowering of the Holy Spirit; where guilty we must seek to humbly confess our sins and to accept and take disciplinary action.
- Individual Christians wherever called upon be a voice for the lower castes, the exploited and oppressed, and that legal advice and personal counsel be given without compromising our Christian commitment; where appropriate joint action may be pursued with other agencies to take a united stand against caste-ism.[58]

This is an excellent list and, sadly, after over four decades, it is still relevant today, especially the last point where we as the church need to speak for the exploited and the oppressed. To this list, I would add a few more practical and active initiatives to bring together castes (and classes) within the church:

1. In terms of our church services, we must look to intentionally worship together with people of other castes, and even eat together. We must especially try our best to have a common communion.
2. In our preaching, teaching, and Bible studies, we must emphasize shared identity, where "Christian" and not "caste-Christian" is the primary identity. This is not to deny caste realities, or ignore those who are oppressed, but to recognize that in Christ we are truly equal. In the same way we must emphasize ideas of "self-worth," "value," and "interdependence" that come because of Christ and through the Spirit.

---

58. Asia Theological Association and Evangelical Fellowship of India Theological Commission, "Editorial: Declaration on Caste and the Church."

3. Through our church ministries, we must also address the socioeconomic problems facing lower caste, economically poor Christians. For instance, while selling all our possessions and sharing may be too high a demand, churches can help develop capability, where those who are less privileged get assistance in education and other skills that will be useful for surviving in society. Churches can help lower caste members to improve in trades and gain exposure to increase earning potential. These are not unspiritual concerns but appropriate for people who are economically downtrodden.
4. Similarly, churches can further aspire to break the socioeconomic divide by having more shared resources and responsibilities. Lower caste members can "co-own" church properties and share in leadership duties. This could result in a significant shift in how lower caste members perceive themselves and encourage more parity with the privileged church members.
5. Members of churches must also aspire to live like families. Even if inter-caste marriages are improbable at the moment, it is still possible to invite inter-caste members to attend marriage services and share in food and blessing. The idea is to live like large Indian families, where birth, marriage, and death are community affairs that include those we love. This could be a good way to practically get various castes into shared spaces that matter.

A HOPEFUL STORY

I close this paper with a personal story. Recently, I led a Bible study for about fifteen pastors from various parts of Karnataka (a southern state in India). It turned out that unknown to me, one of the pastors was from a lower caste, and another from a higher caste. Both were first-generation Christians, and both were evangelists and pastors. However, the higher caste pastor, from south Karnataka was well-read and vocal. His church was large, and he had a good support base. In contrast, the lower caste pastor from north Karnataka did not have a big congregation. He was struggling financially, and he was not able to express himself well. In addition, because he was unable to preach to the upper caste communities, his church remained a lower caste church. On the surface, differences could be quickly seen without knowing why. The higher caste pastor had more confidence, and he looked more secure. The lower caste pastor barely spoke and lacked confidence.

By some providence, in a group discussion activity I put these two pastors together in one group. It was only then that one of the organizers told me that they were from opposite sides of the caste spectrum. I was immediately concerned, fearing that the upper caste pastor would dominate the discussion and not allow the other pastor to speak. But what happened surprised me, and others, deeply. The pastor from south Karnataka encouraged the north Karnataka pastor to become the group leader. In addition, the north Karnataka pastor was given charge of explaining the views of others. What I thought could be a negative experience became an opportunity of empowerment. Eventually the north Karnataka pastor grew in confidence and started taking more initiative in class, to the point that he came up with insightful comments of his own.

What I saw that day was Christians actively being "in Christ." Regardless of the caste (and class) divisions that do exist, I saw two pastors engage respectfully with one another, and one uplift the other. In Christ, this was possible.

CONCLUSION

To summarize, I state that caste is not simply a religious category; it is influenced by many factors that play out in society. As a result, we Christians must be careful not to simplify it as a religious problem alone. Yes, it remains a problem, and it has seeped into the life and worship of several churches. However, to challenge this phenomenon, Christians cannot resort simply to the concept of *imago Dei*, as if the fact that we are all created equal warrants equality. Rather, we must move toward the New Testament concept of "in Christ" that extends, even corrects, isolationist thinking and encourages a more active engagement to break and overcome caste (and class) boundaries.

QUESTIONS FOR DISCUSSION

1. While the caste system has been uniquely identified with Hindu India, are there other social stratification systems in your context that are similarly unjust and oppressive?
2. This article argues that the concept of *imago Dei* (image of God) is not enough to tackle caste, and we need to further see how Jesus Christ transforms social relations. Do you agree? What other theological tools do you think could help tackle oppressive stratifications in culture?

3. In addition to the proposals in this article to tackle caste at a local level, what further practical suggestions would you give the Indian church to tackle caste in Christianity?

BIBLIOGRAPHY

Ambedkar, B. R. *Annihilation of Caste: The Annotated Critical Edition*, edited by S. Anand. Navayana Publishing, 2014.

Asia Theological Association and Evangelical Fellowship of India Theological Commission, "Editorial: Declaration on Caste and the Church," 9–12 February 1984. https://journals.sagepub.com/doi/pdf/10.1177/026537888500200201.

Balagangadhara, S. N. *"The Heathen in His Blindness. . . ."*: *Asia, the West and the Dynamic of Religion*. Leiden: Brill, 1994.

Bayly, Susan. *The New Cambridge History of India. Vol. 4. Pt. 3, Caste, Society and Politics in India from the Eighteenth Century to the Modern Age*. Cambridge: Cambridge University Press, 1999.

Clooney, Francis X. "Finding One's Place in the Text: A Look at the Theological Treatment of Caste in Traditional India." *The Journal of Religious Ethics* 17, no. 1 (1989): 1–29. http://www.jstor.org/stable/40017778.

Farek, Martin, Dunkin Jalki, Sufiya Pathan, and Prakash Shah, eds. *Western Foundations of the Caste System*. Cham, Switzerland: Palgrave Macmillan, 2017. eBook.

Fletcher, George P. "In God's Image: The Religious Imperative of Equality under Law." *Columbia Law Review* 99, no. 6 (1999): 1608–29. https://doi.org/10.2307/1123550.

Jeremiah, Anderson. "Dalits and Religion: Towards a Synergetic Proposal." *Black Theology* 17, no. 1 (2019): 40–51.

Kamala, Gethzi Chella. "The Expulsion of the Outcaste Women of the Land: Re-reading of Ezra 9–10 from a Dalit Perspective." PhD diss., Flinders University, Adelaide, 2014.

Kumar, Nigel Ajay. *What is Religion? A Theological Answer*. South Asian ed. Bengaluru: SAIACS Press, 2013.

Merrill, E. H. "Image of God," in *Dictionary of Old Testament: Pentateuch*, edited by T. Desmond Alexander and David W. Baker, 441–45. Downers Grove: InterVarsity Press, 2003.

Mosse, David. "Caste and Christianity," *India-Seminar*, 2012, https://www.india-seminar.com/2012/633/633_david_mosse.htm.

National Council of Educational Research & Training (NCERT), *Indian Society: Textbook in Sociology for Class XII*, Chapter 3, "Social Institutions: Continuity and Change," 2022–23, https://ncert.nic.in/textbook/pdf/lesy103.pdf.

Rajkumar, Peniel. *Dalit Theology and Dalit Liberation: Problems, Paradigms and Possibilities*. Farnham, Surrey: Ashgate Publishing, 2010.

Ramachandra, Vinoth. "Globalisation: Towards a Theological Perspective and Critique." *Queretaro*, September 2003.

Restakis, John. *Civilizing the State: Reclaiming Politics for the Common Good*. Gabriola Island, Canada: New Society Publishers, 2021. eBook.

Roy, Ajit. "Caste and Class: An Interlinked View." *Economic and Political Weekly* 14, no. 7/8 (1979): 297–312, http://www.jstor.org/stable/4367350.

Saraswati, (Pandita) Ramabai. *The High-Caste Hindu Woman*. New Edition, New York: Fleming H. Revell Company, (1887) 1901.

Singh, Avni. "The Channar Revolt: The Fight for A Dignified Existence," *Feminism in India* 5 August (2019), https://feminisminindia.com/2019/08/05/the-channar-revolt-dignified-existence/.

Stott, John. *Human Rights and Human Wrongs: Major Issues for A New Century*. Grand Rapids: Baker Books, 1999.

Vishwanath, Rupa. *The Pariah Problem: Caste, Religion, and the Social in Modern India*. New York: Columbia University Press, 2014. eBook.

WCC, "Indian Christian leaders call for an end to caste-based discrimination, also within churches," *Oikoumene*, 30 September 2009. https://www.oikoumene.org/news/indian-christian-leaders-call-for-an-end-to-caste-based-discrimination-also-within-churches.

The Wire Staff, "NCERT to Drop Chapters on Caste Struggles, Colonialism from Class 9 History Book," *The Wire*, 18 March 2019, https://thewire.in/education/ncert-history-textbook-caste-struggles-colonialsm.

CHAPTER 14

THE MISSION OF THE CHURCH

Just Peacemaking and Reconciliation

Rula Khoury Mansour

This chapter proceeds in three parts. I begin with an introduction to peace ethics describing *just peacemaking theory*. In the second section, I briefly introduce *church mission*. I describe and explore church mission in three case studies of oppressed churches. The first two cases are often thought to be post-conflict: the "Black church" in the American civil rights movement and the "Black church" in apartheid South Africa. The third case is the Palestinian church in the ongoing Israeli–Palestinian conflict. The experiences of the three cases illustrate that the mission of the oppressed church as a prophetic voice could bring about signs of the kingdom – liberation, healing, and restoration. Finally, I proceed to analyze and evaluate the three cases using two different approaches: reconciliation theology and peace ethics. I draw on reconciliation theology to explore the church's theology in its struggle against injustice. I engage with the results to illustrate how the church's context shapes its mission and theology amid conflict. Then, in terms of peace ethics, I apply just peacemaking theory in order to examine the effectiveness of this paradigm in situations of injustice.

JUST PEACEMAKING THEORY

The discipline of Christian ethics has three main approaches to violence, war, and peacemaking: (1) just war,[1] (2) nonviolence/pacifism,[2] and (3) just peace-

---

[1]. A foundational point in just war theory is that to justify killing in war, there must be an important reason that overrides the truth that killing people is wrong. Legitimate Christian use of just war should always be established on nonviolence and justice, as taught by Jesus, and should be seen as a way of minimizing violence and injustice, not as a means of rationalizing war. Glen Stassen and David Gushee, *Kingdom Ethics: Following Jesus in Contemporary Context* (Downers Grove: InterVarsity Press, 2003), 158–65.

[2]. *Nonviolence/Pacifism* from a Christian view seeks to be faithful to the way of Jesus, who taught nonviolence exemplified by his life and death on the cross. John Howard Yoder points out that some people wrongly confuse pacifism with passivism. However, Jesus's teachings are not mere

making. Jesus's way of peacemaking is the basis for all three ethics.[3] In what follows, I elaborate on just peacemaking theory.

Just Peacemaking Theory

Just peacemaking theory arose out of a desire to move beyond discussions of whether war is ever justifiable, to a positive theology of peacemaking and war-prevention. Stassen and Gushee present ten practices of just peacemaking[4] that are divided into three thematic parts that emphasize their Christian theological foundation:[5] peacemaking initiatives, justice, love, and community.[6]

Peacemaking Initiatives

For Christians, peacemaking embodies a Christology that emphasizes Jesus's teachings. In the Sermon on the Mount, Jesus provides a vision of peacemaking that precludes both violence and passive withdrawal from society and instead offers ways to restore damaged relationships.[7] Just peacemaking thus emphasizes taking proactive steps to create and sustain peace, to confront evil in society, and to prevent violence.[8] The practices of just peacemaking under this theme are: (1) support nonviolent direct action, (2) take independent initiatives to reduce threat, (3) use co-operative conflict resolution, (4) acknowledge responsibility for conflict and injustice; seek repentance and forgiveness.

Justice

In just peacemaking, justice and peace are intimately linked and expressed by the biblical concept of shalom. Shalom expresses God's fundamental intention

---

prohibitions but active initiatives. Yoder asserts that the point of discipleship is faithfulness, not effectiveness. John Howard Yoder, *The Politics of Jesus* (Grand Rapids: Eerdmans, 1972; 1994, chap. 12).
3. Stassen and Gushee, *Kingdom Ethics*.
4. The aftermath of the two world wars, the potential devastation from nuclear weapons, the threat of terrorism, among others, provided the context for the growth of just peacemaking theory. From 1993 Glen Stassen worked with twenty-three scholars to identify practical peacemaking strategies and he compiled and edited *Just Peacemaking* based on their work. Just peacemaking theory has emerged as a powerful and practical method for considering war, peace, and justice and promoting peacebuilding. It is a theory that does not replace but works alongside pacifism and just war theory. See Glen Stassen, *Just Peacemaking: The New Paradigm for the Ethics of Peace and War* (Cleveland: Pilgrim, 2008).
5. Stassen and Gushee, *Kingdom Ethics*, 170–73.
6. Stassen and Gushee, 170–73.
7. Matt 5:23–26.
8. Anna Scheid, *Just Revolution: A Christian Ethic of Political Resistance and Social Transformation* (Lexington Books: Lanham, 2015), 30.

for humanity that people live in a "right" state in all areas of their lives: in their relationship with God, themselves, others, and nature. Peace cannot be lived without justice and justice cannot be achieved by non-peaceful means.[9] The next two practices are based on the prophets' and Jesus's teachings that eliminating injustice is crucial for peace: (5) promote democracy, human rights, and religious liberty, (6) foster just and sustainable economic development.

Love and Community

Peacemaking is contiguous with building relationships across boundaries and addressing structural inequalities and injustices that lead to conflict. Christians see love as a radical force for building community that includes enemies and the marginalized.[10] Belonging to a church community involves commitment to "conversation" and "active participation" in community life,[11] which provides a model for conflict resolution in the world, where active listening, negotiation, and participation are crucial to peacemaking.

Just peacemaking practices under the theme of love and community are: (7) work with emerging cooperative forces in the system, (8) strengthen the United Nations and international organizations, (9) reduce offensive weapons and weapon trade, (10) encourage grassroots peacemaking groups and voluntary associations.

THE MISSION OF THE OPPRESSED CHURCH: THREE CASE STUDIES

This section defines the term "church mission" as a prophetic role and gives three case studies as examples of how an oppressed church as a prophetic voice could apply the principles of shalom in specific contexts. The case studies are: (1) the Black church(es) during and post-apartheid South Africa, (2) the Black church(es) in the American civil rights movement, and (3) the Palestinian church within the ongoing Israeli–Palestinian conflict.

---

9. Chris Marshall, *Little Book of Biblical Justice: A Fresh Approach to the Bible's Teachings on Justice* (Intercourse, PA: Good Books, 2005), 12–13.
10. Matt 5:43–48.
11. Pamela Brubaker et al. "Introduction: Just Peacemaking as the New Ethic for Peace and War," in *Just Peacemaking: The New Paradigm for Peace and War*, ed. Stassen. (Cleveland: Pilgrim Press, 2008), 31.

The Church Mission: A Prophetic Role

Mission has its origin in God's heart. There is mission because God loves people.[12] Hence, the church's mission, similar to Jesus's, involves being sent to the world to love, serve, teach, heal, save, and free.[13] Contemporary mission has five marks: (1) to proclaim the good news of the kingdom of God, (2) to teach, baptize, and nurture new believers, (3) to respond to human need by loving service, (4) to transform unjust structures of society, to challenge violence of every kind, and to pursue peace and reconciliation, (5) to strive to safeguard the integrity of creation and to sustain and renew the life of the earth.[14] Mission, then, is the tool by which the love of God is expressed to God's creation everywhere.

Therefore, the church of God should seek to apply the principles of shalom in society through taking active steps to (1) create and sustain peace, (2) confront injustice in society, and (3) prevent violence. The prophetic ministry of the church is to link the gospel to major events and daily issues.[15] As Archbishop Tutu puts it, the church must serve as the conscience of society.[16] Considering the foregoing, how can the church have a prophetic role in situations of injustice?

Case Study 1 – The Role of the Black Church(es) in Apartheid South Africa

When English settlers arrived in Africa in the early nineteenth century, missionary activity grew. Archbishop Tutu, however, saw this growth differently, saying, "When the missionaries came to Africa, they had the Bible and we had the land. They said, 'Let us pray.' We closed our eyes. When we opened them, we had the Bible and they had the land."[17] In South Africa, at the time

---

12. David J. Bosch, *Transforming Mission: Paradigm Shift in Theology of Mission* (New York: Orbis Books, 1991), 392.
13. David J. Bosch, "Reflection on Biblical Models of Mission," in *Landmark Essays in Mission and World Christianity*, Gallagher and Hertig (eds.) (New York: Orbis, 2009), 3–16.
14. The five marks of mission have been developed by the Anglican Consultative Council since 1984. Anne Richards et al. *Five Marks of Mission*, The Church of England, updated (1984) 2018, https://www.churchofengland.org/sites/default/files/2017-11/MTAG%20The%205%20Marks%20Of%20Mission.pdf.
15. Miroslav Volf, "The Church as a Prophetic Community and a Sign of Hope," *European Journal of Theology* 2 (1993): 9–30.
16. Desmond Tutu, "My Creed," 235, In Michael Battle, *Ubuntu: I in You and You in Me* (New York: Seabury, 2009), 32.
17. Steven D. Gish, *Desmond Tutu: A Biography* (Westport, CT: Greenwood Press, 2004), 101.

of country liberation in 1994, eighty percent of the fertile lands previously belonging to Black owners had ended up in the hands of the White minority.[18]

Apartheid means "separateness" in Afrikaans. It is the system of racial segregation through which the White minority ruled in South Africa from 1948 until it was abolished between 1990–1993. Apartheid laws classified people into ethnic groups according to their skin color: Black, White, Colored, and Indian.[19] The violent and systematic implementation of this system had devastating effects on the South African community.

The Church's Position during Apartheid – The Kairos Document and Other Statements

The South African church under the apartheid system was divided between churches who supported the apartheid government such as the Dutch Reformed Church, and churches who struggled against apartheid such as the Anglicans, Methodists, and Catholics. A foremost figure in the struggle was Archbishop Tutu, Secretary General of the South African Council of Churches (SACC) from 1978–1985, who with SACC, took a public stand against apartheid and supported the idea of a South Africa where people of all races would be reconciled to one another.[20]

Archbishop Tutu modeled an approach to Christian salvation which celebrates ethnic diversity, is free from all oppression and subjugation, reflects the values of God's kingdom, and is full of the love of God.[21] For forty years, the pulpits of the church were relatively safe places addressing government policies and abuses. However, many of those who spoke out against these violations were prohibited from preaching, others were imprisoned, even killed.[22]

---

18. Maano Ramutsindela and Paballo Abel Chauke, "Biodiversity, Wildlife and the Land Question in Africa," 201.
19. Implemented since the early 1940's apartheid led to the following: Black people were unable to vote in white South Africa; their ancestral lands were seized by the government and sold to White citizens; Black homelands were placed in the most distant and least economically viable areas of the country; education, health and other services were segregated and Black people were only able to access unskilled jobs.
20. Desmond Tutu, "Address to the Provincial Synod of the Anglican Church in Southern Africa," 35–36. SACC was rooted in a biblical worldview of liberation from oppression.
21. Dion Forster, "The Role of the Church in Reconciliation in South Africa," 2010; http://www.lausanneworldpulse.com/themedarticles-php/1267/04-2010.
22. Forster, "Reconciliation."

Despite this, the church issued prophetic pronouncements, for example: the Cottesloe Declaration,[23] which rejected unjust discrimination in its various forms; the Belhar Confession,[24] which asserted that apartheid is a sin; and the Kairos Document,[25] which challenged the response of the churches to the evil policies of the apartheid state.

During the apartheid period, the Black church's focus was on seeking justice and liberation.

The Church's Position Post-Apartheid: The Truth and Reconciliation Commission

When apartheid ended in 1994 after the first fully inclusive democratic elections in South Africa, a groundbreaking reconciliation process spearheaded by a "Truth and Reconciliation Commission" (TRC) under the leadership of Archbishop Tutu, was launched across the country.

As an official body, the TRC held court-like "hearings," where victims of human rights violations were invited to make statements about their abuse, and some were selected to be witnesses for public hearings. Perpetrators were also given the opportunity to testify and apply for amnesty for their crimes.[26] TRC promoted truth-telling in exchange for less harsh sentencing to encourage repentance and forgiveness.[27] As Peter Storey argues, the experiences of the TRC point "beyond conventional retribution into a realm where justice and mercy coalesce and both victim and perpetrator must know pain if healing is

---

23. The Cottesloe Consultation was held in 1960 in Cottesloe, South Africa. The conference was sponsored by the World Council of Churches. During the consultations, member bodies were urged to push the South African government towards more inclusion of Black people in political positions. See https://en.wikipedia.org/wiki/Cottesloe_Consultation.
24. The *Belhar Confession* is a 1982 statement of Christian faith. According to the Confession, unity is God's gift to the church; and this means unity of Christians of different races. Individual, racial, and social segregation is a sin, and all forms of separation lead to hostility and hatred. https://en.wikipedia.org/wiki/Belhar_Confession.
25. *Kairos* is a theological statement issued in 1985 by Black South African theologians. It challenged the churches' response to the evil policies of the apartheid state. *Kairos* is a prominent example of contextual theology and libertarian theology, and became the model for statements issued in Latin America, Zimbabwe, India, and Palestine. https://en.wikipedia.org/wiki/Kairos_Document.
26. Truth and Reconciliation Commission (South Africa), *Wikipedia*. http://en.wikipedia.org/wiki/Truth_and_Reconciliation_Commission_(South_Africa).
27. However, reconciliation did not include an apology from those responsible. For *Kairos* theologians, reconciliation had been manipulated in South Africa and justice also was not represented. Thus, the remaining concept was truth.

to happen. It is an area more consistent with Calvary than the courtroom."[28] From this perspective, it can be said that in the post-apartheid period the church's focus was on *forgiveness and peace*.

Case Study 2 – The Role of the Black Churches in the American Civil Rights Movement (1954–1968)

The American civil rights movement (CRM) aimed to restore African Americans' rights and was one of the most influential social movements of the twentieth century. With the passing of the Civil Rights Act in 1964, the children of former slaves began to be treated as citizens.[29]

The Black churches played a key role in the CRM, which birthed the civil rights organizations and leaders of the movement.[30] They provided the movement with the following: an organized mass base; activist clergymen skilled in managing people and resources; a financial base through which protest was funded; meeting places where the masses planned tactics and strategies; a symbol of identity with a collective commitment to the struggle; a cultural center; and a shelter.

Why Was the Church Successful in Leading the Civil Rights Movement?
The success of the Black churches in taking the leadership role is attributable to a combination of historic and tactical factors.
   a) Black churches styled themselves as churches of the oppressed. Their history and the painful experiences of African Americans in American society[31] placed the Black churches in a strategically dominant position for functioning as organizers – and the people responded to the churches' efforts.
   b) The Black churches provided a guiding philosophy of the movement. This was accomplished through multiple means:
      • Linking the goal of the movement with Christian teachings. Martin Luther King Jr.'s (MLK) speeches resonated with appeals to the cultural ideology and faith of the people via the

---

28. Peter Storey, "A Different Kind of Justice: Truth and Reconciliation in South Africa," *The Christian Century* 114 (1997): 788–793.
29. Allison Calhoun-Brown, "Upon This Rock: The Black Church, Nonviolence, and the Civil Rights Movement," *Political Science and Politics*, 33 (2000): 168–174, 169.
30. Supad Kumar Ghose, "The Role of the Black Church in the American Civil Rights Movement," *UITS Journal* 5, no. 1 (2017): 59.
31. Gunnar Myrdal, *An American Dilemma* (New York: Harper and Brothers, 1944).

biblical image of slaves being set free from bondage in Egypt and entering the Promised Land.[32] African Americans thus saw their faith as a struggle for liberation, and they joined the movement as a way of being fully involved in their religion.[33]

- Developing a philosophy of nonviolent resistance which mirrored[34] the way that believers had fought against injustice in the early church. This method was believed to still be effective.[35]
- Urging people to accept the concept of redemptive suffering as sacred, because suffering is deeply rooted in Christian faith.[36]
- Using biblical stories to show that serving the oppressed is God's will and a means of serving God.[37]

c) The Black churches provided an appropriate environment for personal and social education and development. Because their people were prevented from participating in mainstream American institutions, Black churches developed to contain elements of politics, the arts, education, economic development, social services, civic organization, and leadership opportunities. A shared sense of spiritual culture encouraged people to listen and actively take part in political education as part of their religious culture. The songs, teachings, prayers, and rituals of the Black churches reinforced the revolutionary message that all are equal before God.[38]

d) The Black churches provided financial support for the movement. Fundraising confirmed the material influence of the church, as well as local churches' role as financiers of the movement.[39]

---

32. Aldon D. Morris, *The Origins of the Civil Rights Movement: Black Communities Organizing for Change* (New York: The Free Press, 1984), 4–17.
33. Ghose, "The Role of the Black Church in the American Civil Rights Movement," 60.
34. Calhoun-Brown, "Upon This Rock: The Black Church, Nonviolence, and the Civil Rights Movement," 168–74.
35. Martin Luther King, Jr. encountered Gandhi's philosophy during his theological studies. He explained that Christ showed us the way and Gandhi showed it could work. See Nojeim, *Gandhi and King*, for a comparison between Gandhi and King.
36. The concept that there is positive "redemptive" quality in suffering is laid out in detail in the work: Anthony Pinn, *Moral Evil and Redemptive Suffering* (Gainesville: University of Florida Press, 2002).
37. Calhoun-Brown, "Upon This Rock: The Black Church, Nonviolence, and the Civil Rights Movement," 168–74.
38. Ghose, "The Role of the Black Church in the American Civil Rights Movement," 62.
39. Morris, *The Origins of the Civil Rights Movement*, 117.

The Mission of the Church

e) The Black churches provided shelter for the movement's activists involved in various protest activities, because they were the *only* institutions able to do this at necessary moments.
f) The church worked as a central organization in stimulating Black society because it fulfilled the spiritual and social needs of Black people therefore their culture developed around the church. The Black churches also had extensive communication networks that easily helped in mobilizing community support, as was the case during the mass boycott of buses, public transport, and some businesses owned by racially discriminatory White people.[40]
g) The Black churches collaborated with other organizations within the community. The United Defense League was formed to provide the civil rights movement with the support of non-ecclesiastical organizations within the community. It sought to engage all segments of society, while maximizing collective cohesion. Likewise, other non-ecclesiastical institutions such as the National Association for the Advancement of Colored People (NAACP) needed to align with the church for mutual benefit.[41]
h) The role of the clergy, especially charismatic ministers, was fundamental in producing relationships between the churches and in leading churches in the struggle for Black rights. Ministers also established an interdenominational alliance so they could consult and work together on significant issues regarding the Black community.[42]

To conclude, the Black church(es) in creative ways became a "movement church."[43] It was an integral part of the civil rights movement that: (1) defined the goals of the movement – the equality of Black people in the eyes of God as described by Christian teaching; (2) decided on nonviolent procedures as the movement's technique; (3) coordinated the overall movement,

---

40. Morris, 4–17.
41. The NAACP had common interests with the churches because they were both participating in the struggle for black equality in American society. Ghose, "The Role of the Black Church in the American Civil Rights Movement," 65.
42. Clarence Taylor, *Black Religious Intellectuals: The Fight for Equality from Jim Crow to the Twenty-First Century* (New York: Routledge, 2002), 88–100.
43. Ghose, "The Role of the Black Church in the American Civil Rights Movement," 63–64.

including different groups; and (4) played an important role in educating the Black masses.

Case Study 3 – The Role of the Palestinian Church within the Ongoing Israeli–Palestinian Conflict

Background and Challenges

The creation of Israel in 1948 caused the displacement of more than 700,000 Palestinian Arabs and the destruction of more than 400 Palestinian villages and towns.[44] Palestinians scattered and divided in different places. Many rounds of war and violence have taken place during the ongoing Israeli–Palestinian conflict. Seven decades later, two million Palestinians live under siege in Gaza, three million live under occupation in the West Bank,[45] and two million Palestinians are second-class citizens within Israel.[46] Six million Palestinians live in the diaspora or in refugee camps in neighboring countries.

A Historically Oppressed Church

Palestinian Christians include some of the oldest Christian communities in the world; their presence in the Holy Land dates back to early Christianity (Acts 2:11).[47] These Christians were isolated from much of their Arab culture throughout centuries of Muslim rule and survived by paying *jizya* tax to keep their religion, though this did not always guarantee their safety. Since the late nineteenth century, Arab Christians have contributed significantly to the renaissance of Arabic culture through Arab Christian intellectuals.

Under Ottoman rule, Christians were confined to being second-class citizens,[48] subject to legal restrictions within the framework of the *millet* sys-

---

44. This event is known in the Palestinian narrative as the *nakba*, the period of war itself and events affecting Palestinians from December 1947 to January 1949. See Ilan Pappé, *The Forgotten Palestinians: A History of the Palestinians in Israel* (New Haven: Yale University Press, 2011), and Walid Khalidi, ed., *All That Remains: The Palestinian Villages Occupied and Depopulated by Israel in 1948* (Washington, DC: Institute for Palestine Studies, 1992).
45. The West Bank and Gaza strip was occupied by Israel in 1967.
46. Uri Benziman and Mansour Atallah, *Dayare mishneh* [Sub-tenants] (Jerusalem: Keter, 1992). Some laws are declaratively discriminatory on religious-ethnic ground, such as the Nationality Law, which aimed at marginalization and alienation.
47. B. Sabella, "The Emigration of Christian Arabs: Dimensions and Causes of the Phenomenon," in *Christian Communities in the Arab Middle East: The Challenge of the Future*, A. Pacini, ed. (Oxford: Oxford University Press, 1998), 127–28.
48. The modernization of the Ottoman Empire led to a new era of Arab political activism. This offered Arab Christians the means of escape from their *dhimmi* status. Influenced to some extent by education conducted by missionaries, Christians were at the forefront of efforts to create

tem[49] that gave each Christian denomination limited authority to administer themselves. However, millets further isolated the Christian minority, and their use was undoubtedly a political strategy to "divide and conquer" Christian communities. In the early twentieth century the millet system was adapted by the British Mandate and, later, by the State of Israel. Today, Palestinian Arab Christians in Israel and the Occupied Territories number only 183,000 divided into twenty denominations.[50] Most denominational leadership is foreign and headquartered in foreign countries.[51] It should be noted that due to more than 100 years of large-scale displacement and emigration, the number of Palestinian Christians has decreased from ten percent of the total population in 1921 to two percent in 2020.[52]

A Numerical Minority

As ethnic minorities among Jews in Israel (twenty percent)[53] and as religious minorities among Arab Muslims (eight percent in Israel and one percent in the West Bank), Palestinian Arab Christians form a unique numerical minority. Palestinian Christians tend to perceive themselves positively as a distinct social group; this collective self-esteem is partly due to the educational and economic level Christians have achieved despite their difficulties.[54] As a resourceful minority, they have played an important role in shaping a Palestinian national

---

secular, nationalistic political orders. See Ye'or, *Islam and Dhimmitude*; Cragg, *Arab Christian*; Sharkey, "Christianity in the Middle East"; Jenkins, *Lost History of Christianity*; Khūry, *A'rab masihiyūn*; and Mansour, *Narrow Gate Churches*.
49. The word millet comes from the Arabic word millah and means "nation." It refers to the separate legal courts under which communities (Muslims, Christians or Jews abiding by sharia, canon or halakha law, respectively) were allowed to rule themselves under their own system.
50. The main denominations are: Catholic (6 denominations); Orthodox (2 denominations); Oriental Orthodox (4 denominations); Mainline Protestants (3 denominations); and Evangelical (5 denominations).
51. For example, the Catholic in Rome, Orthodox in Greece. The role of the Palestinian clergy in the struggle is limited since the local churches are controlled by foreign churches and vocal clergy have been asked to move from their influential positions.
52. Bader Mansour, "Christians," http://www.comeandsee.com/ar/post/2880450.
53. Rabinowitz describes the Palestinian citizens of Israel as a "trapped minority," which is a "segment of a larger group spread across at least two states. Citizens . . . alienated from political power. Unable to influence the definition of public goods or enjoy them, its members are at the same time marginal within their mother nation abroad." Danny Rabinowitz, "The Palestinian Citizens of Israel, the Concept of Trapped Minority and the Discourse of Transnationalism in Anthropology," *Ethnic and Racial Studies* 24 (2001): 64–85.
54. G. Horenczyk and S. Munayer, "Acculturation Orientations toward Two Majority Groups: The Case of Palestinian Arab Christian Adolescents in Israel," *Journal of Cross Cultural Psychology* 38 (2007): 76–86.

identity, with a political and cultural influence within Palestinian society that far exceeds their numbers.

The ongoing Israeli–Palestinian conflict, the failed peace process, the fact that Palestinians are geographically scattered between the West Bank, Gaza, Israel, and surrounding countries, the general political instability of the region, the rise of Islamist groups,[55] and the exodus of Christian populations have shaped the political identity of Palestinian Christians, causing a split in their loyalties. Some embrace traditional secular nationalism, others work for a Christian religio-communal revitalization, or focus on apolitical escapism.[56] Some Palestinian Christian citizens of Israel favor alignment with Jews in Israel, while others take a role through involvement with parachurch organizations.

Christian Zionism[57]

Major conservative evangelical denominations in the world openly support Zionism and the State of Israel, without any consideration for the implications that this support has for the suffering of the Palestinians, the indigenous population. This ideology is a key contributing factor to the tremendous amount of injustice experienced by the Palestinian communities in Israel–Palestine. As a result, the Palestinian struggle does not have enough international church support which would be effective in helping to end the conflict. It is worth noting that while American Black churches used Old Testament passages for liberation, these texts have been used against Palestinians in Zionist theology.

Opportunities and Initiatives through the Different Stages of the Conflict

The first way minorities relate to majority groups is typically through integration. Palestinian Christians, however, do not seek to integrate, which may be related to their characteristics of being highly religious, supported by strong church and school structures, having a long history of survival in the Middle

---

55. Such as ISIS (Islamic State of Iraq and Syria), which kills Christians who refuse to convert to Islam or pay the *jizya*.
56. Loren Lybarger, "For Church or Nation? Islamism, Secular-Nationalism and the Transformation of Christian Identities in Palestine," *American Academy of Religion* 75, no. 4 (2007): 777–813.
57. Christian Zionism is a belief among some Christians that the establishment of the State of Israel in 1948 was in fulfilment of Biblical prophecy. They believe that the gathering of Jews in Israel precedes the second coming of Jesus, hence they actively support immigration of the Jews to Israel.

East, and their heightened investment in Arab Nationalism.[58] Throughout the different stages of the conflict, as I will elaborate, the Palestinian church has been active in taking a stance against the occupation and injustices. Church initiatives include successful and less successful efforts.

Shock and Resignation Stages (1948–1967)[59]

During the nakba, Palestinians in Israel were stunned when, within a short period, they became a minority and refugees in their own land. The new government imposed a martial law to control their movement and confiscate their land. The Palestinians' main attitude was one of acceptance, as the state had developed a sophisticated "system of control," with which to manipulate the Arab minority and control it effectively. During these stages, the church hosted many refugee families from evacuated towns and villages and provided shelter for both Muslims and Christians. The church took the role of relief work; its buildings became shelters and health and educational centers.

Awakening Stage (1967–1989)[60]

In 1967, Israel occupied the West Bank and the Gaza Strip. During this stage, Palestinians in Israel, the West Bank, and Gaza, began to increasingly resist injustices against them. Prior to and during the First Intifada in 1987, Mubarak Awad (the "Gandhi of Palestine") and the Palestinian Center for the Study of Nonviolence sponsored various Christian nonviolent actions including: civil disobedience, planting olive trees on Israeli settlements, tax-strikes, and boycotting Israeli products. Additionally, the patriarchs of churches in Jerusalem issued many statements against injustices. They called for nonviolent resistance by Palestinian Christian communities and for international involvement for solving the conflict through dialogue.

Palestinian Christians struggled in this situation; they were fighting against Israeli occupation, Palestinian violent resistance, and Christian Zionism. As a result, several Palestinian theologians started to develop contextual theology,[61]

---

58. Salim Munayer and Gabriel Horenczyk, "Multi-Group Acculturation Orientations in a Changing Context: Palestinian Christian Arab Adolescents in Israel after the Lost Decade," *International Journal of Psychology* 49, no. 5 (2014): 364–70.
59. Naim Ateek, *Justice and Only Justice: A Palestinian Theology of Liberation* (Maryknoll, NY: Orbis, 1989), 32–37.
60. Ateek, *Justice and Justice Only*, 38–49.
61. Such as Mitri Raheb, *I Am a Palestinian Christian*, Ruth Gritsch, trans. (Minneapolis: Fortress, 1995).

liberation theology,[62] nonviolent theology,[63] and, later, a theology of the land,[64] and reconciliation theology.[65]

Demanding Justice (1989–Today)

After the failure of the Oslo Accords[66] (peace talks between Israel and the Palestinians in the 1990s), Palestinian voices started to demand justice through less traditional political methods. Palestinian Christians played a significant role during this period, which was characterized by a new generation using new means to fight for their rights. Besides protests and demonstrations, civil disobedience was employed in the West Bank against unjust laws. Several Palestinian Christian villages, such as Beit Sahour, organized citywide resistance – refusing to pay tax to Israel and boycotting Israeli products. More Palestinian Christian scholars wrote about justice and peace; they also developed various ecumenical and inter-religious parachurch organizations.

In 2006, a group of patriarchs and heads of Palestinian churches issued the Jerusalem Declaration on Christian Zionism,[67] a statement which rejects Christian Zionism as a false doctrine that corrupts the biblical truths of love, justice, and reconciliation. The Declaration does not specifically oppose political Zionism in terms of challenging the reality of Israel's presence, but it condemns Christian Zionism for identifying with the one-sided political ideology of Zionism. The Declaration criticizes Christian Zionist support for Israel's territorial expansion and expresses a clear belief that Israelis and Palestinians can live together in peace.

In 2009, an unprecedented collaboration of thirteen Palestinian Christian communities led to the creation of Kairos Palestine; this movement declares that the Israeli occupation of the Palestinian Territories is a "sin against God

---

62. Such as Ateek's, *Justice and Only Justice* and *Palestinian Theology of Liberation*.
63. Ateek, *Justice and Only Justice*.
64. Such as that provided by Katanacho and Isaac who advocate a Christological ownership of the land and provide a biblical study responding to dispensational Zionism. Katanacho, *The Land of Christ*, and Isaac, *From Land to Lands*.
65. See Rula Khoury Mansour, *Theology of Reconciliation in the Context of Church Relations: A Palestinian Christian Perspective in Dialogue with Miroslav Volf* (Carlisle: Langham Monographs, 2020). Also Salim Munayer and Lisa Loden, *Through My Enemy's Eyes: Envisioning Reconciliation in Israel-Palestine* (Milton Keynes, UK: Paternoster, 2014).
66. The Oslo Accords are a pair of agreements between Israel and the Palestine Liberation Organization aimed at achieving a peace based on United Nations Security Council Resolutions 242 and 338 and at fulfilling the "right of the Palestinian people to self-determination." https://en.wikipedia.org/wiki/Oslo_Accords.
67. https://imeu.org/article/the-jerusalem-declaration-on-christian-zionism.

and humanity" and urges Christians everywhere to nonviolently intervene to end its injustices. It insists that the mission of the church is to proclaim the kingdom of God – a kingdom of justice, peace, and dignity – seeing injustice resistance with love as its logic, as a right and duty for Christians. It encourages Palestinian and international social and religious organizations to urge companies and states to take part in boycotts, divestment, and sanctions against the Israeli occupation.[68]

Despite the challenges of being an historically oppressed church and a marginalized numerical minority, the Palestinian church has effectively shaped contextual theology related to their struggle. They have been successful in drawing widespread attention to the injustices through their emerging creative nonviolence practices.

RECONCILIATION THEOLOGY AND JUST PEACEMAKING PARADIGMS IN THE CASE STUDIES

After examining the church mission in three case studies, I move to analyze them using two different approaches: (1) Theologically, I draw on *reconciliation theology* in order to explore the church's theology in its struggle against injustice. (2) In terms of *peace ethics*, I use just peacemaking theory in order to examine the effectiveness of this paradigm in situations of injustice.

Reconciliation Theology Adopted by the Churches in the Case Studies

Generally, the church's theologians have focused on vertical reconciliation between humanity and God, with minimal focus on horizontal reconciliation between peoples.[69] Enmity toward God is enmity toward human beings, and the enmity toward human beings is enmity toward God. Hence, reconciliation

---

68. https://www.kairospalestine.ps/index.php/about-kairos/kairos-palestine-document.
69. Some theologians, such as Colin Gunton, "Towards a Theology of Reconciliation," in *The Theology of Reconciliation*, edited by Colin Gunton (London: T&T Clark, 2003), 167–74 and John Webster, "The Ethics of Reconciliation," in *The Theology of Reconciliation*, edited by Colin Gunton, 109–24, discuss reconciliation primarily as a vertical concept with the horizontal seen as a secondary result of personal salvation (vertical). On the other side of the debate are theologians such as Volf, Tutu and DeGruchy, who see the horizontal aspect of reconciliation as being an undeniable part of the vertical and believe there is a danger that reconciliation's social implications are left to politicians while its vertical ideals are exemplified theologically. Leah Robinson, *Embodied Peacebuilding: Reconciliation as Practical Theology* (Oxford: Peter Lang, 2014).

has both a vertical and a horizontal dimension. It contains a turning away from enmity toward people – not just from enmity to God.

Scholars use different terms to define reconciliation theology including repentance, apology, forgiveness, justice, truth, and peace. Some associate reconciliation with forgiveness and repentance. Liechty, in the Northern Ireland context, sees reconciliation as involving the complementary dynamic of forgiveness and repentance.[70] Schreiter takes the same approach, seeing reconciliation as taking place with an initiation from God leading the victim who receives divine healing to forgive – and this forgiveness in turn inspiring repentance.[71]

Other scholars associate reconciliation with justice and truth. DeGruchy, in the South African context, sees reconciliation as the restoration of justice, which means the re-establishment of broken relationships; truth acts as liberator if it works alongside justice and reconciliation.[72] Palestinian liberation theologians Ateek and Raheb also prioritize justice.[73] Ateek calls for his readers to "de-stereotype" Western images of the people of the Middle East, to "de-Zionize" the Bible, and to "de-mythologize" the State of Israel.[74] Raheb argues that post-Auschwitz theology has not paid attention to Palestinian suffering due to hermeneutical flaws, and concludes that the church must promote justice, righteousness, and creative nonviolent resistance when seeking peaceful coexistence between Palestinians and Israelis.

Volf argues against these approaches, believing that a focus only on justice will lead to *in*justice, for justice should be at work under the greater structure of reconciliation.[75] However, Volf and DeGruchy agree that the meaning of the main theological concepts within reconciliation are relative to the particularities of a social context – the South African for DeGruchy and the Croatian for Volf.[76]

---

70. Joseph Liechty, "Putting Forgiveness in Its Place: The Dynamics of Reconciliation" in *Explorations in Reconciliation: New Directions in Theology*, David Tombs and Joseph Liechty, eds. (Aldershot: Ashgate, 2006), 59–68.
71. Robert Schreiter, *The Ministry of Reconciliation: Spirituality and Strategies* (Maryknoll, NY: Orbis, 1998).
72. John DeGruchy, *Reconciliation: Restoring Justice* (London: SCM, 2002).
73. Ateek, *Justice and Only Justice*. Ateek, *Palestinian Theology of Liberation*; Raheb, *I Am a Palestinian Christian*.
74. Ateek, *Justice and Only Justice*, 159.
75. Miroslav Volf, "The Social Meaning of Reconciliation," *Transformation* 16 (1999): 7–12.
76. Robinson, *Embodied Peacebuilding*.

Comparison between the Case Studies in Terms of Reconciliation Theology

There are some differences between the positions of the churches in the case studies, primarily due to the different contexts. Robinson, through her work on reconciliation in Northern Ireland, proposes a model that considers the influence of the social context on theological understandings of reconciliation. This model uses the four most common concepts from reconciliation theology: truth, justice, repentance, and forgiveness. The concepts are divided into two tendencies: truth and justice (liberating tendencies) and repentance and forgiveness (atoning tendencies), all of which exist under the umbrella of reconciliation theology. Influenced by social context, the movement within the theology of reconciliation is seen in a modified version of Lederach's model which utilizes a sliding scale between an emphasis on liberating tendencies (truth and justice) with the goal of freedom to an emphasis on atoning tendencies (repentance and forgiveness) with the goal of peace.

An emphasis on one tendency in any given context is based on the goal of those who are adhering to the theology. When the goal is freedom in each context then there is a move toward liberating tendencies – as we saw in the cases of the Black churches in the USA, the churches in South Africa during apartheid, and the Palestinian church. If the desired goal is peace/healing, then one sees a movement toward atoning tendencies – as we saw in the South African church's position post-apartheid and in the establishing of the Truth and Reconciliation Commission.[77] When the context changed, the church in South Africa responded differently. During apartheid, the church focused on justice to seek freedom; post-apartheid, the church focused on forgiveness for the sake of healing and peace.

Just Peacemaking Practices for Resisting Oppression in the Case Studies

Drawing on the case studies, I characterize resistance strategies used by the oppressed church under the following practices of just peacemaking theory:

---

77. As a community, forgiving and restoring the humanity of both the victim and the perpetrator and embracing them back into community (restorative justice), was one of the basic principles of the commission's work. In my article "Communities of Forgiveness," I proposed an integrated approach to forgiveness that combines the significant work of God with the work of the community. God works in the lives of forgivers through a community that makes the practice of forgiveness meaningful. Rula Khoury Mansour, "Communities of Forgiveness: A Palestinian Christian Perspective," *Ex Auditu: An International Journal for the Theological Interpretation of Scripture* 35 (2019): 122–150 (Pickwick, 2020).

supporting nonviolent direct action; advancing democracy, human rights, and interdependence; and encouraging grassroots peacemaking groups and voluntary associations.

Supporting Nonviolent Direct Action[78]

Gandhi's thoughts provide a rich resource for just peacemaking. He developed the concept of *satyagraha*[79] (holding onto truth in a determined but nonviolent resistance to evil) and deployed it during both the Indian independence movement and his earlier struggles in South Africa for Indian rights. Satyagraha includes preparation for direct action by raising awareness, strategizing resistance, and taking direct action in various forms – marches, demonstrations, sit-ins, strikes, economic boycotts, and civil disobedience regarding unjust laws central to the issue at hand.[80] Gandhian thought influenced MLK during the civil rights movement, Nelson Mandela's struggle against apartheid in South Africa, and Mubarak Awad in Palestine.[81]

The American and South African Black churches' experiences illustrate that nonviolent direct action is significant in exposing tensions rooted in unjust systems, and thereby directly confronting them. It requires large numbers of participants to reveal the will of the oppressed to the regime and the

---

78. Nonviolent resistance has been influential in the last decades of the previous century. The 1980s saw successful movements in Poland, the German Democratic Republic, and what is now the Czech Republic in Eastern Europe; the former Soviet Union; Burma (now named Myanmar); Guatemala; South Africa; the Philippines and more. These struggles were productive against heavily armed military regimes; they won revolutions without bloodshed. Michael J. Nojeim, *Gandhi and King: The Power of Nonviolent Resistance* (Westport: Praeger Publishers), 2004.

79. *Satyagraha* means "truth force." It is a particular form of nonviolent resistance or civil resistance. To learn more about Gandhi's concepts see D. Gerson and D. Van Soest, "Relevance of Gandhi to a peaceful and just world society," in *New Global Development: Journal of Global and International Comparative Social Welfare*.

80. For instance, in 1930, Gandhi and 80 volunteers marched 200 miles to the sea to produce salt from seawater in opposition to British Salt Laws, which taxed the sale of salt. Around 60,000 Indians were imprisoned for salt-making. Gandhi ended the civil disobedience campaign after negotiating a truce with the British government's representative, Lord Irwin. However, Irwin's successor resumed political repression. Gandhi revived the *satyagraha* movement and was soon imprisoned again. While in prison, Gandhi fasted against the policy of separate electorates for "untouchables," India's lowest caste, within India's new constitution. The fast resulted in a historic resolution making discrimination against untouchables illegal. See Nojeim, *Gandhi and King*.

81. Gandhian nonviolence had made its way into pacifists and war-resisters of the West. See Leilah Danielson, "'In My Extremity I Turned to Gandhi': American Pacifists, Christianity, and Gandhian Nonviolence, 1915–1941," *Church History: Studies in Christianity and Culture*, 72 (2003): 361–88, and Glyn Richards, "Faith and Praxis in Liberation Theology, Bonhoeffer and Gandhi," *Modern Theology* 3, no. 4 (1987): 359–73.

international community.[82] As MLK argued: "We who engage in nonviolent direct action are not the creators of tension. We merely bring [it] to the surface . . . where it can be seen and dealt with."[83]

Unjust laws are exposed as people simultaneously claim their rights and commit civil disobedience by breaking these laws. For example, during the civil rights movement, African Americans exposed the injustice of segregation, claiming their right to equal treatment by sitting at the Whites-only counter. By performing the desegregation they demanded, activists demonstrated both the injustice of segregation and the justice and equality they requested.[84]

The participatory character of nonviolent direct action makes it an effective and appealing nonviolent revolutionary strategy. Large protests and demonstrations were evident in the Black churches, clearly illustrating the majority's will. African Americans also boycotted public transport and the businesses of racially discriminatory White owners. As part of the anti-apartheid nonviolent resistance, activists organized major boycotts of companies invested in South Africa with targeted economic sanctions. Just peacemaking theorists view this particular boycott as the most impressive example of global boycott.

During the First Intifada in Israel–Palestine, Christian organizations and churches employed a range of nonviolent initiatives. In 2002, based on an appeal from local church leaders, the World Council of Churches created the Ecumenical Accompaniment Program in Palestine and Israel. This established an international presence in the countries, accompanied the local people and communities, offered a protective presence, and witnessed to their daily struggles.

In 2005, the Boycott, Divestment, and Sanctions movement (BDS), a Palestinian-led movement modeled after South Africa's anti-apartheid movement, was established. It aims to pressure Israel to meet its obligations under international law: withdrawing from the occupied territories, removing the separation barrier in the West Bank, providing full equality for Palestinian citizens of Israel, and protecting the rights of Palestinian refugees. Since the BDS call, there has been an increase in nonviolent strategies as various groups have participated at some level, including several international Christian denominations, Israeli human rights organizations, American Jewish organizations,

---

82. Scheid, *Just Revolution*, 41–42.
83. Martin Luther King, Jr., "Letter from a Birmingham Jail" (1963). Available at http://www.africa.upenn.edu/Articles_Gen/Letter_Birmingham.html.
84. Scheid, *Just Revolution*, 41.

religious institutions, student groups, and Palestinian civil society groups. The BDS movement, which has gained international support, has been criticized by Israel.[85]

Advance Democracy, Human Rights, Interdependence

South Africans and African Americans worked to promote democracy and human rights within both their own movements and their nations. They demonstrated how just revolutions should prevision the participation and respect for human rights that revolutionaries wish to instill nationally. For example, the Cottesloe Declaration, Belhar Confession, Kairos Document, and Freedom Charter[86] articulate a vision for human rights in South Africa that provide a model for other movements.

Kairos Palestine is modeled after the anti-apartheid movement in South Africa. It emphasizes that the separation wall, the expansion of settlements, the closure of Gaza, the refugees, the imprisonment of thousands of Palestinians, and the emptying of Jerusalem of its Palestinian residents contradict "the will of God for this land." The land's "universal mission" is to be a place of "reconciliation, peace, and love" and the church's prophetic mission is to stand with the oppressed. It encourages the worldwide church to intervene to help bring a just peace to Palestinians. It also criticizes those Western theologians who give theological legitimacy to the infringement of Palestinian rights.[87]

Encourage Grassroots Peacemaking Groups and Voluntary Associations

The SACC promotes social justice. Friesen notes that, "Bishop Desmond Tutu and the SACC were in the forefront in advocating nonviolence in the struggle in South Africa."[88] Together, they showed how religious organizations, as grassroots groups, can empower people to engage in nonviolent direct action. Similarly, the Black church(es) in America became a "movement church" that supported members and the CRM via a multiplicity of methods, as discussed

---

85. As a result, the Israel Allies Foundation (an Israeli government-funded lobby group) has succeeded in passing laws banning state agencies from contracting with BDS supporters in 25 American states. https://bdsmovement.net/.
86. The *Freedom Charter* declares ten categories of human rights, which can be grouped under the headings of civil-political rights, social-economic rights, and cultural rights. https://en.wikipedia.org/wiki/Freedom_Charter.
87. https://www.kairospalestine.ps/index.php/about-kairos/kairos-palestine-document.
88. Duane Friesen, "Encourage Grassroots Peacekeeping Groups and Voluntary Associations," in *Just Peacemaking: The New Paradigm for the Ethics of Peace and War*, Stassen, ed. (Cleveland: Pilgrim Press, 2008).

above. In the Palestinian case, several grassroots parachurch organizations – led by pastors, theologians, and activists – have taken various approaches toward peacebuilding. One is Sabeel,[89] a liberation theology movement that has been contributing to the rebuilding and growth of Palestinian society post-Intifada through developing a Christian nonviolent theo-political approach.[90] Another is the Diyar consortium[91] – a peacebuilding movement that works with Palestinian young people from all religious backgrounds in a praxis-oriented, socio-political, and educational-culturally programmed approach.[92] Al-Liqa,[93] a Palestinian contextual theology movement, has been focused on developing a sustainable dialogue between Muslims and Christians in Palestine-Israel, with the initiative being taken by the native Christian ecumenical community.

Other movements working toward nonviolent reconciliation are: the Holy Land Trust which promotes the teaching of nonviolence;[94] Musalaha Ministry of Reconciliation which fosters interfaith dialogue between Palestinians and messianic Jews;[95] the Nazareth Center for Peace Studies; Come and See, a leading online forum; Bethlehem Bible College[96] (including the Christ at the Checkpoint conferences); and Nazareth Evangelical College[97] which engages in contextual theology focusing on peace and justice.

CONCLUSION

Mission and peacemaking are inherently connected; without mission, there is no peace that reconciles and makes whole; without peacemaking, there is no mission that is authentic and worthy of the gospel of Jesus Christ.[98] In this chapter, I explored the peacemaking mission of the church in three case studies: two largely post-conflict cases and one ongoing conflict. I also analyzed

---

89. https://sabeel.org/.
90. *Sabeel* also organizes ecumenical meetings between Palestinian Christians and Westerners, alongside encounters between the various local churches and communities in the region.
91. https://www.diyar.ps/.
92. *Diyar's* aim is to equip the next generation to work towards the goal of building a sustainable and self-reliant nation-state for the Palestinian people. It also raises awareness among Western churches of the ecumenical implications of their work in the West Bank. Kuruvilla, "Contextual Theological Praxis as Resistance: Palestinian Christian Peacebuilding in the Occupied West Bank," 10.
93. http://www.al-liqacenter.org.ps/eng/.
94. https://www.holylandtrust.org/.
95. http://www.musalaha.org/.
96. https://bethbc.edu/ and – https://christatthecheckpoint.bethbc.edu/.
97. https://www.nazcol.org/.
98. Willard M. Swartley, *Covenant of Peace: The Missing Peace in New Testament Theology and Ethics* (Grand Rapids: Eerdmans, 2006).

the cases in terms of reconciliation theology and just peacemaking paradigms. These cases demonstrate how the church could apply the principles of shalom in its context through its prophetic mission.

For the church to live its vision as an agent of peace, it needs, first, to conceptualize reconciliation theology in its own context. If the goal in each context is liberation, then there will be a move toward seeking justice, as seen in all three cases. If the desired goal is healing/peace, then forgiveness should become the focus, as seen in the church's position post-apartheid. Second, the church should engage in peacemaking through education, stimulating collective public engagement, developing peace movements, and practicing nonviolent resistance that seeks peace. Large and coordinated numbers of people are needed to participate in revolutionary movements that confront unjust systems. The just peacemaking paradigm serves well as a conceptual framework for justly using nonviolent tactics against oppression.

QUESTIONS FOR DISCUSSION

1. What is the foundation of our ethical practices as peacemakers?
2. Give examples of how the oppressed church as a prophetic voice could apply the principles of shalom in its context.
3. What is a theology of reconciliation? What implications would it have for church mission amid injustice and oppression?
4. Explain how the just peacemaking paradigm assists the oppressed church in confronting unjust systems.

BIBLIOGRAPHY

Ateek, Naim. *Justice and Only Justice: A Palestinian Theology of Liberation*. Maryknoll, NY: Orbis, 1989.

———. *A Palestinian Theology of Liberation: The Bible, Justice, and the Palestine-Israel Conflict*. Maryknoll, NY: Orbis, 2017.

Battle, Michael. *Ubuntu: I in You and You in Me*. New York: Seabury, 2009.

Benziman, Uri, and Mansour Atallah. *Dayare mishneh* [Sub-tenants]. Jerusalem: Keter, 1992.

Bosch, David J. "Reflection on Biblical Models of Mission," in *Landmark Essays in Mission and World Christianity*, edited by Gallagher and Hertig, 3–16. New York: Orbis, 2009.

———. *Transforming Mission: Paradigm Shift in Theology of Mission*. New York: Orbis Books, 1991.

Brubaker, Pamela, James B. Burke, Duane K. Friesen, John Langan, S.J., and Glen Stassen. "Introduction: Just Peacemaking as the New Ethic for Peace and War," in *Just Peacemaking: The New Paradigm for Peace and War*, edited by Glen Stassen, 1–40. Cleveland: Pilgrim Press, 2008.

Cahill, Lisa Sowle. *Love Your Enemies: Discipleship, Pacifism, and Just War Theory*. Minneapolis: Augsburg Fortress, 1994.

Calhoun-Brown, Allison. "Upon This Rock: The Black Church, Nonviolence, and the Civil Rights Movement," *Political Science and Politics* 33 (2000): 168–74.

Danielson, Leilah. "'In My Extremity I Turned to Gandhi': American Pacifists, Christianity, and Gandhian Nonviolence, 1915–1941." *Church History: Studies in Christianity and Culture* 72 (2003): 361–88.

DeGruchy, John. *Reconciliation: Restoring Justice*. London: SCM, 2002.

Forster, Dion. "The Role of the Church in Reconciliation in South Africa," *Lausanne World Pulse Archives* 4, 2010. http://www.lausanneworldpulse.com/themedarticles-php/1267/04-2010.

Friesen, Duane. "Encourage Grassroots Peacekeeping Groups and Voluntary Associations," in *Just Peacemaking: The New Paradigm for the Ethics of Peace and War*. Cleveland: Pilgrim Press, 2008.

Gerson, David, and Dorothy Van Soest. "Relevance of Gandhi to a Peaceful and Just World Society: Lessons for Social Work Practice and Education." *New Global Development* 15, no. 1 (1999): 8–22.

Ghose, Supad Kumar. "The Role of the Black Church in the American Civil Rights Movement," *UITS Journal* 5, no. 1 (2017): 58–68.

Gish, Steven D. *Desmond Tutu: A Biography*. Westport, CT: Greenwood Press, 2004.

Glyn, Richards. "Faith and Praxis in Liberation Theology, Bonhoeffer and Gandhi," *Modern Theology* 3, no. 4 (1987): 359–73.

Gunton, Colin. "Towards a Theology of Reconciliation." In *The Theology of Reconciliation*, edited by Colin Gunton, 167–74. London: T&T Clark, 2003.

Horenczyk, G., and S. Munayer. "Acculturation Orientations toward Two Majority Groups: The Case of Palestinian Arab Christian Adolescents in Israel." *Journal of Cross-Cultural Psychology* 38 (2007): 76–86.

Isaac, Munther. *From Land to Lands, from Eden to the Renewed Earth: A Christ-Centred Biblical Theology of the Promised Land*. Carlisle, UK: Langham Monographs, 2015.

Katanacho, Yohanna. *The Land of Christ: A Palestinian Cry*. Eugene: Pickwick, 2013.

Khalidi, Walid, ed. *All That Remains: The Palestinian Villages Occupied and Depopulated by Israel in 1948*. Washington, DC: Institute for Palestine Studies, 1992.

Khoury Mansour, Rula. *Theology of Reconciliation in the Context of Church Relations: A Palestinian Christian Perspective in Dialogue with Miroslav Volf.* Carlisle: Langham Monographs, 2020.

———. "Communities of Forgiveness: A Palestinian Christian Perspective." *Ex Auditu: An International Journal for the Theological Interpretation of Scripture* 35 (2019): 122–50. Pickwick, 2020.

Kumar Yadav, Ajay. "Structural Violence and Human Security: Gandhi's Visions." In *Peace and Conflict: The South Asian Experience*, edited by Priyankar Upadhyaya and Samrat Schmiem Kumar, 122-39. Foundation Books, 2014. https://doi.org/10.1017/9789384463076

Kuruvilla, Samuel. "Contextual Theological Praxis as Resistance: Palestinian Christian Peace-building in the Occupied West Bank" in *Mary's Well Occasional Papers*, 3:1, January. Israel: Nazareth Evangelical Theological Seminary, 2014.

Lederach, John Paul. *Building Peace: Sustainable Reconciliation in Divided Societies.* Washington, DC: United States Institute of Peace Press, 1997.

Liechty, Joseph. "Putting Forgiveness in Its Place: The Dynamics of Reconciliation." In *Explorations in Reconciliation: New Directions in Theology*, edited by David Tombs and Joseph Liechty, 59–68. Aldershot: Ashgate, 2006.

Lybarger, Loren. "For Church or Nation? Islamism, Secular-Nationalism and the Transformation of Christian Identities in Palestine." *American Academy of Religion* 75, no. 4 (2007): 777–813.

Marshall, Chris. *Little Book of Biblical Justice: A Fresh Approach to the Bible's Teachings on Justice.* Intercourse, PA: Good Books, 2005.

Morris Aldon D. *The Origins of the Civil Rights Movement: Black Communities Organizing for Change.* New York: The Free Press, 1984.

Munayer, Salim, and Gabriel Horenczyk. "Multi-Group Acculturation Orientations in a Changing Context: Palestinian Christian Arab Adolescents in Israel after the Lost Decade." *International Journal of Psychology* 49, no. 5 (2014): 364–70.

Munayer, Salim, and Lisa Loden. *Through My Enemy's Eyes: Envisioning Reconciliation in Israel–Palestine.* Milton Keynes, UK: Paternoster, 2014.

Myrdal, Gunnar. *An American Dilemma.* New York: Harper and Brothers, 1944.

Nojeim, Michael J., *Gandhi and King: The Power of Nonviolent Resistance.* Westport: Praeger Publishers, 2004.

Pappé, Ilan. *The Forgotten Palestinians: A History of the Palestinians in Israel.* New Haven: Yale University Press, 2011.

Pinn, Anthony. *Moral Evil and Redemptive Suffering.* Gainesville: University of Florida Press, 2002.

Rabinowitz, Danny. "The Palestinian Citizens of Israel, the Concept of Trapped Minority and the Discourse of Transnationalism in Anthropology." *Ethnic and Racial Studies* 24 (2001): 64–85.

Raheb, Mitri. *I Am a Palestinian Christian*. Translated by Ruth Gritsch. Minneapolis: Fortress, 1995.

Ramutsindela, Maano, and Paballo Abel Chauke, "Biodiversity, Wildlife and the Land Question in Africa," in *Africa and the Sustainable Development Goals* (Sustainable Development Goals Series) edited by Ramutsindela and Mickler, 197–205. Springer International Publishing, 2020.

Robinson Leah. *Embodied Peacebuilding: Reconciliation as Practical Theology*. Oxford: Peter Lang, 2014.

Sabella, B. "The Emigration of Christian Arabs: Dimensions and Causes of the Phenomenon," in *Christian Communities in the Arab Middle East: The Challenge of the Future*, edited by Andrea Pacini, 127–8. Oxford: Oxford University Press, 1998.

Scheid, Anna. *Just Revolution: A Christian Ethic of Political Resistance and Social Transformation*. Lanham: Lexington Books, 2015.

Schreiter, Robert. *The Ministry of Reconciliation: Spirituality and Strategies*. Maryknoll: Orbis, 1998.

Stassen, Glen. *Just Peacemaking: The New Paradigm for the Ethics of Peace and War*. Cleveland: Pilgrim, 2008.

Stassen, Glen, and David Gushee. *Kingdom Ethics: Following Jesus in Contemporary Context*. Downers Grove:InterVarsity Press, 2003.

Storey, Peter. "A Different Kind of Justice: Truth and Reconciliation in South Africa." *The Christian Century* 114 (1997): 788–93.

Swartley, Willard M. *Covenant of Peace: The Missing Peace in New Testament Theology and Ethics*. Grand Rapids: Eerdmans, 2006.

Taylor, Clarence. *Black Religious Intellectuals: The Fight for Equality from Jim Crow to the Twenty-First Century*, New York: Routledge, 2002.

Tutu, Desmond. "Address to the Provincial Synod of the Anglican Church in Southern Africa." In *Rainbow People of God: The Making of a Peaceful Revolution*, John Allen, ed., New York: Doubleday, 1994.

———. "My Creed." In *Living Philosophies: Reflections of some of the Eminent Men and Women of Our Time*, Clifton Fadiman ed., New York: Doubleday, 1990.

Volf, Miroslav. "The Church as a Prophetic Community and a Sign of Hope." *European Journal of Theology* 2 (1993): 9–30.

———. *Exclusion and Embrace: A Theological Exploration of Identity, Otherness and Reconciliation*. Nashville: Abingdon Press, 1996.

———. "The Social Meaning of Reconciliation." *Transformation* 16 (1999): 7–12.

Webster, John. "The Ethics of Reconciliation." In *The Theology of Reconciliation*, edited by Colin Gunton, 109–24. London: T&T Clark, 2003.

Yoder, John Howard. *The Politics of Jesus*. Grand Rapids: Eerdmans, 1972; 1994.

———. *The War of the Lamb: The Ethics of Nonviolence and Peacemaking*. Brazos Press, 2009.

CHAPTER 15

RELIGIOUS PLURALISM

How Should Asian Christians Behave That Just Peace May Prevail?

Paulus S. Widjaja

A PERPETUAL PROBLEM: RELIGIOUS PARTICULARISM VERSUS RELIGIOUS PLURALISM

I am writing this chapter when the entire world is anxious due to the worldwide transmission of the COVID-19 virus. By the end of January 2022, according to a World Health Organization (WHO) report, the COVID-19 virus had infected 364,191,494 people worldwide and spread in over 200 countries, with the death toll reaching 5,631,457 people.[1] This pandemic reminds me of the old wisdom: a hazard can easily turn into a disaster when those impacted do not have enough capacity to anticipate and overcome it, while at the same time they are also suffering from a certain level of vulnerability. Those involved in Disaster Risk Reduction are surely familiar with the formula:

$$D = \frac{H \times V}{C}$$

D = Disaster; H = Hazard; V = Vulnerability; C = Capacity

This equation reminds us that a hazard can take place anywhere at any time. But a hazard does not necessarily turn into a disaster. It all depends on the capacity those impacted have to anticipate and overcome the hazard and on their level of vulnerability. This formula is also relevant to social disasters, as we shall see.

---

1. World Health Organization, WHO Coronavirus (COVID-19) Dashboard, accessed January 30, 2022, https://covid19.who.int.

Since the origins of their faith two thousand years ago, Christians have faced the issue of religious pluralism. Simply put, religious pluralism is "the state of being where every individual in a religiously diverse society has the rights, freedoms, and safety to worship, or not, according to their conscience."[2] The main problem that determines the attitude and behavior of religious people toward people of other faiths, however, is not primarily about the civil human rights one should endow, but about the perception of the salvific nature of religions. On the one hand, some want to draw a clear line between the saved and the unsaved to the extent of excluding those who are different. On the other, some want to eradicate the line altogether to say that there is no distinction between those who believe in Jesus Christ as their savior and those who do not – to the extent of accepting everybody without any critical judgment. The former is claiming that there is only one truth and only one way to reach that truth while, for the latter, there are many ways to the truth – some even say that all ways lead to it. The former believes that "the 'unsaved' mind fails to know God's purpose or nature because it lies outside the knowledge of God as disclosed in Jesus Christ,"[3] while the latter prefers to stretch "the dynamic impact of the saving grace erupted through the event of Jesus of Nazareth to other traditions."[4]

The problem with both approaches, however, is that they start from arbitrary a priori standpoints. The particularists have absolutized religious differences to the extent that there seems to be no commonality whatsoever between religions. The pluralists, on the other hand, have absolutized religious commonalities to the extent of killing all kinds of discussion. From an ethical standpoint, the issue at stake in this dilemma is a contestation between defending a Christian particular identity or opening that identity to embrace and include others.[5] Amid this contestation, how should Christians, especially Asian Christians, behave so that just peace may prevail? Should we follow either the particularists or the pluralists, or can we create another approach to the problem? It should be clear from the outset, though, that the focus of this writing is not to discuss the doctrine of salvation per se and its implications

---

2. "Religious Pluralism 101," The Aspen Institute, July 18, 2019, https://www.aspeninstitute.org/blog-posts/religious-pluralism-101/.
3. Alan Race, *Making Sense of Religious Pluralism* (London: SPCK, 2013), 26.
4. Race, 33.
5. M. Sastrapratedja, S.J., "Hospitalitas Dalam Dialog Interreligius: Belajar Dari E. Levinas, J. Derrida Dan Paul Ricoer," in *Islam, Agama-Agama, Dan Nilai Kemanusiaan: Festschrift Untuk M. Amin Abdullah*, ed. Moch Nur Ichwan and Ahmad Muttaqin (Yogyakarta: CISForm UIN Sunan Kalijaga, 2013), 149.

to people of faith, Christians and non-Christians alike, but about the ethical attitude and behavior of Christians amid the reality of religious plurality. After all, who we are that we assume we have the right and authority to decide who are saved and who are not, albeit under the jargon that the Bible tells us so. Yet, we must first answer this question: what are the hazards and vulnerabilities of which we must be cautious, so they do not turn into a disaster?

THE HAZARD: RELIGIOUS VIOLENCE AND RELIGIOUS NATIONALISM

In my other writings, I have pointed out that globalization has brought significant impact around the world and religious communities are not exempted.[6] For one, it has hardened group identities since too many people are terrified of having their particular and unique identities crushed and swept away by the wave of globalization. Coupled with the growth of individualization, there has been the evaporation of many identity markers and organizations. The clear socio-cultural identity that many had in the past has lost its stability, and thus it is affecting their sense of belonging.[7] This situation, in turn, has triggered the emergence of identity politics, in which groups in society utilize their group identity to strive for redistribution of goods, political power, and recognition of their respective group.

But there are times when identity politics turns into a dangerous primordialism that creates negative attitudes and behaviors toward others who are different. Primordialism, which refers to the characteristics and personality traits of a group of people that exist in or persist from the very beginning of the respected group, is an inevitable reality of human beings. It is a natural construction of identity, including religious identity, by which one shares solidarities with and loyalties to others within the same collective, group consciousness of one's community. It has deep cultural and historical roots and is passed down from generation to generation.[8] Thus a person who is born in a

---

6. Paulus S. Widjaja, "Recognizing the Other's Insecurity," in *At Peace and Unafraid: Public Order, Security, and the Wisdom of the Cross*, ed. Duane K. Friesen and Gerald W. Schlabach (Scottdale: Herald Press, 2005), 261–74; see also Peter C. Phan, "Peacekeeping, Peacemaking, Peacebuilding: An Interreligious Spirituality for Just Peace," in *Violence, Religion, Peacemaking* (New York: Palgrave Macmillan, 2016), 22.
7. Peter Jonkers, "How to Break the Ill-Fated Bond between Religious Truth and Violence," in *Religious Truth and Identity in an Age of Plurality*, ed. Peter Jonkers and Oliver J. Wiertz (London and New York: Routledge, 2019), 246.
8. John Coakley, "'Primordialism' in Nationalism Studies: Theory or Ideology?," *Nations and Nationalism* 24, no. 2 (April 2018): 327–47, https://doi.org/10.1111/nana.12349; Laura

Christian family and grows up in a Christian community and environment will naturally tend to be and behave as a Christian, similarly to one born in a Muslim family and community or a Hindu family and community, and so forth. This is the primary primordialism. As such, it does not necessarily pose any threat to society. It threatens the cohesiveness of society only when it turns into the so-called secondary primordialism by which people of a certain primordial group perceive themselves as the truest, purest, and holiest – the only group with the right to exist in society, "the one." It then becomes exclusive and seeks to eliminate or marginalize others.[9]

Such dynamics are inevitable when we speak about religion since religion is always tied with the search for truth. It is the drive that is internal in any religion; it is based not mainly on rational grounds, but a psychological one. Members of each community become attached to their religion and accept it as truth, simply because they feel it is theirs. This will naturally drive them "to adopt an attitude of superiority and exclusivism with regard to other religions or secular worldviews."[10] Furthermore, it encourages religious people to enforce what they perceive as religious truth upon those they consider infidels or heretics, often based on what, for them, is an altruistic reason, namely, the salvation of the latter.[11]

When my colleagues and I examined the level at which the behavior of the religious people in the public sphere in the Special Region of Yogyakarta, Indonesia, is indicative of identity politics, we found out that the level is to be as much as 29.6%.[12] This figure shows that identity politics, in its negative use of the term, do not strongly impact the respondents. Yet the figure should not be underestimated either. It is even surprising considering that Yogyakarta has long been known as a well-educated and multicultural region, where people from all religious backgrounds live together. My

---

Yeghiazaryan, "Which of the Three Main Ethnic Conflict Theories Best Explains the Ethnic Violence in the Post-Soviet States of Azerbaijan, Georgia, and Moldova?," *Undergraduate Journal of Political Science* 3, no. 1 (Spring 2018): 46–63.
9. Frans Magnis-Suseno, "Persatuan Indonesia: Pancasila, Paham Kebangsaan Dan Integritas Nasional," in *Pancasila Sebagai Ideologi Terbuka: Problema Dan Tantangannya*, ed. Alex Lanur (Yogyakarta: Kanisius, 1995), 57–59; see also Kementerian Agama RI, Moderasi Beragama (Jakarta: Badan Litbang dan Diklat Kementerian Agama RI, 2019), 48.
10. Jonkers, "How to Break the Ill-Fated Bond between Religious Truth and Violence," 247.
11. Jonkers, 246–49.
12. Paulus Sugeng Widjaja, Djoko Prasetyo Adi Wibowo, and Imanuel Geovasky, "Politik Identitas Dan Religiusitas Perdamaian Berbasis Pancasila Di Ruang Publik," *GEMA TEOLOGIKA: Jurnal Teologi Kontekstual Dan Filsafat Keilahian* 6, no. 1 (April 30, 2021): 95–126, https://doi.org/10.21460/gema.2021.61.658.

colleagues, Handi Hadiwitanto and Carl Sterkens have also confirmed similar findings. Researching the behavior toward religious plurality among Muslim and Christian students in Ambon and Yogyakarta, they found out that, while the students from both religions are, in principle, inclusive they are nevertheless still exclusive in attitude. Hadiwitanto and Sterkens called this behavior a kind of monism since each group believes that its respective religion is, in the end, the one true and right one; while the other religions either have been replaced by their respective religion (replacement monism) or their respective religion has fulfilled the other religions (fulfillment monism).[13]

The danger of the rise of such identity politics is that religious groups in society will strive and compete for political power. Indeed, socio-cultural diversity often goes hand-in-hand with various kinds of inequalities that, in turn, create social conflicts. People may be indifferent to their socio-cultural others, or they may become exclusive in how they define their socio-cultural identity.[14] Yet, there is more. Iannaccone and Berman have pointed out that when religious groups in society no longer stick with their core business, namely, supernatural questions, but strive and compete over political power, the situation will turn from good to deadly, and religious militancy and group loyalty can transform themselves into religious extremism. The problem becomes worse when the state favors one religious group over another. Dominant religious groups will then use their influence to gain benefits for their group while pushing aside other religious groups to the periphery.[15] The collective consciousness of the dominant religious group becomes very rigid as collective religious identities collide with political affiliations, and religious truth claims penetrate politics.[16] Religious extremism and religious violence disguise themselves under the veil of religious nationalism.

In such situations, harassment by the dominant religious group toward other religious groups in society soon changes into harassment by the state.

---

13. Handi Hadiwitanto and Carl Sterkens, "Sikap Terhadap Pluralitas Agama: Studi Perbandingan-Empiris Mahasiswa Muslim Dan Kristen Di Indonesia," *Gema Teologi* 36, no. 2 October (2012), http://journal-theo.ukdw.ac.id/index.php/gema/article/view/143.
14. Jonkers, "How to Break the Ill-Fated Bond between Religious Truth and Violence," 246.
15. Laurence R. Iannaccone and Eli Berman, "Religious Extremism: The Good, The Bad, and The Deadly," *Public Choice* 128, July (2006): 109–29.
16. Ahmad Muttaqin, "Meneguhkan Harmoni Muslim-Kristen: Mengayuh Di Antara Problem Dan Potensi," in *Islam, Agama-Agama*, Dan Nilai Kemanusiaan: Festschrift Untuk M. Amin Abdullah, ed. Moch Nur Ichwan and Ahmad Muttaqin (Yogyakarta: CISForm UIN Sunan Kalijaga, 2013), 140, 142–43; See also IRIN, "How to Reverse Buddhism's Radical Turn in Southeast Asia?," *Refworld*, July 16, 2013. https://www.refworld.org/docid/51e9102b4.html.

These trends away from democracy occur because when a dominant religious group gains enough political power and intends to maintain the status quo for their interest, religious nationalism will naturally be perceived as the safeguard for their identity. Even in countries with secular constitutions, citizenship often goes hand-in-hand with the religious affiliation of the dominant group, becoming like two sides of one coin.[17] Thus, Filipino means Catholic, Malay means Muslim, Thai means Buddhist, Indian means Hindu, and so forth. The repression and persecution of minority religious groups correspondingly go in disguise as religion-related regulations, such as the law against religious blasphemy, for instance. Social fragility and religious violence naturally follow.[18]

Nilay Saiya gives an example of how religious blasphemy laws in Pakistan have been used to persecute, even punish, those who are accused of challenging the dominance of the religious majority group. Far from what Muhammad Jinnah, the founder of Pakistan, envisioned in 1947 about the establishment of a country that would provide freedom for those of minority faiths, modern Pakistan, in Saiya's view, has been tainted by religious nationalism. The blasphemy code that can be found in Section XV of the Pakistan Penal Code has been used arbitrarily to eliminate those who are perceived as a threat to the dominant religious group. The code has been interpreted in such a loose way that it encourages, rather than prevents, social hostilities against religious minority groups to the extent of terminating, officially or unofficially, alleged violators of the code such as Aasia Bibi, Salman Taseer, Shahbaz Bhatti, Rashid Rehman, and others.[19] This only proves that the problem is not so much located in religion per se, as in the political power that dominant religious groups enjoy.

The identity crisis due to globalization brings yet another twist. The instability, indeed, the vacuum of identity that many people are experiencing is often filled in by charismatic leaders, religious and secular alike,[20] such as Osama Bin Laden, Abu Bakr al-Baghdadi, Abu Sayyaf, U-Wirathu, Benny Hinn, Donald Trump, Jair Bolsonaro, to mention just a few. Unfortunately,

---

17. Muttaqin, "Meneguhkan Harmoni Muslim-Kristen: Mengayuh Di Antara Problem Dan Potensi," 140.
18. Nilay Saiya, "Pluralism and Peace in South Asia," *The Review of Faith & International Affairs* 17, no. 4 (2019):12–13, https://doi.org/10.1080/15570274.2019.1681779.
19. Saiya, 19–21; see also Dicky Sofjan and Ewa Trojnar, "The Challenge of Building a Multi-Ethnic State in Malaysia," *Hémisphères* 26 (2011): 1–15.
20. Alvin Toffler, *Future Shock* (New York: Bantam Books, 1972); Alvin Toffler, *The Third Wave* (Clerkenwell, London: Pan Books, 1981); John Naisbitt, *Megatrends 2000* (New York: HarperCollins, 1991).

people are not critical of the contents of what these charismatic leaders give to them. The most important matter for the people is that they (re)gain a sense of identity.

In the light of this hazard and vulnerability, how should we Asian Christians respond so that just peace, especially just peace among religious people, may prevail? To this, we now turn.

CAPACITY: PEACEKEEPING, PEACEMAKING, AND PEACEBUILDING

As has been said before, the way to prevent a hazard from turning into a disaster is to reduce a community's vulnerability and increase its capacity. Hence, we need to identify what capacities Asian Christians need to develop to block the threats of religious violence and religious nationalism.

Years ago, the political scientist Samuel Huntington posed a controversial thesis, that people in the post-Cold War world will inevitably engage in conflicts and wars along communal lines.[21] The hard facts of the world, however, do not necessarily support his thesis. Asian countries such as Singapore, Japan, South Korea, Vietnam, and some others can demonstrate how people of different ethnicities and religions can live side by side relatively well, despite the assumed perception of many people toward these countries as mono-ethnic ones and some problems of discriminatory to minorities which still exist in these countries. The clash happens more within civilizations than between civilizations.[22] Hence, when people of the world are now talking about the new normal in the post-COVID-19 era, so are the Christians regarding Christian attitude and behavior toward people of other faiths. We need to understand and demonstrate religion not as a source of conflict, but as a resource for peace while acknowledging what Scott R. Appleby calls "the ambivalence of the sacred."[23]

Understanding and demonstrating religion as a resource for peace, however, is not an easy task. The secularization school of thought argued that religion will eventually either disappear from human societies or be absorbed

---

21. Samuel P. Huntington, *The Clash of Civilizations and the Remaking of World Order* (New York: Simon and Schuster, 2007).
22. Saiya, "Pluralism and Peace in South Asia," 13.
23. Scott R. Appleby, *The Ambivalence of the Sacred: Religion, Violence, and Reconciliation* (Lanham: Rowman & Littlefield Publishers, 1999).

into other aspects or dimensions of life.[24] Many times, religion has also been considered either irrelevant or too complex, to the extent that it is ignored altogether in peace endeavors. What has often been forgotten is the fact that religion is tied to all parts of human life and each will inevitably impact either conflict or peace in its way.[25] Religion, in Habermas' words, has (re)gained "a new, hitherto unexpected political importance."[26]

In this sense, we Christians need to understand and demonstrate religion, specifically Christianity, in a more positivistic and optimistic view. We need not live in a perpetual state of contestation and rivalry between religious particularism and religious pluralism. Such contestations do not help anybody to build just peace among people of different faiths. Religious people, Christians included, must walk away from the contestation between the two seemingly unbridgeable positions related to the reality of religious plurality. Instead, we must start thinking and striving for a just peace to overcome religious violence. This approach understands peace from a more positive perspective, in which we intentionally work to create conditions that just peace may prevail.[27]

To begin with, we must remember that the calling of the church is rooted in Jesus Christ himself. In the great intercession Jesus offered before he left his disciples, he prayed, "As you sent me into the world, I have sent them into the world" (John 17:18).[28] The calling of the church is always intertwined with the calling of Jesus. In this conviction, there is an acknowledgment and understanding that Jesus Christ is the center of the Christian life. It is in Jesus that we may know who God is, his character, and his will so that we can carry forward Jesus's mission. Jesus himself said, "Anyone who has seen me has seen the Father" (John 14:9).

This, above all else, is a conviction[29] that when one commits and declares her/himself to be a follower of Jesus Christ, that commitment entails a conviction of Jesus Christ as God's revelation of himself. It is a love language that

---

24. Douglas Irvin-Erickson, "Introduction: Interfaith Contributions to Nurturing Cultures of Peace," in *Violence, Religion, Peacemaking* (New York: Palgrave Macmillan, 2016), 9–10.
25. Christine Schliesser, "Religion and Peace: Anatomy of a Love-Hate Relationship," *Religions* 11, no. 219 (2020): 3–5, https://doi.org/10.3390/rel11050219.
26. Jürgen Habermas, "Religion in the Public Sphere," *European Journal of Philosophy* 14, no. 1 (2006): 1–25, https://doi.org/10.1111/j.1468-0378.2006.00241.x.
27. Paulus S. Widjaja, "Peace," in *Dictionary of Mission Theology: Evangelical Foundations,* ed. John Corrie, Juan F. Martinez, and Simon Chan (Nottingham, England; Downers Grove: IVP Academic, 2007), 279–81.
28. All Biblical quotations based on the New Revised Standard Version (1989).
29. James Wm McClendon, Jr and James M. Smith, *Convictions: Defusing Religious Relativism*, Revised edition (Eugene: Wipf & Stock, 2002).

we, as Christians, employ in our intimate relationship with Jesus. It has claims on God, based on a personal relationship of the respective people and God, without necessarily undermining, let alone, disrespecting other love languages that belong to other people of faiths. By the same token, it is in Jesus Christ we may see the example, par excellence, of how God intends human beings to be. That is why Jesus repeatedly says to his disciples, "Follow me" (Matt 4:19). This is a call to imitate Jesus and to live as he did.

But what is exactly the essence of Jesus's calling, indeed Jesus's mission, in the world? In Mark 1:15, Jesus said, "The time has come . . . The kingdom of God has come near. Repent and believe the good news!" A very intriguing question to be asked, however, is, where did Jesus get the very term "kingdom of God"? Nowhere does the Old Testament use the term. Yet in the Targum Isaiah 52:7, there is a statement of "the kingdom of your God is revealed." If Jesus had this verse in mind when he spoke about the kingdom of God, then, for Jesus, the kingdom of God is well connected to peace (שָׁלוֹם), the good news (טוֹב), and salvation (יְשׁוּעָה).[30] Jesus does not speak about power or dominance, let alone violence. Of course, this verse does not address the issue of religious pluralism per se. Yet this verse conveys a strong message about the characteristics of the kingdom of God, namely, peace, the good news, and salvation. This is what lies in the heart of Jesus's mission in the world that all Christians, Asian Christians included, need to carry forward. It is this mission that must shape what we can call "interreligious spirituality," that is, "a way of living that promotes peacekeeping, peacemaking, and peacebuilding"[31] among people of different religions. In such a living, Asian Christians need to not merely recognize the reality of religious plurality, but to make religious pluralism the approach[32] to carry forward Jesus's mission in the world that just peace as Jesus has envisioned may prevail. Indeed, it corresponds to the very existence of the church in the world as what I have written about elsewhere as "the Church of the Descended Christ, the Church of the Crucified Christ, and the Church of the Risen Christ."[33]

---

30. Willard M. Swartley, *Covenant of Peace: The Missing Peace in New Testament Theology and Ethics* (Grand Rapids:Eerdmans, 2006), 13–17.
31. Phan, "Peacekeeping, Peacemaking, Peacebuilding: An Interreligious Spirituality for Just Peace," 22.
32. Saiya, "Pluralism and Peace in South Asia," 13.
33. See a more thorough elaboration of this theme in Paulus S. Widjaja, *Character Formation and Social Transformation: An Appeal to The Indonesian Churches Amidst the So-Called Chinese Problem* (Saarbrücken: VDM Verlag Dr. Müller, 2010).

PEACEKEEPING: THE CHURCH OF THE DESCENDED CHRIST

Peacekeeping is an effort to enter conflict situations to limit the violence so that it does not spread to many places and areas of life. Translated into the situation of religious pluralism, this means an effort to break into the vicious cycle of religious violence that has made religious pluralism problematic in society, as elaborated earlier. But what is exactly the theological basis for that? What is the right Christian attitude and behavior to break the vicious cycle of religious violence so that just peace may prevail?

First, we must remember that Christian confession of God as the creator of the universe and everything within it can only mean that all areas of this universe, inside and outside of the church, are under God's reign and sovereignty. This implies a conviction that there can be no part and no person in the whole universe, which/who is not under Christ's reign since he is "the firstborn over all creation. For in him all things were created (Col 1:15–16).[34]

There is no dualism whatsoever. We should not remove ourselves from the world based on an a priori that the world outside the church, including people of other faiths, is bad and has nothing to do with the church, except to be conquered for Christ. Moreover, creation itself is not a once for all act of God. By immersing ourselves in the world, we take part in God's work of creation, just as Jesus said, "My Father is always at his work to this very day, and I too am working" (John 5:17). Hence all Christians must develop adaptive skills, by which we adapt to new environments of plurality in society, be they cultural, ethnic, or religious ones. This is the social intelligence we all must cultivate.[35]

It is by coming to and embracing people of other faiths, without prior judgments, that we can be faithful to our mission. Jesus descended to the world to embrace, not to exclude, others. This is demonstrated very well in the story of Jesus's table fellowship in the Gospels. He shows that the kingdom of God is an open commensality where there is acceptance and respect for those who are excluded and considered sinful. Jesus even embraces them before they make any commitment to him. His embrace precedes any kind of truth of others

---

34. In Paulus S. Widjaja, "Apakah Aku Penjaga Saudaraku?: Mencari Etika Ekologis Kristiani Yang Panentheistik Dan Berkeadilan," *Gema Teologika: Jurnal Teologi Kontekstual Dan Filsafat Keilahian* 3, no. 2 (2018): 167–84. I have pointed out that the Lordship of Christ even includes non-human creation, as well.
35. Zuly Qodir, "Etika Sosial Dan Dialog Antaragama Di Indonesia," in *Islam, Agama-Agama, Dan Nilai Kemanusiaan: Festschrift Untuk M. Amin Abdullah*, ed. Moch Nur Ichwan and Ahmad Muttaqin (Yogyakarta: CISForm UIN Sunan Kalijaga, 2013), 209.

and any judgment about them.[36] It is true that Jesus also condemns, as will be elaborated on later, but he does not do it simply based on prior judgments.

Inspired by the thoughts of Emanuel Levinas, Jacques Derrida, and Paul Ricoeur, Sastrapratedja proposes what he calls "hospitality in interreligious dialogue."[37] In this proposal, Sastrapratedja reminds all religious people that we should avoid the mistakes made by both realism and idealism that have reduced plurality, based on prior judgments, into a unity of the "same." By so doing we have erased the otherness of others since that otherness has been squeezed and extracted into one totality of the "same." This is ontology in which the others are experienced as surprising, and therefore they must be incorporated into the "same."[38] In the history of Christianity, such thinking manifests itself in both simple pluralism and hardcore particularism. In both cases, there are no longer any "others."

Sastrapratedja further says that ethics must challenge such thinking since ethics always precedes ontology. The incapacity to embrace others is, in its very essence, an act of excluding them. We must accept and respect all others as the "other," with their "otherness," as friends on the same journey, and not as strangers who demand anybody's response. In this perspective, our relationship with the other is an epiphany, an encounter with a "face" with otherness and vulnerability. Violence only happens when the other is seen and understood as a threat.[39] It is such hospitality that will renew the Christian mission, no longer as a conquest of those who are different, but as reconciliation with others.[40]

---

36. See Chapter two of Widjaja, *Character Formation and Social Transformation* for the interpretation of the stories of Jesus's table fellowship in the Gospel of Luke that shows how Jesus consistently takes the initiative to embrace others, independent of any judgment about the truth of others and their commitment to him.
37. Sastrapratedja, S.J., "Hospitalitas Dalam Dialog Intereligius: Belajar Dari E. Levinas, J. Derrida Dan Paul Ricoer," 149–62.
38. See Sindhunata, *Kambing Hitam: Teori René Girard* (Jakarta: Gramedia Pustaka Utama, 2006) for the elaboration of Rene Girard's theory of scapegoat in the Indonesian context. Sindhunata shows that in Javanese culture, any kind of difference is understood as dangerous and is a threat for the whole society; therefore, it has to be eliminated. During the New Regime era under the leadership of the late President Suharto, for instance, any kind of conversation and action that evoked the issue of SARA (Suku, Agama, Ras, Antargolongan – Ethnicity, Religion, Race, Intergroup) was considered dangerous, and people who were involved in it could be detained by the State.
39. Sastrapratedja, S.J., "Hospitalitas Dalam Dialog Intereligius: Belajar Dari E. Levinas, J. Derrida Dan Paul Ricoer," 152–57.
40. Paulus S. Widjaja, "Mission As Reconciliation Amidst Religious Extremism: An Indonesian Christian Perspective," in *Overcoming Violence in Asia*, ed. Donald Eugene Miller, Gerard Guiton, and Paulus S. Widjaja (Ontario: Pandora Press, 2011), 159–72. See also Jozef Mepibozef Nelsun Hehanussa, "New Challenges for Christian Mission in the Context of Religious

It implies that we take the risk of accepting more than what we might think we are capable of, and thus brings forward a question about safety, including the safety of our very identity. The word "dialogue" itself conveys the idea of a flow of meaning between two or more parties.[41] For the flow to happen reciprocally, it must start from a willingness of all parties to be interrupted by the otherness of others.[42]

The operation of such thought can be seen clearly in the famous parable of the good Samaritan in Luke 10:25–37. In that story, the lawyer who comes to Jesus is asking the very question that many Christians ask when talking about people of other faiths, "And who is my neighbor?" (Luke 10:29). Behind this question, there is a strong, confident assumption, even prejudice, that one who poses the question is the party who decides who her/his neighbor is and who is not.

Interestingly, after recounting the different attitudes and behaviors of the priest, the Levite, and the Samaritan, Jesus asks the lawyer, "Which of these three do you think was a neighbor to the man who fell into the hands of robbers?" (Luke 10:36). Jesus changes and transforms the lawyer's standpoint. He criticizes the arrogance of the lawyer for his self-centered perspective. Instead of deciding who can be considered our neighbor and who is not, Jesus turns the tide. It is not the position of the lawyer that should become the standpoint to judge, but the "other's." No community, Christians included, has the right to decide who should be in and who should be out, who should be embraced as a neighbor, and who should be not. It is precisely the other's standpoint and perspective that becomes the locus to judge whether Christians can be considered and called neighbors, indeed fellow human beings, or not.

PEACEMAKING: THE CHURCH OF THE CRUCIFIED CHRIST

Peacemaking is an effort to negotiate between parties and establish justice so that the hazard does not become a disaster. The church must lead the way to offer solutions to the problems around religious plurality so that religion can be a resource for peace rather than a source of violence. As has been said earlier, we must engage proactively with the created world of God; immerse

---

Fundamentalism and Radicalism: Learning from the Indonesian Context," in *Mission Still Possible? Global Perspectives on Mission and Mission Theology*, ed. Jochen Motte and Andar Parlindungan (Germany: United Evangelical Mission [UEM], 2017), 47–66.
41. "What Is Dialogue?," Clark University, accessed January 29, 2022, https://www2.clarku.edu/difficultdialogues/learn/index.cfm.
42. Sastrapratedja, 157–60.

ourselves within it, and not run away from it. This does not, however, mean that we must always be positive toward the created world of God, and accept it for what it is. We need to realize that the good world God created has fallen into sin. When Christ was crucified, he also brought judgment to the sinful world (John 5:22, 27, 30), as well as its remedy.

Such is the call of the church, namely, to bring a critical evaluation of the reality of the world. And this is to be done using a clear criterion – God's revelation in Jesus Christ. The confession of the church that "Jesus Christ is Lord" (Phil 2:11) is the oldest Christian confession. This confession expresses the church's confirmation that Jesus's norms are universal. We do not need to feel ashamed or embarrassed for this confession, lest our witness becomes too general, thin, and shallow, due to its lack of clear criteria. We can give witness to Christ in the world only if we have a clear position and opinion. The challenge of the church is not how to delete or disguise Christ in our witness to the world, but to make it bolder.

The church must recall her calling to be the church of the crucified Christ. Such a church will immerse herself in the world with a clear judgment of right and wrong. As the psalmist said, "Love and faithfulness meet together; righteousness and peace kiss each other" (Ps 85:10). There is a slight problem with the translation of this verse in English. The word "faithfulness" comes from the Hebrew word "אֱמֶת," which is more accurately translated as "truth." It is from this very word that the word "Amen" (= truly) comes. The word "righteousness" is from the Hebrew word "צֶדֶק," which is also more accurately translated as "justice." Hence Psalms 85:10 wants to convey the idea of two pairs of moral norms that should be held together, even within the reality of religious plurality. The individual norm in each pair should not be omitted and separated from its pair, lest it loses its meaning altogether.

Love has truth as its complement. We need to love everybody, including people of other faiths, without any prior judgment. But love should not be separated from its pair, truth. Love without truth will only bring us into permissiveness. Loving others does not mean ratifying everything that others do. When somebody or a group of people engages in religious violence, even in the name of God, then truth must be upheld. We should not accept this kind of attitude and behavior in the name of love. The story in 1 Samuel 15 when Samuel hewed King Agag into pieces in the name of God is a good example of religious extremism. It is violent religious vengeance done in the name of God. This is also the story of suicide bombers or anyone who kills others who are perceived as the enemies of God, or people who bomb an abortion clinic or injure people of other colors in the name of God.

The struggle for truth means that we must work to establish the facts of wrongdoing, disclose the lies and the pattern of violence, and make the case public.[43] When discussing forgiveness and reconciliation regarding violence in politics, Donald W. Shriver Jr. reminds us that the first thing we need to do is to not withhold moral judgment. It all starts from the remembrance of the evil that has happened and posing moral judgment on that evil based on truth. By doing so the parties involved will not merely accuse each other for no reason. Everybody should face the facts before assuming that they can overcome what has happened.[44] Hannah Arendt has also profoundly pointed out that any discussion on violence and its remedy is useless until all the parties involved are willing to listen to the voice of the victims.[45]

By the same token, truth should not be separated from love, lest it brings Christians into a mere constant judgment of others. This is the situation shown by the proponents of religious particularism. In the name of religious truth claims, they easily judge people of other faiths a priori, even before they engage with them, and try to learn the meaning of faith in their lives. In the name of love, Christians should respect people of other faiths, and embrace them without any prior judgments about their fate and faith.

Presenting *philia* as the noblest kind of love, Prasetya and Sasongko argue that it is "a love which expresses the joyful relationships of all beings with one another and with the wellspring of being – the God of life." It is this kind of friendly love that lies behind the idea of perichoretic identity. This is the kind of identity which we, as Christians, should develop, for it stems from the kind of identity that the triune God has demonstrated. What really matters is the relationship. The word perichoresis means "moving around the space." As the imagery of Eastern tradition of Christianity conveys, when all persons of the triune God dance around the empty space a sacred milieu is created, and the space which is opened upholds them simultaneously together and apart. Our

---

43. Phan, "Peacekeeping, Peacemaking, Peacebuilding: An Interreligious Spirituality for Just Peace," 46; see also Robert J. Schreiter, *Reconciliation: Mission and Ministry in a Changing Social Order* (Maryknoll; Boston: Orbis Books and Boston Theological Institute, 2015) who reminds us about the danger of "narrative of the lie."
44. Donald W. Shriver, *An Ethic for Enemies: Forgiveness in Politics* (Oxford: Oxford University Press, 1995), 7, 128, 157.
45. Hannah Arendt, *On Violence* (Boston: Houghton Mifflin Harcourt, 1970).

identity, correspondingly, is always "determined by space that we share with the others."[46]

So also should peace not be separated from justice. Peace without justice only brings oppression. People are asked to stay quiet and not challenge the status quo for the sake of simple harmony. This is certainly a false understanding of peace. The history of oppression in the name of religion in the past should become a strong reminder to every living being that the powerful can easily disguise their crude reason in conquering others behind religious jargon. The apartheid system, colonialism in the name of "God-Gold-Glory," slavery, and so forth, just to mention a few, are examples of evil deeds practiced in the name of peace. Hence, peace must be achieved with justice. It is just peace.

God's main concern of just peace is evident in the life and ministry of Jesus. In his inaugural address as recorded in Luke 4:16–30, Jesus cites Isaiah 61 and 58 about the fulfillment of shalom justice. There are some word substitutions and omissions that we need to pay attention to as can be shown in the table below.

Isaiah 61:1–2	Luke 4:18–19	Isaiah 58:6
the poor	the poor	
the brokenhearted	*omitted*	
the captives	the captives	
the prisoners	the oppressed of Isa 58:6 (*substituted*)	the oppressed (רְצוּצִים)
	the blind (*added*)	
the year of the LORD's favor	the year of the LORD's favor	
the day of vengeance of our God	*omitted*	

Jesus only mentions "the poor" and omits "the brokenhearted" of Isaiah 61 to emphasize his attention to people who are physically and economically poor. He also substitutes "the prisoners" of Isaiah 61 with "the oppressed" of Isaiah

---

46. Joas Adiprasetya and Nindyo Sasongko, "A Compassionate Space-making: Toward a Trinitarian Theology of Friendship," *The Ecumenical Review* 71, no. 1–2 (January 2019): 21–31; see also Joas Adiprasetya, "Pastor as Friend: Reinterpreting Christian Leadership," *Dialog* 57, no. 1 (2018): 47–52, https://doi.org/10.1111/dial.12377.

58 since the word "רְצוּצִים" in Isaiah 58 carries the meaning of people who are being crushed, ill-treated, and abused. It brings the notion of people who have been treated unjustly and violently. Jesus also adds "the blind" since, in his days, people who did not have sight were excluded from their community. Finally, the omission of "the day of vengeance of our God" shows Jesus is here talking about the kingdom of God that is characterized by peace, not violence.

All this shows that Jesus is emphasizing the theme of shalom justice which promotes the liberation of those who have physical and material problems. Jesus is here proclaiming the healing, freeing, and redeeming presence of God to the people at their greatest pain due to the unjust treatment of them. In Jesus's life and ministry, the good news becomes manifested in concrete acts of care for the poor and the outcast; these result in substantive changes in circumstances such that the poor and the outcast might enjoy the chance for a new beginning.[47]

On the other hand, justice without peace will only bring a bloody and violent revolution. People who strive for justice, but without the orientation to peace, tend to be motivated by the desire to take revenge on the powerful and to take them down at any cost. It will only live up to the ancient barbaric mechanism – violence begets violence. Justice without peace is an endeavor based on hatred, not love. And non-hatred is more important than, and it takes precedence over, nonviolence in any pursuit of a just peace. That is why justice must be paired with peace.

There is no doubt that the churches around the globe are quite advanced in promoting love and peace. Yet the churches are sometimes not that strong in advocating truth and justice. Worse yet, the churches sometimes do speak and advocate for truth and justice, but only when the church's interests are at stake. Hence the establishment of church-related institutions that are geared toward the advancement of truth and justice in a pluralistic society is one example of something concrete that can be done. Those institutions should work not only for the benefit of the church, such as when the churches are striving for an official permit from the government or when Christians are persecuted but for the benefit of all people in society regardless of their religious affiliations.

---

47. See Paulus S. Widjaja, *Keadilan Allah Dalam Kitab-Kitab Injil Sinoptik* (Semarang: Pustaka Muria, 2013) for the elaboration of justice in the life and ministry of Jesus as witnessed in the synoptic gospels.

PEACEBUILDING: THE CHURCH OF THE RISEN CHRIST

Peacebuilding is an effort to create a long-term alternative that just peace may prevail continuously and sustainably.[48] Here is where creative imagination becomes very crucial.[49] As Christians, we believe that the resurrection of Jesus Christ from death gives witness to the world that nothing and no one can hinder or fail the creative salvation work of God. There is now an alternative to the world's vicious cycle of violence. At the same time, resurrection is also proof that God has legitimated Jesus's deeds and life as righteous. In this line of thought, the church of Jesus Christ should become an alternative community that can offer concrete alternatives to the world, to demonstrate herself as a social manifestation of the reign of Christ who has been risen. We should not simply follow the currents lest we are drawn into evil. Yet we do not need to simply oppose the current, either, lest we are crushed since our power may not be as strong as that of the current. What we need to do is to creatively and constructively create an alternative – a new current.

To become an alternative community means that we must exercise servanthood, not power. Our life orientation should not be to control and dominate others while serving ourselves but to serve others, especially those who suffer, regardless of their religious backgrounds. We need to learn the reality of life from below, so that we may understand what people at the bottom of society are suffering. This can only be done by our presence among those who suffer, through our participation in advocating just peace, and doing concrete actions to help them. Indeed, it is not simply about the preferential option for the poor, but a preferential option *with* the poor across religions. We need to transform our Diakonia from Diakonia to fellow Christians, to Diakonia to people of other faiths, and then to Diakonia *with* people of other faiths.

When a big earthquake hit the Special Region of Yogyakarta in 2006, the Mennonite church in Yogyakarta worked hand-in-hand with the Muslims, including the Hezbollah Corps, to help those who were impacted by the earthquake. Before that, the Mennonites and the Hezbollah Corps joined hands in helping the 2004 tsunami victims in the Special Region of Aceh, the

---

48. John Paul Lederach, *The Little Book of Conflict Transformation*, The Little Books of Justice & Peacebuilding (Intercourse, PA: Good Books, 2003).
49. John Paul Lederach, *The Moral Imagination: The Art and Soul of Building Peace*, Reprint edition (Oxford: Oxford University Press, 2010).

province in Indonesia where the Islamic Syariah Law is officially practiced and implemented for the whole society.[50]

Being the church of the risen Christ also means that we need to empower all religious people to leave behind that which drives us to disrespect and eliminate others, and move toward what Milton Bennett has termed "ethnorelativism," a belief that stems from a deep and genuine respect for other cultures that all cultures, subcultures, and groups are inherently equal, that will enable us to be integrated with people of other faiths. This occurs through six stages, namely: denial, defence, minimization, acceptance, adaptation, and integration.[51]

> Denial – We need to empower those among us who live in the denial stage by way of creating the awareness that there are others outside of our group. Activities such as multicultural education teaching about cultural and religious sensitivities can be very helpful.
>
> Defence – Those who live in the stage of defense can be empowered through education and what Paulo Freire termed "conscientization,"[52] a way to bring people coming into consciousness so that they can realize that each religious group has its unique qualities, and all have commonalities that we share. Activities such as giving help to people of other faiths when in extremis, such as during and after natural disasters, and on more normal, less dramatic occasions, can be effective.
>
> Minimization – In this stage, we can empower religious people to locate their own and others' attitudes and behaviors in particular cultural contexts, and neither generalize nor universalize them. Informal gathering for sharing or sincere interfaith dialogue is an example.

---

50. For a more complete elaboration of these stories see Agus Suyanto and Paulus Hartono, *The Radical Muslim and Mennonite: A Muslim-Christian Encounter for Peace in Indonesia*, trans. Agnes Chen (Semarang: Pustaka Muria, 2015).
51. Milton J. Bennett, "Towards Ethnorelativism: A Developmental Model of Intercultural Sensitivity," in *Education for the Intercultural Experience*, ed. R. Michael Paige (Yarmouth: Intercultural Press, 1993), 21–71. The British spellings come from Bennett's article and are therefore maintained as such.
52. Paulo Freire, *Pedagogy of the Oppressed* (London and New York: Continuum, 1993).

Acceptance – When religious people can move forward, they will start a journey in ethnorelativism beginning with acceptance. Here we need to empower religious people so that they can create and develop intercultural communication with people of other faiths. There will then be a paradigm migration, by which they are willing to come out of their perspective and learn to see and understand reality from the perspective of others. Activity such as "live-in," a term uniquely used by the Indonesians referring to the opportunity to live for several days or weeks with a family or residential school belonging to a different religious community, or an intensive study together with people of other faiths is useful.

Adaptation – In this stage, we can empower religious people to enhance intercultural communication to become intercultural interactions. It is here that formal interreligious networking is established and joint actions between people of different faiths can be done.[53]

Integration – When religious people arrive in the final stage we may expect that they have already developed perichoretic identities as has been elaborated earlier. They can easily move in and out among different religious groups since they have developed the capability to have multiple frameworks.[54]

CONCLUDING REMARKS

I started this chapter by stating that hazards in our life do not necessarily turn into disasters. A hazard would turn into a disaster only if those affected do not have enough capacity to anticipate and overcome the hazard, coupled with a certain degree of vulnerability.

The most dangerous hazard [greatest danger] in a religiously pluralistic society that I have identified is religious violence, which in many Asian

---

53. See Jeniffer Pelupessy-Wowor, "The Role of Religious Education in Promoting Religious Freedom: A Mutual Enrichment Between 'My Story,' 'Your Story,' and 'Our Stories,'" *The Review of Faith & International Affairs* 14, no. 4 (October 1, 2016): 98–106, https://doi.org/10.1080/15570274.2016.1248527 for a proposal of religious education that can promote collaboration among people of different faiths for religious freedom.

54. Paulus S. Widjaja, "Tantangan Dan Prospek Relasi Antarumat Beragama Di Indonesia," in *Meretas Diri, Merengkuh Liyan, Berbagi Kehidupan: Bunga Rampai Penghargaan Untuk Pdt. Aristarchus Sukarto*, ed. Paulus S. Widjaja and Wahyu Satrio Wibowo (Jakarta: BPK Gunung Mulia, Fakultas Teologi UKDW, Sinode GKMI, 2020), 328–54.

countries, indeed worldwide, often also takes in the form of religious nationalism. This happens when religious people are busy gaining political power in society for the sake of maintaining their dominance and influence, and the other religious groups are therefore seen as threats to their identity and existence. To overcome such a hazard, religious people, including Christians, must develop a capacity to proactively and continuously engage in the efforts of peacekeeping, peacemaking, and peacebuilding so that just peace may prevail amid religious plurality.

The effort to engage in peacekeeping corresponds to our call to become the church of the descended Christ. Just as Jesus Christ was willing to descend to the sinful world to embrace others without any a priori judgment, so must Christians engage the world. Our Christian mission is not to proselytize people of other faiths and make them the object of our conquest, for whatever reason. We do have to proactively engage in evangelism. It is the DNA of every Christian. But evangelism is neither proselytization nor conquest. Evangelism means we manifest the reign of God in our everyday lives through words, thoughts, actions, and any other forms. And we can do it only when we start by accepting and embracing people of other faiths without any prior judgment. We even need to cultivate a deep understanding within ourselves that the purpose of being with the "others" is precisely to change both of us, not just one party. This is the way to cut off the vicious cycle of religious violence.

The effort to engage in peacemaking corresponds to our call to become the church of the crucified Christ. Just as Jesus exposes the sin of the world and passes judgment on it when he is crucified, so do we. The drive to embrace others, including people of other faiths, does not mean that we simply ratify whatever is. Instead, we must simultaneously practice and manifest love and truth, peace, and justice. They are pairs that should not be separated. One cannot be advocated without the other. Last, the effort to engage in peacebuilding corresponds to our call to become the church of the risen Christ. This call is an acknowledgment and a confession that Jesus's resurrection demonstrates that the power of death has been defeated and that God has legitimated Jesus's life. Accordingly, our life should also be as such that just peace may prevail. We need not simply follow the current of the world nor oppose it, but we are called to creatively create a new alternative, a new current so that a new creation emerges, and a new heaven and new earth come into existence.

In short, amid the reality of religious plurality, we, Asian Christians, need to *ACT*, that is, to *accept* people of other faiths without any prior judgment, to *condemn* any wrongdoings done in the name of God or religion that are against what Jesus taught and demonstrated to us, and to *transform* everybody, including ourselves, so that just peace may prevail and the reign of God be manifested.

QUESTIONS FOR DISCUSSION

1. When you sincerely look at yourself, do you find yourself more inclined toward the exclusive side or the inclusive one concerning religious pluralism? Why? Are you satisfied with that position, or do you want to transform it? How?
2. What is your opinion concerning religious violence and religious nationalism? Is there something that you and your church want to do about it?
3. What are examples of best practices for Christians in functioning as the church of the descended Christ (peacekeeping), the church of the crucified Christ (peacemaking), and the church of the risen Christ (peacebuilding) in the context of religious pluralism that you have experienced? Why do you consider them as best practices? What lessons have you learned from those experiences?

BIBLIOGRAPHY

Adiprasetya, Joas. "Pastor as Friend: Reinterpreting Christian Leadership." *Dialog* 57, no. 1 (2018): 47–52. https://doi.org/10.1111/dial.12377.

Adiprasetya, Joas, and Nindyo Sasongko. "A Compassionate Space-making: Toward a Trinitarian Theology of Friendship," *The Ecumenical Review* 71, no. 1–2 (January 2019): 21–31.

Appleby, Scott R. *The Ambivalence of the Sacred: Religion, Violence, and Reconciliation*. Lanham: Rowman & Littlefield Publishers, 1999.

Arendt, Hannah. *On Violence*. Boston: Houghton Mifflin Harcourt, 1970.

Bennett, Milton J. "Towards Ethnorelativism: A Developmental Model of Intercultural Sensitivity." In *Education for the Intercultural Experience*, edited by R. Michael Paige, 21–71. Yarmouth: Intercultural Press, 1993.

Clark University. "What Is Dialogue?" Accessed January 29, 2022. https://www2.clarku.edu/difficultdialogues/learn/index.cfm.

Coakley, John. "'Primordialism' in Nationalism Studies: Theory or Ideology?" *Nations and Nationalism* 24, no. 2 (April 2018): 327–47. https://doi.org/10.1111/nana.12349.

Freire, Paulo. *Pedagogy of the Oppressed*. London and New York: Continuum, 1993.

Habermas, Jürgen. "Religion in the Public Sphere." *European Journal of Philosophy* 14, no. 1 (2006): 1–25. https://doi.org/10.1111/j.1468-0378.2006.00241.x.

Hadiwitanto, Handi, and Carl Sterkens. "Sikap Terhadap Pluralitas Agama: Studi Perbandingan-Empiris Mahasiswa Muslim Dan Kristen Di Indonesia." *Gema Teologi* 36, no. 2 (October 31, 2012). http://journal-theo.ukdw.ac.id/index.php/gema/article/view/143.

Huntington, Samuel P. *The Clash of Civilizations and the Remaking of World Order*. New York: Simon and Schuster, 2007.

Iannaccone, Laurence R, and Eli Berman. "Religious Extremism: The Good, The Bad, and The Deadly." *Public Choice* 128 (July 28, 2006): 109–29.

IRIN. "How to Reverse Buddhism's Radical Turn in Southeast Asia?" Refworld, July 16, 2013. https://www.refworld.org/docid/51e9102b4.html.

Irvin-Erickson, Douglas. "Introduction: Interfaith Contributions to Nurturing Cultures of Peace." In *Violence, Religion, Peacemaking*, 1–19. New York: Palgrave Macmillan, 2016.

Jonkers, Peter. "How to Break the Ill-Fated Bond between Religious Truth and Violence." In *Religious Truth and Identity in an Age of Plurality*, edited by Peter Jonkers and Oliver J. Wiertz, 246–63. London and New York: Routledge, 2019.

Kementerian Agama RI. *Moderasi Beragama*. Jakarta: Badan Litbang dan Diklat Kementerian Agama RI, 2019.

Lederach, John Paul. *The Little Book of Conflict Transformation*. The Little Books of Justice & Peacebuilding. Intercourse: Good Books, 2003.

———. *The Moral Imagination: The Art and Soul of Building Peace*. Reprint edition. Oxford: Oxford University Press, 2010.

Magnis-Suseno, Frans. "Persatuan Indonesia: Pancasila, Paham Kebangsaan Dan Integritas Nasional." In *Pancasila Sebagai Ideologi Terbuka: Problema Dan Tantangannya*, edited by Alex Lanur. Yogyakarta: Kanisius, 1995.

McClendon, Jr., James Wm,, and James M. Smith. *Convictions: Defusing Religious Relativism*. Revised edition. Eugene: Wipf & Stock, 2002.

Muttaqin, Ahmad. "Meneguhkan Harmoni Muslim-Kristen: Mengayuh Di Antara Problem Dan Potensi." In *Islam, Agama-Agama, Dan Nilai Kemanusiaan: Festschrift Untuk M. Amin Abdullah*, edited by Moch Nur Ichwan and Ahmad Muttaqin, 133–48. Yogyakarta: CISForm UIN Sunan Kalijaga, 2013.

Naisbitt, John. *Megatrends 2000*. New York: HarperCollins, 1991.

Pelupessy-Wowor, Jeniffer. "The Role of Religious Education in Promoting Religious Freedom: A Mutual Enrichment Between 'My Story,' 'Your Story,' and 'Our Stories.'" *The Review of Faith & International Affairs* 14, no. 4 (October 1, 2016): 98–106. https://doi.org/10.1080/15570274.2016.1248527.

Phan, Peter C. "Peacekeeping, Peacemaking, Peacebuilding: An Interreligious Spirituality for Just Peace." In *Violence, Religion, Peacemaking*, 21–60. New York: Palgrave Macmillan, 2016.

Qodir, Zuly. "Etika Sosial Dan Dialog Antaragama Di Indonesia." In *Islam, Agama-Agama, Dan Nilai Kemanusiaan: Festschrift Untuk M. Amin Abdullah*, edited by Moch Nur Ichwan and Ahmad Muttaqin, 203–19. Yogyakarta: CISForm UIN Sunan Kalijaga, 2013.

Race, Alan. *Making Sense of Religious Pluralism*. London: SPCK, 2013.

Saiya, Nilay. "Pluralism and Peace in South Asia." *The Review of Faith & International Affairs* 17, no. 4 (2019): 12–22. https://doi.org/10.1080/15570274.2019.1681779.

Sastrapratedja, S.J., M. "Hospitalitas Dalam Dialog Intereligius: Belajar Dari E. Levinas, J. Derrida Dan Paul Ricoer." In *Islam, Agama-Agama, Dan Nilai Kemanusiaan: Festschrift Untuk M. Amin Abdullah*, edited by Moch Nur Ichwan and Ahmad Muttaqin, 149–62. Yogyakarta: CISForm UIN Sunan Kalijaga, 2013.

Schliesser, Christine. "Religion and Peace: Anatomy of a Love-Hate Relationship." *Religions* 11, no. 219 (2020). https://doi.org/10.3390/rel11050219.

Schreiter, Robert J. *Reconciliation: Mission and Ministry in a Changing Social Order*. Maryknoll; Boston: Orbis Books and Boston Theological Institute, 2015.

Shriver, Donald W. *An Ethic for Enemies: Forgiveness in Politics*. Oxford: Oxford University Press, 1995.

Sindhunata. *Kambing Hitam: Teori René Girard*. Jakarta: Gramedia Pustaka Utama, 2006.

Sofjan, Dicky, and Ewa Trojnar. "The Challenge of Building a Multi-Ethnic State in Malaysia." *Hémisphères* 26 (2011): 1–15.

Suyanto, Agus, and Paulus Hartono. *The Radical Muslim and Mennonite: A Muslim-Christian Encounter for Peace in Indonesia*. Translated by Agnes Chen. Semarang: Pustaka Muria, 2015.

Swartley, Willard M. *Covenant of Peace: The Missing Peace in New Testament Theology and Ethics*. Grand Rapids: Eerdmans, 2006.

The Aspen Institute. "Religious Pluralism 101," July 18, 2019. https://www.aspeninstitute.org/blog-posts/religious-pluralism-101/.

Toffler, Alvin. *Future Shock*. New York: Bantam Books, 1972.

———. *The Third Wave*. Clerkenwell, London: Pan Books, 1981.

"WHO Coronavirus (COVID-19) Dashboard." Accessed January 30, 2022. https://covid19.who.int.

Widjaja, Paulus S. "Apakah Aku Penjaga Saudaraku?: Mencari Etika Ekologis Kristiani Yang Panentheistik Dan Berkeadilan." *Gema Teologika: Jurnal Teologi Kontekstual Dan Filsafat Keilahian* 3, no. 2 (2018): 167–84.

———. *Character Formation and Social Transformation: An Appeal to The Indonesian Churches Amidst the So-Called Chinese Problem*. Saarbrücken: VDM Verlag Dr. Müller, 2010.

———. *Keadilan Allah Dalam Kitab-Kitab Injil Sinoptik*. Semarang: Pustaka Muria, 2013.

———. "Mission As Reconciliation Amidst Religious Extremism: An Indonesian Christian Perspective." In *Overcoming Violence in Asia*, edited by Donald Eugene Miller, Gerard Guiton, and Paulus S. Widjaja, 159–72. Ontario: Pandora Press, 2011.

———. "Peace." In *Dictionary of Mission Theology: Evangelical Foundations*, edited by John Corrie, Juan F. Martinez, and Simon Chan, 279–81. Nottingham, England; Downers Grove: IVP Academic, 2007.

———. "Recognizing the Other's Insecurity." In *At Peace and Unafraid: Public Order, Security, and the Wisdom of the Cross*, edited by Duane K. Friesen and Gerald W. Schlabach, 261–74. Scottdale: Herald Press, 2005.

———. "Tantangan Dan Prospek Relasi Antarumat Beragama Di Indonesia." In *Meretas Diri, Merengkuh Liyan, Berbagi Kehidupan: Bunga Rampai Penghargaan Untuk Pdt. Aristarchus Sukarto*, edited by Paulus S. Widjaja and Wahyu Satrio Wibowo, 328–54. Jakarta: BPK Gunung Mulia, Fakultas Teologi UKDW, Sinode GKMI, 2020.

Widjaja, Paulus Sugeng, Djoko Prasetyo Adi Wibowo, and Imanuel Geovasky. "Politik Identitas Dan Religiusitas Perdamaian Berbasis Pancasila Di Ruang Publik." *GEMA TEOLOGIKA: Jurnal Teologi Kontekstual Dan Filsafat Keilahian* 6, no. 1 (April 30, 2021): 95–126. https://doi.org/10.21460/gema.2021.61.658.

Yeghiazaryan, Laura. "Which of the Three Main Ethnic Conflict Theories Best Explains the Ethnic Violence in the Post-Soviet States of Azerbaijan, Georgia, and Moldova?" *Undergraduate Journal of Political Science* 3, no. 1 (Spring 2018): 46–63.

CONTRIBUTORS

Shang-Jen Chen (PhD, Princeton Theological Seminary) is Associate Professor in Christian Ethics at Taiwan Graduate School of Theology and the President of Taiwan Theological Association. He was the former president of Taiwan Theological College and Seminary (2010–2019). The Seminary has been accredited by the Ministry of Education of Taiwan since 2015 and has a new name as Taiwan Graduate School of Theology (TGST). His publications include *Recasting A Covenant Ethics for the Family in Taiwan: A Dialogue between Christianity and Chinese Culture* (VDM Verlag, 2009) and *Pastoral Ethics in the 21st Century* (Campus Evangelical Fellowship, 2021), and numerous essays.

Agnes S. Chiu was born and raised in Hong Kong. Dr. Chiu is a licensed attorney in California and an adjunct professor. She received her Bachelor of Arts degree from the University of California, Irvine, majoring in Social Ecology with a criminology specialization. Then, she received her Juris Doctor degree from the University of California, School of Law, Los Angeles. Dr. Chiu has practiced employment law, business law, and estate planning since 1992. In 2010, Dr. Chiu received her Master of Arts degree in Biblical Studies from Fuller Theological Seminary. Dr. Chiu continued with her theological education and studied under the mentorship of the late Dr. Glen Stassen, and then Dr. Richard Mouw and Dr. George Harinck. In 2017, Dr. Chiu received her Doctor of Philosophy in Christian Ethics. Dr. Chiu served as the assistant professor of systematic theology and ethics 2016–2019 at the China Evangelical Seminary North America. Since 2020, Dr. Chiu has served as the Law Agape Center's managing attorney and teaches as an adjunct professor. Dr. Chiu has published articles on Neo-Calvinism, labor reforms in China, and public theology. Dr. Chiu has served on the boards of various Christian organizations.

Dick Osita Eugenio is a Filipino theologian. He received his PhD from the University of Manchester, UK in 2011. He currently serves as Dean of the School of Leadership and Advanced Studies of Wesleyan University, Philippines. He lectures in theology and religion, equips writers, and helps theological institutions local and international. His primary interest is in making theology relevant to the contemporary situation. Aside from many articles and book chapters, he has published three books, namely *Communion with the Triune God* (2014), *The Gift of Life* (2019), and *The Christian Life* (2019). He is happily married to Mary Ann and blessed with two young children: Heloise and Jed. They currently live in Cabanatuan City, Philippines.

Athena E. Gorospe is Professor and Chair in Biblical Studies and Director of the PhD program in Contextual Theology at Asian Theological Seminary, Manila, Philippines. As an Asian scholar, her research interests lie in Scripture's interface with philosophy, culture, and the social context. She has written *Narrative and Identity: An Ethical Reading of Exodus 4* (Brill) and a commentary on the book of Judges for the *Asia Bible Commentary Series*, as well as articles on various social issues in the light of Scripture. She has a PhD in Theology (Old Testament) from Fuller Theological Seminary, California, USA.

Nigel Ajay Kumar is a theological education consultant based in Bengaluru, India. Until recently, he was the Head of the Department of Theology, at SAIACS. Currently, he assists church organisations to develop training curriculum for grassroot pastors and lay leaders. He completed his PhD at SAIACS in 2012. His dissertation was published as *What is Religion? A Theological Answer* (Pickwick, 2012; SAIACS Press, 2014). His research interests include biblical theology, contextual theology, and theological research methodology. He has most recently published a book to help intermediate and advanced theological students with research and writing expectations called *Think Write: A Theological Handbook for Critical Thinking, Research Methodology, and Academic Writing* (SAIACS Press, 2022). Nigel is an elder at The Gospel Church, Bengaluru, an inter-denominational church that ministers to local and migrant communities. He is married and has one daughter.

Kiem-Kiok Kwa is Lecturer in missiology and interdisciplinary studies at Biblical Graduate School of Theology, Singapore. A lawyer by training, she earned her PhD at Asbury Theological Seminary, Kentucky, USA, looking at public theology, and has been teaching since 2009. Outside the seminary, she sits on several medical ethics boards, and is involved with Micah Singapore. She has published on a diverse range of subjects including a contextual commentary on Matthew for the *Asia Bible Commentary Series*, contributed to the *Dictionary of Christian Spirituality* (Zondervan, 2011) as well as religious harmony in *Faith in an Age of Terror* (BGST, 2018). She and her husband, a Methodist pastor, enjoy listening to classical music and walking in the outdoors.

Jean Lee is Abundant Grace Professor (Theological Studies) at the China Graduate School of Theology, Hong Kong. She was initially trained in accounting and was designated a Chartered Accountant in Ontario, Canada. She has done auditing and business advisory work in Canada and Hong Kong. She has also served as a director of companies listed on the Hong Kong and Australia stock exchanges and acted as the Chief Executive Officer of a technology company. In 2002, Dr. Lee left her work to study theology; after obtaining her MDiv she served as a church minister. She obtained her PhD in 2010 from the University of Edinburgh, where her research focused on the interface between theology and economics. Dr. Lee is author of *The Two Pillars of the Market: A Paradigm for Dialogue between Theology and Economics* (Peter Lang, 2011), 職場繁星 *Shine for Jesus in the Marketplace* (CCL, 2014), 職場敘事 *Vocation as Narratives* (CCL, 2019), and a number of other books and articles.

Rula Khoury Mansour is a Palestinian Christian from Nazareth, Israel. She received her PhD from the Oxford Center for Mission Studies, UK, in 2018. She is the founder and director of Nazareth Center for Peace Studies and associate professor of theology and peace studies at Nazareth Evangelical College. She lectures, trains and consults churches and different institutions locally and internationally. She has published many articles and a book, *Theology of Reconciliation in the Context of Church Relations* (Langham Monographs, 2020). Currently, she is working on her post-doctoral research with Langham Scholars.

Previously, having earned her law degree from the Hebrew University of Jerusalem and Masters in Conflict Resolution (Cum laude) from Tel-Aviv University, she worked for over a decade as a public prosecutor and was the deputy head of the prosecution office in northern Israel.

Rula and her husband, Bader, live in Nazareth with their three sons: Adi, Rami and Sami.

Aldrin M. Peñamora obtained his PhD in Theology with a concentration in Christian Ethics at Fuller Theological Seminary, California, USA. He is the Executive Director of the Justice, Peace and Reconciliation Commission and the Theological Commission of the Philippine Council of Evangelical Churches (PCEC). He also serves as the Executive Director of the Center for the Study of Christian-Muslim Relations (CSCMR) and Interim Program Director of the PhD in Peace Studies Program of Asia Graduate School of Theology (AGST)/International Graduate School of Leadership (IGSL) in the Philippines. Aldrin teaches theology and ethics at AGST, IGSL and Asian Theological Seminary (ATS). He is co-editor of *Christology, Cultures and Religions* (OMF Lit / ATA, 2016) and *Faith and Bayan: Evangelical Christian Engagement in the Philippine Context* (Langham Global Library, 2022). Aldrin is married to Christine Ching Peñamora.

Vinoth Ramachandra, (PhD, University of London) lives in Colombo, Sri Lanka, and serves as the Secretary for Dialogue & Social Engagement with the International Fellowship of Evangelical Students. His work mainly involves helping students, professors, and graduates engage Christianly with the social, ideological, and political challenges they face in their universities and nations. He has also been involved with the Faraday Institute for Science & Religion, Micah Global, the civil rights movement in Sri Lanka and A Rocha. He has authored several essays and books including *Faiths in Conflict?* (IVP, 1999), *Subverting Global Myths* (SPCK, 2008), *Gods That Fail* (Wipf & Stock, 2016) and *Sarah's Laughter: Doubt, Tears and Christian Hope* (Langham Global Library, 2020).

ShinHyung Seong (PhD, Garrett-Evangelical Theological Seminary) is an Assistant Professor at Baird College of General Education at Soongsil University, Seoul, Korea. He also teaches Philosophy at the Graduate School of Christianity at Soongsil University. He is an ordained minister with the Presbyterian Church in Korea. His publications include *Otherness and Ethics* (Wipf & Stock, 2018), *Participation and Responsibility: An Ethical Discourse of Tillich and Levinas* (Handel, 2017), and numerous academic articles. He is currently working on a translation of Tillich's *Morality and Beyond*, to be completed in 2022.

Florian M. P. Simatupang (PhD, Regent University) is a Pastor-Theologian planted firmly in the Church and the Academy. He and his wife are lead pastors of IES Christ the King, an international congregation which is a part of the Gereja Sidang-Sidang Jemaat Allah (The Indonesian Assemblies of God). He is also a Lecturer at Sekolah Tinggi Teologi (STT) Satyabhakti teaching systematic theology and research methodology. He published an article with *Pneuma* (2019) titled, "Christian Hospitality in the Celebration of 'Id al-Fitr." His research interests include Pentecostal theology, sacramental theology, ecclesiology, pneumatology, postcolonial theology, feminist theology, and indigenous religion. His dissertation focused on constructing a theology of the Eucharist, and he is in the process of turning it into a monograph.

Paulus S. Widjaja (PhD, Fuller Theological Seminary, School of Theology) is an Assistant Professor in Christian Ethics and Peace Studies at the Faculty of Theology, Universitas Kristen Duta Wacana, Yogyakarta, Indonesia. He is the former Dean of the Faculty (2015–2019) and is currently the Director of the Master of Divinity Studies Program. An ordained minister with the Gereja Kristen Muria Indonesia, a Mennonite denomination, he is also an adjunct lecturer at the Indonesian Consortium for Religious Studies, an international PhD program offered collaboratively by Duta Wacana Christian University, Gajah Mada University, and Sunan Kalijaga Islamic State University. His publications include *Dampak Politik Identitas Terhadap Perilaku Umat Kristen Di Ruang Publik Di Daerah Istimewa Yogyakarta* (TPK, 2020) which he co-wrote with Djoko Prasetyo, Imanuel Geovasky, and Edy Nugroho; *Keadilan Allah Dalam Kitab-kitab Injil Sinoptik* (Pustaka Muria, 2013); *Character Formation and Social Transformation: An Appeal To The Indonesian Churches Amidst The So-called Chinese Problem* (VDM Verlag Dr. Muller Aktiengesellschaft & Co, 2010); *Who Do You Say That I Am? The Quest of Historical Jesus From Hermann Samuel Reimarus to Marcus J. Borg* (TPK, 2009); *Engaging the State: 16th Century Anabaptist View of the State* (TPK, 2008); *A Culture of Peace: God's Vision for the Church* (Good Books, 2005) which he co-wrote with Alan and Eleanor Kreider; and numerous essays.

Bernard K. Wong (PhD, Garrett-Evangelical Theological Seminary) is President and S. Y. King Associate Professor of China Graduate School of Theology, Hong Kong. His research interests include the theology of marriage and family, bioethics, creation care, and the intersection between faith and technology. An ordained pastor of the Christian and Missionary Alliance Church, he is also involved in Christian organizations such as Cedarfund Hong Kong and the Christian Forum for Reconciliation in Northeast Asia. His publications include *Beginning from Man and Woman: Witnessing Christ in the Family* (Langham Monographs, 2017), *Communio: A Biblical Reflection on Relationship and Community* (FES Hong Kong, 2018), and *A Theological Reflection on Singleness, Marriage, and the Family* (Campus Taiwan, 2022).

Hwa Yung is a Bishop Emeritus of the Methodist Church in Malaysia. He served as a pastor and Principal of the Malaysia Theological Seminary (STM) for many years, and has also taught at Trinity Theological College, Singapore. Although no longer officially involved, he was previously engaged in the work of the Oxford Centre for Mission Studies Council, the International Lausanne Board, and IFES. He maintains an active ministry of preaching and writing today.

Asia Theological Association
54 Scout Madriñan St. Quezon City 1103, Philippines
Email: ataasia@gmail.com Telefax: (632) 410 0312

OUR MISSION

The Asia Theological Association (ATA) is a body of theological institutions, committed to evangelical faith and scholarship, networking together to serve the Church in equipping the people of God for the mission of the Lord Jesus Christ.

OUR COMMITMENT

The ATA is committed to serving its members in the development of evangelical, biblical theology by strengthening interaction, enhancing scholarship, promoting academic excellence, fostering spiritual and ministerial formation and mobilizing resources to fulfill God's global mission within diverse Asian cultures.

OUR TASK

Affirming our mission and commitment, ATA seeks to:

- **Strengthen** interaction through inter-institutional fellowship and programs, regional and continental activities, faculty and student exchange programs.
- **Enhance** scholarship through consultations, workshops, seminars, publications, and research fellowships.
- **Promote** academic excellence through accreditation standards, faculty and curriculum development.
- **Foster** spiritual and ministerial formation by providing mentor models, encouraging the development of ministerial skills and a Christian ethos.
- **Mobilize** resources through library development, information technology and infra-structural development.

To learn more about ATA, visit www.ataasia.com or facebook.com/AsiaTheologicalAssociation

Langham Literature, along with its publishing work, is a ministry of Langham Partnership.

Langham Partnership is a global fellowship working in pursuit of the vision God entrusted to its founder John Stott –

> *to facilitate the growth of the church in maturity and Christ-likeness through raising the standards of biblical preaching and teaching.*

Our vision is to see churches in the Majority World equipped for mission and growing to maturity in Christ through the ministry of pastors and leaders who believe, teach and live by the word of God.

Our mission is to strengthen the ministry of the word of God through:
- nurturing national movements for biblical preaching
- fostering the creation and distribution of evangelical literature
- enhancing evangelical theological education

especially in countries where churches are under-resourced.

Our ministry

Langham Preaching partners with national leaders to nurture indigenous biblical preaching movements for pastors and lay preachers all around the world. With the support of a team of trainers from many countries, a multi-level programme of seminars provides practical training, and is followed by a programme for training local facilitators. Local preachers' groups and national and regional networks ensure continuity and ongoing development, seeking to build vigorous movements committed to Bible exposition.

Langham Literature provides Majority World preachers, scholars and seminary libraries with evangelical books and electronic resources through publishing and distribution, grants and discounts. The programme also fosters the creation of indigenous evangelical books in many languages, through writer's grants, strengthening local evangelical publishing houses, and investment in major regional literature projects, such as one volume Bible commentaries like the *Africa Bible Commentary* and the *South Asia Bible Commentary*.

Langham Scholars provides financial support for evangelical doctoral students from the Majority World so that, when they return home, they may train pastors and other Christian leaders with sound, biblical and theological teaching. This programme equips those who equip others. Langham Scholars also works in partnership with Majority World seminaries in strengthening evangelical theological education. A growing number of Langham Scholars study in high quality doctoral programmes in the Majority World itself. As well as teaching the next generation of pastors, graduated Langham Scholars exercise significant influence through their writing and leadership.

To learn more about Langham Partnership and the work we do visit **langham.org**

www.ingramcontent.com/pod-product-compliance
Lightning Source LLC
Chambersburg PA
CBHW071951220426
43662CB00009B/1085